ASCENDANCE OF A BOOKWORM
I'll do anything to become a librarian!

Part 1 If there aren't any books, I'll just have to make some!

Volume 5

Author: **Miya Kazuki** / Artist: **Suzuka**
Character Designer: **You Shiina**

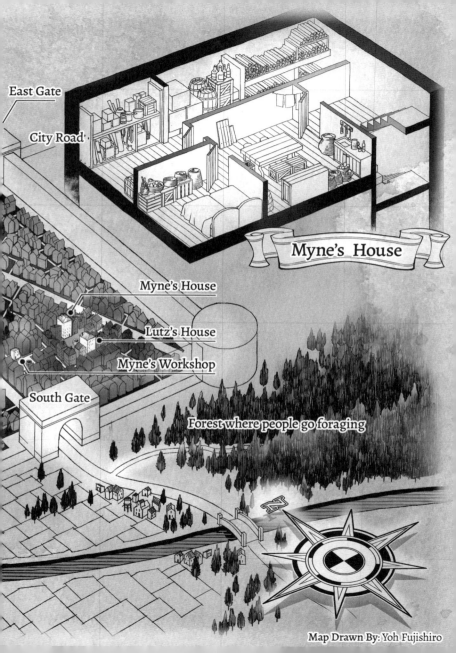

East Gate

City Road

Myne's House

Myne's House

Lutz's House

Myne's Workshop

South Gate

Forest where people go foraging

Map Drawn By: Yoh Fujishiro

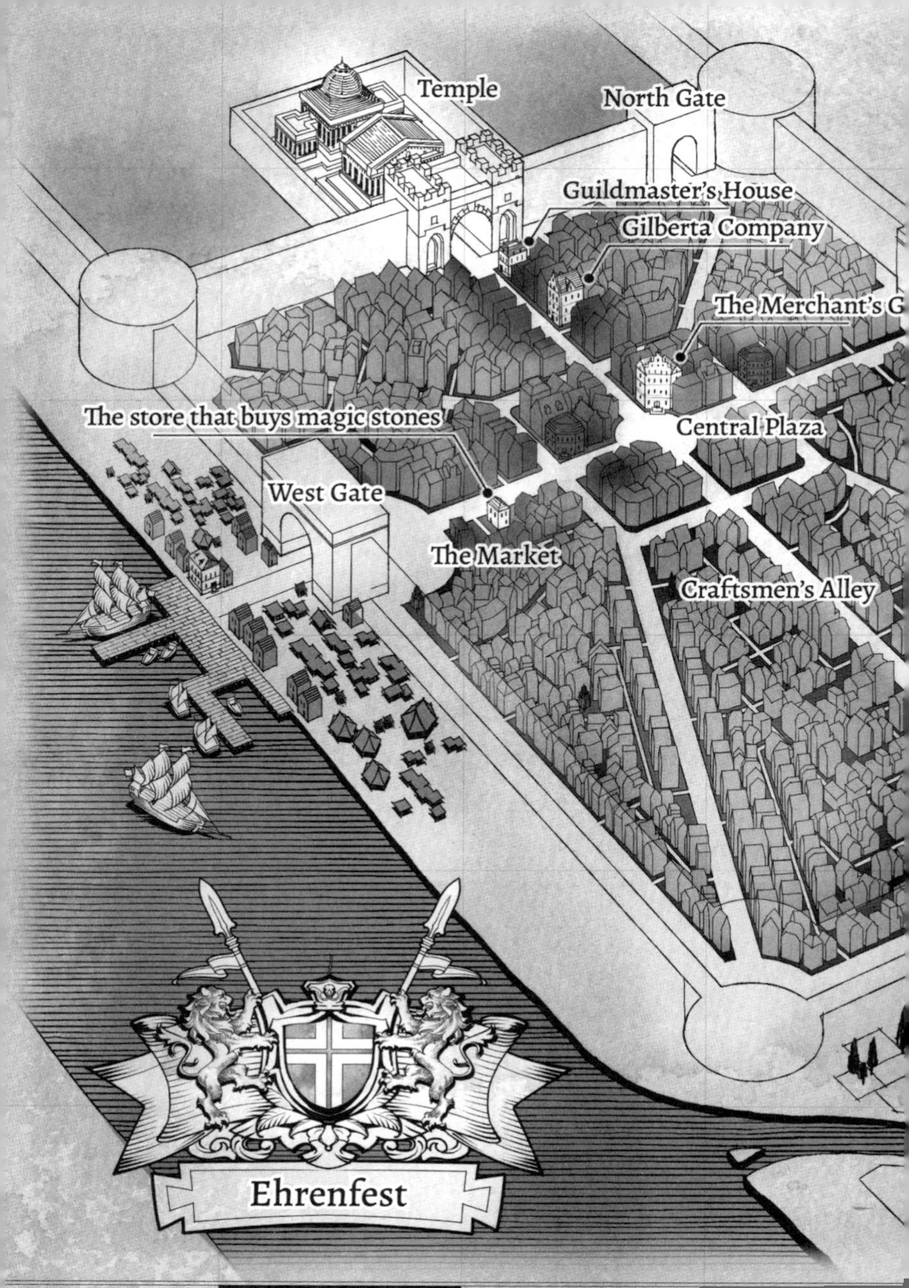
Temple
North Gate
Guildmaster's House
Gilberta Company
The Merchant's G
The store that buys magic stones
Central Plaza
West Gate
The Market
Craftsmen's Alley
Ehrenfest

CON TENTS

ASCENDANCE OF A BOOKWORM
I'll do anything to become a librarian!
Part 1 If there aren't any books, I'll just have to make some!

Ch.20 The Guildmaster's Granddaughter

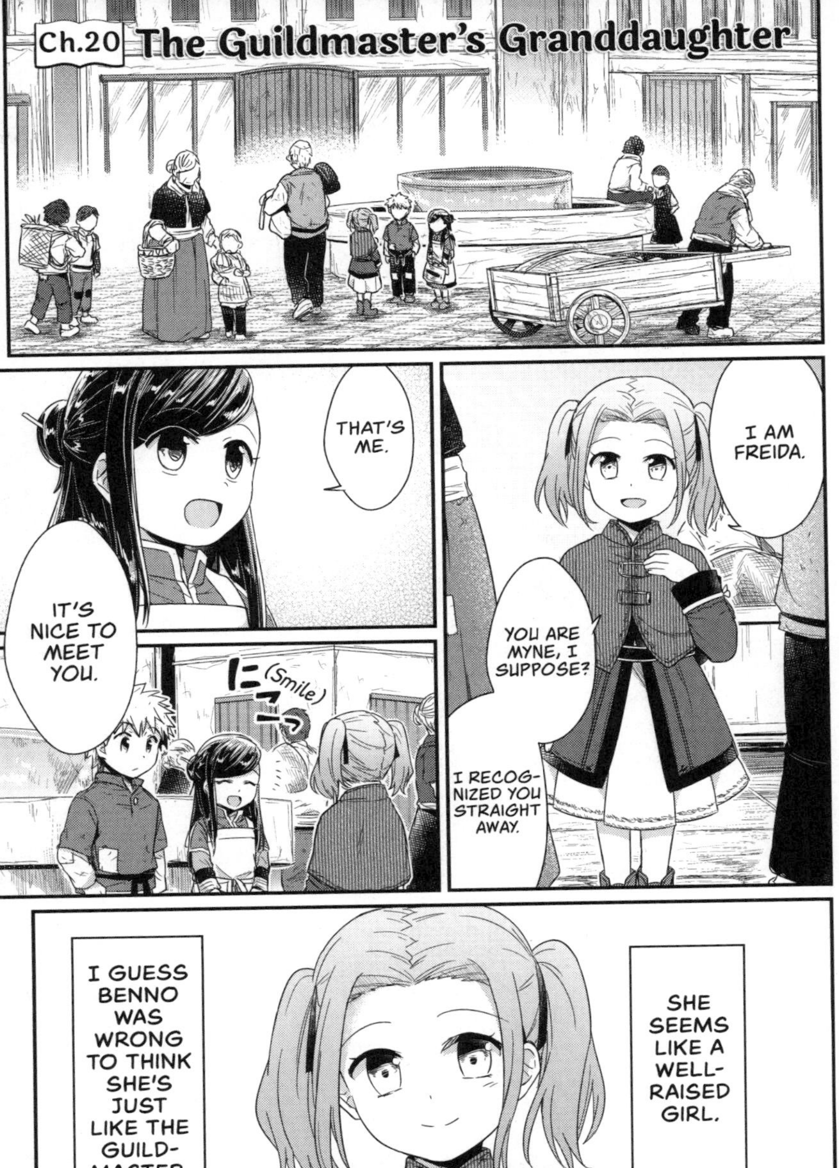
I AM FREIDA.
YOU ARE MYNE, I SUPPOSE?
I RECOG-NIZED YOU STRAIGHT AWAY.
THAT'S ME.
IT'S NICE TO MEET YOU.
に (Smile)
SHE SEEMS LIKE A WELL-RAISED GIRL.
I GUESS BENNO WAS WRONG TO THINK SHE'S JUST LIKE THE GUILD-MASTER.

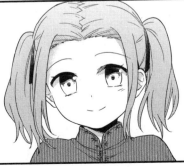

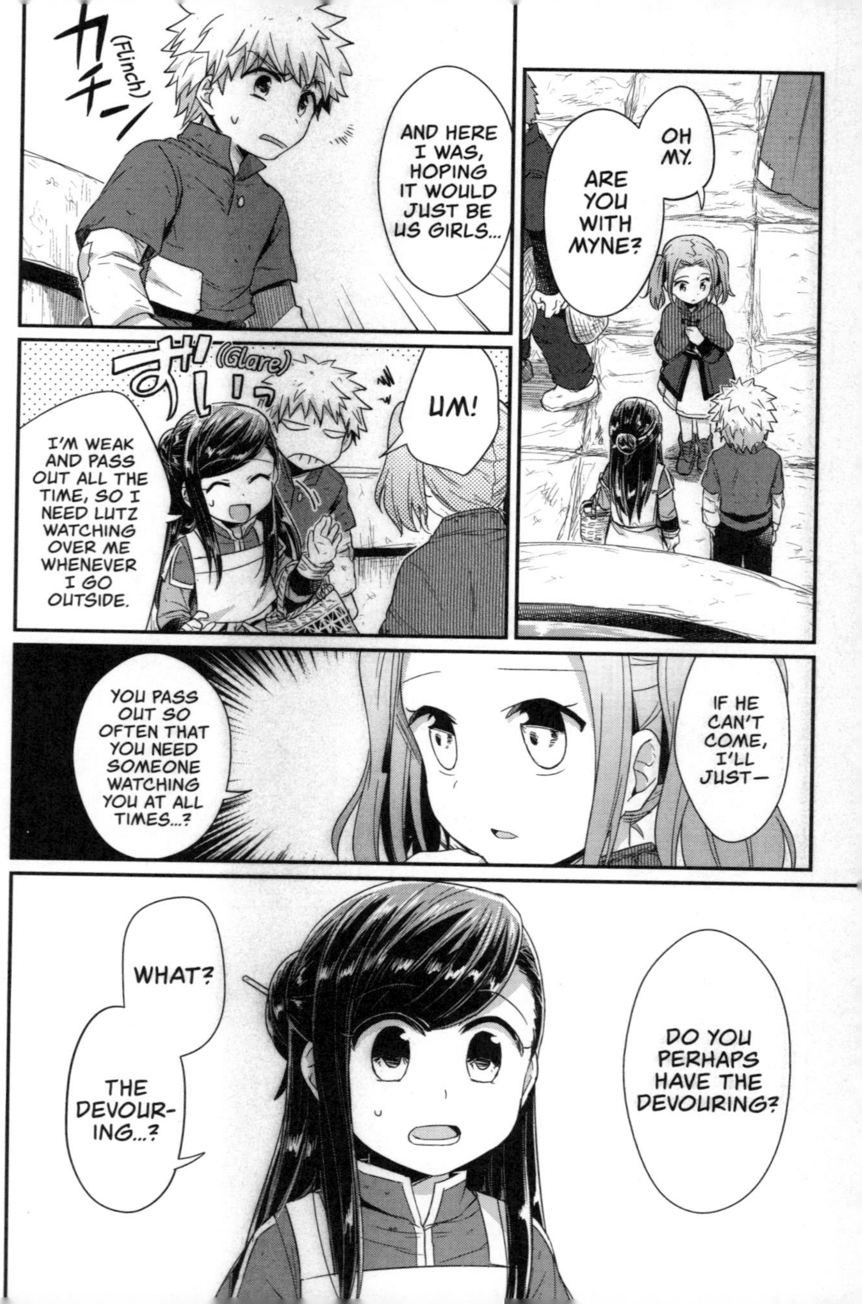
OH MY.
ARE YOU WITH MYNE?
AND HERE I WAS, HOPING IT WOULD JUST BE US GIRLS...
カチーン (Flinch)
UM!
(Glare)
I'M WEAK AND PASS OUT ALL THE TIME, SO I NEED LUTZ WATCHING OVER ME WHENEVER I GO OUTSIDE.
IF HE CAN'T COME, I'LL JUST—
YOU PASS OUT SO OFTEN THAT YOU NEED SOMEONE WATCHING YOU AT ALL TIMES...?
DO YOU PERHAPS HAVE THE DEVOURING?
WHAT?
THE DEVOURING...?

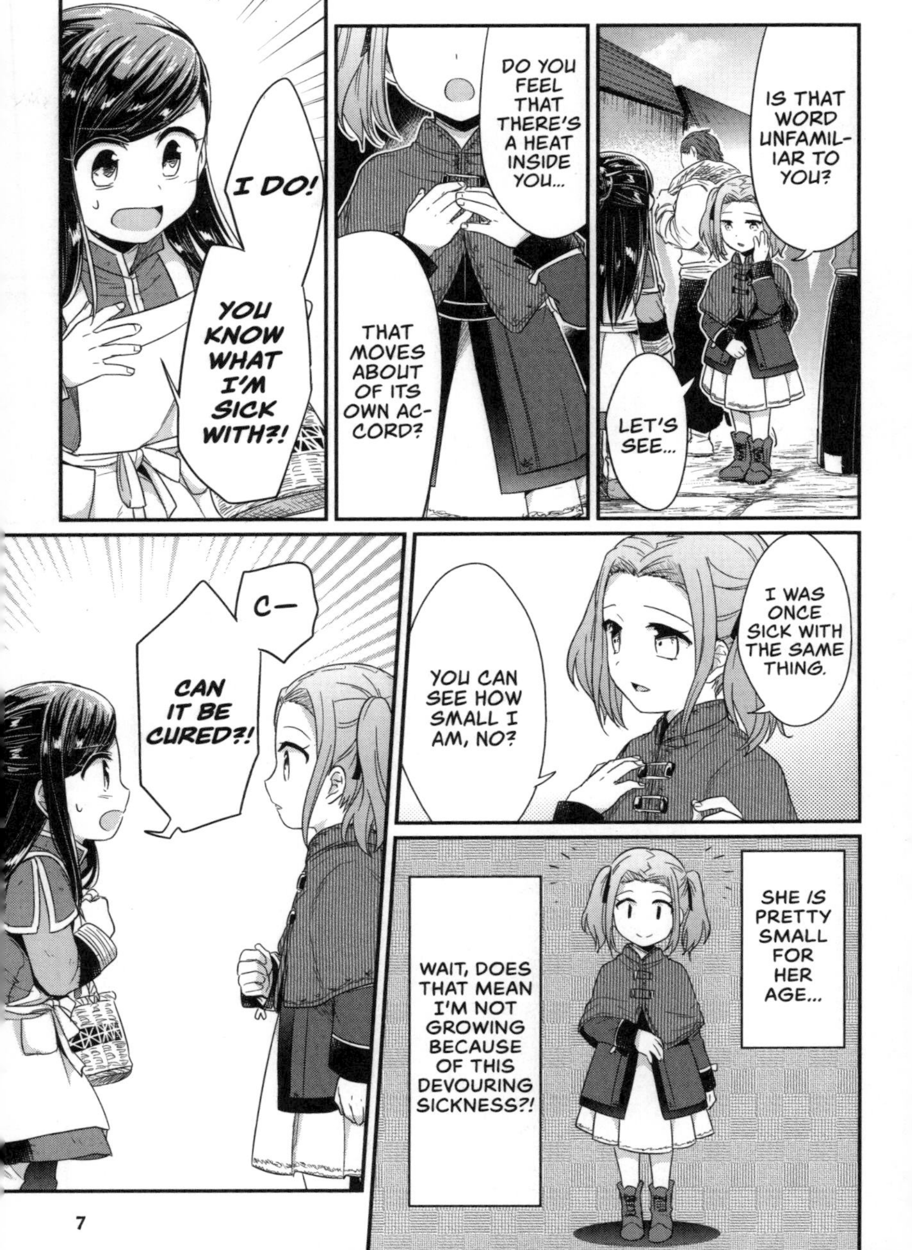
IS THAT WORD UNFAMILIAR TO YOU?
LET'S SEE...
DO YOU FEEL THAT THERE'S A HEAT INSIDE YOU...
THAT MOVES ABOUT OF ITS OWN ACCORD?
I DO!
YOU KNOW WHAT I'M SICK WITH?!
I WAS ONCE SICK WITH THE SAME THING.
YOU CAN SEE HOW SMALL I AM, NO?
SHE *IS* PRETTY SMALL FOR HER AGE...
WAIT, DOES THAT MEAN I'M NOT GROWING BECAUSE OF THIS DEVOURING SICKNESS?!
C—
CAN IT BE CURED?!

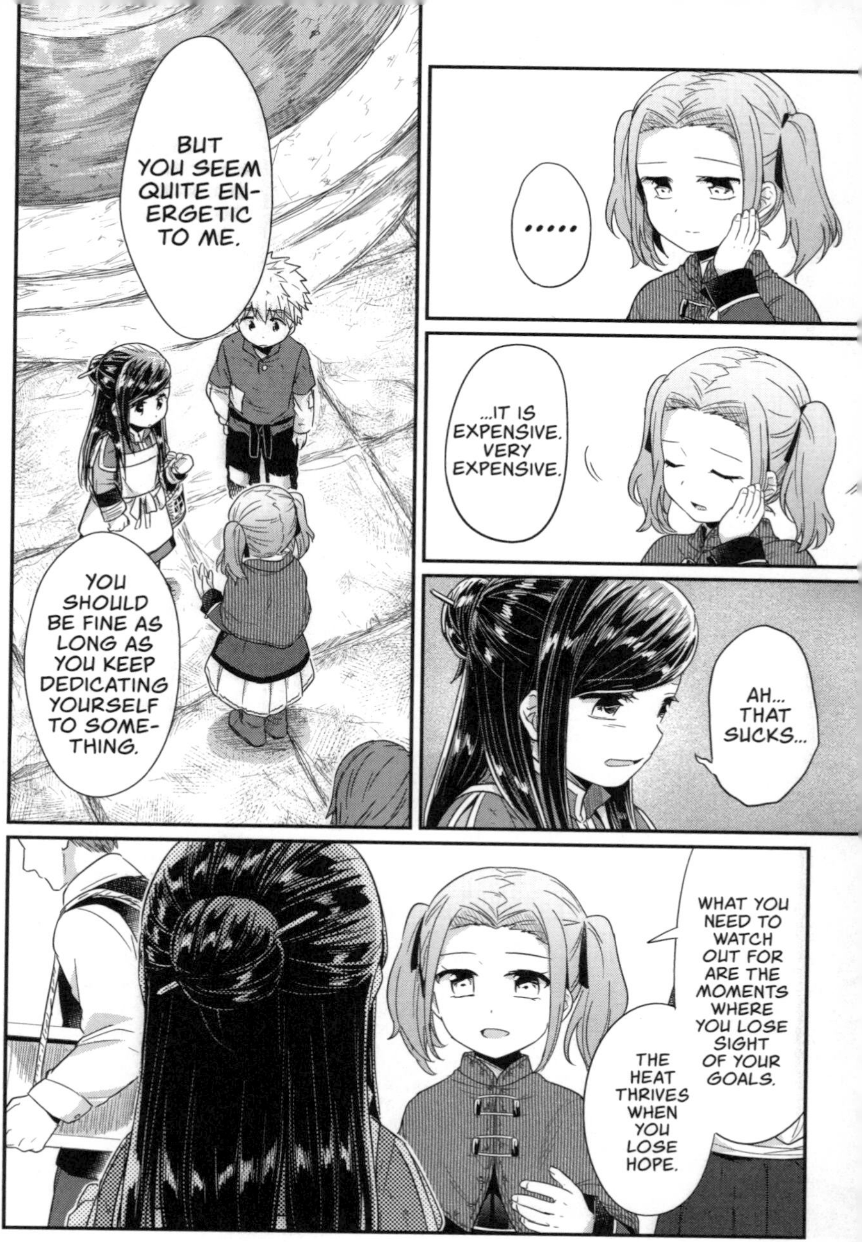

.....
...IT IS EXPENSIVE. VERY EXPENSIVE.
AH... THAT SUCKS...
BUT YOU SEEM QUITE EN-ERGETIC TO ME.
YOU SHOULD BE FINE AS LONG AS YOU KEEP DEDICATING YOURSELF TO SOME-THING.
WHAT YOU NEED TO WATCH OUT FOR ARE THE MOMENTS WHERE YOU LOSE SIGHT OF YOUR GOALS.
THE HEAT THRIVES WHEN YOU LOSE HOPE.

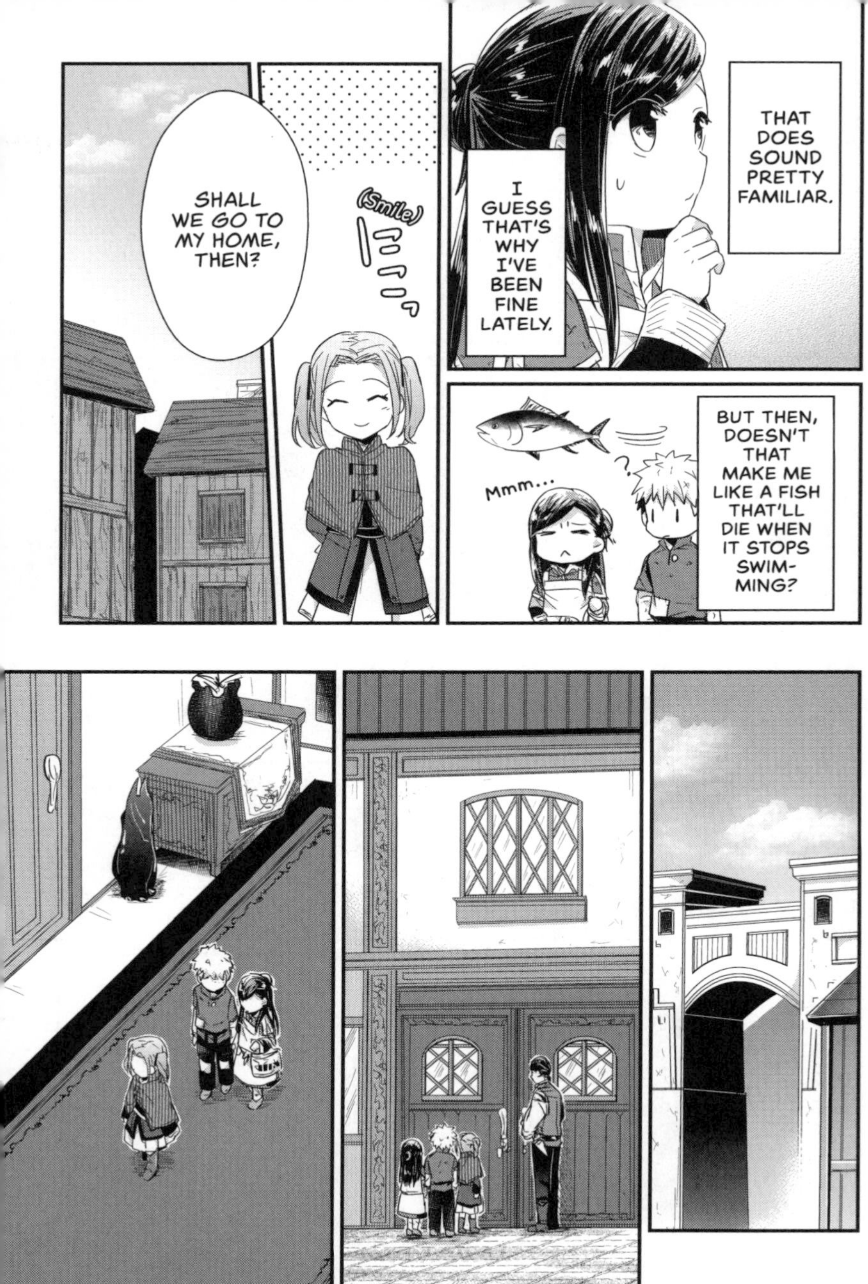
THAT DOES SOUND PRETTY FAMILIAR.
I GUESS THAT'S WHY I'VE BEEN FINE LATELY.
BUT THEN, DOESN'T THAT MAKE ME LIKE A FISH THAT'LL DIE WHEN IT STOPS SWIMMING?
Mmm...
(Smile)
SHALL WE GO TO MY HOME, THEN?

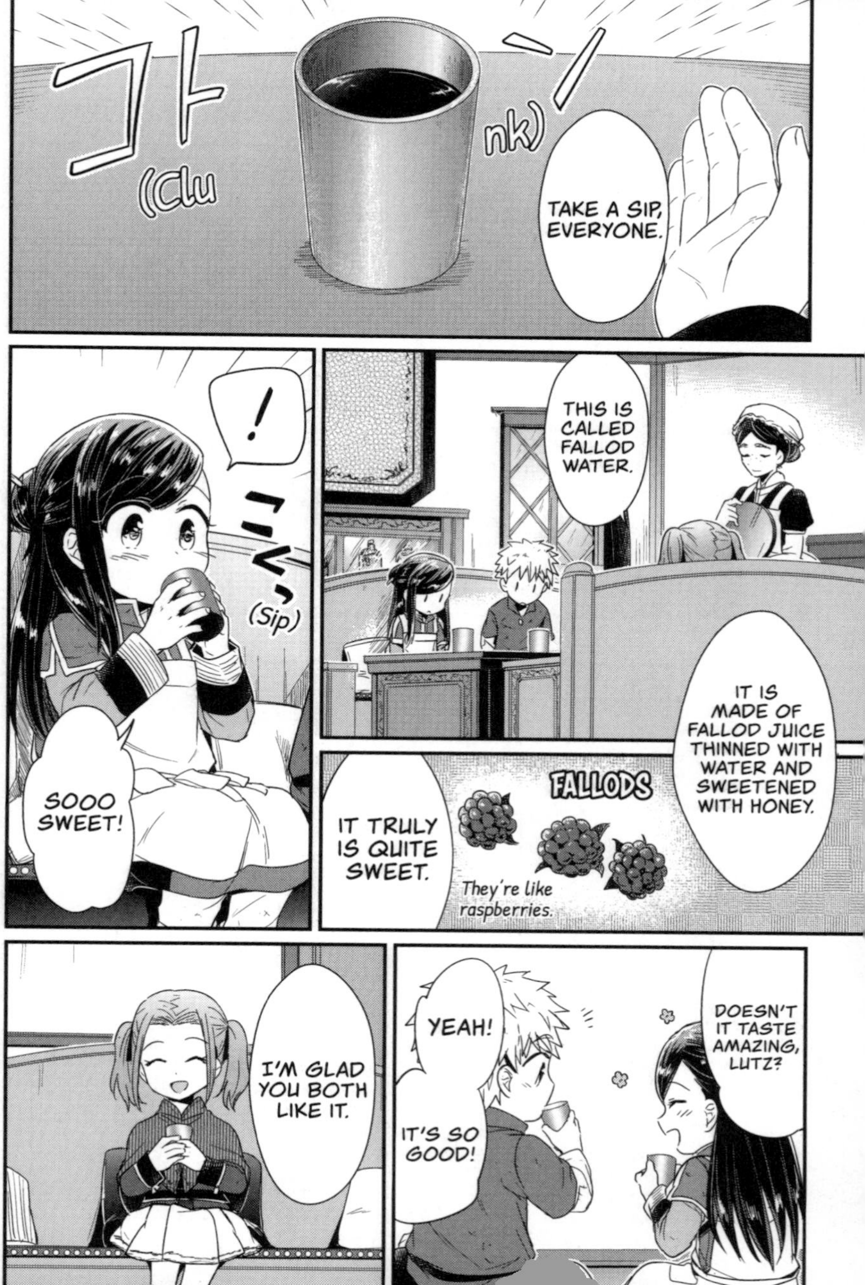
TAKE A SIP, EVERYONE.
コト
(Clunk)
THIS IS CALLED FALLOD WATER.
IT IS MADE OF FALLOD JUICE THINNED WITH WATER AND SWEETENED WITH HONEY.
FALLODS
IT TRULY IS QUITE SWEET.
They're like raspberries.
!
こくっ
(Sip)
SOOO SWEET!
DOESN'T IT TASTE AMAZING, LUTZ?
YEAH!
IT'S SO GOOD!
I'M GLAD YOU BOTH LIKE IT.

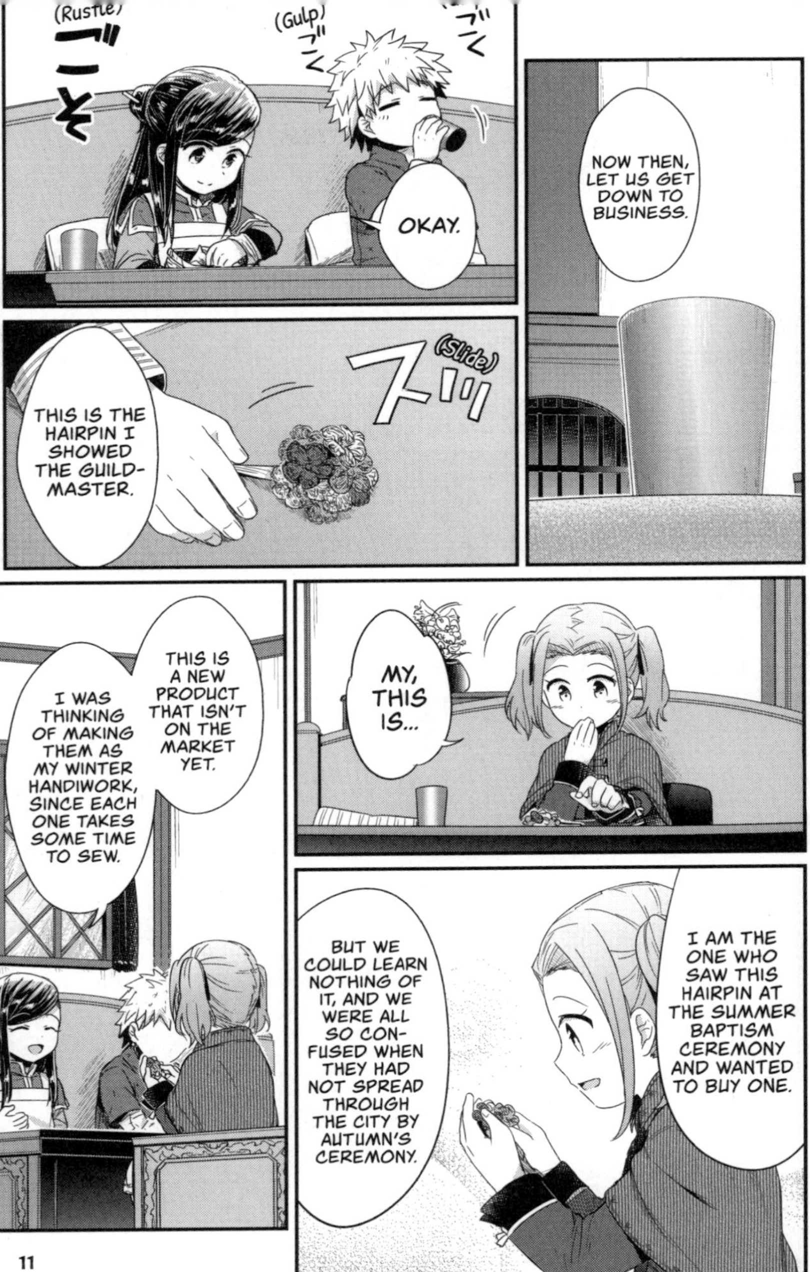
NOW THEN, LET US GET DOWN TO BUSINESS.
(Rustle)
ごそ
(Gulp)
ごく ごく
OKAY.
(Slide)
スッ
THIS IS THE HAIRPIN I SHOWED THE GUILD-MASTER.
MY, THIS IS...
I AM THE ONE WHO SAW THIS HAIRPIN AT THE SUMMER BAPTISM CEREMONY AND WANTED TO BUY ONE.
BUT WE COULD LEARN NOTHING OF IT, AND WE WERE ALL SO CON-FUSED WHEN THEY HAD NOT SPREAD THROUGH THE CITY BY AUTUMN'S CEREMONY.
THIS IS A NEW PRODUCT THAT ISN'T ON THE MARKET YET.
I WAS THINKING OF MAKING THEM AS MY WINTER HANDIWORK, SINCE EACH ONE TAKES SOME TIME TO SEW.

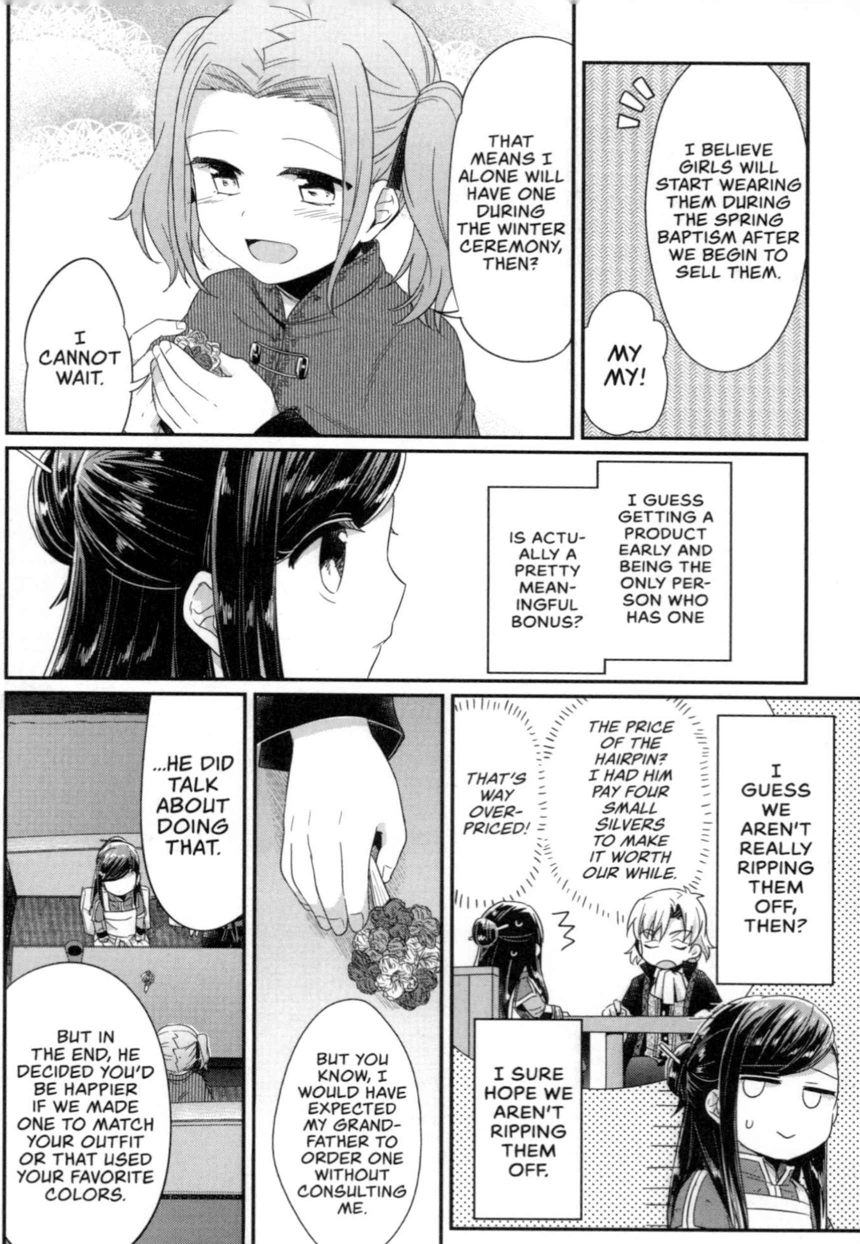
I BELIEVE GIRLS WILL START WEARING THEM DURING THE SPRING BAPTISM AFTER WE BEGIN TO SELL THEM.
MY MY!
THAT MEANS I ALONE WILL HAVE ONE DURING THE WINTER CEREMONY, THEN?
I CANNOT WAIT.
I GUESS GETTING A PRODUCT EARLY AND BEING THE ONLY PERSON WHO HAS ONE
IS ACTUALLY A PRETTY MEANINGFUL BONUS?
I GUESS WE AREN'T REALLY RIPPING THEM OFF, THEN?
THE PRICE OF THE HAIRPIN? I HAD HIM PAY FOUR SMALL SILVERS TO MAKE IT WORTH OUR WHILE.
THAT'S WAY OVERPRICED!
I SURE HOPE WE AREN'T RIPPING THEM OFF.
BUT YOU KNOW, I WOULD HAVE EXPECTED MY GRANDFATHER TO ORDER ONE WITHOUT CONSULTING ME.
...HE DID TALK ABOUT DOING THAT.
BUT IN THE END, HE DECIDED YOU'D BE HAPPIER IF WE MADE ONE TO MATCH YOUR OUTFIT OR THAT USED YOUR FAVORITE COLORS.

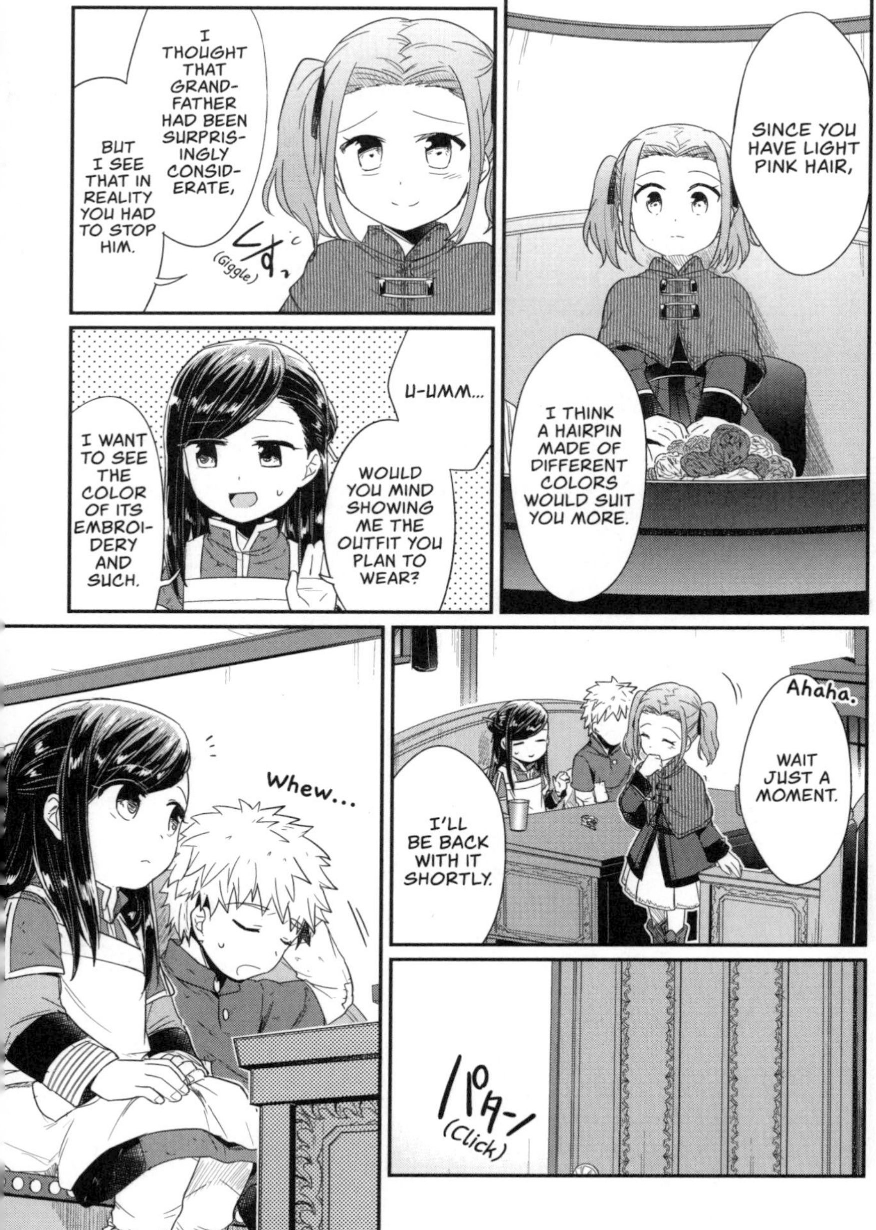
SINCE YOU HAVE LIGHT PINK HAIR,
I THINK A HAIRPIN MADE OF DIFFERENT COLORS WOULD SUIT YOU MORE.
I THOUGHT THAT GRAND-FATHER HAD BEEN SURPRIS-INGLY CONSID-ERATE,
BUT I SEE THAT IN REALITY YOU HAD TO STOP HIM.
くすっ
(Giggle)
U-UMM...
WOULD YOU MIND SHOWING ME THE OUTFIT YOU PLAN TO WEAR?
I WANT TO SEE THE COLOR OF ITS EMBROIDERY AND SUCH.
Ahaha.
WAIT JUST A MOMENT.
I'LL BE BACK WITH IT SHORTLY.
パタン
(Click)
Whew...

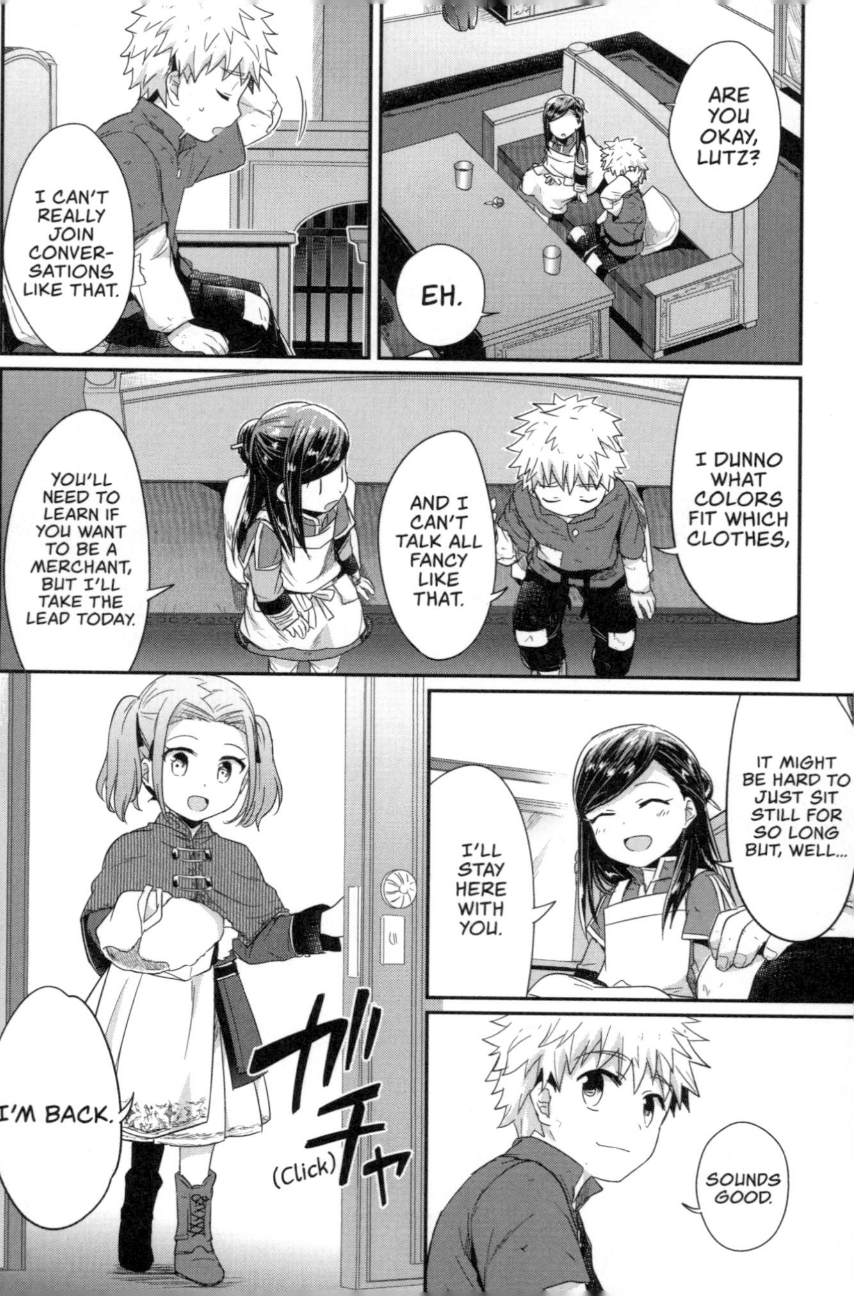
ARE YOU OKAY, LUTZ?
EH.
I CAN'T REALLY JOIN CONVER-SATIONS LIKE THAT.
I DUNNO WHAT COLORS FIT WHICH CLOTHES,
AND I CAN'T TALK ALL FANCY LIKE THAT.
YOU'LL NEED TO LEARN IF YOU WANT TO BE A MERCHANT, BUT I'LL TAKE THE LEAD TODAY.
IT MIGHT BE HARD TO JUST SIT STILL FOR SO LONG BUT, WELL...
I'LL STAY HERE WITH YOU.
SOUNDS GOOD.
ガチャ
(Click)
I'M BACK.

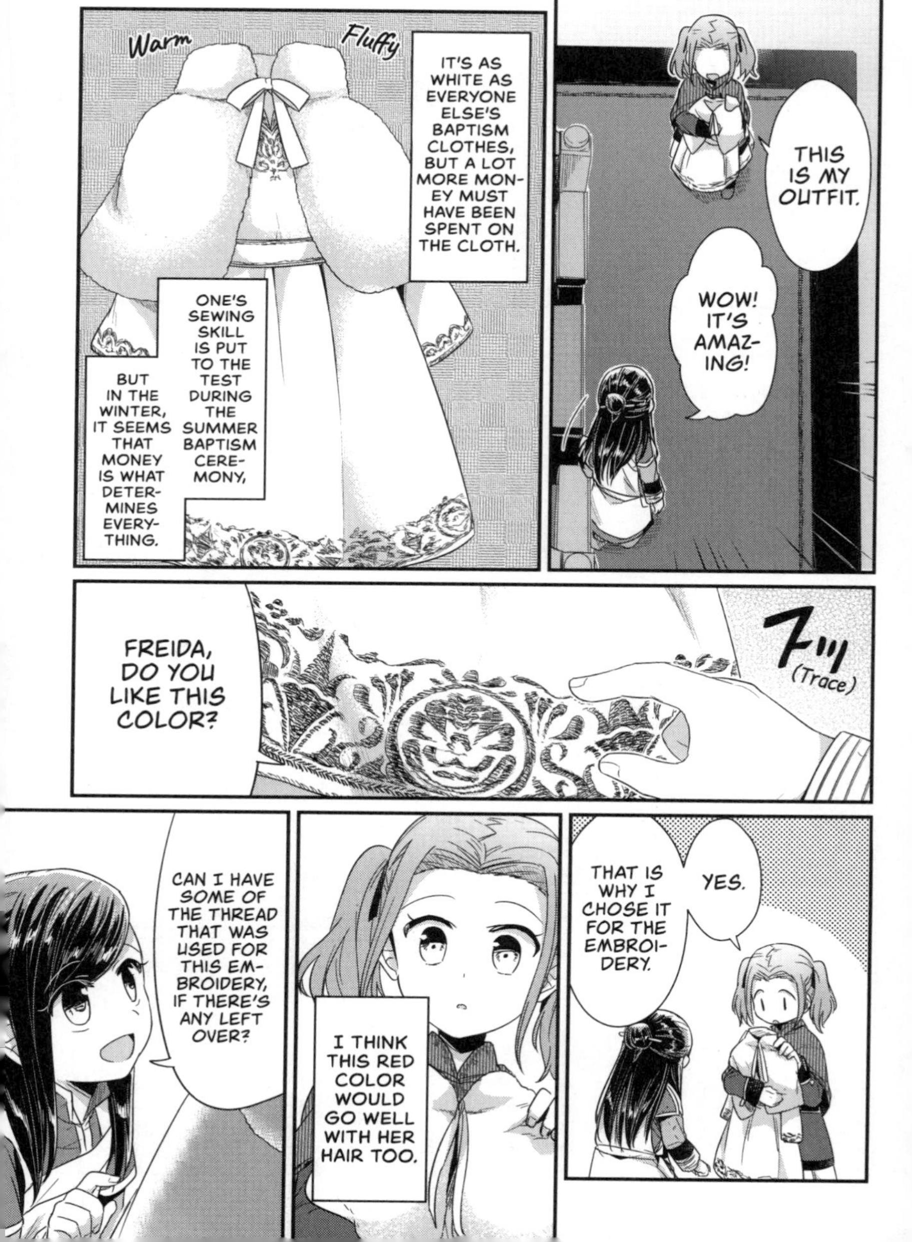
THIS IS MY OUTFIT.
WOW! IT'S AMAZ-ING!
Fluffy
Warm
IT'S AS WHITE AS EVERYONE ELSE'S BAPTISM CLOTHES, BUT A LOT MORE MON-EY MUST HAVE BEEN SPENT ON THE CLOTH.
ONE'S SEWING SKILL IS PUT TO THE TEST DURING THE SUMMER BAPTISM CERE-MONY,
BUT IN THE WINTER, IT SEEMS THAT MONEY IS WHAT DETER-MINES EVERY-THING.
フッ
(Trace)
FREIDA, DO YOU LIKE THIS COLOR?
YES.
THAT IS WHY I CHOSE IT FOR THE EMBROI-DERY.
I THINK THIS RED COLOR WOULD GO WELL WITH HER HAIR TOO.
CAN I HAVE SOME OF THE THREAD THAT WAS USED FOR THIS EM-BROIDERY, IF THERE'S ANY LEFT OVER?

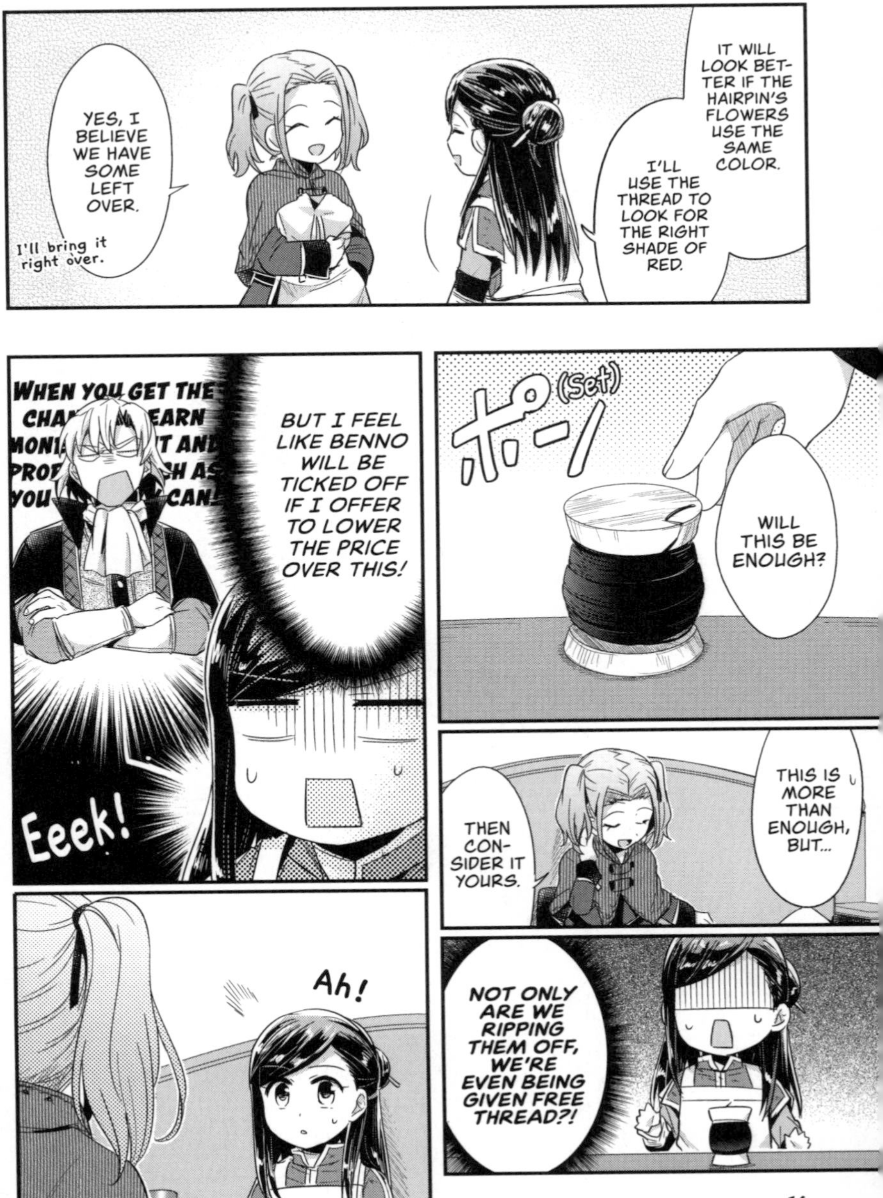
IT WILL LOOK BET-TER IF THE HAIRPIN'S FLOWERS USE THE SAME COLOR.
I'LL USE THE THREAD TO LOOK FOR THE RIGHT SHADE OF RED.
YES, I BELIEVE WE HAVE SOME LEFT OVER.
I'll bring it right over.
(Set)
WILL THIS BE ENOUGH?
THIS IS MORE THAN ENOUGH, BUT...
THEN CON-SIDER IT YOURS.
WHEN YOU GET THE
BUT I FEEL LIKE BENNO WILL BE TICKED OFF IF I OFFER TO LOWER THE PRICE OVER THIS!
Eeek!
NOT ONLY ARE WE RIPPING THEM OFF, WE'RE EVEN BEING GIVEN FREE THREAD?!
Ah!

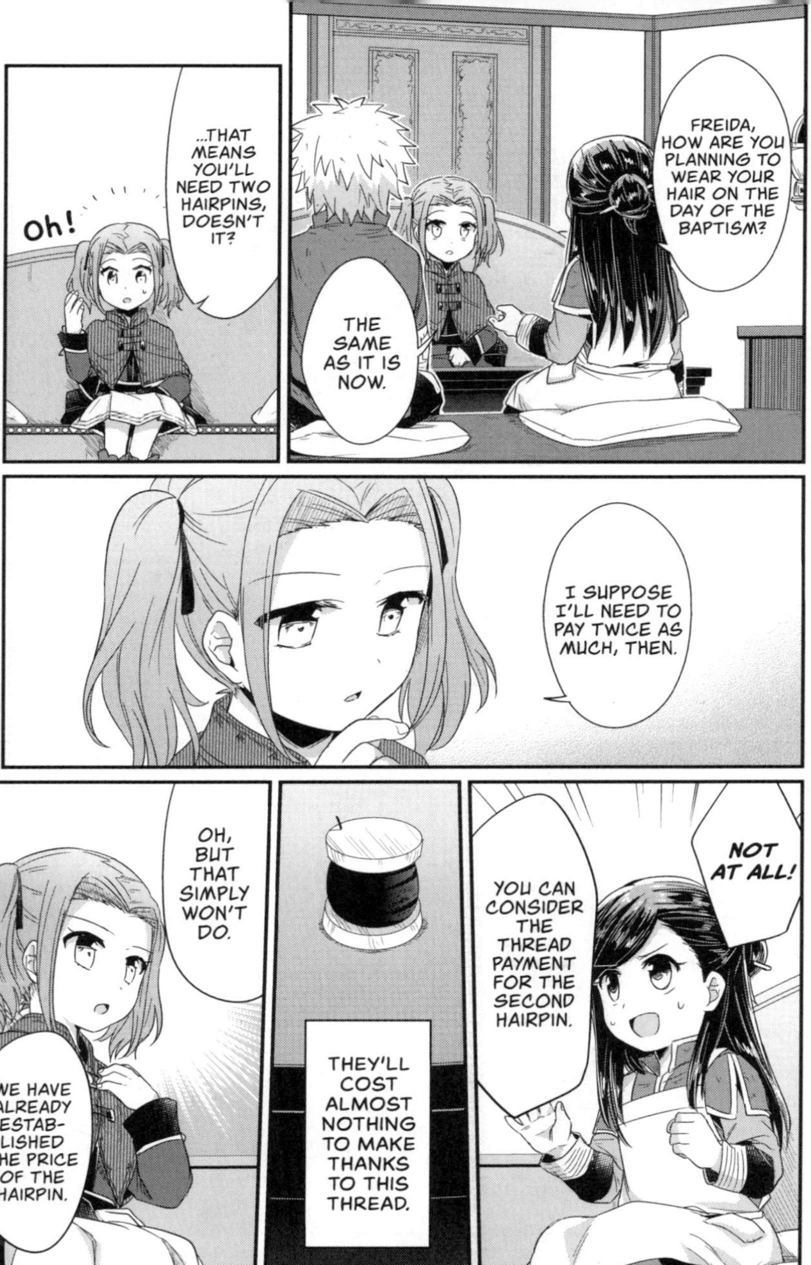
FREIDA, HOW ARE YOU PLANNING TO WEAR YOUR HAIR ON THE DAY OF THE BAPTISM?
THE SAME AS IT IS NOW.
...THAT MEANS YOU'LL NEED TWO HAIRPINS, DOESN'T IT?
Oh!
I SUPPOSE I'LL NEED TO PAY TWICE AS MUCH, THEN.
NOT AT ALL!
YOU CAN CONSIDER THE THREAD PAYMENT FOR THE SECOND HAIRPIN.
THEY'LL COST ALMOST NOTHING TO MAKE THANKS TO THIS THREAD.
OH, BUT THAT SIMPLY WON'T DO.
WE HAVE ALREADY ESTAB-LISHED THE PRICE OF THE HAIRPIN.

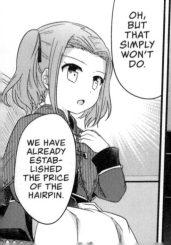

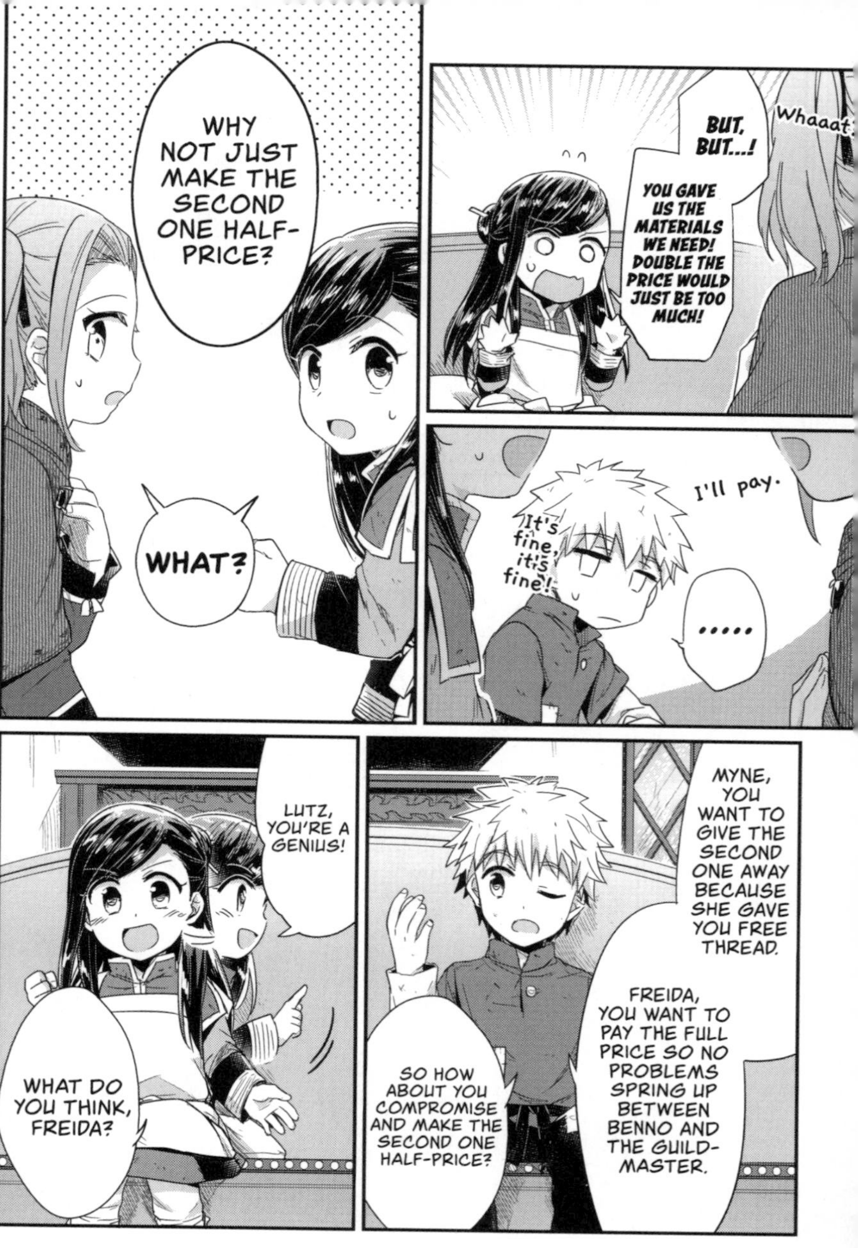
Whaaat!
BUT, BUT...!
YOU GAVE US THE MATERIALS WE NEED! DOUBLE THE PRICE WOULD JUST BE TOO MUCH!
I'll pay.
It's fine, it's fine!
.....
WHY NOT JUST MAKE THE SECOND ONE HALF-PRICE?
WHAT?
MYNE, YOU WANT TO GIVE THE SECOND ONE AWAY BECAUSE SHE GAVE YOU FREE THREAD.
FREIDA, YOU WANT TO PAY THE FULL PRICE SO NO PROBLEMS SPRING UP BETWEEN BENNO AND THE GUILD-MASTER.
SO HOW ABOUT YOU COMPROMISE AND MAKE THE SECOND ONE HALF-PRICE?
LUTZ, YOU'RE A GENIUS!
WHAT DO YOU THINK, FREIDA?

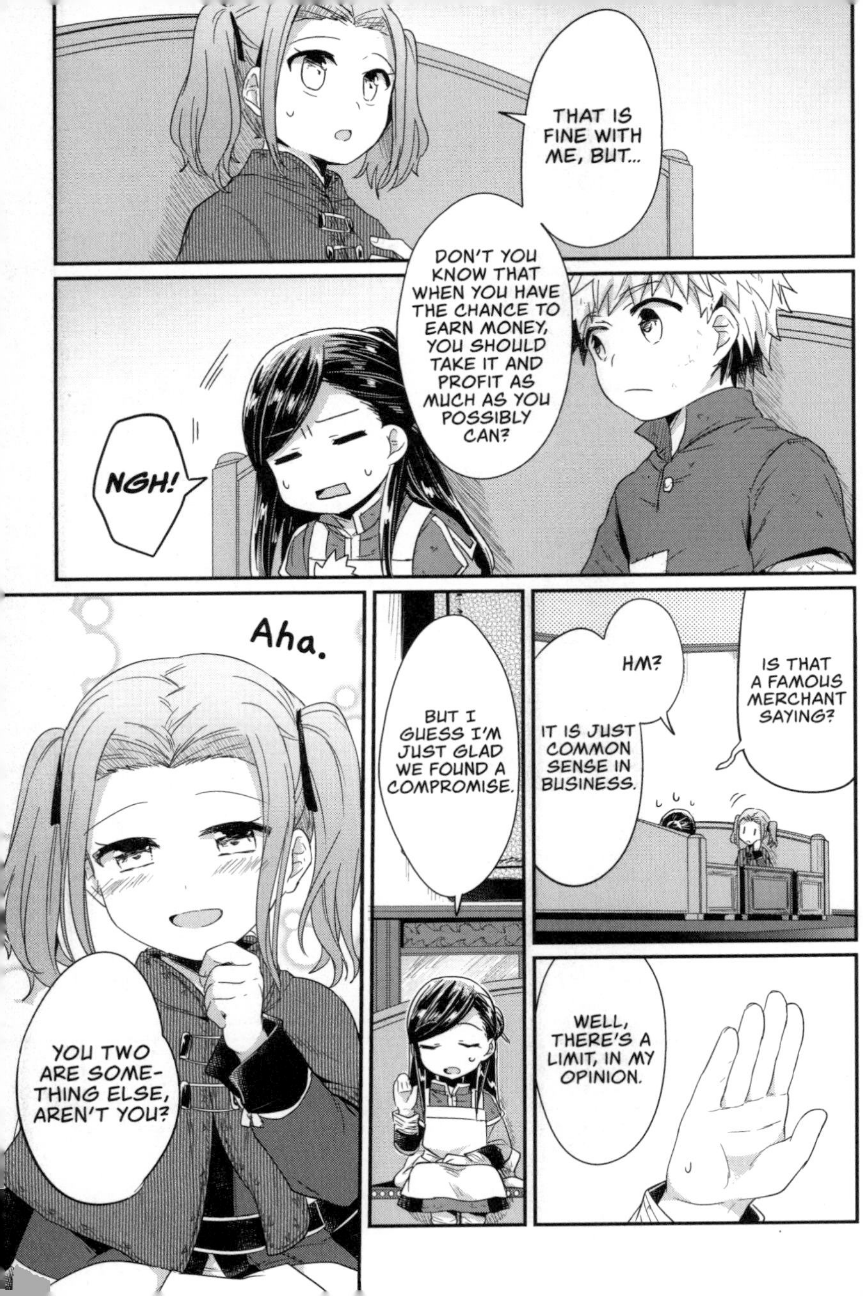
THAT IS FINE WITH ME, BUT...
DON'T YOU KNOW THAT WHEN YOU HAVE THE CHANCE TO EARN MONEY, YOU SHOULD TAKE IT AND PROFIT AS MUCH AS YOU POSSIBLY CAN?
NGH!
IS THAT A FAMOUS MERCHANT SAYING?
HM?
IT IS JUST COMMON SENSE IN BUSINESS.
WELL, THERE'S A LIMIT, IN MY OPINION.
BUT I GUESS I'M JUST GLAD WE FOUND A COMPROMISE.
Aha.
YOU TWO ARE SOME-THING ELSE, AREN'T YOU?

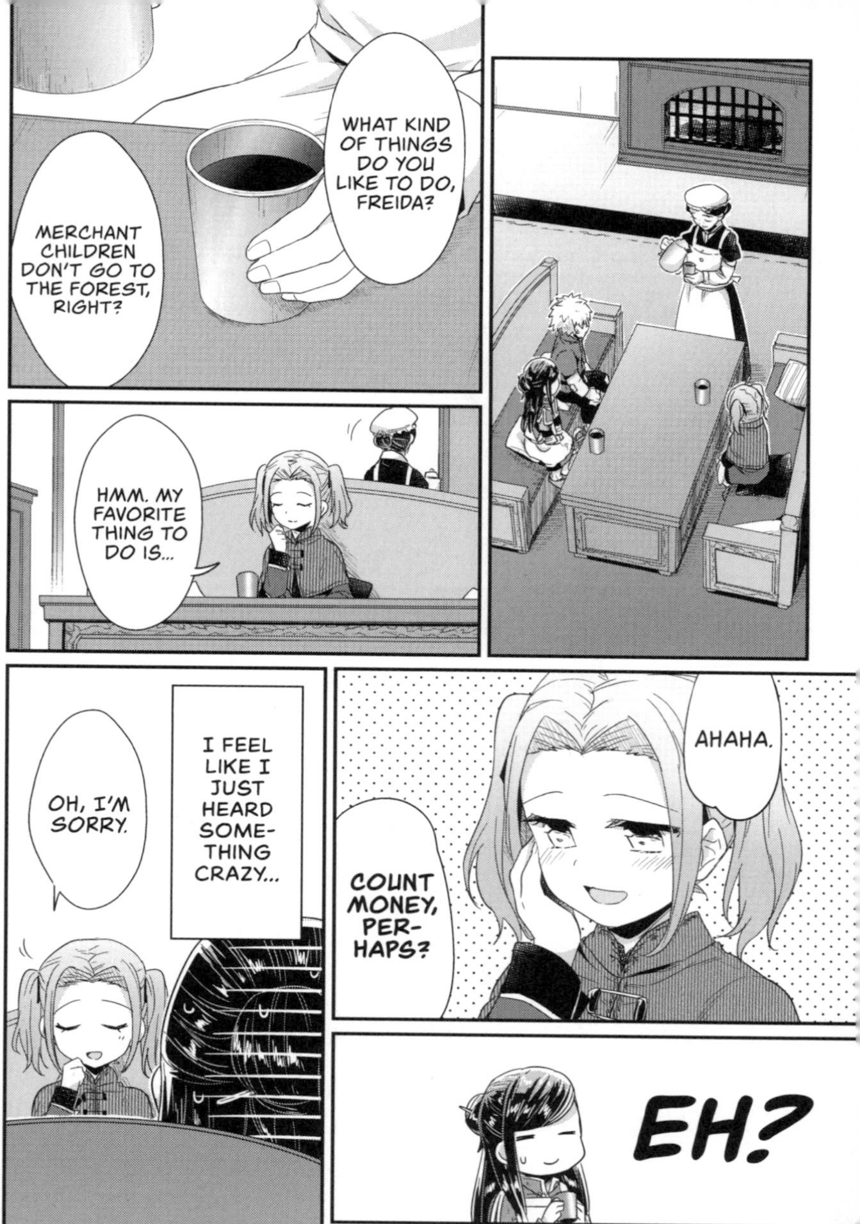
WHAT KIND OF THINGS DO YOU LIKE TO DO, FREIDA?
MERCHANT CHILDREN DON'T GO TO THE FOREST, RIGHT?
HMM. MY FAVORITE THING TO DO IS...
AHAHA.
COUNT MONEY, PER-HAPS?
EH?
I FEEL LIKE I JUST HEARD SOME-THING CRAZY...
OH, I'M SORRY.

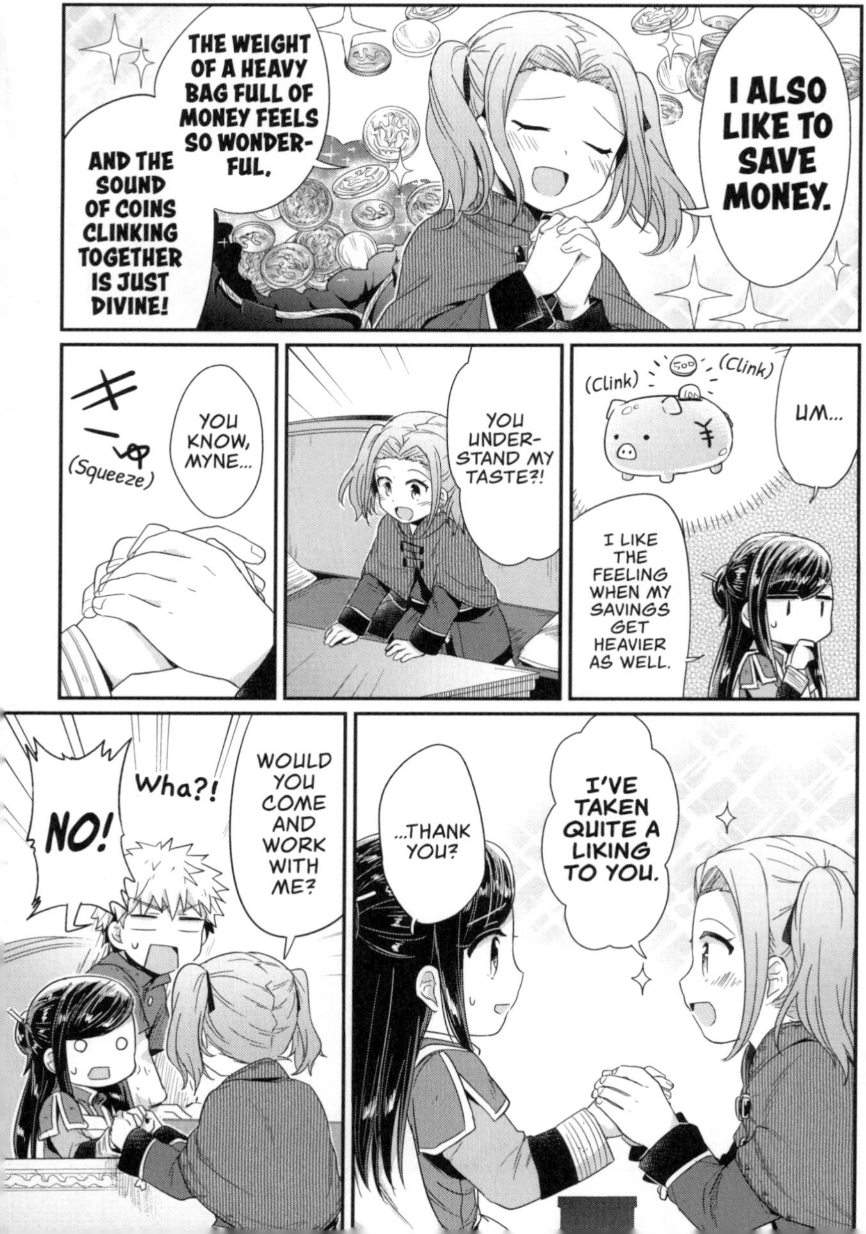
I ALSO LIKE TO SAVE MONEY.
THE WEIGHT OF A HEAVY BAG FULL OF MONEY FEELS SO WONDER-FUL,
AND THE SOUND OF COINS CLINKING TOGETHER IS JUST DIVINE!
UM...
(Clink)
(Clink)
I LIKE THE FEELING WHEN MY SAVINGS GET HEAVIER AS WELL.
YOU UNDER-STAND MY TASTE?!
YOU KNOW, MYNE...
(Squeeze)
I'VE TAKEN QUITE A LIKING TO YOU.
...THANK YOU?
WOULD YOU COME AND WORK WITH ME?
Wha?!
NO!

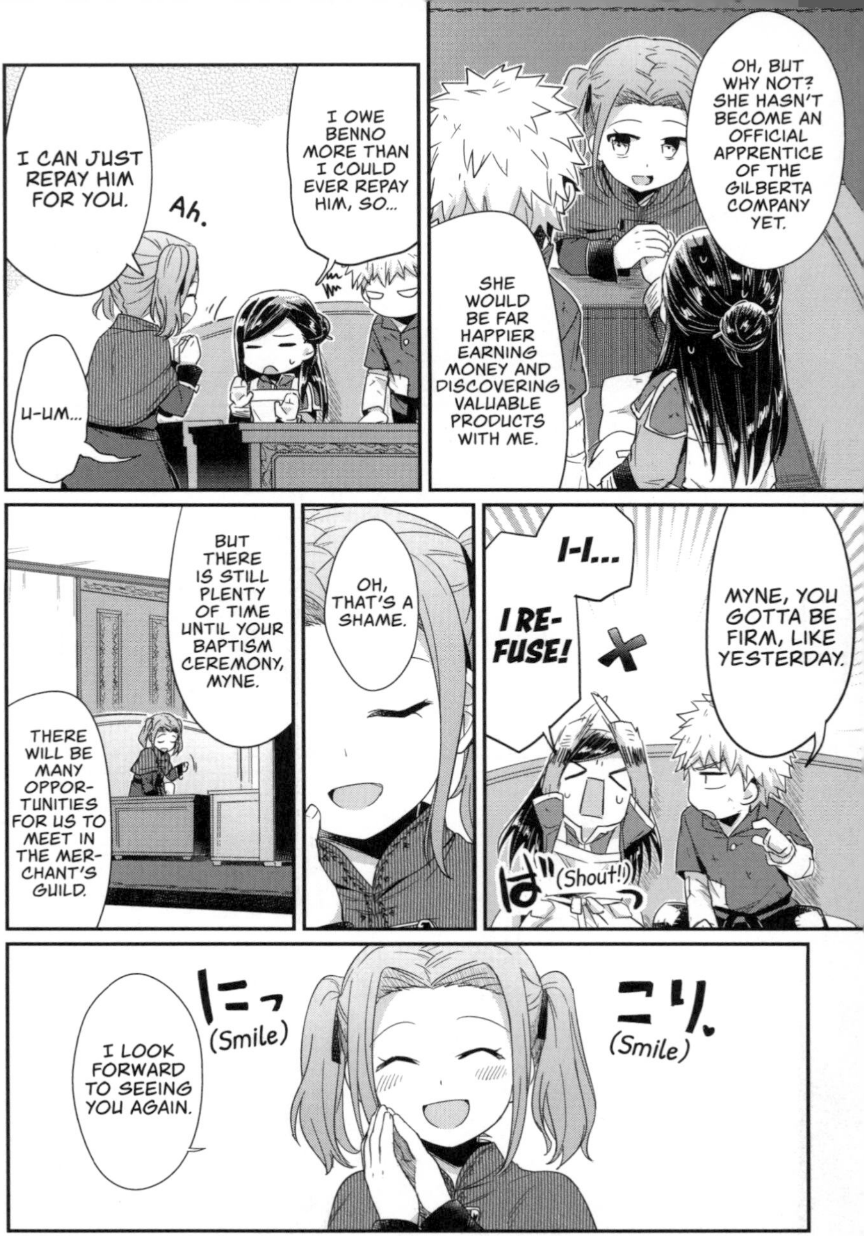

OH, BUT WHY NOT? SHE HASN'T BECOME AN OFFICIAL APPRENTICE OF THE GILBERTA COMPANY YET.
SHE WOULD BE FAR HAPPIER EARNING MONEY AND DISCOVERING VALUABLE PRODUCTS WITH ME.
I OWE BENNO MORE THAN I COULD EVER REPAY HIM, SO...
I CAN JUST REPAY HIM FOR YOU.
Ah.
U-UM...
MYNE, YOU GOTTA BE FIRM, LIKE YESTERDAY.
I-I...
I RE-FUSE!
(Shout!)
OH, THAT'S A SHAME.
BUT THERE IS STILL PLENTY OF TIME UNTIL YOUR BAPTISM CEREMONY, MYNE.
THERE WILL BE MANY OPPOR-TUNITIES FOR US TO MEET IN THE MER-CHANT'S GUILD.
こり。
(Smile)
にっ
(Smile)
I LOOK FORWARD TO SEEING YOU AGAIN.

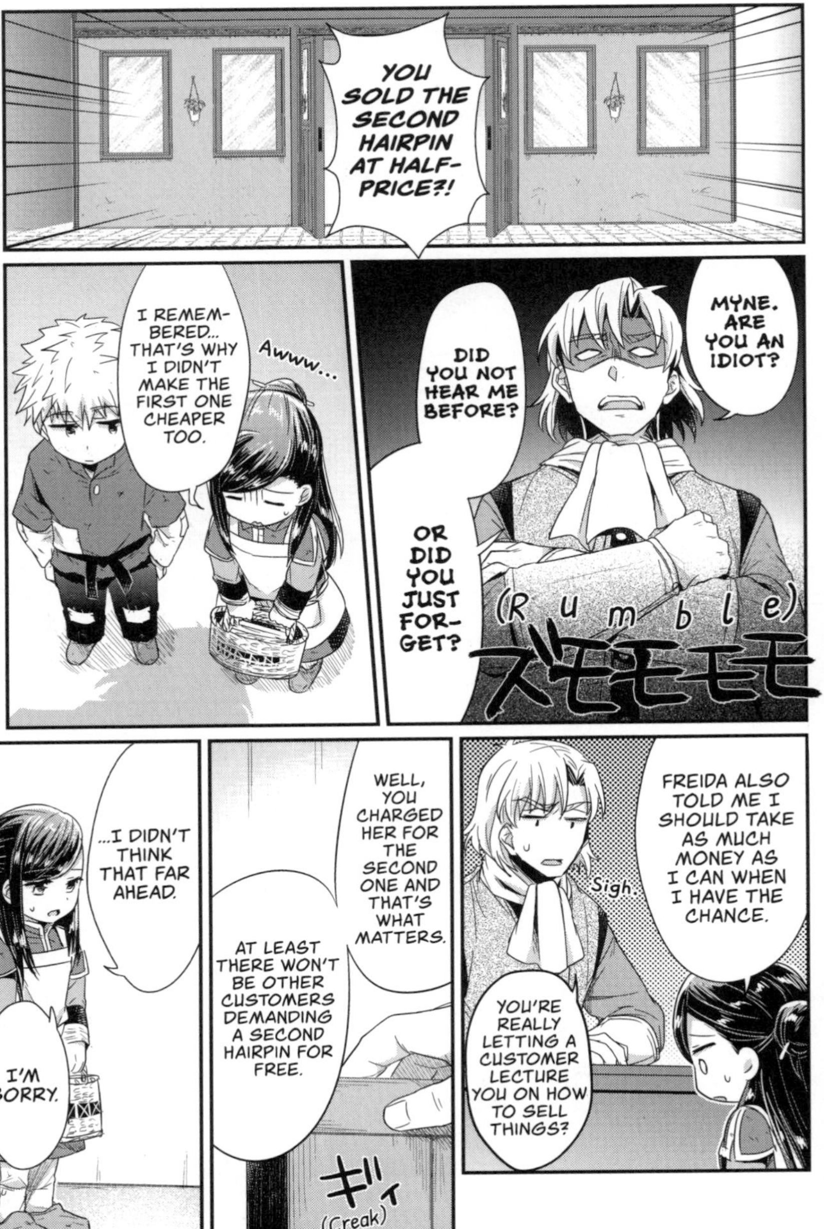
YOU SOLD THE SECOND HAIRPIN AT HALF-PRICE?!
MYNE. ARE YOU AN IDIOT?
DID YOU NOT HEAR ME BEFORE?
OR DID YOU JUST FORGET?
(Rumble)
ズモモモモ
Awww...
I REMEM-BERED... THAT'S WHY I DIDN'T MAKE THE FIRST ONE CHEAPER TOO.
FREIDA ALSO TOLD ME I SHOULD TAKE AS MUCH MONEY AS I CAN WHEN I HAVE THE CHANCE.
Sigh.
YOU'RE REALLY LETTING A CUSTOMER LECTURE YOU ON HOW TO SELL THINGS?
WELL, YOU CHARGED HER FOR THE SECOND ONE AND THAT'S WHAT MATTERS.
AT LEAST THERE WON'T BE OTHER CUSTOMERS DEMANDING A SECOND HAIRPIN FOR FREE.
ギィ
(Creak)
...I DIDN'T THINK THAT FAR AHEAD.
I'M SORRY.

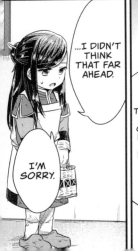

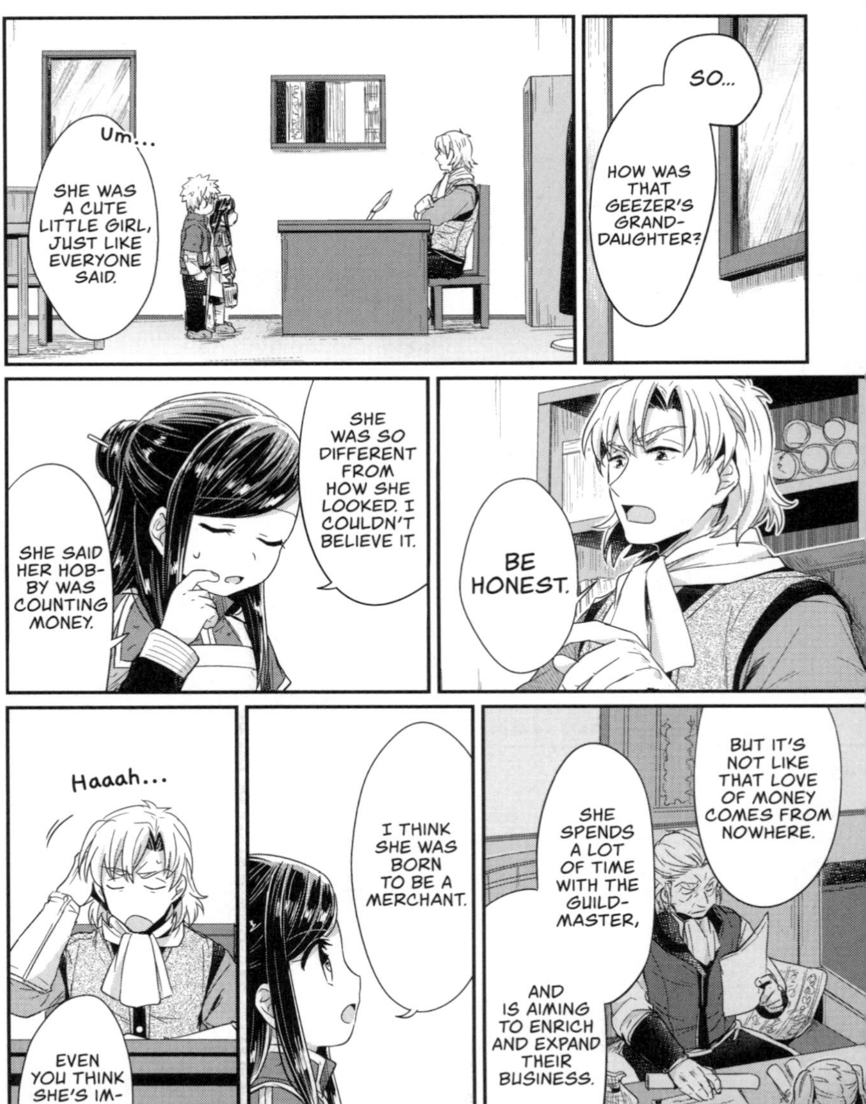
SO...
HOW WAS THAT GEEZER'S GRAND-DAUGHTER?
Um...
SHE WAS A CUTE LITTLE GIRL, JUST LIKE EVERYONE SAID.
BE HONEST.
SHE WAS SO DIFFERENT FROM HOW SHE LOOKED. I COULDN'T BELIEVE IT.
SHE SAID HER HOB-BY WAS COUNTING MONEY.
BUT IT'S NOT LIKE THAT LOVE OF MONEY COMES FROM NOWHERE.
SHE SPENDS A LOT OF TIME WITH THE GUILD-MASTER,
AND IS AIMING TO ENRICH AND EXPAND THEIR BUSINESS.
I THINK SHE WAS BORN TO BE A MERCHANT.
Haaah...
EVEN YOU THINK SHE'S IM-PRESSIVE, HUH?

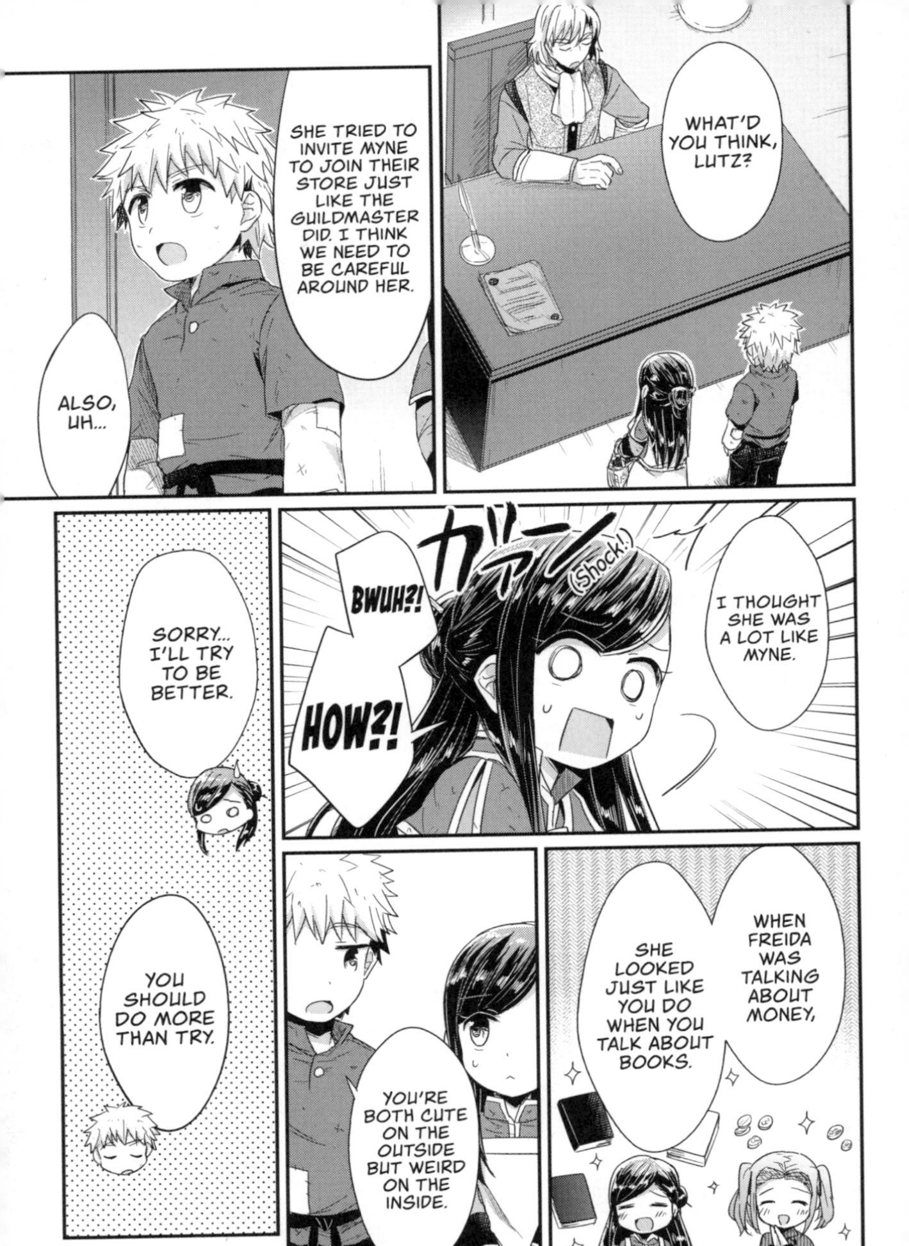
WHAT'D YOU THINK, LUTZ?
SHE TRIED TO INVITE MYNE TO JOIN THEIR STORE JUST LIKE THE GUILDMASTER DID. I THINK WE NEED TO BE CAREFUL AROUND HER.
ALSO, UH...
I THOUGHT SHE WAS A LOT LIKE MYNE.
(Shock!)
BWUH?!
HOW?!
WHEN FREIDA WAS TALKING ABOUT MONEY,
SHE LOOKED JUST LIKE YOU DO WHEN YOU TALK ABOUT BOOKS.
YOU'RE BOTH CUTE ON THE OUTSIDE BUT WEIRD ON THE INSIDE.
SORRY... I'LL TRY TO BE BETTER.
YOU SHOULD DO MORE THAN TRY.

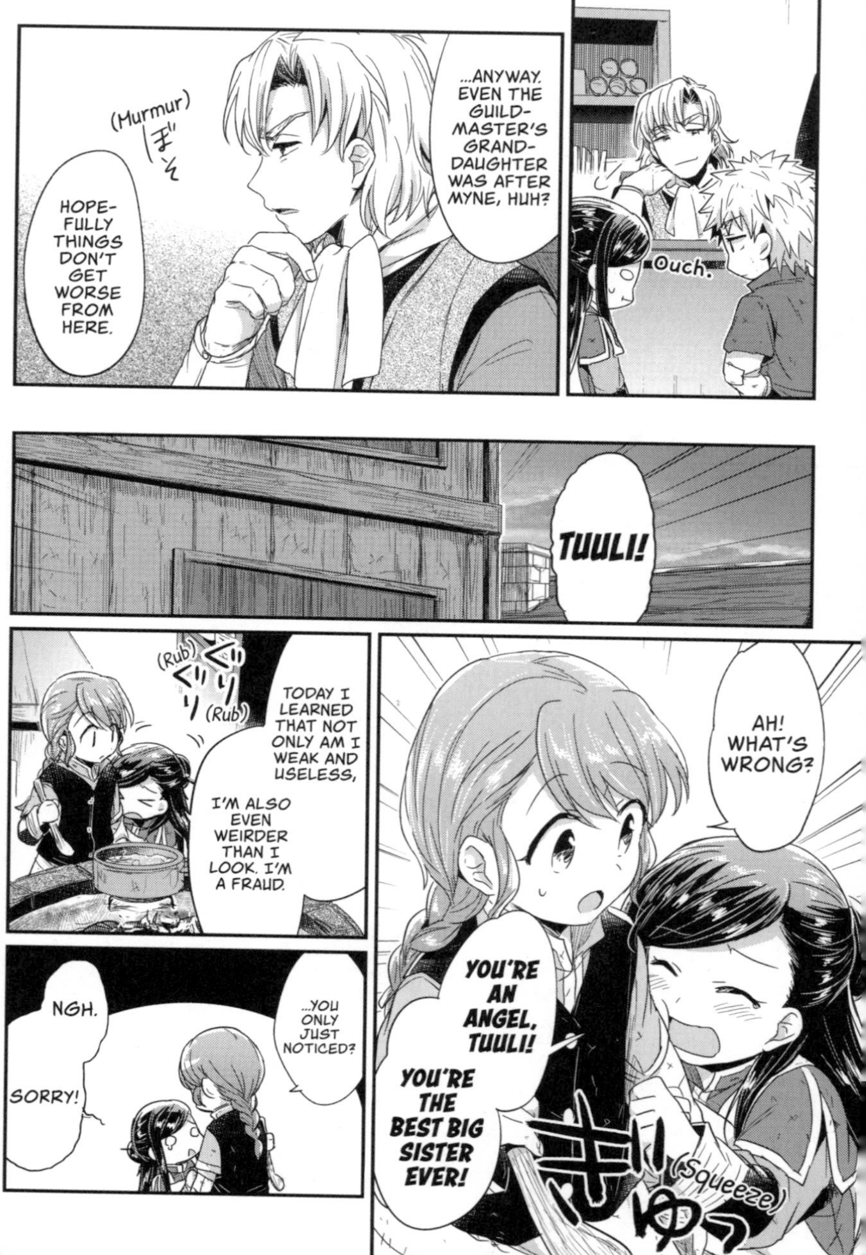
Ouch.
...ANYWAY. EVEN THE GUILD-MASTER'S GRAND-DAUGHTER WAS AFTER MYNE, HUH?
(Murmur)
HOPE-FULLY THINGS DON'T GET WORSE FROM HERE.
TUULI!
AH! WHAT'S WRONG?
YOU'RE AN ANGEL, TUULI!
YOU'RE THE BEST BIG SISTER EVER!
(Squeeze)
(Rub) (Rub)
TODAY I LEARNED THAT NOT ONLY AM I WEAK AND USELESS,
I'M ALSO EVEN WEIRDER THAN I LOOK. I'M A FRAUD.
...YOU ONLY JUST NOTICED?
NGH.
SORRY!

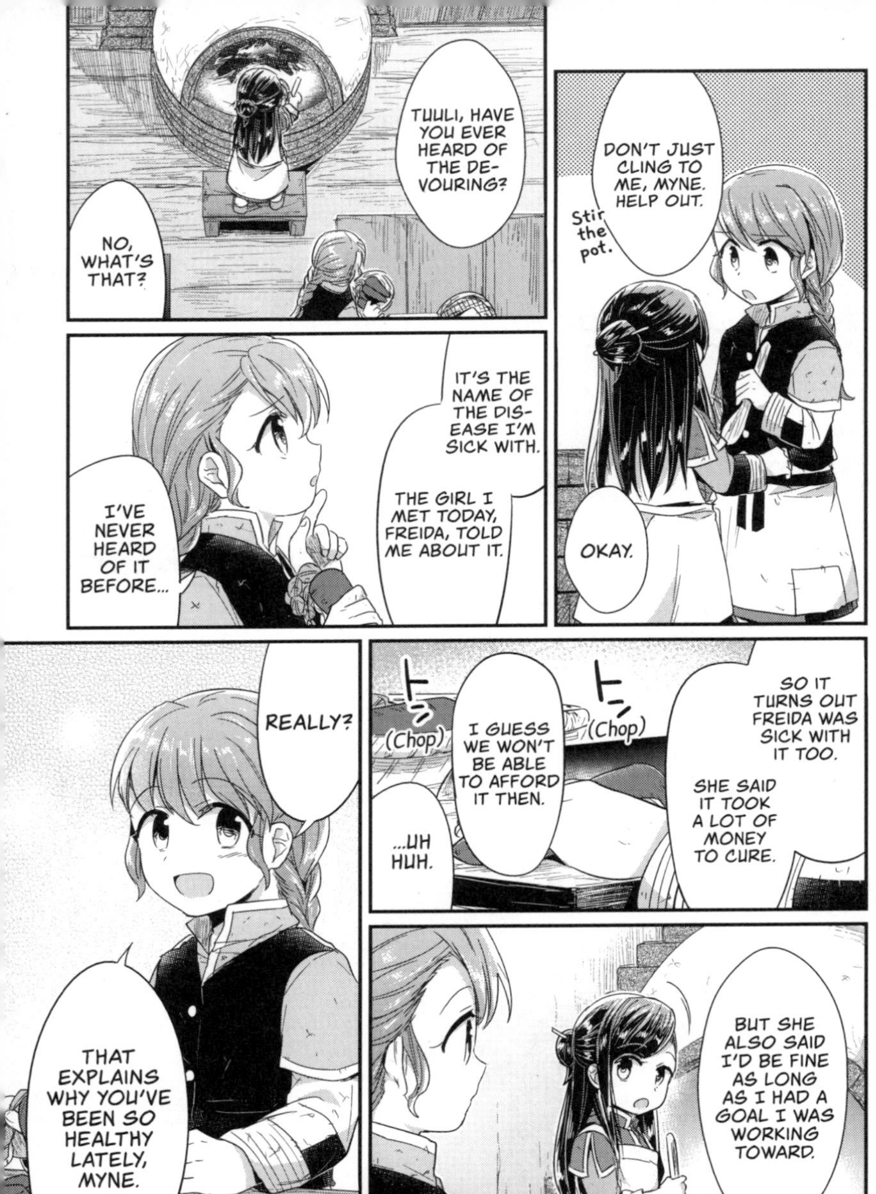
DON'T JUST CLING TO ME, MYNE. HELP OUT.
Stir the pot.
OKAY.
TUULI, HAVE YOU EVER HEARD OF THE DE-VOURING?
NO, WHAT'S THAT?
IT'S THE NAME OF THE DIS-EASE I'M SICK WITH.
THE GIRL I MET TODAY, FREIDA, TOLD ME ABOUT IT.
I'VE NEVER HEARD OF IT BEFORE...
SO IT TURNS OUT FREIDA WAS SICK WITH IT TOO.
SHE SAID IT TOOK A LOT OF MONEY TO CURE.
(Chop)
I GUESS WE WON'T BE ABLE TO AFFORD IT THEN.
(Chop)
...UH HUH.
BUT SHE ALSO SAID I'D BE FINE AS LONG AS I HAD A GOAL I WAS WORKING TOWARD.
REALLY?
THAT EXPLAINS WHY YOU'VE BEEN SO HEALTHY LATELY, MYNE.

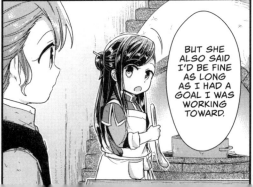

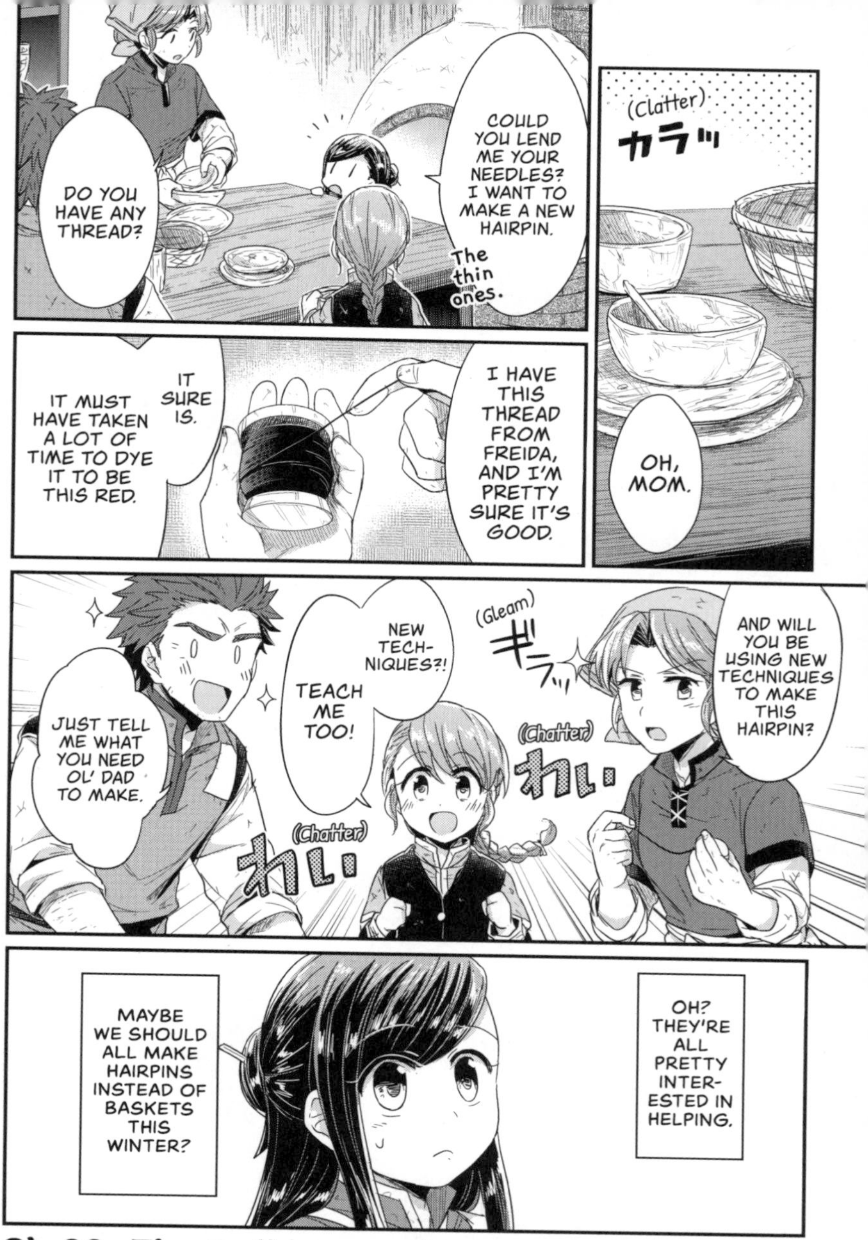
(Clatter)
カラッ
OH, MOM.
COULD YOU LEND ME YOUR NEEDLES? I WANT TO MAKE A NEW HAIRPIN.
The thin ones.
DO YOU HAVE ANY THREAD?
I HAVE THIS THREAD FROM FREIDA, AND I'M PRETTY SURE IT'S GOOD.
IT SURE IS.
IT MUST HAVE TAKEN A LOT OF TIME TO DYE IT TO BE THIS RED.
AND WILL YOU BE USING NEW TECHNIQUES TO MAKE THIS HAIRPIN?
(Gleam)
ギラッ
(Chatter)
わい
NEW TECH-NIQUES?!
TEACH ME TOO!
(Chatter)
わい
JUST TELL ME WHAT YOU NEED OL' DAD TO MAKE.
OH? THEY'RE ALL PRETTY INTER-ESTED IN HELPING.
MAYBE WE SHOULD ALL MAKE HAIRPINS INSTEAD OF BASKETS THIS WINTER?

Ch.20: The Guildmaster's Granddaughter End

Ch.21 Freida's Hairpins

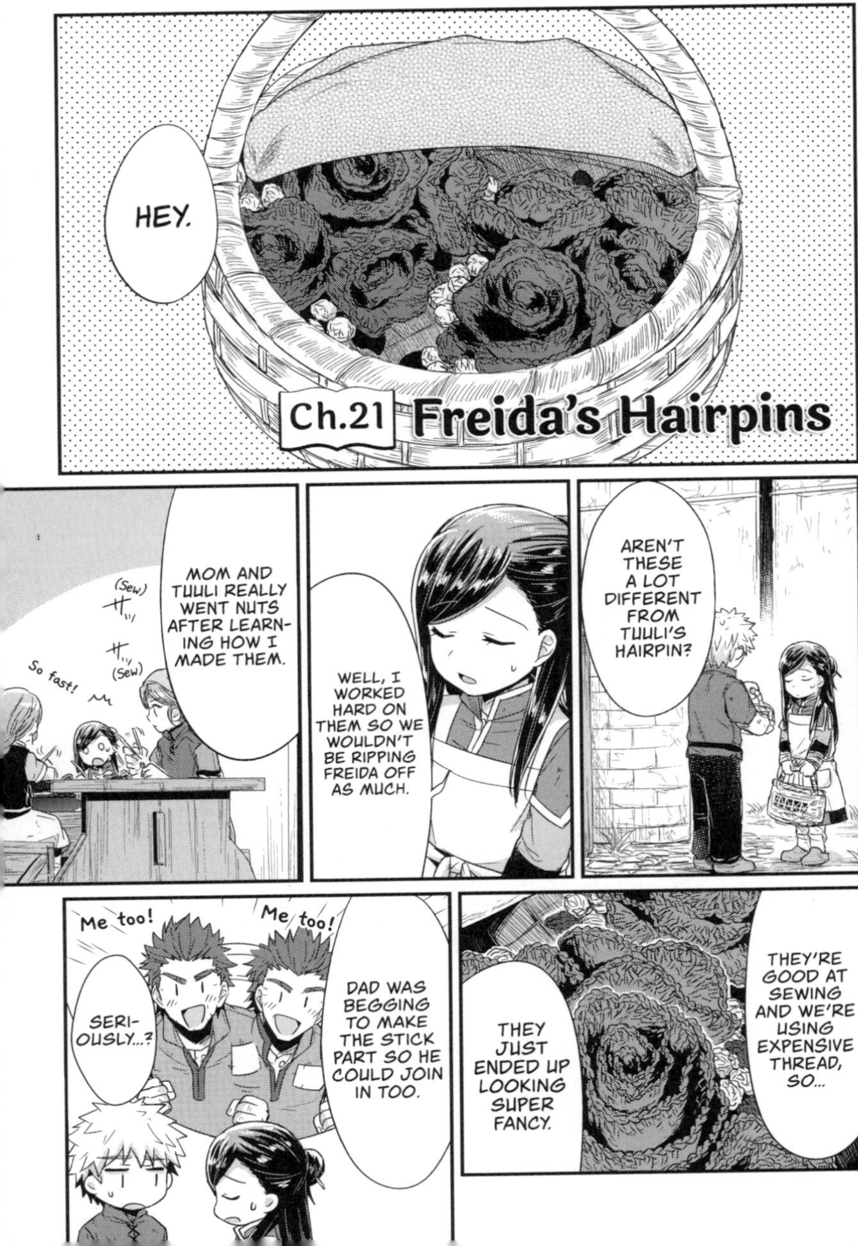
HEY.
AREN'T THESE A LOT DIFFERENT FROM TUULI'S HAIRPIN?
WELL, I WORKED HARD ON THEM SO WE WOULDN'T BE RIPPING FREIDA OFF AS MUCH.
MOM AND TUULI REALLY WENT NUTS AFTER LEARNING HOW I MADE THEM.
(Sew)
(Sew)
So fast!
THEY'RE GOOD AT SEWING AND WE'RE USING EXPENSIVE THREAD, SO...
THEY JUST ENDED UP LOOKING SUPER FANCY.
DAD WAS BEGGING TO MAKE THE STICK PART SO HE COULD JOIN IN TOO.
Me too!
Me too!
SERI-OUSLY...?

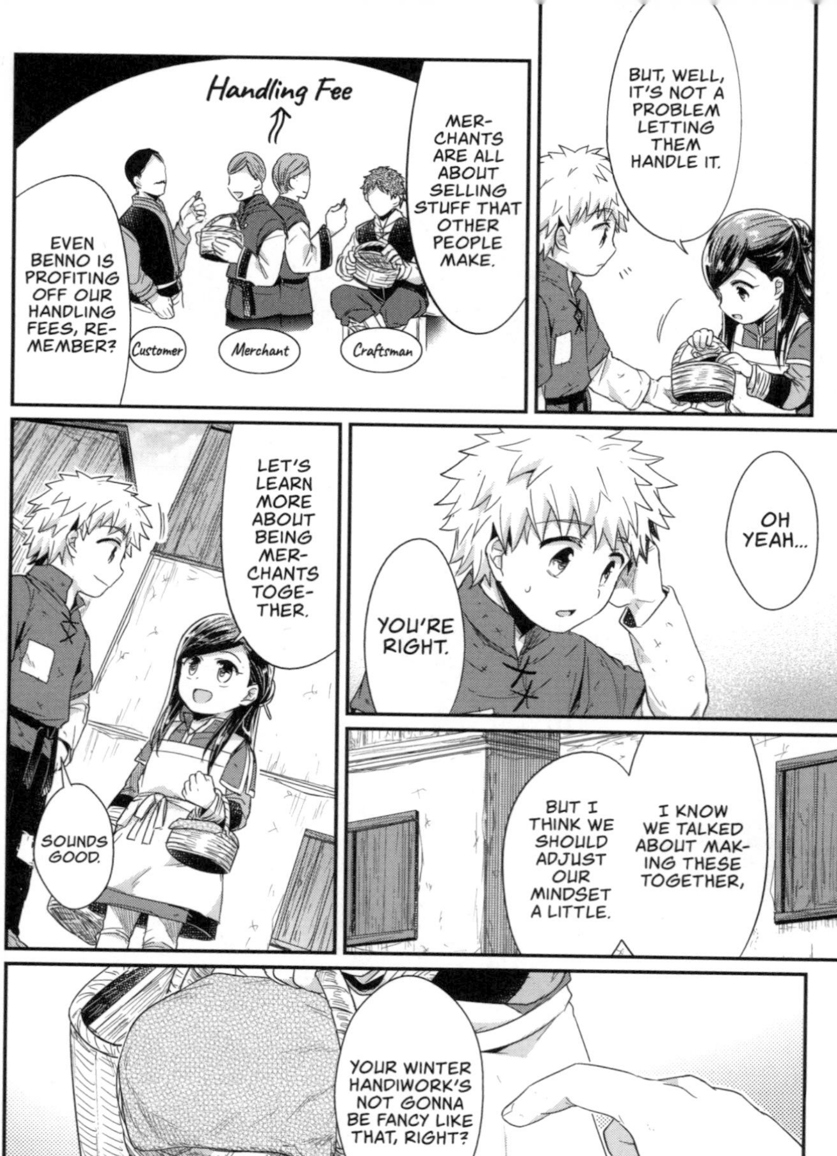
BUT, WELL, IT'S NOT A PROBLEM LETTING THEM HANDLE IT.
Handling Fee
MER-CHANTS ARE ALL ABOUT SELLING STUFF THAT OTHER PEOPLE MAKE.
EVEN BENNO IS PROFITING OFF OUR HANDLING FEES, RE-MEMBER?
Customer
Merchant
Craftsman
OH YEAH...
YOU'RE RIGHT.
I KNOW WE TALKED ABOUT MAK-ING THESE TOGETHER,
BUT I THINK WE SHOULD ADJUST OUR MINDSET A LITTLE.
LET'S LEARN MORE ABOUT BEING MER-CHANTS TOGE-THER.
SOUNDS GOOD.
YOUR WINTER HANDIWORK'S NOT GONNA BE FANCY LIKE THAT, RIGHT?

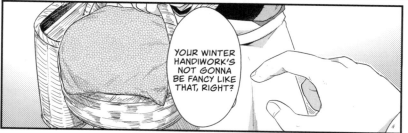

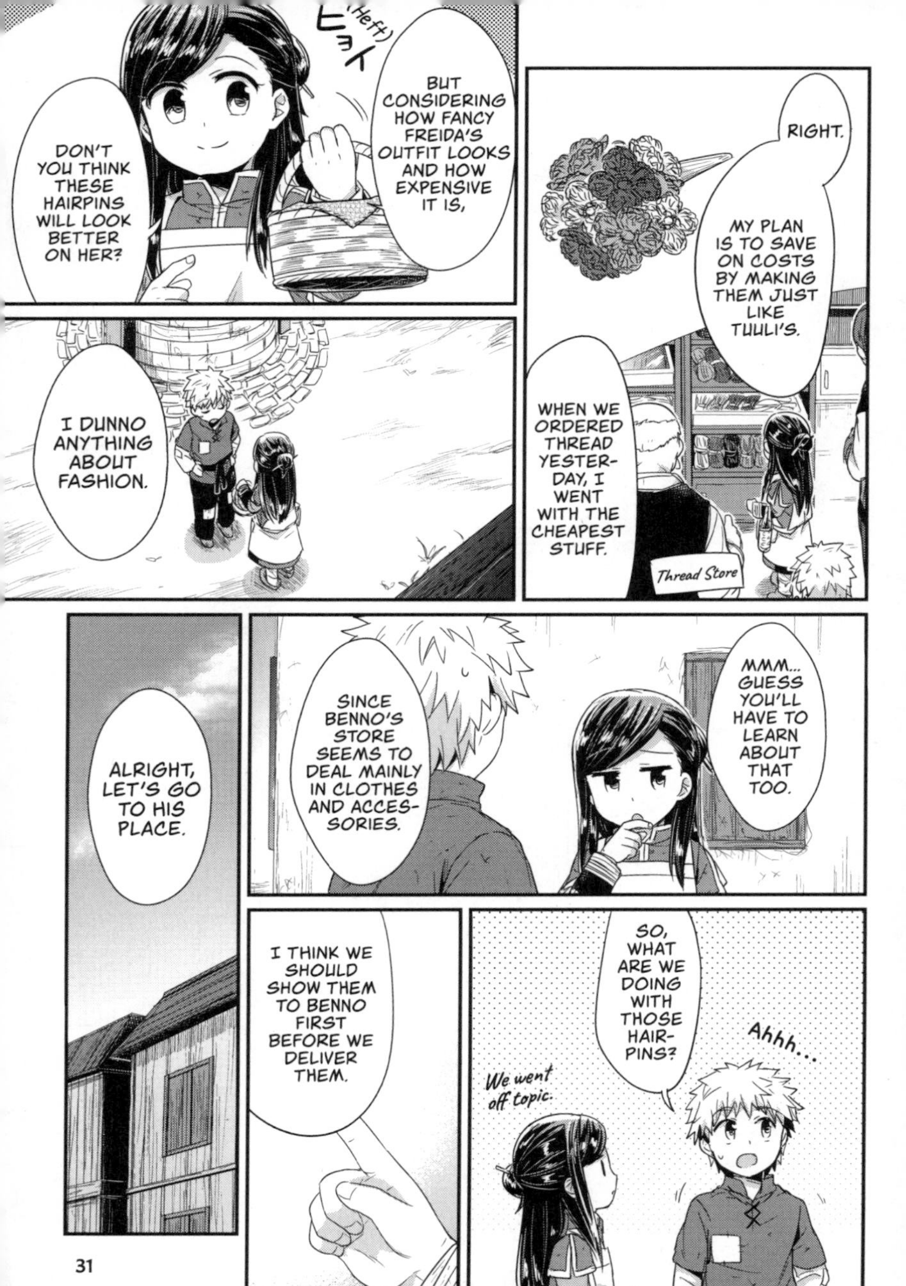
RIGHT.
MY PLAN IS TO SAVE ON COSTS BY MAKING THEM JUST LIKE TUULI'S.
WHEN WE ORDERED THREAD YESTER-DAY, I WENT WITH THE CHEAPEST STUFF.
Thread Store
ヒョイ (Heft)
BUT CONSIDERING HOW FANCY FREIDA'S OUTFIT LOOKS AND HOW EXPENSIVE IT IS,
DON'T YOU THINK THESE HAIRPINS WILL LOOK BETTER ON HER?
I DUNNO ANYTHING ABOUT FASHION.
MMM... GUESS YOU'LL HAVE TO LEARN ABOUT THAT TOO.
SINCE BENNO'S STORE SEEMS TO DEAL MAINLY IN CLOTHES AND ACCES-SORIES.
SO, WHAT ARE WE DOING WITH THOSE HAIR-PINS?
Ahhh...
We went off topic.
I THINK WE SHOULD SHOW THEM TO BENNO FIRST BEFORE WE DELIVER THEM.
ALRIGHT, LET'S GO TO HIS PLACE.

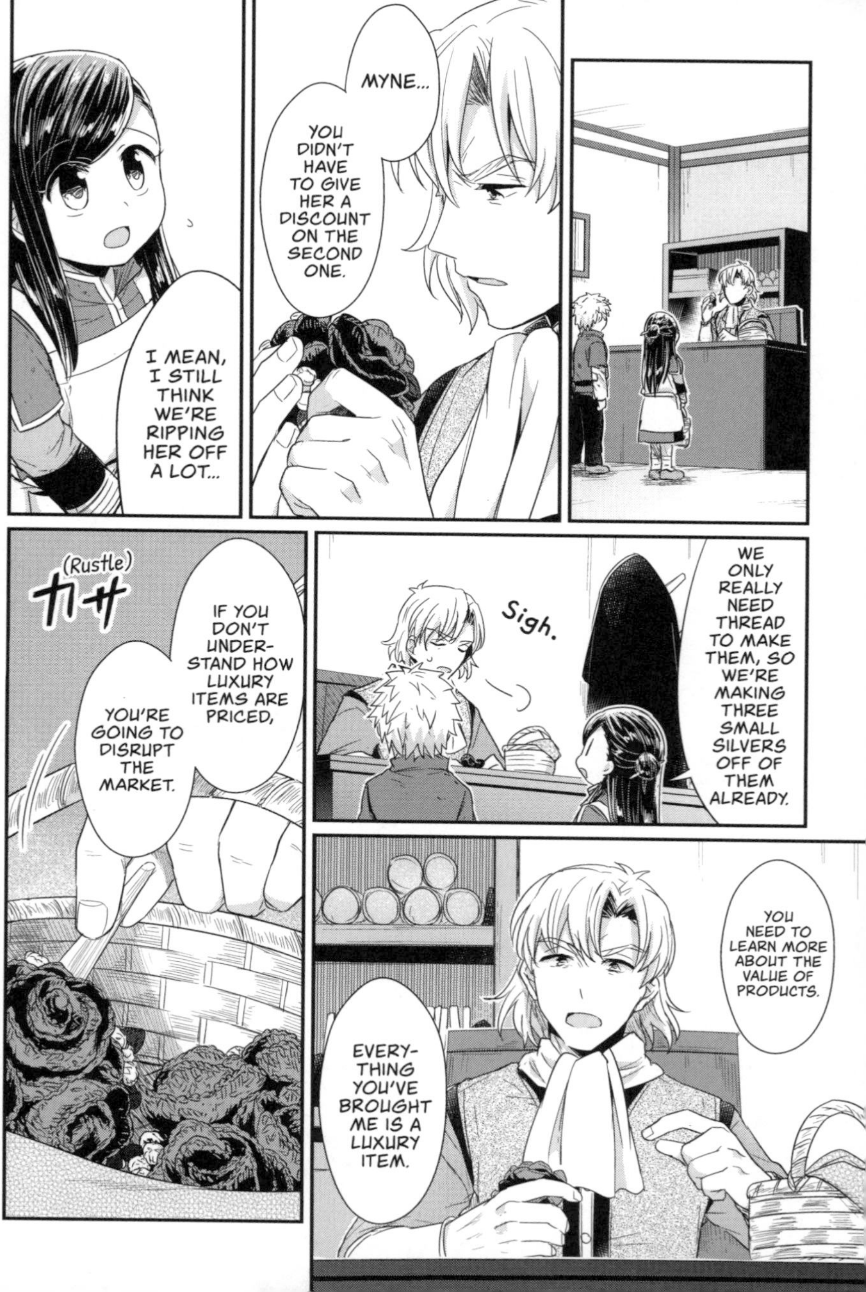
MYNE...
YOU DIDN'T HAVE TO GIVE HER A DISCOUNT ON THE SECOND ONE.
I MEAN, I STILL THINK WE'RE RIPPING HER OFF A LOT...
WE ONLY REALLY NEED THREAD TO MAKE THEM, SO WE'RE MAKING THREE SMALL SILVERS OFF OF THEM ALREADY.
Sigh.
YOU NEED TO LEARN MORE ABOUT THE VALUE OF PRODUCTS.
EVERYTHING YOU'VE BROUGHT ME IS A LUXURY ITEM.
(Rustle)
カサ
IF YOU DON'T UNDERSTAND HOW LUXURY ITEMS ARE PRICED,
YOU'RE GOING TO DISRUPT THE MARKET.

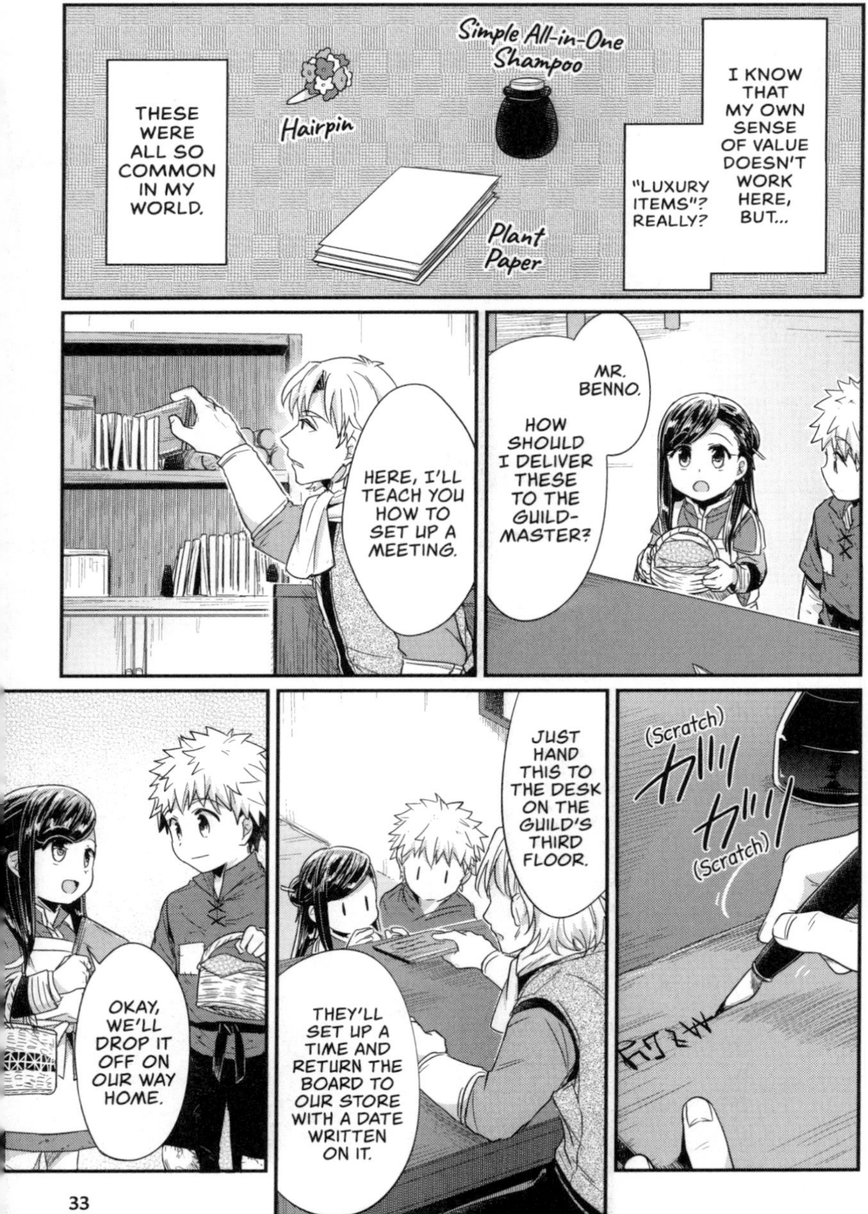
I KNOW THAT MY OWN SENSE OF VALUE DOESN'T WORK HERE, BUT...
"LUXURY ITEMS"? REALLY?
Simple All-in-One Shampoo
Hairpin
THESE WERE ALL SO COMMON IN MY WORLD.
Plant Paper
MR. BENNO.
HOW SHOULD I DELIVER THESE TO THE GUILD-MASTER?
HERE, I'LL TEACH YOU HOW TO SET UP A MEETING.
(Scratch)
(Scratch)
JUST HAND THIS TO THE DESK ON THE GUILD'S THIRD FLOOR.
THEY'LL SET UP A TIME AND RETURN THE BOARD TO OUR STORE WITH A DATE WRITTEN ON IT.
OKAY, WE'LL DROP IT OFF ON OUR WAY HOME.

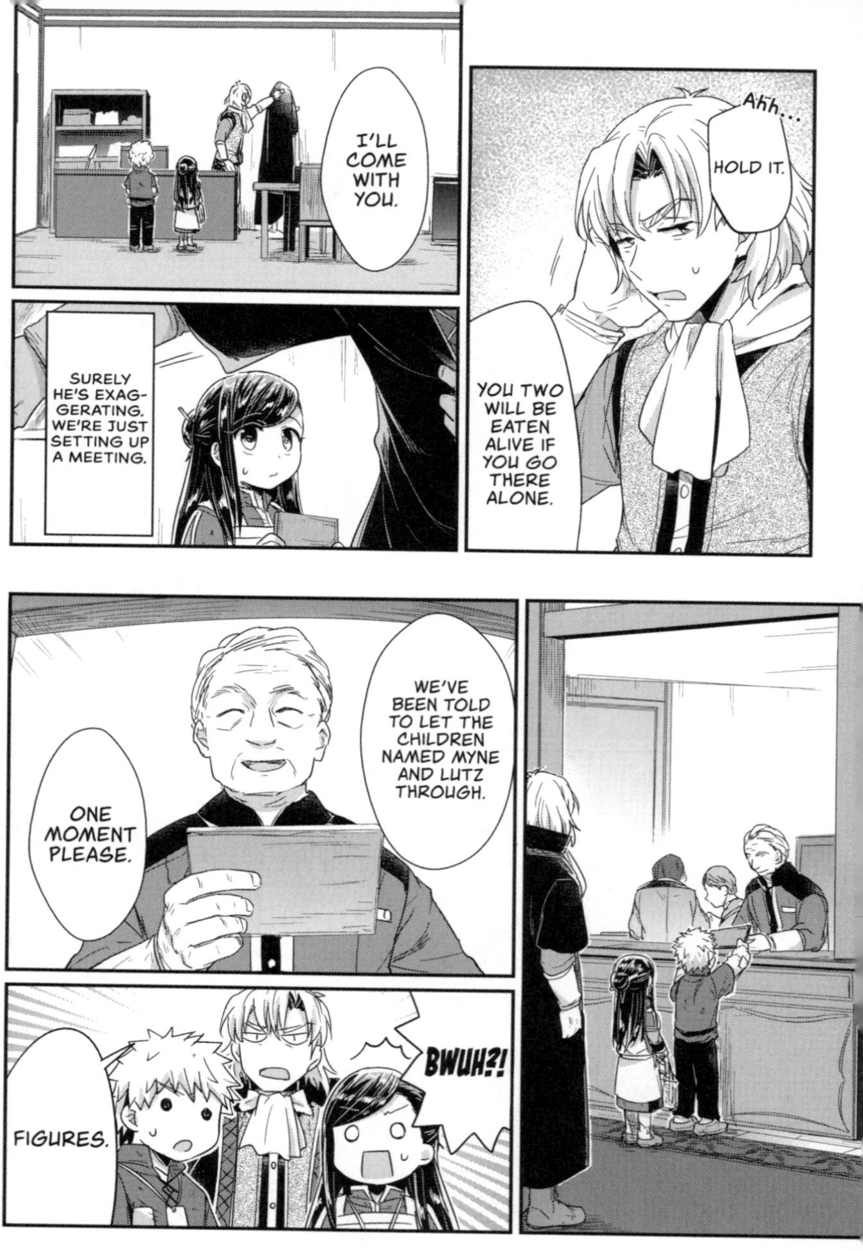
Ahh...
HOLD IT.
YOU TWO WILL BE EATEN ALIVE IF YOU GO THERE ALONE.
I'LL COME WITH YOU.
SURELY HE'S EXAG-GERATING. WE'RE JUST SETTING UP A MEETING.
WE'VE BEEN TOLD TO LET THE CHILDREN NAMED MYNE AND LUTZ THROUGH.
ONE MOMENT PLEASE.
BWUH?!
FIGURES.

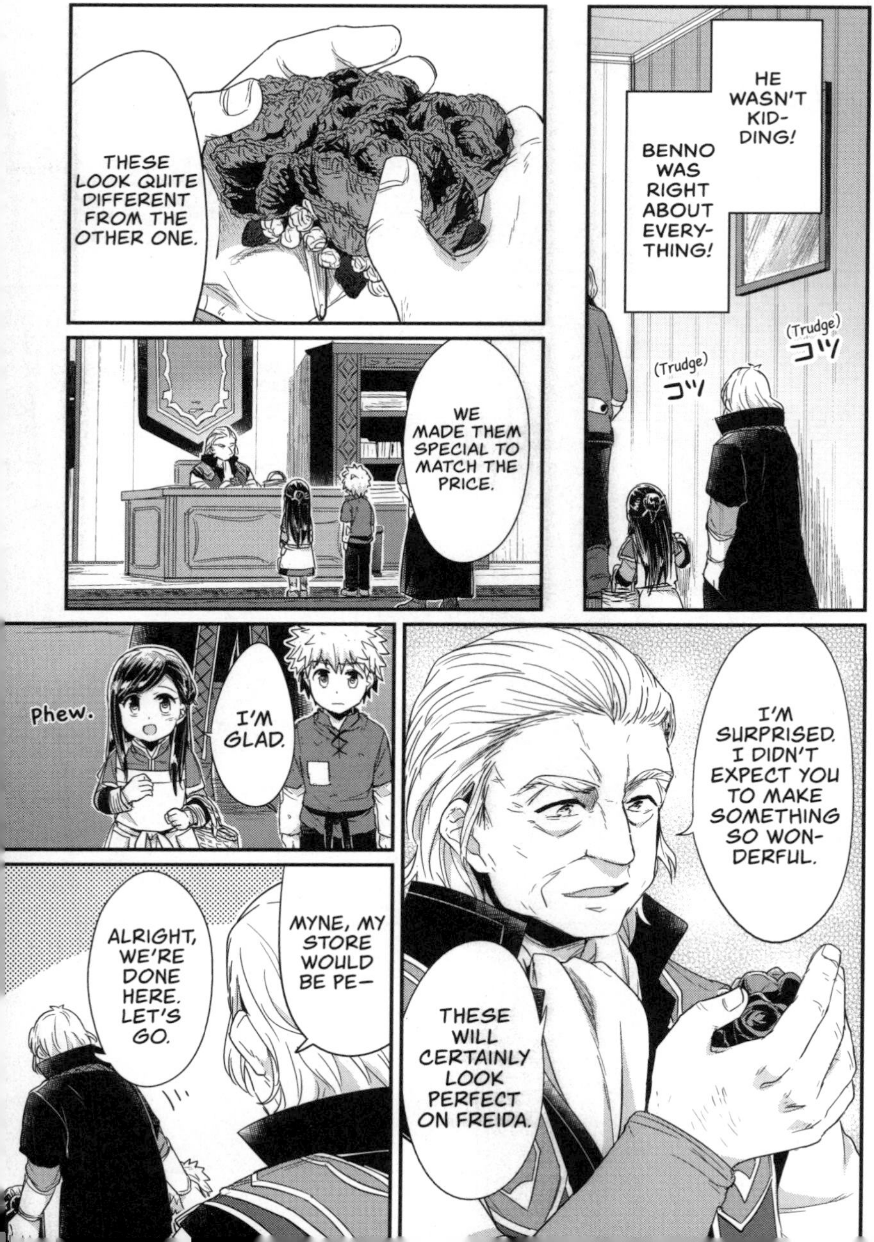

HE WASN'T KID-DING!
BENNO WAS RIGHT ABOUT EVERY-THING!
(Trudge) コツ
(Trudge) コツ
THESE LOOK QUITE DIFFERENT FROM THE OTHER ONE.
WE MADE THEM SPECIAL TO MATCH THE PRICE.
I'M SURPRISED. I DIDN'T EXPECT YOU TO MAKE SOMETHING SO WON-DERFUL.
THESE WILL CERTAINLY LOOK PERFECT ON FREIDA.
I'M GLAD.
Phew.
MYNE, MY STORE WOULD BE PE—
ALRIGHT, WE'RE DONE HERE. LET'S GO.

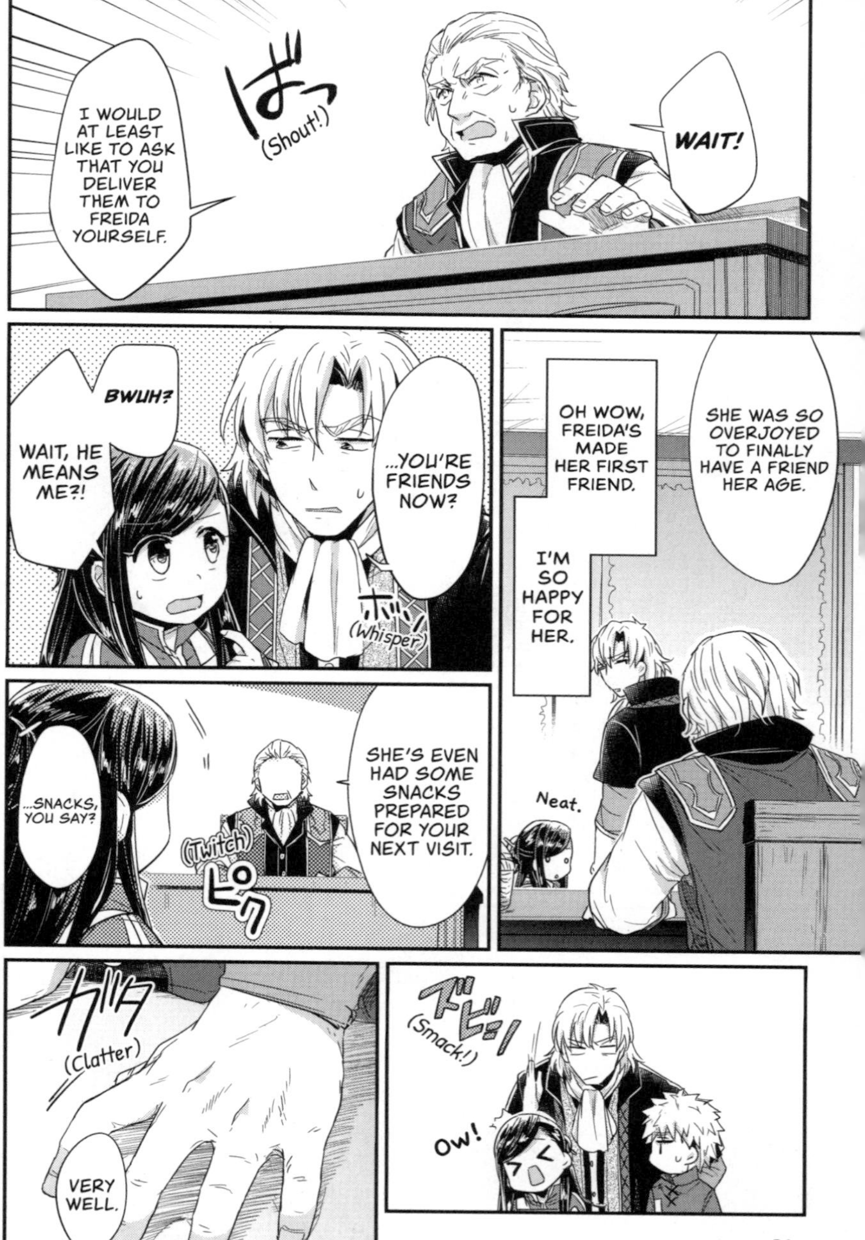
WAIT!
ばっ
(Shout!)
I WOULD AT LEAST LIKE TO ASK THAT YOU DELIVER THEM TO FREIDA YOURSELF.
SHE WAS SO OVERJOYED TO FINALLY HAVE A FRIEND HER AGE.
OH WOW, FREIDA'S MADE HER FIRST FRIEND.
I'M SO HAPPY FOR HER.
Neat.
...YOU'RE FRIENDS NOW?
(Whisper)
BWUH?
WAIT, HE MEANS ME?!
SHE'S EVEN HAD SOME SNACKS PREPARED FOR YOUR NEXT VISIT.
(Twitch)
ピク
...SNACKS, YOU SAY?
(Smack!)
Ow!
(Clatter)
VERY WELL.

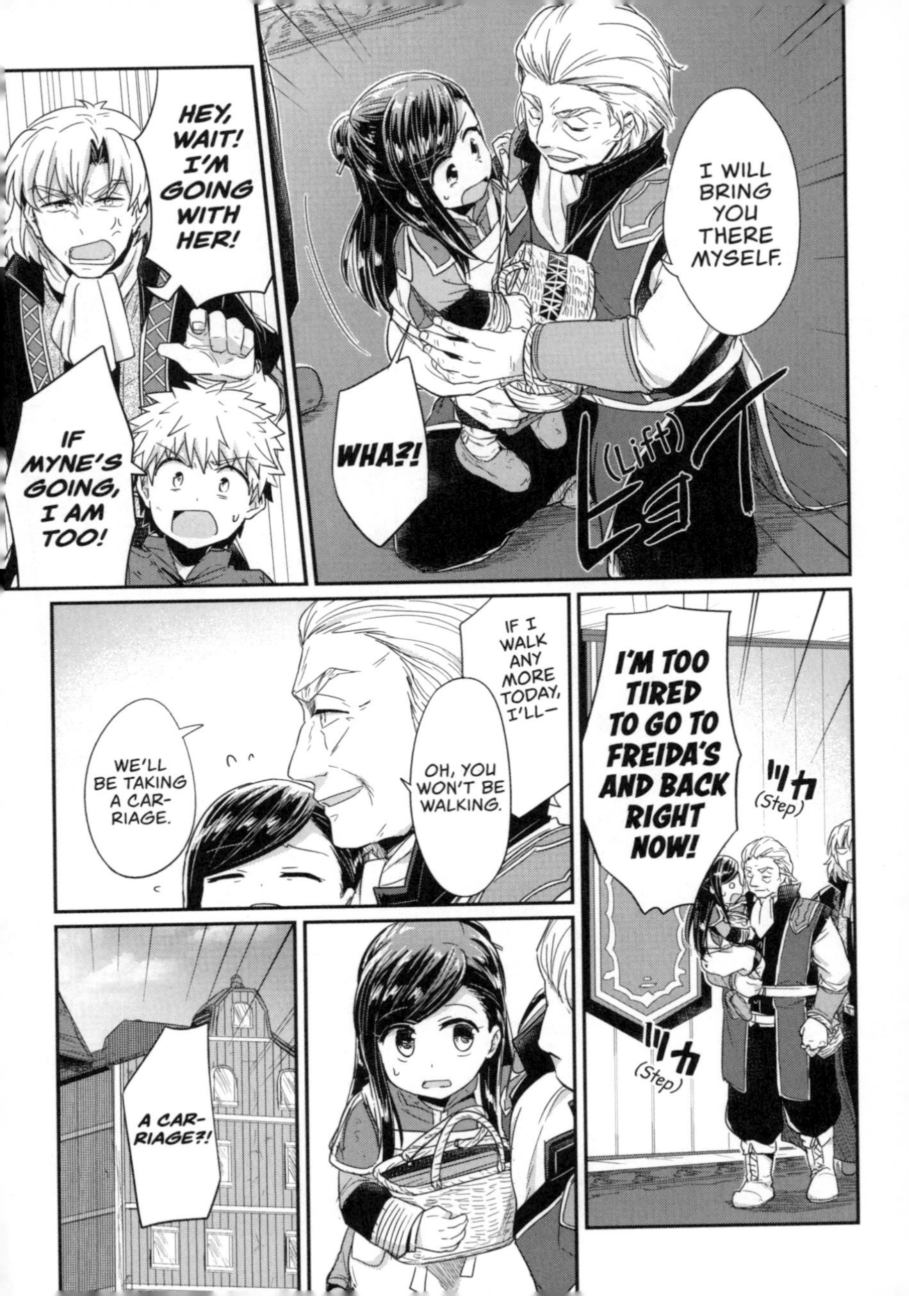
I WILL BRING YOU THERE MYSELF.
ヒョイ (Lift)
WHA?!
HEY, WAIT! I'M GOING WITH HER!
IF MYNE'S GOING, I AM TOO!
I'M TOO TIRED TO GO TO FREIDA'S AND BACK RIGHT NOW!
ツカ (Step)
ツカ (Step)
IF I WALK ANY MORE TODAY, I'LL—
OH, YOU WON'T BE WALKING.
WE'LL BE TAKING A CAR-RIAGE.
A CAR-RIAGE?!

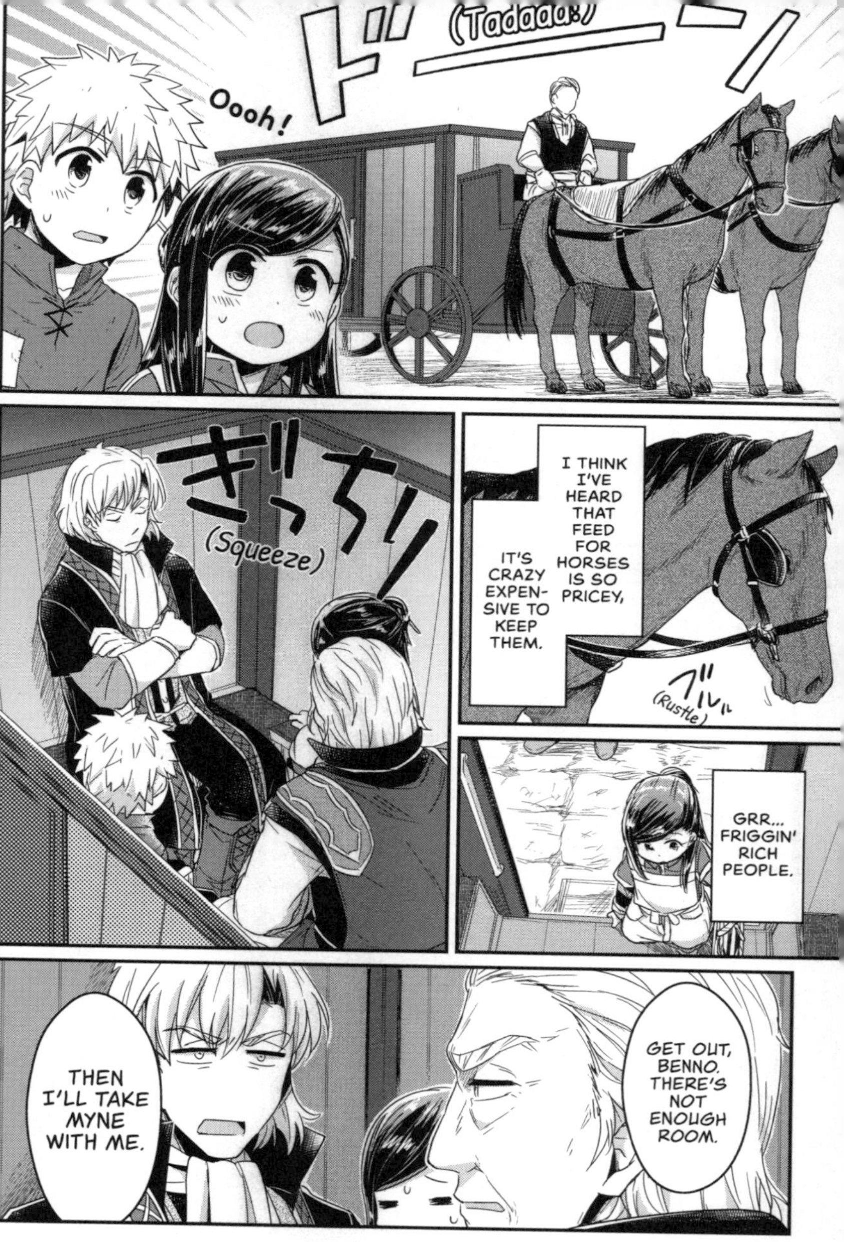
(Tadaaa!)
Oooh!
I THINK I'VE HEARD THAT FEED FOR HORSES IS SO PRICEY,
IT'S CRAZY EXPENSIVE TO KEEP THEM.
(Rustle)
GRR... FRIGGIN' RICH PEOPLE.
(Squeeze)
GET OUT, BENNO. THERE'S NOT ENOUGH ROOM.
THEN I'LL TAKE MYNE WITH ME.

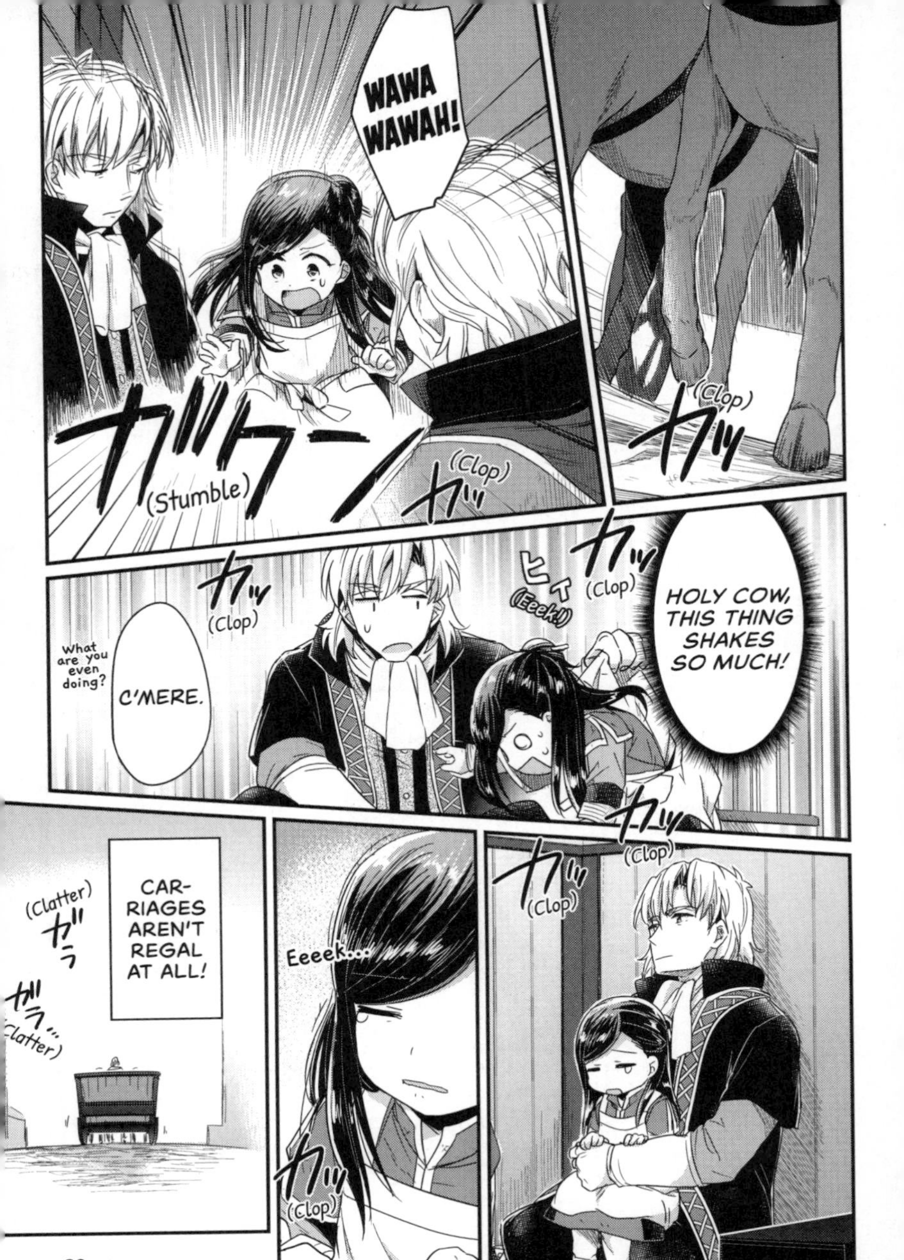
(Clop)
ガッ
WAWA WAWAH!
ガタ〜ン
(Stumble)
(Clop)
ガッ
カッ
(Clop)
HOLY COW, THIS THING SHAKES SO MUCH!
ヒィ
(Eeek!)
カッ
(Clop)
C'MERE.
What are you even doing?
カッ
(Clop)
ガッ
(Clop)
Eeeek...
カッ
(Clop)
CAR-RIAGES AREN'T REGAL AT ALL!
(Clatter)
ガラ
ガラ…
(Clatter)

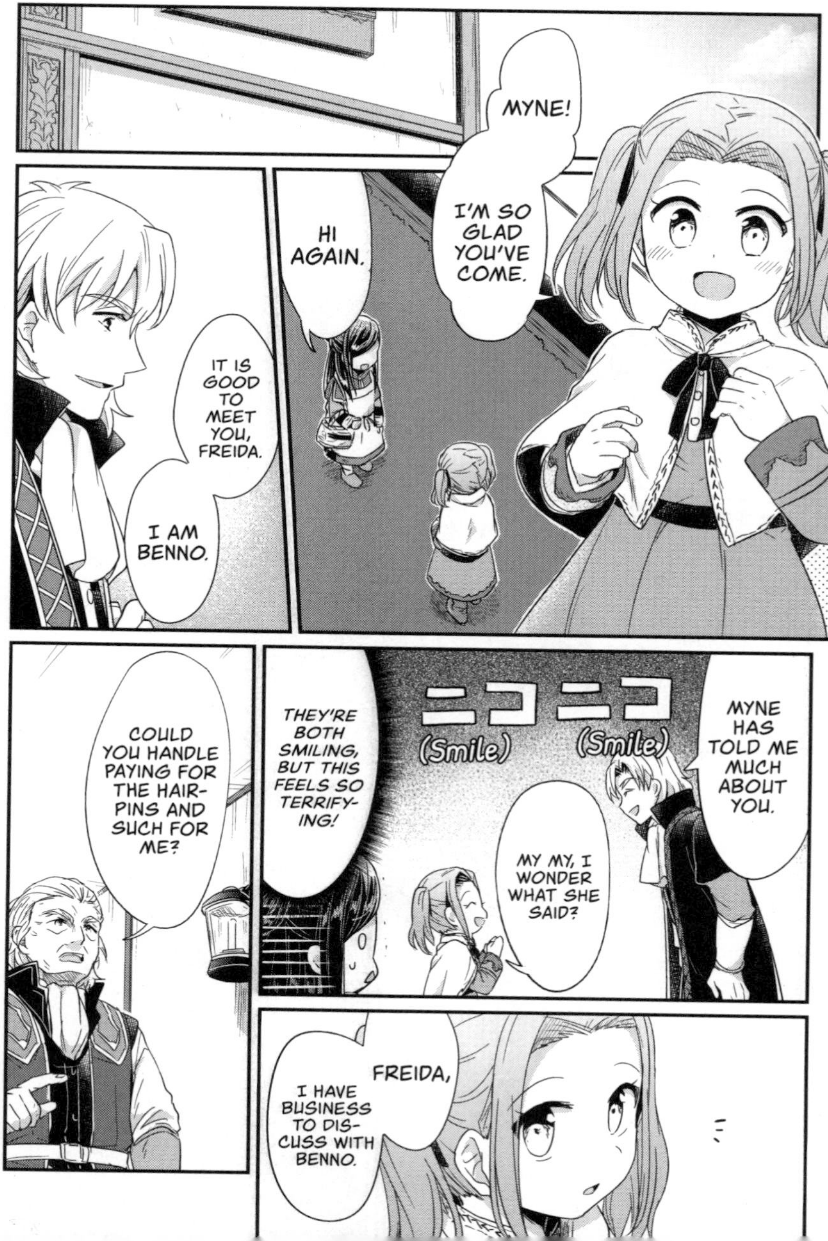
MYNE!
I'M SO GLAD YOU'VE COME.
HI AGAIN.
IT IS GOOD TO MEET YOU, FREIDA.
I AM BENNO.
MYNE HAS TOLD ME MUCH ABOUT YOU.
ニコ (Smile) ニコ (Smile)
MY MY, I WONDER WHAT SHE SAID?
THEY'RE BOTH SMILING, BUT THIS FEELS SO TERRIFY-ING!
FREIDA,
I HAVE BUSINESS TO DIS-CUSS WITH BENNO.
COULD YOU HANDLE PAYING FOR THE HAIR-PINS AND SUCH FOR ME?

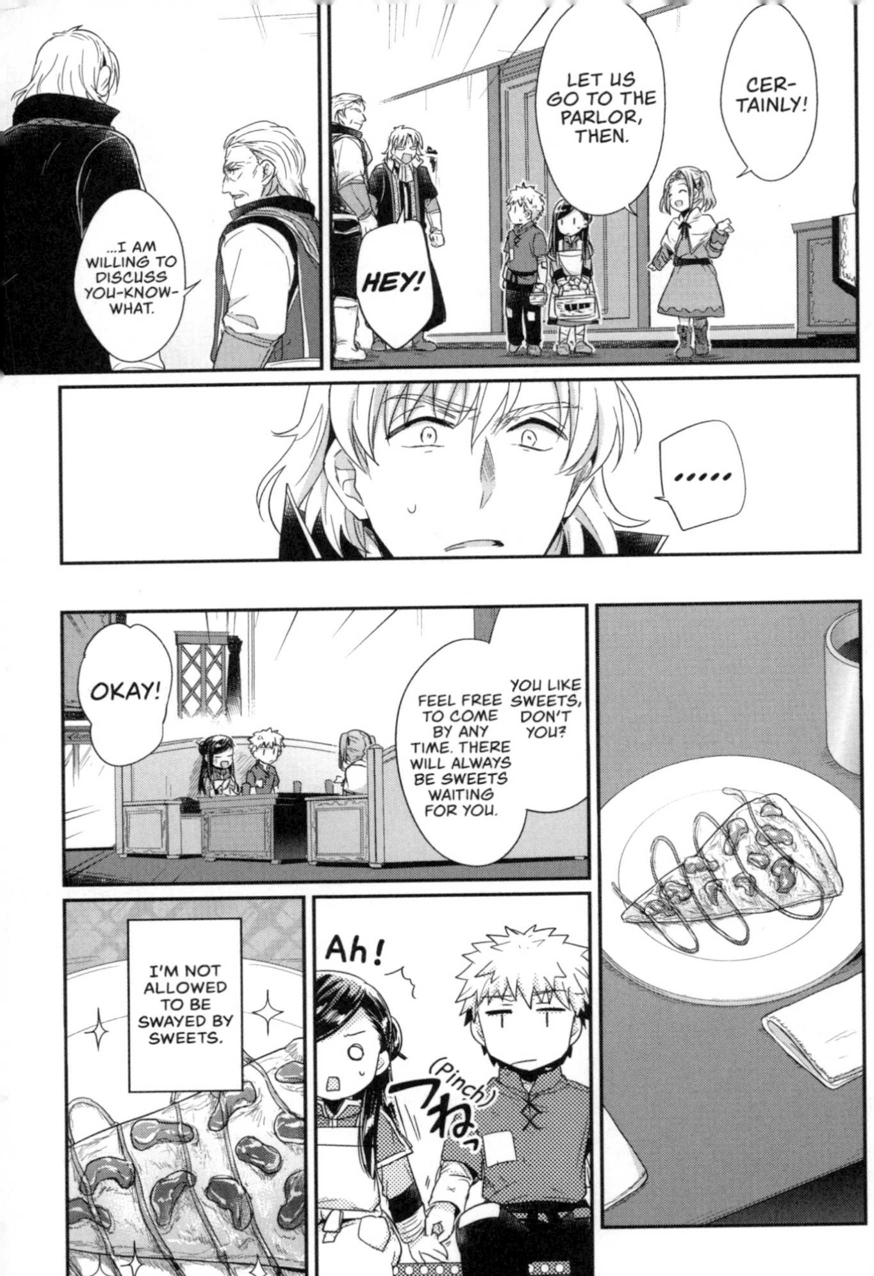
CER-TAINLY!
LET US GO TO THE PARLOR, THEN.
HEY!
...I AM WILLING TO DISCUSS YOU-KNOW-WHAT.
......
YOU LIKE SWEETS, DON'T YOU?
FEEL FREE TO COME BY ANY TIME. THERE WILL ALWAYS BE SWEETS WAITING FOR YOU.
OKAY!
Ah!
(Pinch)
つね
I'M NOT ALLOWED TO BE SWAYED BY SWEETS.

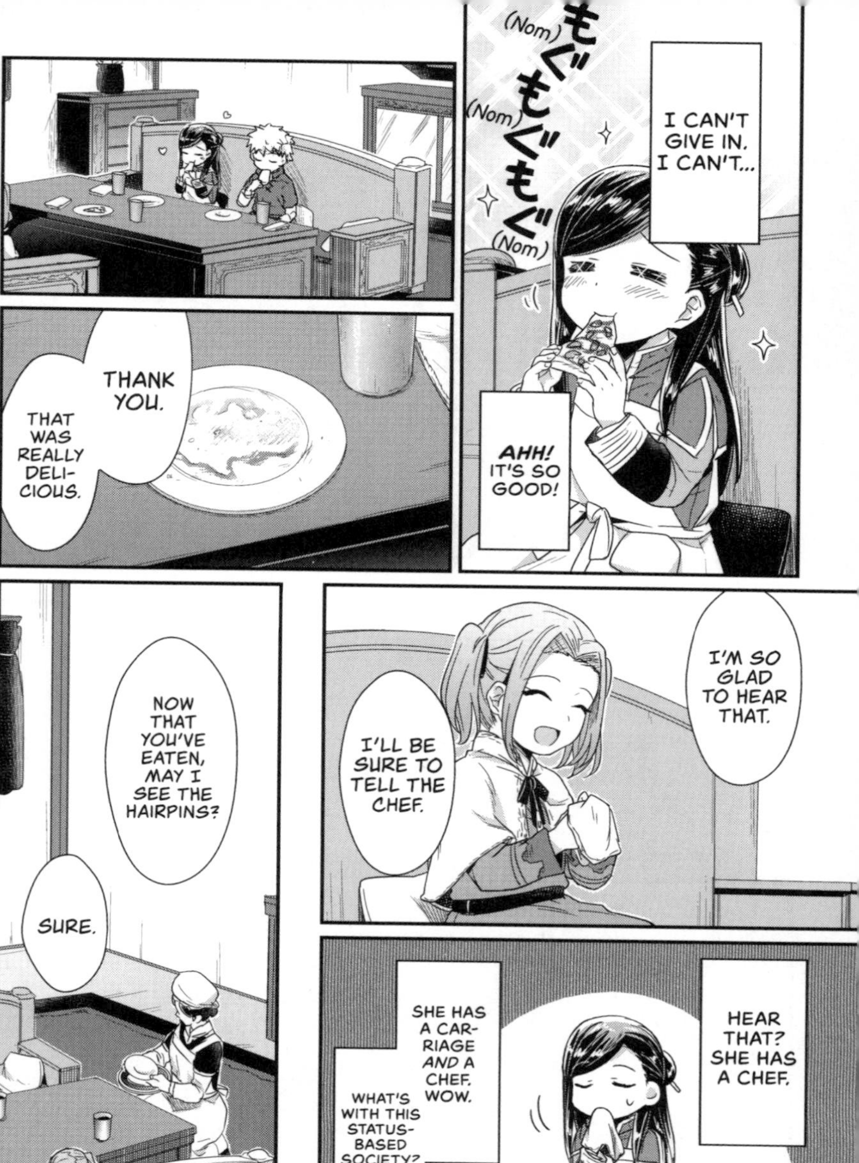
もぐ (Nom) もぐ (Nom) もぐ (Nom)
I CAN'T GIVE IN. I CAN'T...
AHH! IT'S SO GOOD!
THANK YOU.
THAT WAS REALLY DELICIOUS.
I'M SO GLAD TO HEAR THAT.
I'LL BE SURE TO TELL THE CHEF.
HEAR THAT? SHE HAS A CHEF.
SHE HAS A CARRIAGE *AND* A CHEF. WOW.
WHAT'S WITH THIS STATUS-BASED SOCIETY?
NOW THAT YOU'VE EATEN, MAY I SEE THE HAIRPINS?
SURE.

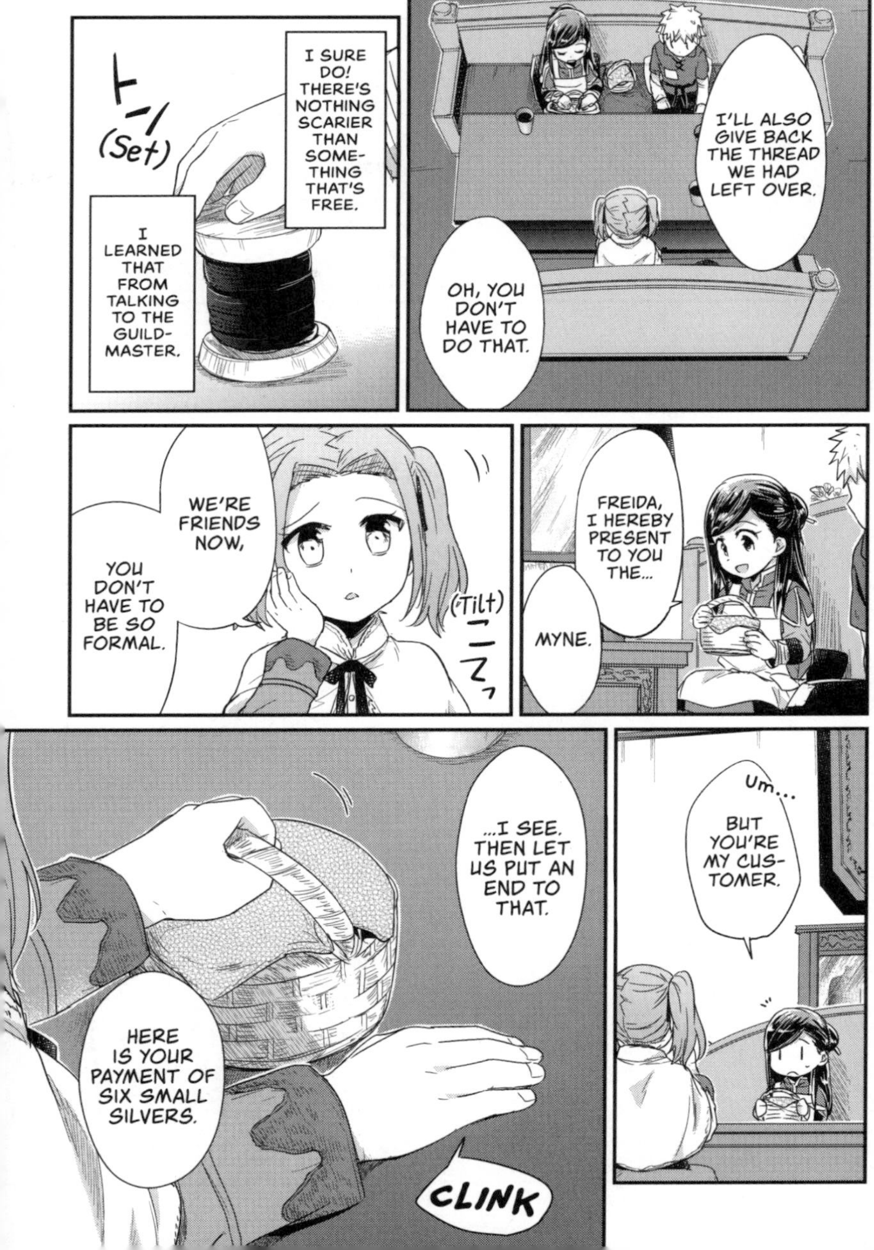
I'LL ALSO GIVE BACK THE THREAD WE HAD LEFT OVER.
OH, YOU DON'T HAVE TO DO THAT.
I SURE DO! THERE'S NOTHING SCARIER THAN SOMETHING THAT'S FREE.
(Set)
I LEARNED THAT FROM TALKING TO THE GUILDMASTER.
FREIDA, I HEREBY PRESENT TO YOU THE...
MYNE.
(Tilt)
WE'RE FRIENDS NOW,
YOU DON'T HAVE TO BE SO FORMAL.
Um...
BUT YOU'RE MY CUSTOMER.
...I SEE. THEN LET US PUT AN END TO THAT.
HERE IS YOUR PAYMENT OF SIX SMALL SILVERS.
CLINK

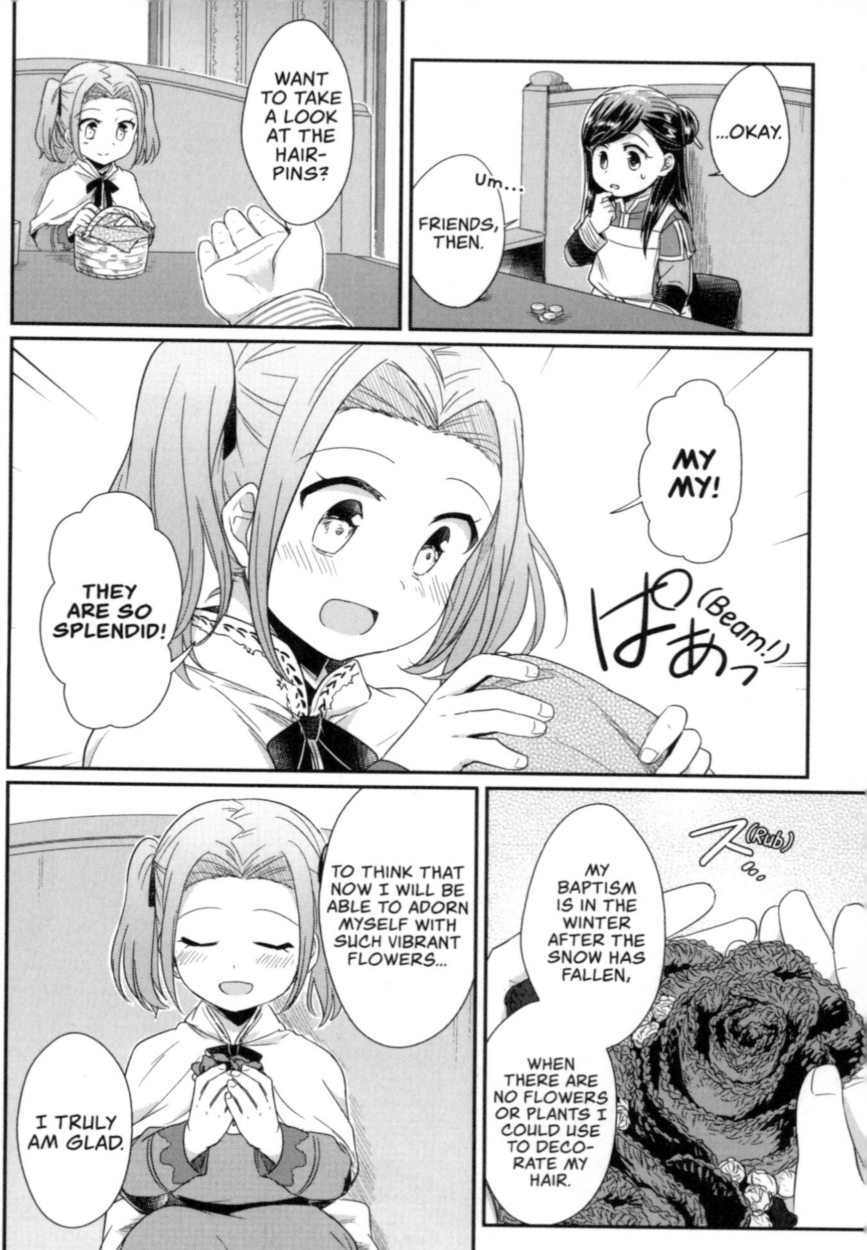
...OKAY.
Um...
FRIENDS, THEN.
WANT TO TAKE A LOOK AT THE HAIR-PINS?
MY MY!
ぱあっ (Beam!)
THEY ARE SO SPLENDID!
ス (Rub)
MY BAPTISM IS IN THE WINTER AFTER THE SNOW HAS FALLEN,
WHEN THERE ARE NO FLOWERS OR PLANTS I COULD USE TO DECO-RATE MY HAIR.
TO THINK THAT NOW I WILL BE ABLE TO ADORN MYSELF WITH SUCH VIBRANT FLOWERS...
I TRULY AM GLAD.

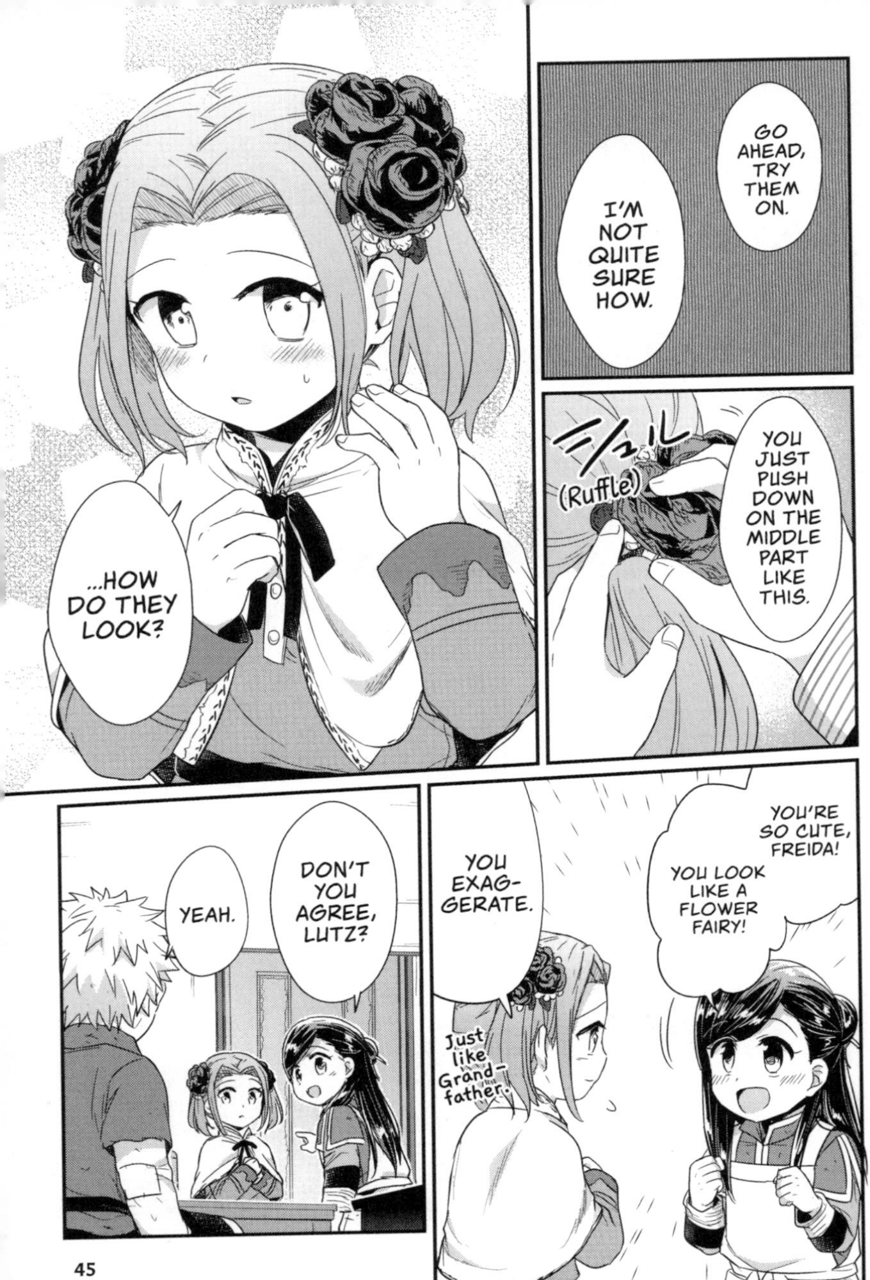
GO AHEAD, TRY THEM ON.
I'M NOT QUITE SURE HOW.
シュル
(Ruffle)
YOU JUST PUSH DOWN ON THE MIDDLE PART LIKE THIS.
...HOW DO THEY LOOK?
YOU'RE SO CUTE, FREIDA!
YOU LOOK LIKE A FLOWER FAIRY!
YOU EXAGGERATE.
Just like Grandfather.
DON'T YOU AGREE, LUTZ?
YEAH.

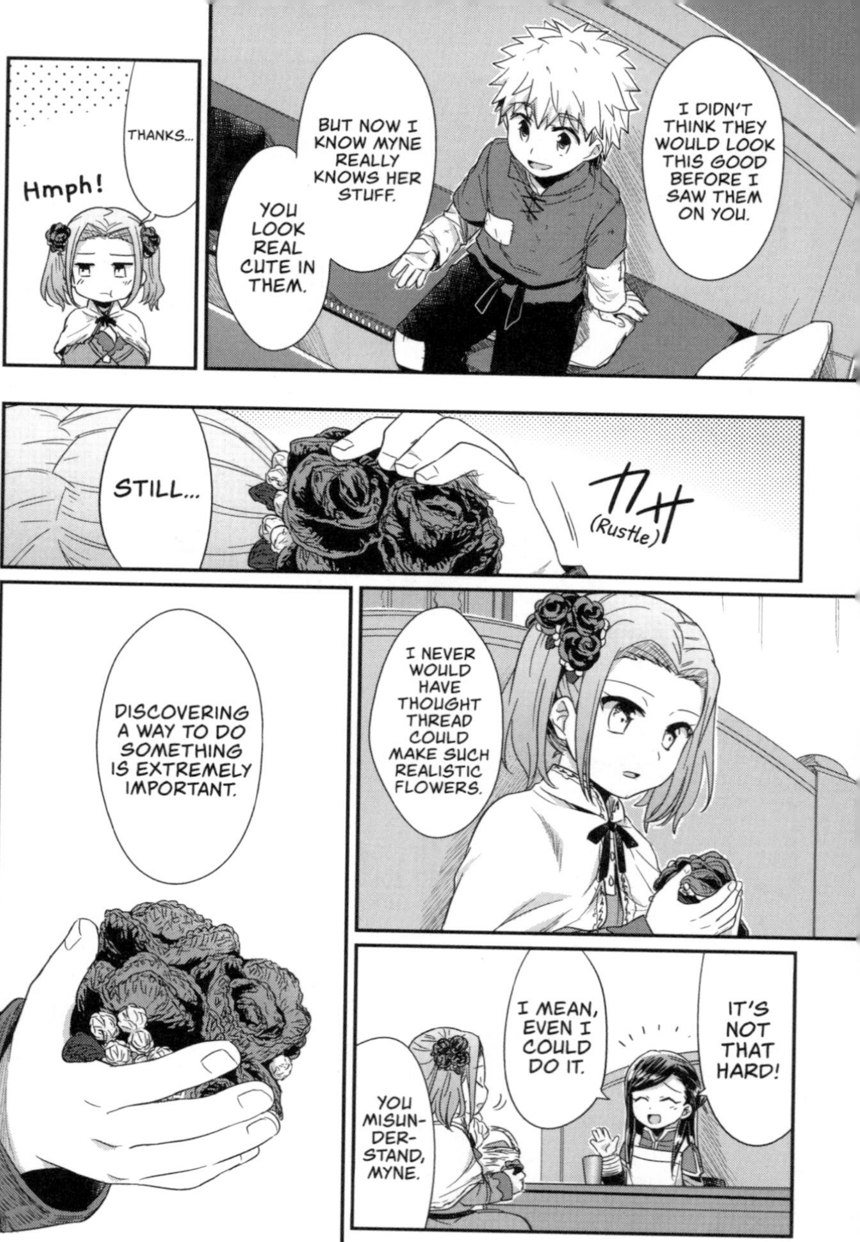
I DIDN'T THINK THEY WOULD LOOK THIS GOOD BEFORE I SAW THEM ON YOU.
BUT NOW I KNOW MYNE REALLY KNOWS HER STUFF.
YOU LOOK REAL CUTE IN THEM.
THANKS...
Hmph!
STILL...
(Rustle)
I NEVER WOULD HAVE THOUGHT THREAD COULD MAKE SUCH REALISTIC FLOWERS.
IT'S NOT THAT HARD!
I MEAN, EVEN I COULD DO IT.
YOU MISUN-DER-STAND, MYNE.
DISCOVERING A WAY TO DO SOMETHING IS EXTREMELY IMPORTANT.

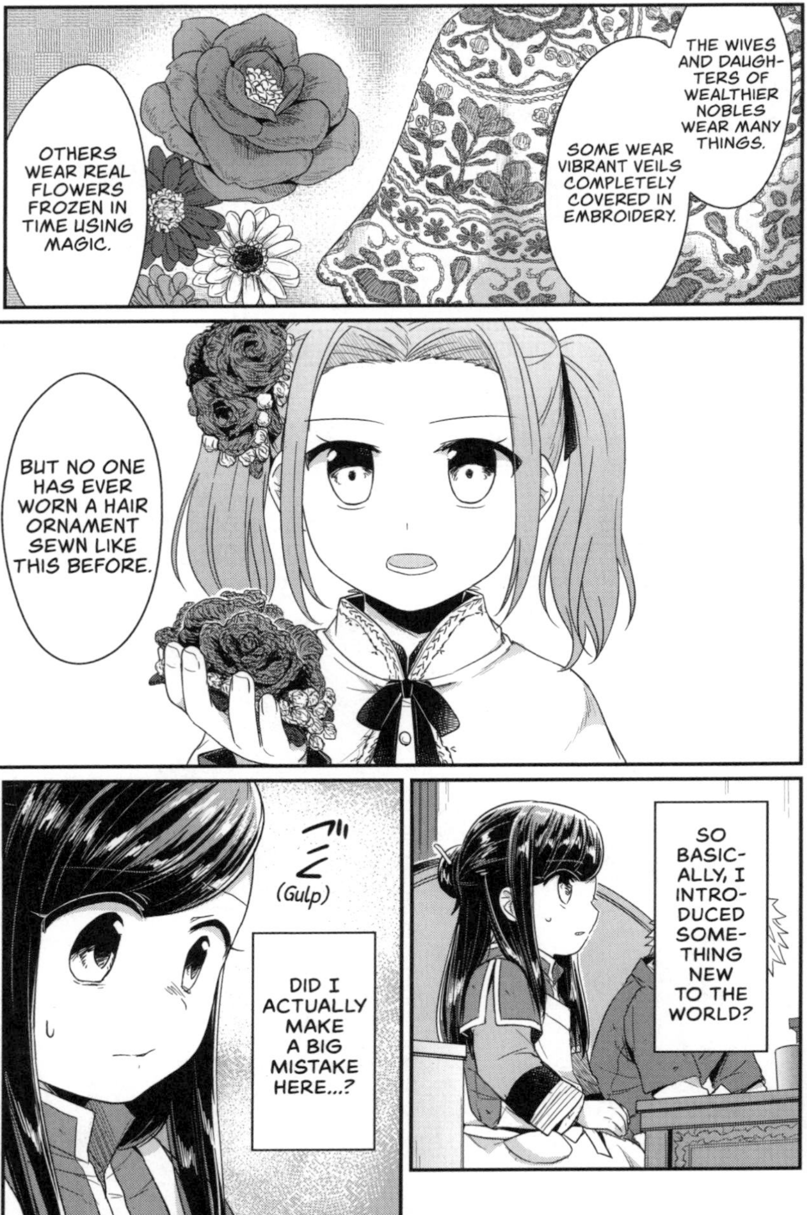
THE WIVES AND DAUGHTERS OF WEALTHIER NOBLES WEAR MANY THINGS.
SOME WEAR VIBRANT VEILS COMPLETELY COVERED IN EMBROIDERY.
OTHERS WEAR REAL FLOWERS FROZEN IN TIME USING MAGIC.
BUT NO ONE HAS EVER WORN A HAIR ORNAMENT SEWN LIKE THIS BEFORE.
SO BASICALLY, I INTRODUCED SOMETHING NEW TO THE WORLD?
(Gulp)
DID I ACTUALLY MAKE A BIG MISTAKE HERE...?

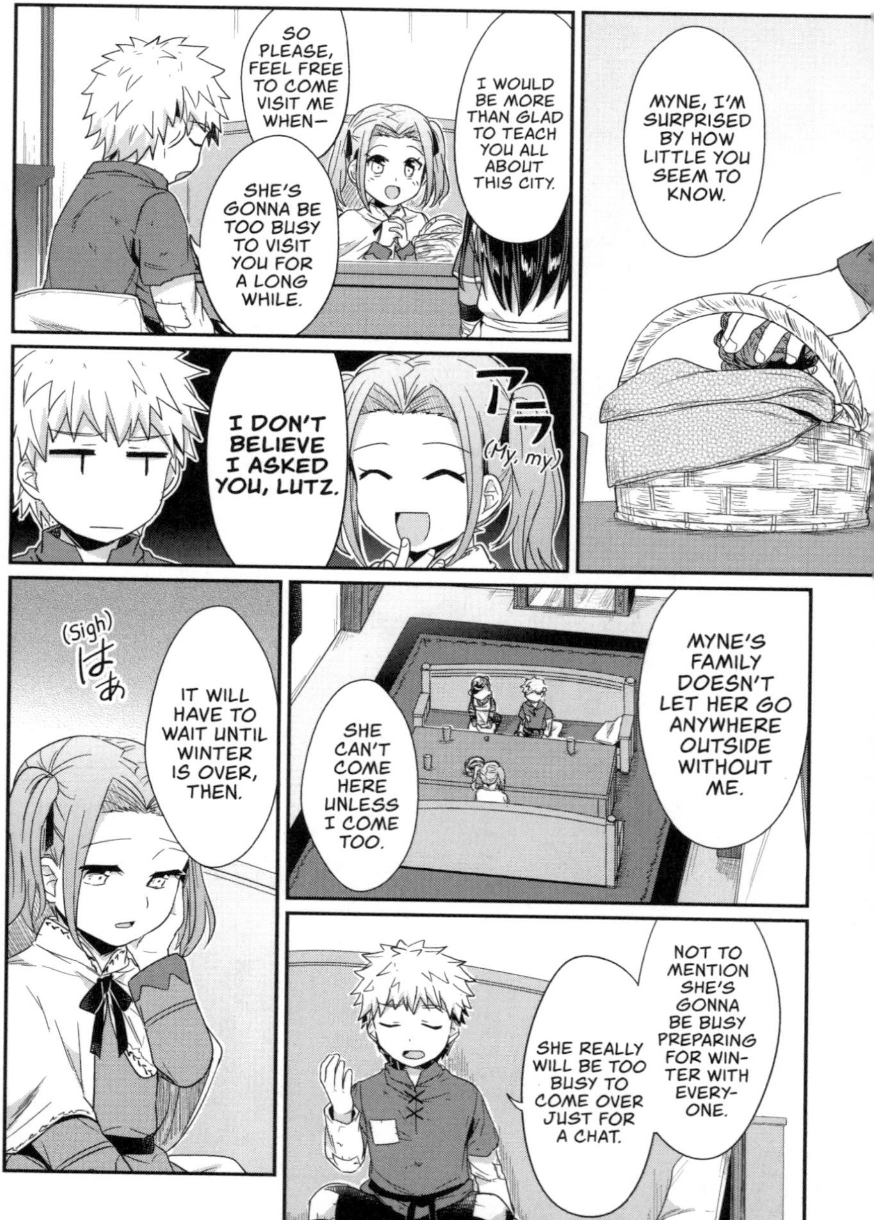
MYNE, I'M SURPRISED BY HOW LITTLE YOU SEEM TO KNOW.
I WOULD BE MORE THAN GLAD TO TEACH YOU ALL ABOUT THIS CITY.
SO PLEASE, FEEL FREE TO COME VISIT ME WHEN—
SHE'S GONNA BE TOO BUSY TO VISIT YOU FOR A LONG WHILE.
アラ
(My, my)
I DON'T BELIEVE I ASKED YOU, LUTZ.
MYNE'S FAMILY DOESN'T LET HER GO ANYWHERE OUTSIDE WITHOUT ME.
SHE CAN'T COME HERE UNLESS I COME TOO.
NOT TO MENTION SHE'S GONNA BE BUSY PREPARING FOR WIN-TER WITH EVERY-ONE.
SHE REALLY WILL BE TOO BUSY TO COME OVER JUST FOR A CHAT.
(Sigh)
はぁ
IT WILL HAVE TO WAIT UNTIL WINTER IS OVER, THEN.

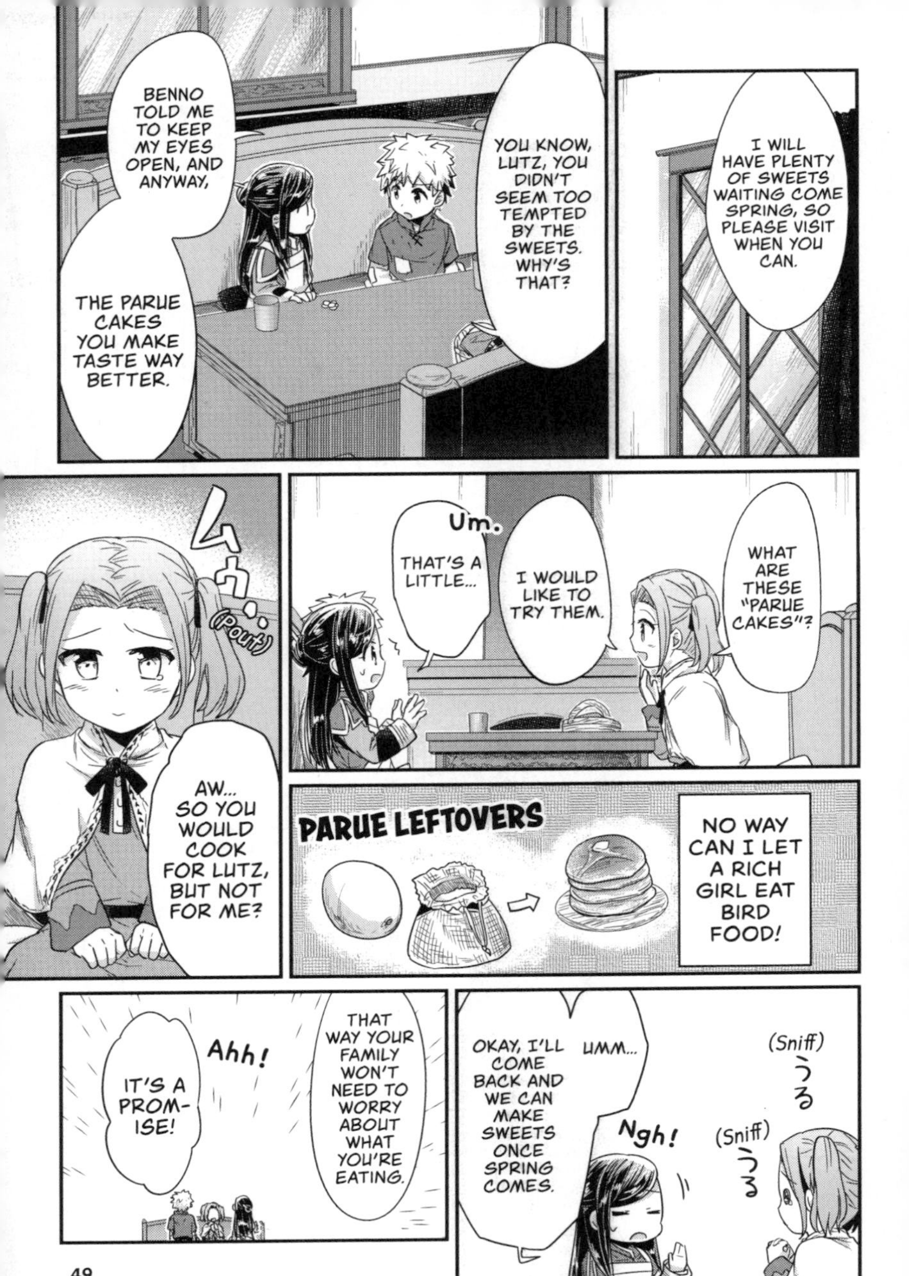
I WILL HAVE PLENTY OF SWEETS WAITING COME SPRING, SO PLEASE VISIT WHEN YOU CAN.
YOU KNOW, LUTZ, YOU DIDN'T SEEM TOO TEMPTED BY THE SWEETS. WHY'S THAT?
BENNO TOLD ME TO KEEP MY EYES OPEN, AND ANYWAY,
THE PARUE CAKES YOU MAKE TASTE WAY BETTER.
WHAT ARE THESE "PARUE CAKES"?
I WOULD LIKE TO TRY THEM.
Um.
THAT'S A LITTLE...
NO WAY CAN I LET A RICH GIRL EAT BIRD FOOD!
PARUE LEFTOVERS
ムゥ
(Pout)
AW... SO YOU WOULD COOK FOR LUTZ, BUT NOT FOR ME?
(Sniff)
うる
(Sniff)
うる
Ngh!
UMM...
OKAY, I'LL COME BACK AND WE CAN MAKE SWEETS ONCE SPRING COMES.
THAT WAY YOUR FAMILY WON'T NEED TO WORRY ABOUT WHAT YOU'RE EATING.
Ahh!
IT'S A PROM-ISE!

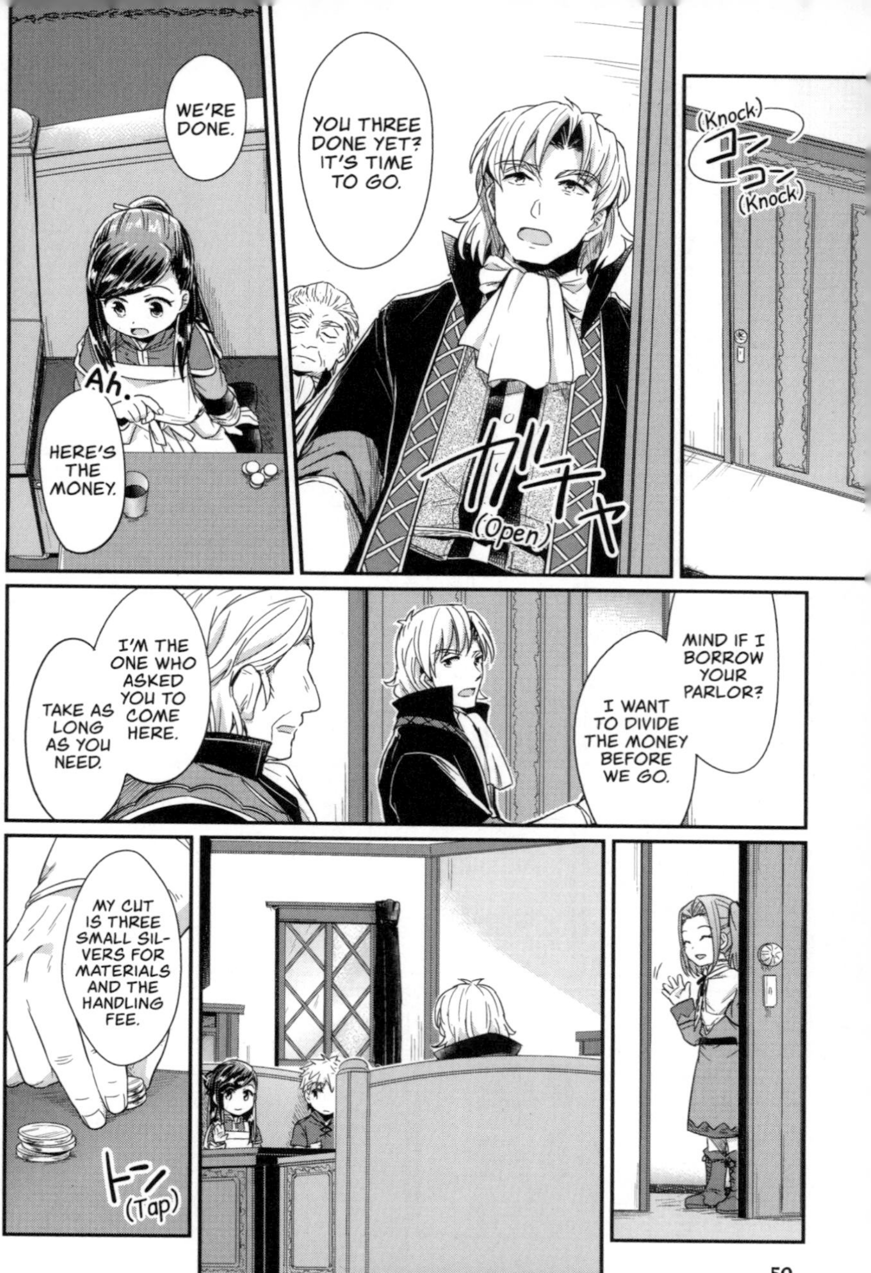
コン (Knock)
コン (Knock)
ガチャ (Open)
YOU THREE DONE YET? IT'S TIME TO GO.
WE'RE DONE.
Ah.
HERE'S THE MONEY.
MIND IF I BORROW YOUR PARLOR?
I WANT TO DIVIDE THE MONEY BEFORE WE GO.
I'M THE ONE WHO ASKED YOU TO COME HERE.
TAKE AS LONG AS YOU NEED.
MY CUT IS THREE SMALL SILVERS FOR MATERIALS AND THE HANDLING FEE.
トン (Tap)

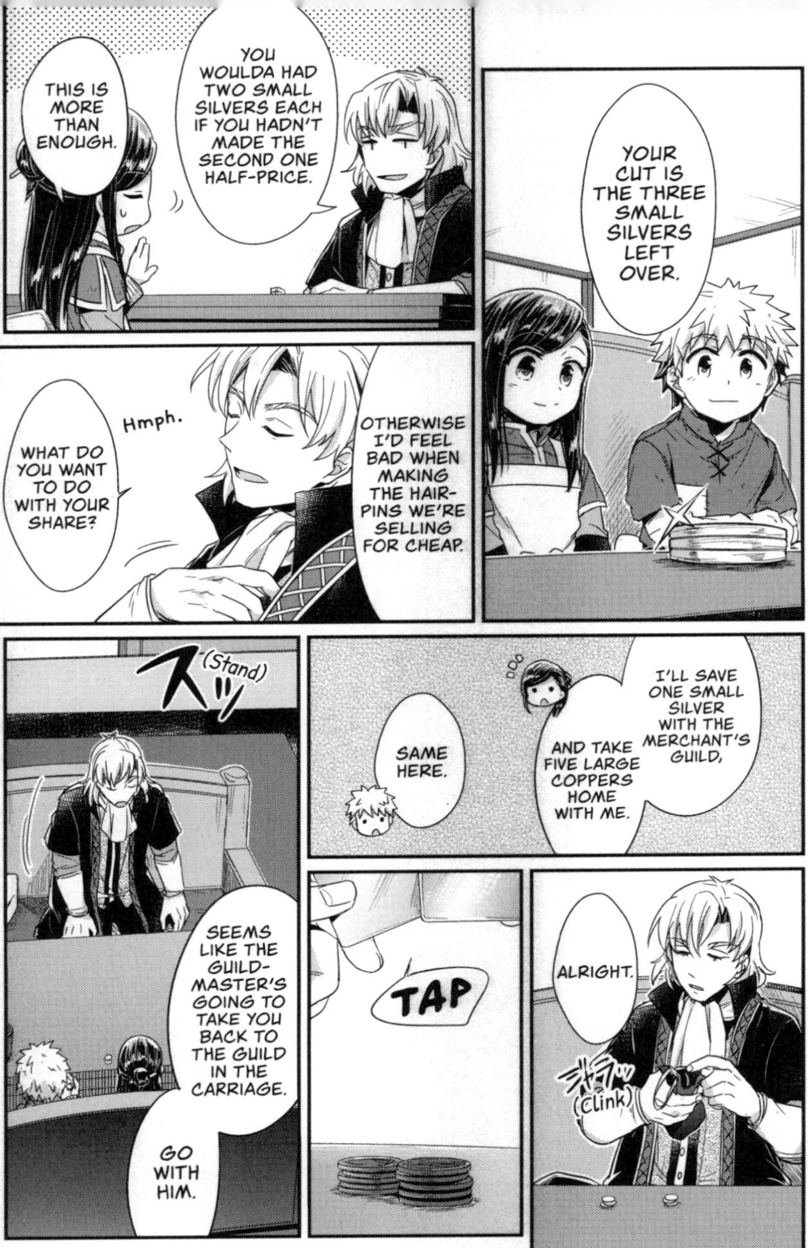
YOUR CUT IS THE THREE SMALL SILVERS LEFT OVER.
YOU WOULDA HAD TWO SMALL SILVERS EACH IF YOU HADN'T MADE THE SECOND ONE HALF-PRICE.
THIS IS MORE THAN ENOUGH.
OTHERWISE I'D FEEL BAD WHEN MAKING THE HAIR-PINS WE'RE SELLING FOR CHEAP.
Hmph.
WHAT DO YOU WANT TO DO WITH YOUR SHARE?
I'LL SAVE ONE SMALL SILVER WITH THE MERCHANT'S GUILD,
AND TAKE FIVE LARGE COPPERS HOME WITH ME.
SAME HERE.
ALRIGHT.
(Clink)
TAP
(Stand)
SEEMS LIKE THE GUILD-MASTER'S GOING TO TAKE YOU BACK TO THE GUILD IN THE CARRIAGE.
GO WITH HIM.

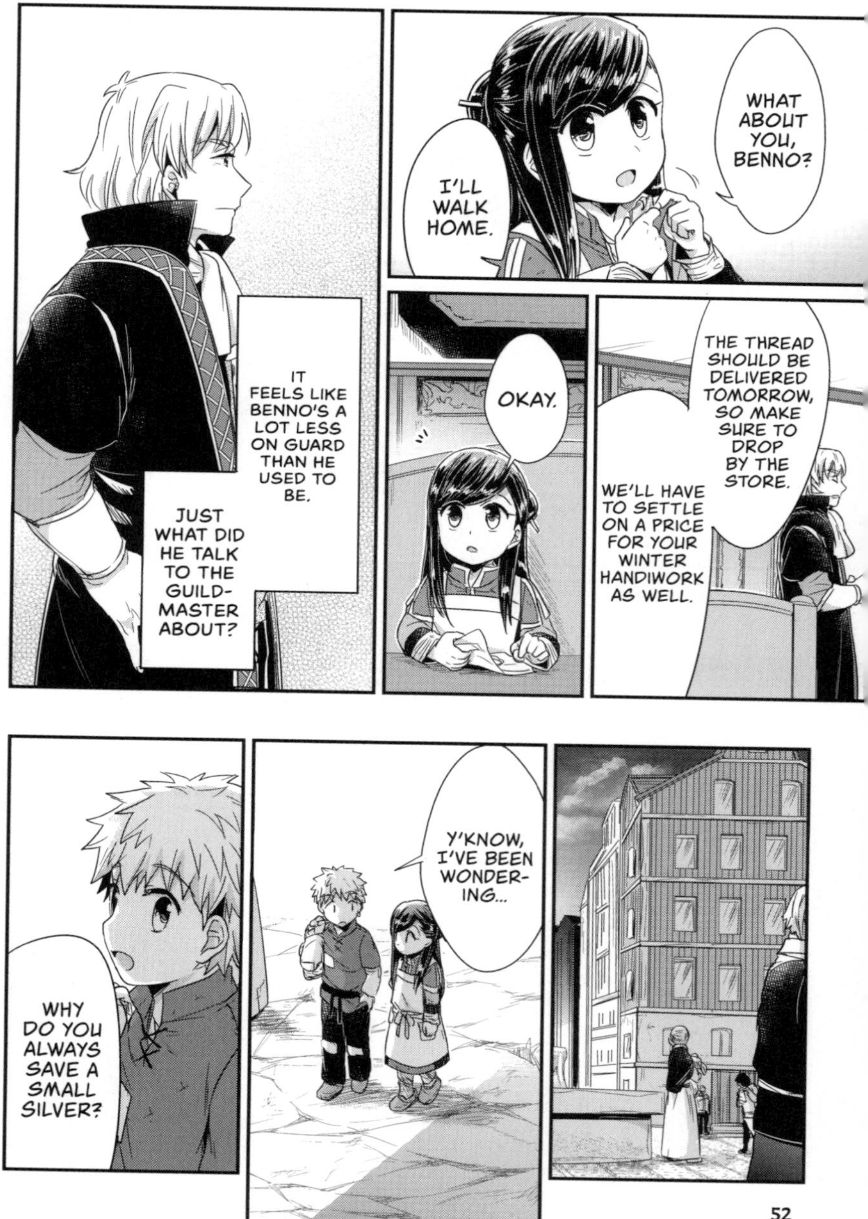
WHAT ABOUT YOU, BENNO?
I'LL WALK HOME.
THE THREAD SHOULD BE DELIVERED TOMORROW, SO MAKE SURE TO DROP BY THE STORE.
WE'LL HAVE TO SETTLE ON A PRICE FOR YOUR WINTER HANDIWORK AS WELL.
OKAY.
IT FEELS LIKE BENNO'S A LOT LESS ON GUARD THAN HE USED TO BE.
JUST WHAT DID HE TALK TO THE GUILD-MASTER ABOUT?
Y'KNOW, I'VE BEEN WONDERING...
WHY DO YOU ALWAYS SAVE A SMALL SILVER?

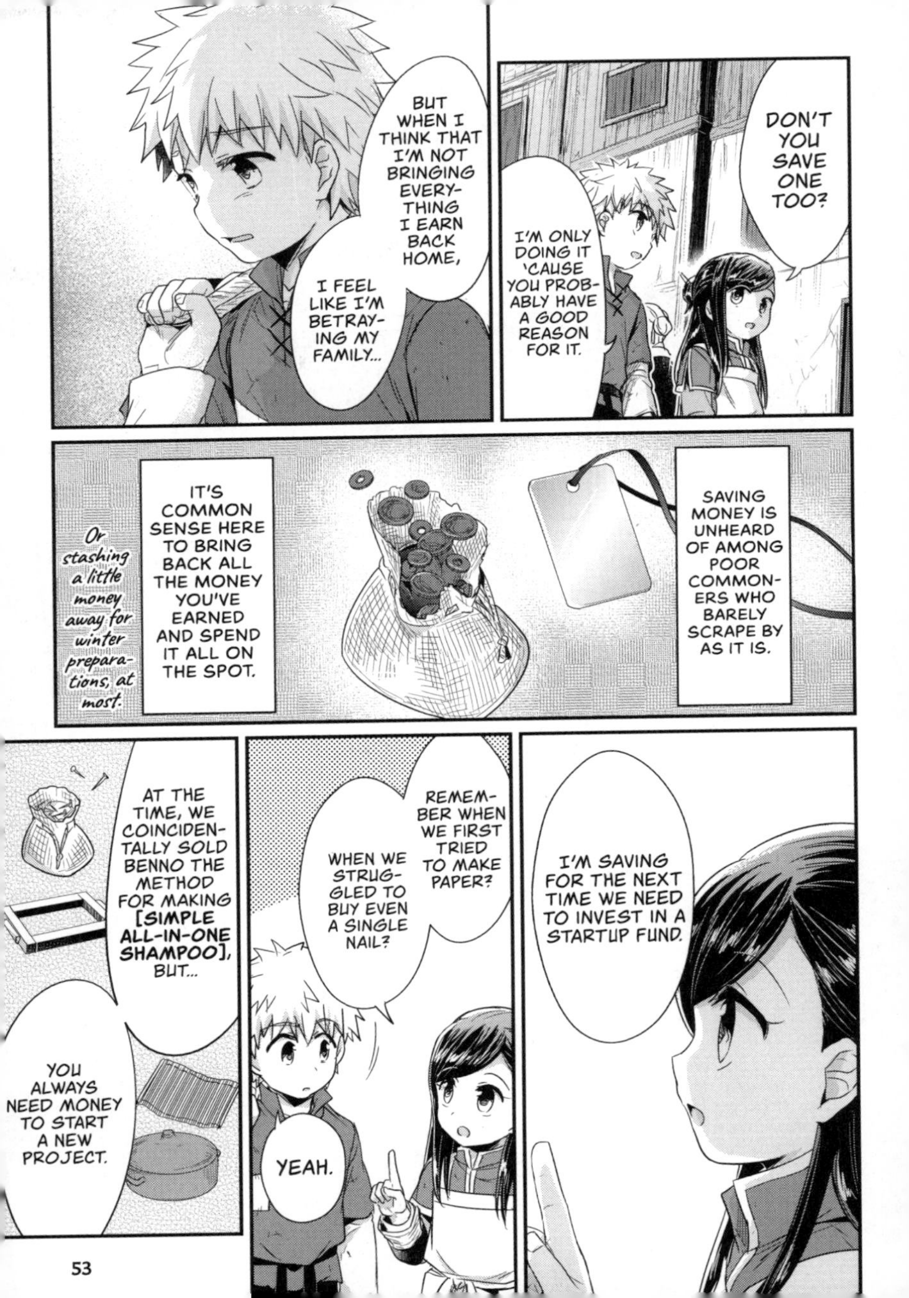
DON'T YOU SAVE ONE TOO?
I'M ONLY DOING IT 'CAUSE YOU PROBABLY HAVE A GOOD REASON FOR IT.
BUT WHEN I THINK THAT I'M NOT BRINGING EVERYTHING I EARN BACK HOME,
I FEEL LIKE I'M BETRAYING MY FAMILY...
SAVING MONEY IS UNHEARD OF AMONG POOR COMMONERS WHO BARELY SCRAPE BY AS IT IS.
IT'S COMMON SENSE HERE TO BRING BACK ALL THE MONEY YOU'VE EARNED AND SPEND IT ALL ON THE SPOT.
Or stashing a little money away for winter preparations, at most.
I'M SAVING FOR THE NEXT TIME WE NEED TO INVEST IN A STARTUP FUND.
REMEMBER WHEN WE FIRST TRIED TO MAKE PAPER?
WHEN WE STRUGGLED TO BUY EVEN A SINGLE NAIL?
YEAH.
AT THE TIME, WE COINCIDENTALLY SOLD BENNO THE METHOD FOR MAKING **[SIMPLE ALL-IN-ONE SHAMPOO]**, BUT...
YOU ALWAYS NEED MONEY TO START A NEW PROJECT.

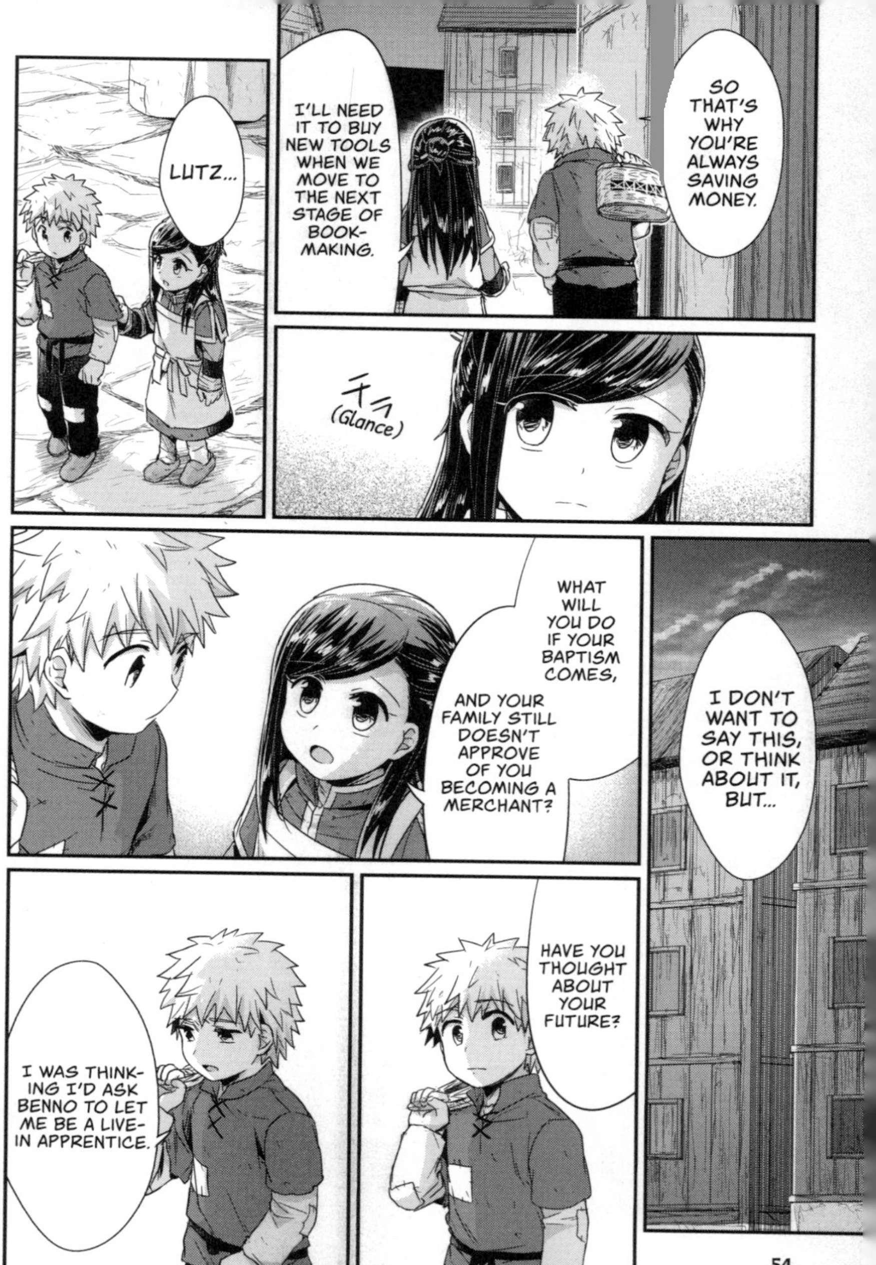
SO THAT'S WHY YOU'RE ALWAYS SAVING MONEY.
I'LL NEED IT TO BUY NEW TOOLS WHEN WE MOVE TO THE NEXT STAGE OF BOOK-MAKING.
チラ
(Glance)
LUTZ...
I DON'T WANT TO SAY THIS, OR THINK ABOUT IT, BUT...
WHAT WILL YOU DO IF YOUR BAPTISM COMES,
AND YOUR FAMILY STILL DOESN'T APPROVE OF YOU BECOMING A MERCHANT?
HAVE YOU THOUGHT ABOUT YOUR FUTURE?
I WAS THINKING I'D ASK BENNO TO LET ME BE A LIVE-IN APPRENTICE.

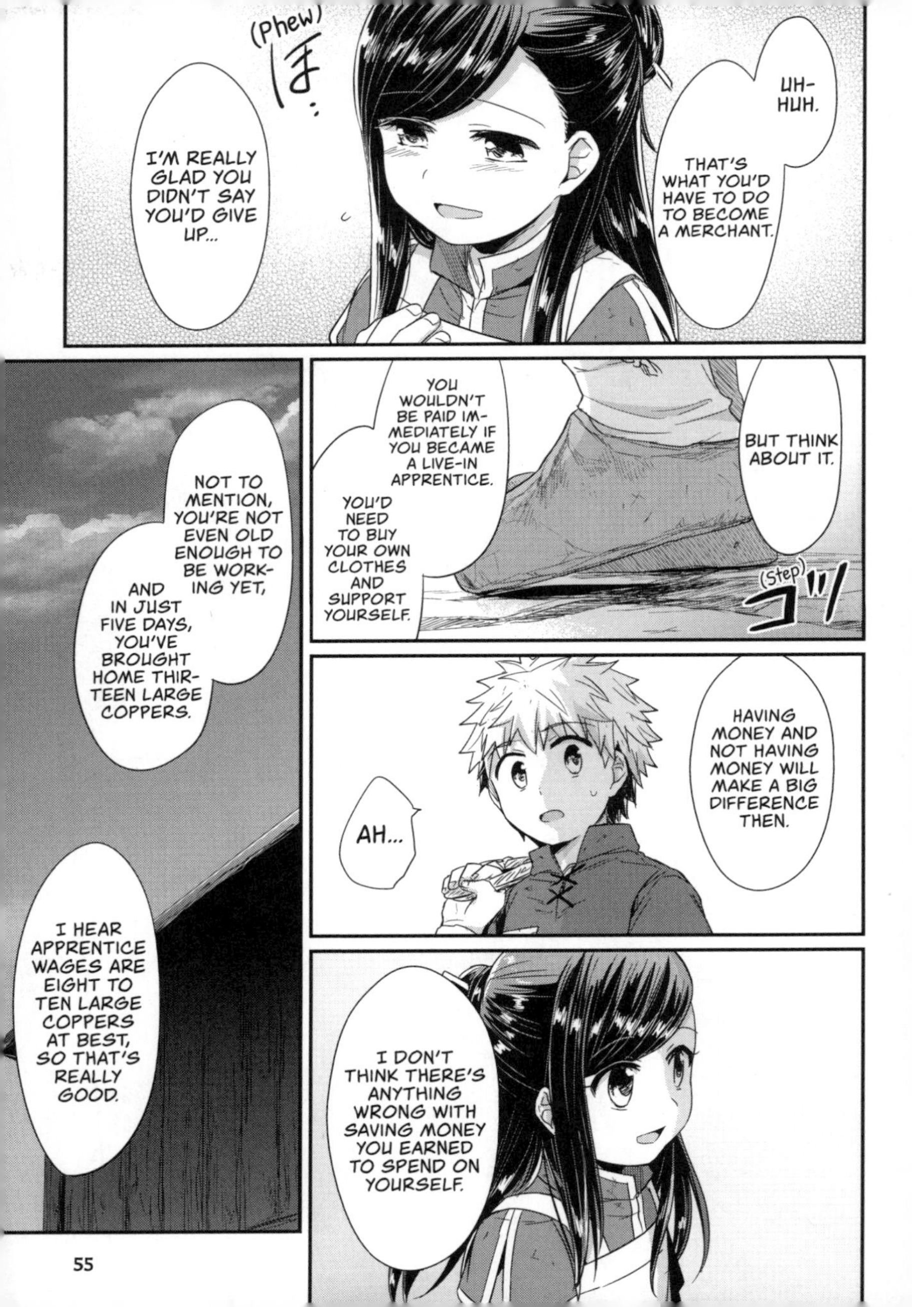
UH-HUH.
THAT'S WHAT YOU'D HAVE TO DO TO BECOME A MERCHANT.
(Phew) ほ
I'M REALLY GLAD YOU DIDN'T SAY YOU'D GIVE UP...
BUT THINK ABOUT IT.
(Step) コツ
YOU WOULDN'T BE PAID IM-MEDIATELY IF YOU BECAME A LIVE-IN APPRENTICE.
YOU'D NEED TO BUY YOUR OWN CLOTHES AND SUPPORT YOURSELF.
HAVING MONEY AND NOT HAVING MONEY WILL MAKE A BIG DIFFERENCE THEN.
AH...
I DON'T THINK THERE'S ANYTHING WRONG WITH SAVING MONEY YOU EARNED TO SPEND ON YOURSELF.
NOT TO MENTION, YOU'RE NOT EVEN OLD ENOUGH TO BE WORK-ING YET,
AND IN JUST FIVE DAYS, YOU'VE BROUGHT HOME THIR-TEEN LARGE COPPERS.
I HEAR APPRENTICE WAGES ARE EIGHT TO TEN LARGE COPPERS AT BEST, SO THAT'S REALLY GOOD.

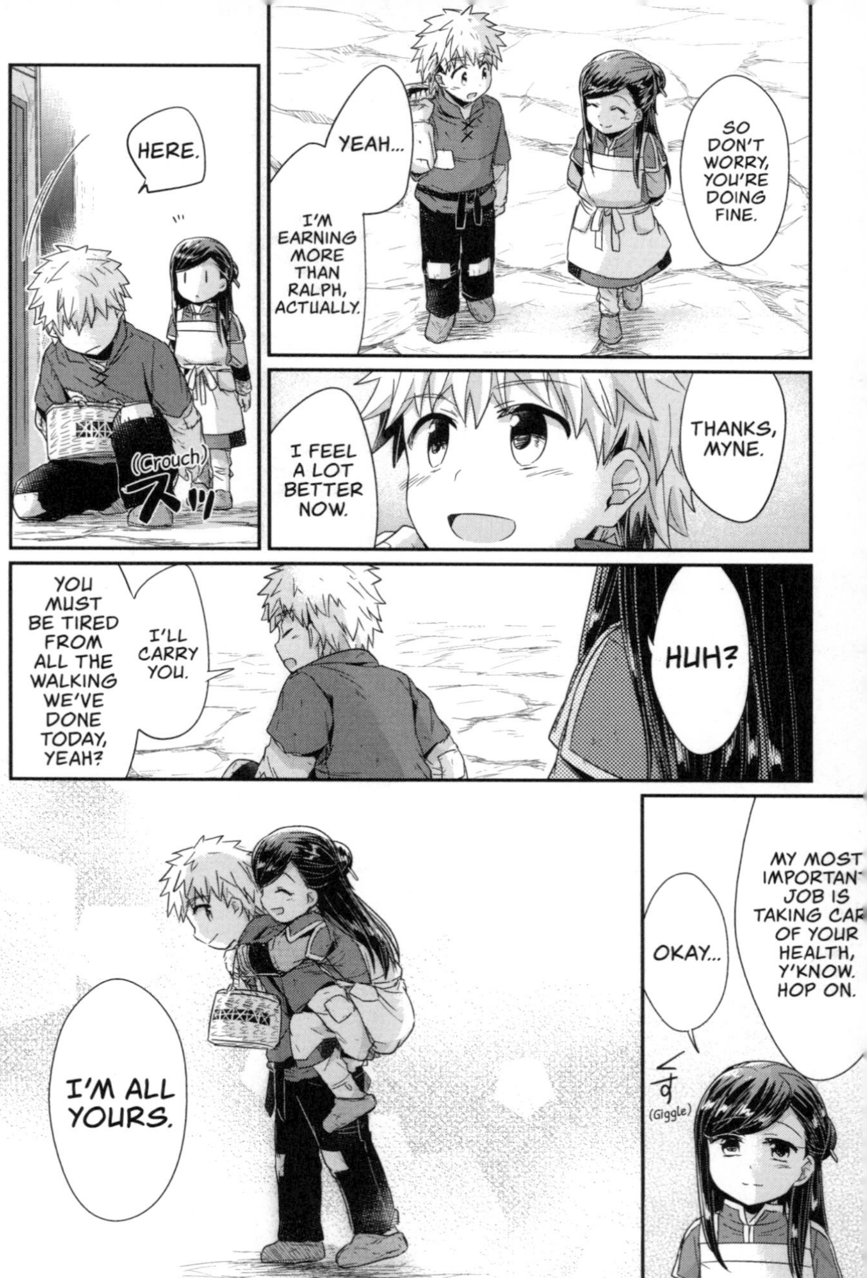
YEAH... I'M EARNING MORE THAN RALPH, ACTUALLY.
SO DON'T WORRY, YOU'RE DOING FINE.
THANKS, MYNE.
I FEEL A LOT BETTER NOW.
HERE.
(Crouch)
スッ
HUH?
YOU MUST BE TIRED FROM ALL THE WALKING WE'VE DONE TODAY, YEAH?
I'LL CARRY YOU.
MY MOST IMPORTANT JOB IS TAKING CAR OF YOUR HEALTH, Y'KNOW. HOP ON.
OKAY...
くす
(Giggle)
I'M ALL YOURS.

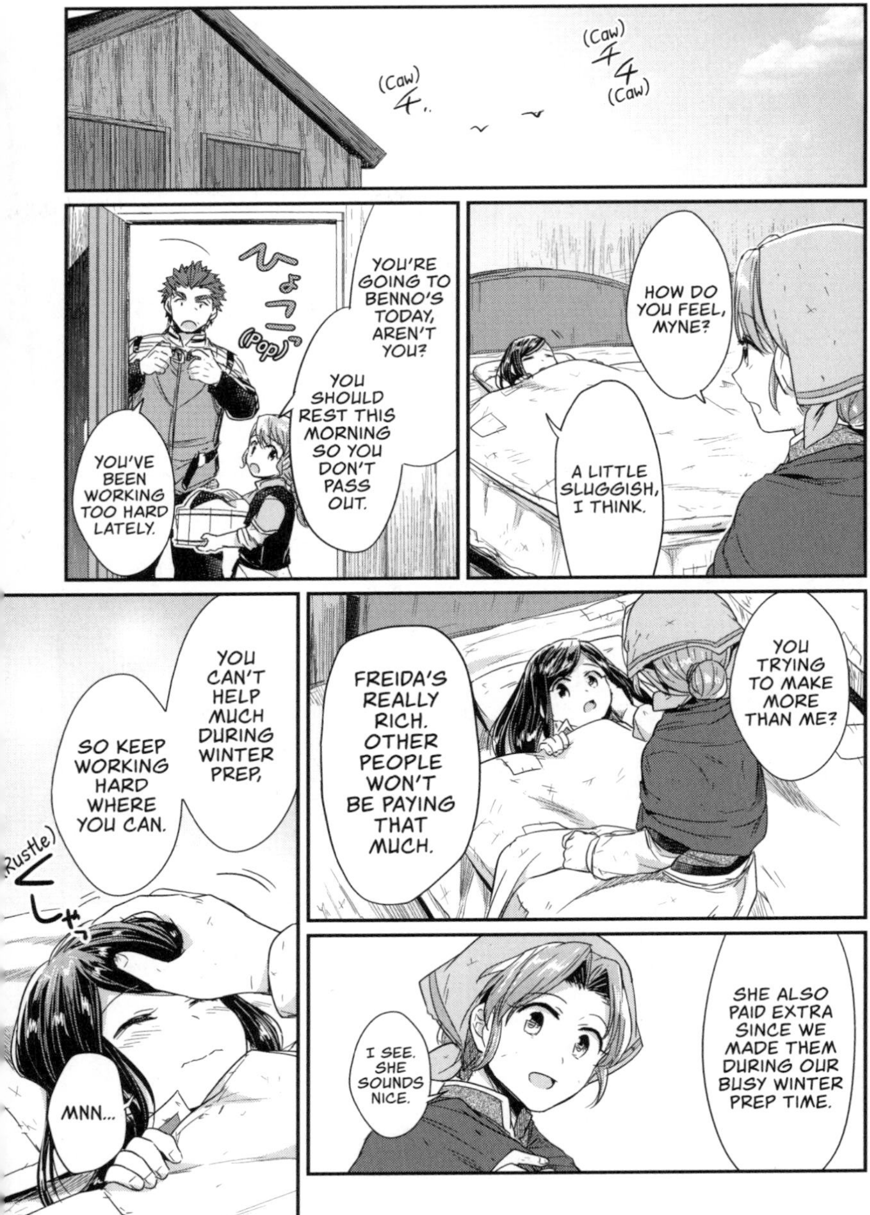

(Caw)
チ
チ
(Caw)
(Caw)
チ..
HOW DO YOU FEEL, MYNE?
A LITTLE SLUGGISH, I THINK.
YOU'RE GOING TO BENNO'S TODAY, AREN'T YOU?
YOU SHOULD REST THIS MORNING SO YOU DON'T PASS OUT.
ひょこっ
(Pop)
YOU'VE BEEN WORKING TOO HARD LATELY.
YOU TRYING TO MAKE MORE THAN ME?
FREIDA'S REALLY RICH. OTHER PEOPLE WON'T BE PAYING THAT MUCH.
SHE ALSO PAID EXTRA SINCE WE MADE THEM DURING OUR BUSY WINTER PREP TIME.
I SEE. SHE SOUNDS NICE.
YOU CAN'T HELP MUCH DURING WINTER PREP,
SO KEEP WORKING HARD WHERE YOU CAN.
(Rustle)
くしゃっ
MNN...

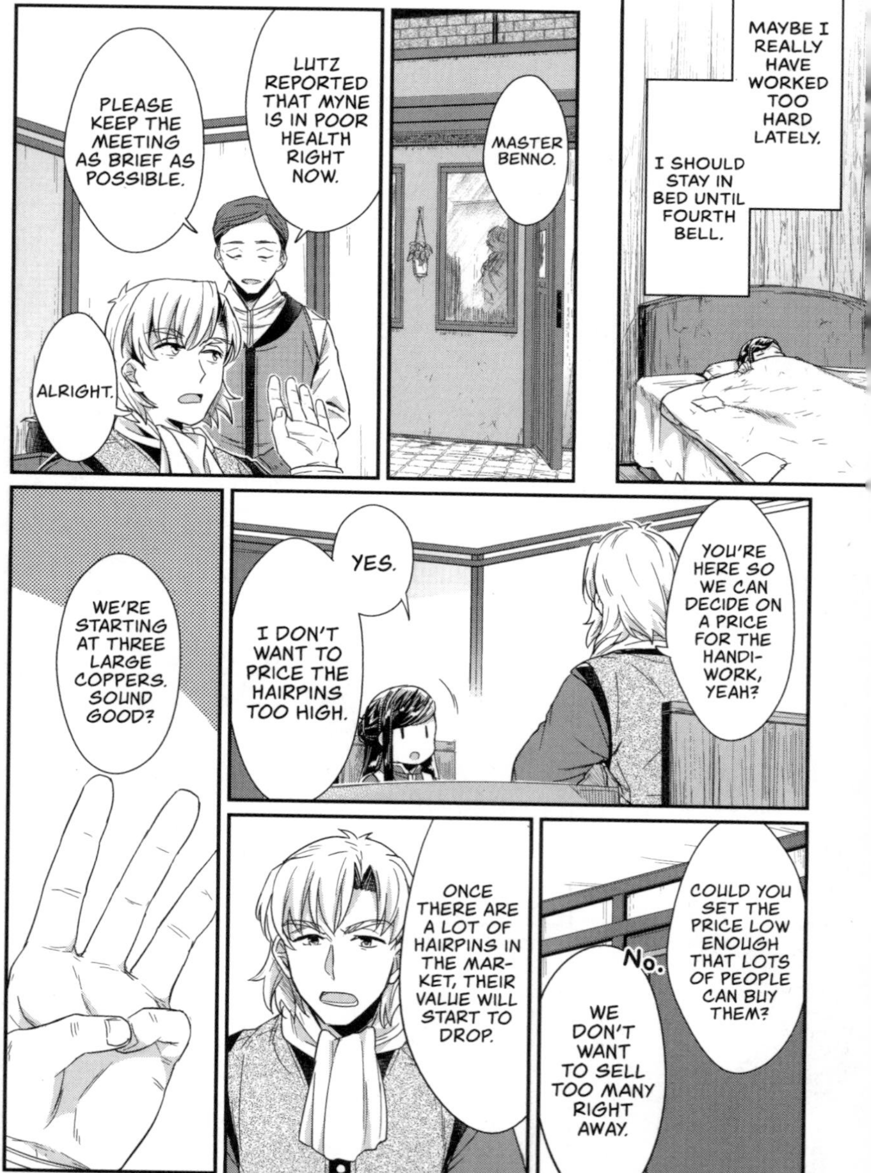
MAYBE I REALLY HAVE WORKED TOO HARD LATELY.
I SHOULD STAY IN BED UNTIL FOURTH BELL.
MASTER BENNO.
LUTZ REPORTED THAT MYNE IS IN POOR HEALTH RIGHT NOW.
PLEASE KEEP THE MEETING AS BRIEF AS POSSIBLE.
ALRIGHT.
YOU'RE HERE SO WE CAN DECIDE ON A PRICE FOR THE HANDI-WORK, YEAH?
YES.
I DON'T WANT TO PRICE THE HAIRPINS TOO HIGH.
COULD YOU SET THE PRICE LOW ENOUGH THAT LOTS OF PEOPLE CAN BUY THEM?
No.
WE DON'T WANT TO SELL TOO MANY RIGHT AWAY.
ONCE THERE ARE A LOT OF HAIRPINS IN THE MAR-KET, THEIR VALUE WILL START TO DROP.
WE'RE STARTING AT THREE LARGE COPPERS. SOUND GOOD?

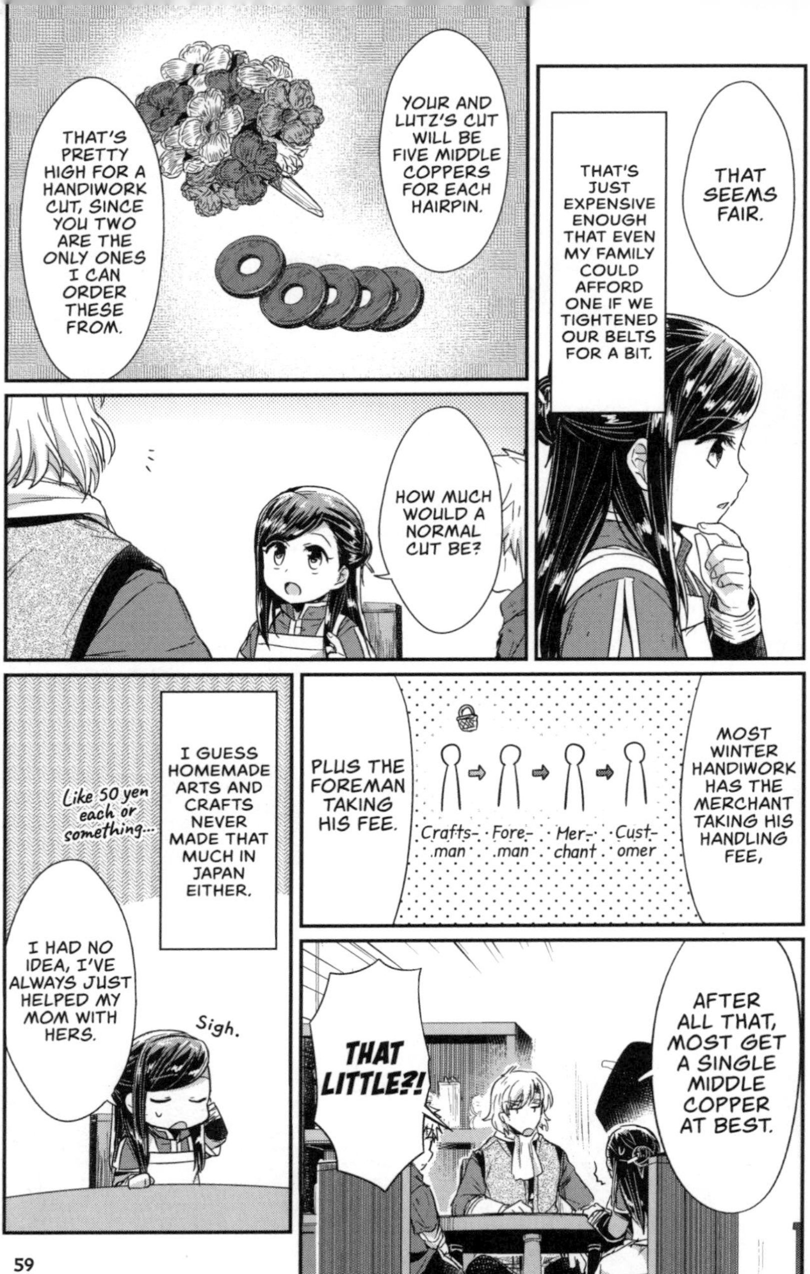
THAT SEEMS FAIR.
THAT'S JUST EXPENSIVE ENOUGH THAT EVEN MY FAMILY COULD AFFORD ONE IF WE TIGHTENED OUR BELTS FOR A BIT.
YOUR AND LUTZ'S CUT WILL BE FIVE MIDDLE COPPERS FOR EACH HAIRPIN.
THAT'S PRETTY HIGH FOR A HANDIWORK CUT, SINCE YOU TWO ARE THE ONLY ONES I CAN ORDER THESE FROM.
HOW MUCH WOULD A NORMAL CUT BE?
MOST WINTER HANDIWORK HAS THE MERCHANT TAKING HIS HANDLING FEE,
Crafts-man
Fore-man
Mer-chant
Cust-omer
PLUS THE FOREMAN TAKING HIS FEE.
AFTER ALL THAT, MOST GET A SINGLE MIDDLE COPPER AT BEST.
THAT LITTLE?!
I GUESS HOMEMADE ARTS AND CRAFTS NEVER MADE THAT MUCH IN JAPAN EITHER.
Like 50 yen each or something...
I HAD NO IDEA, I'VE ALWAYS JUST HELPED MY MOM WITH HERS.
Sigh.

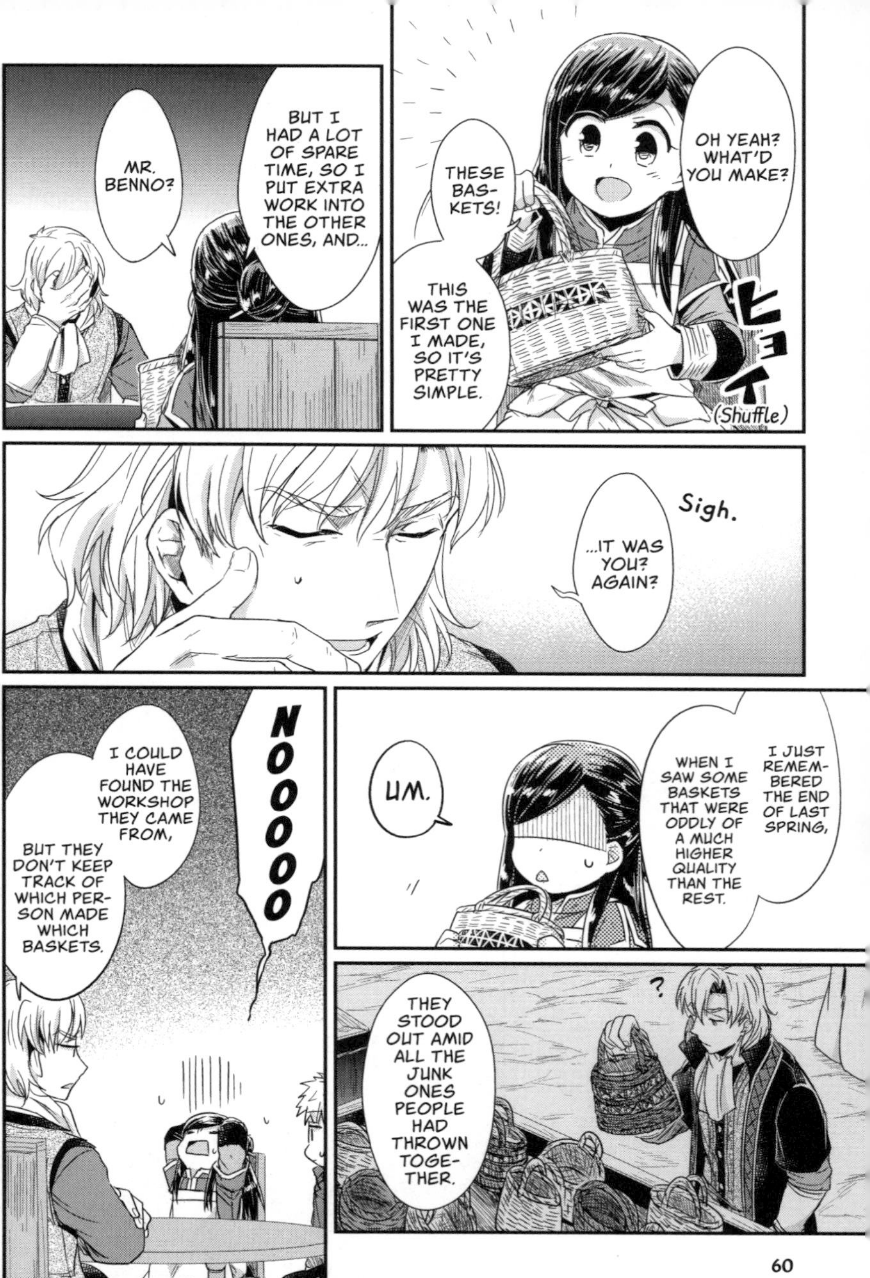
OH YEAH? WHAT'D YOU MAKE?
THESE BAS-KETS!
THIS WAS THE FIRST ONE I MADE, SO IT'S PRETTY SIMPLE.
ヒョイ
(Shuffle)
BUT I HAD A LOT OF SPARE TIME, SO I PUT EXTRA WORK INTO THE OTHER ONES, AND...
MR. BENNO?
Sigh.
...IT WAS YOU? AGAIN?
I JUST REMEM-BERED THE END OF LAST SPRING,
WHEN I SAW SOME BASKETS THAT WERE ODDLY OF A MUCH HIGHER QUALITY THAN THE REST.
UM.
THEY STOOD OUT AMID ALL THE JUNK ONES PEOPLE HAD THROWN TOGE-THER.
NOOOOOO
I COULD HAVE FOUND THE WORKSHOP THEY CAME FROM,
BUT THEY DON'T KEEP TRACK OF WHICH PER-SON MADE WHICH BASKETS.

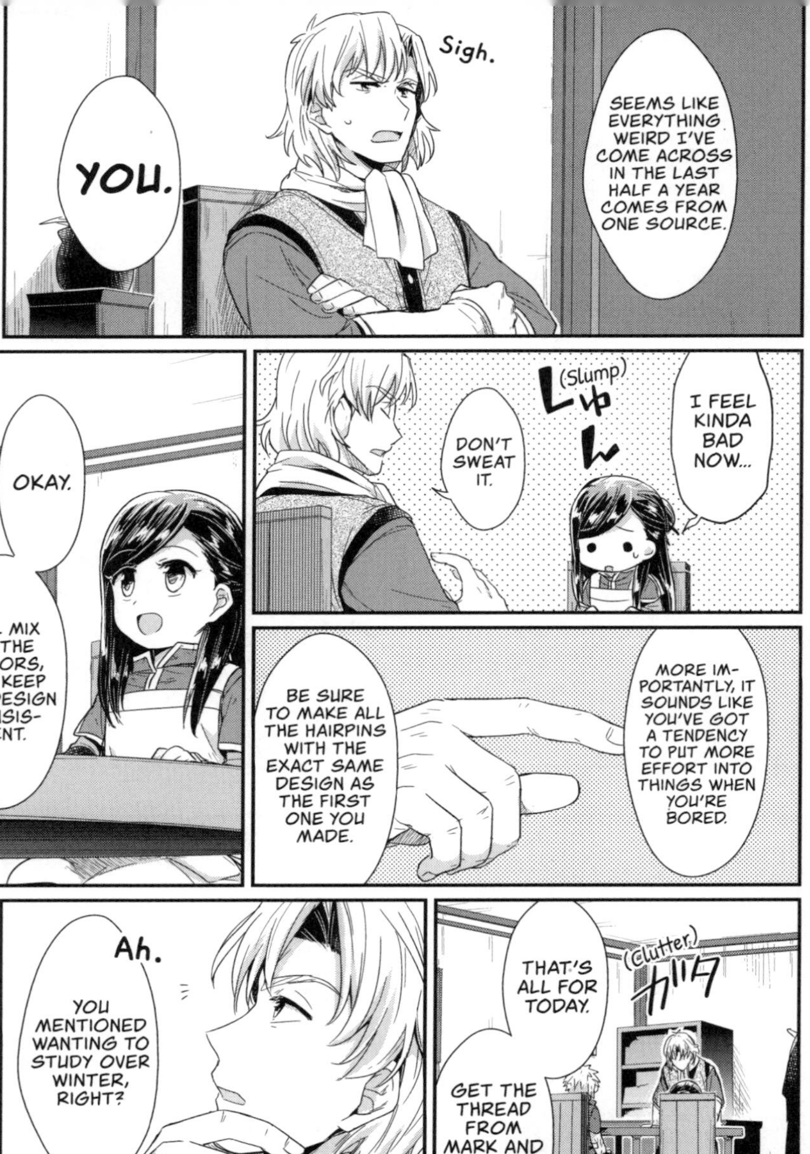
Sigh.
SEEMS LIKE EVERYTHING WEIRD I'VE COME ACROSS IN THE LAST HALF A YEAR COMES FROM ONE SOURCE.
YOU.
I FEEL KINDA BAD NOW...
(Slump) しゅん
DON'T SWEAT IT.
MORE IMPORTANTLY, IT SOUNDS LIKE YOU'VE GOT A TENDENCY TO PUT MORE EFFORT INTO THINGS WHEN YOU'RE BORED.
BE SURE TO MAKE ALL THE HAIRPINS WITH THE EXACT SAME DESIGN AS THE FIRST ONE YOU MADE.
OKAY.
I'LL MIX UP THE COLORS, BUT KEEP THE DESIGN CONSISTENT.
(Clutter) ガタ
THAT'S ALL FOR TODAY.
GET THE THREAD FROM MARK AND HEAD ON HOME.
Ah.
YOU MENTIONED WANTING TO STUDY OVER WINTER, RIGHT?

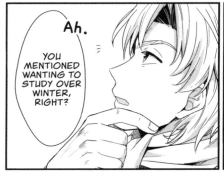

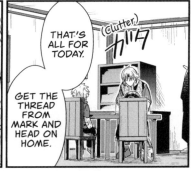

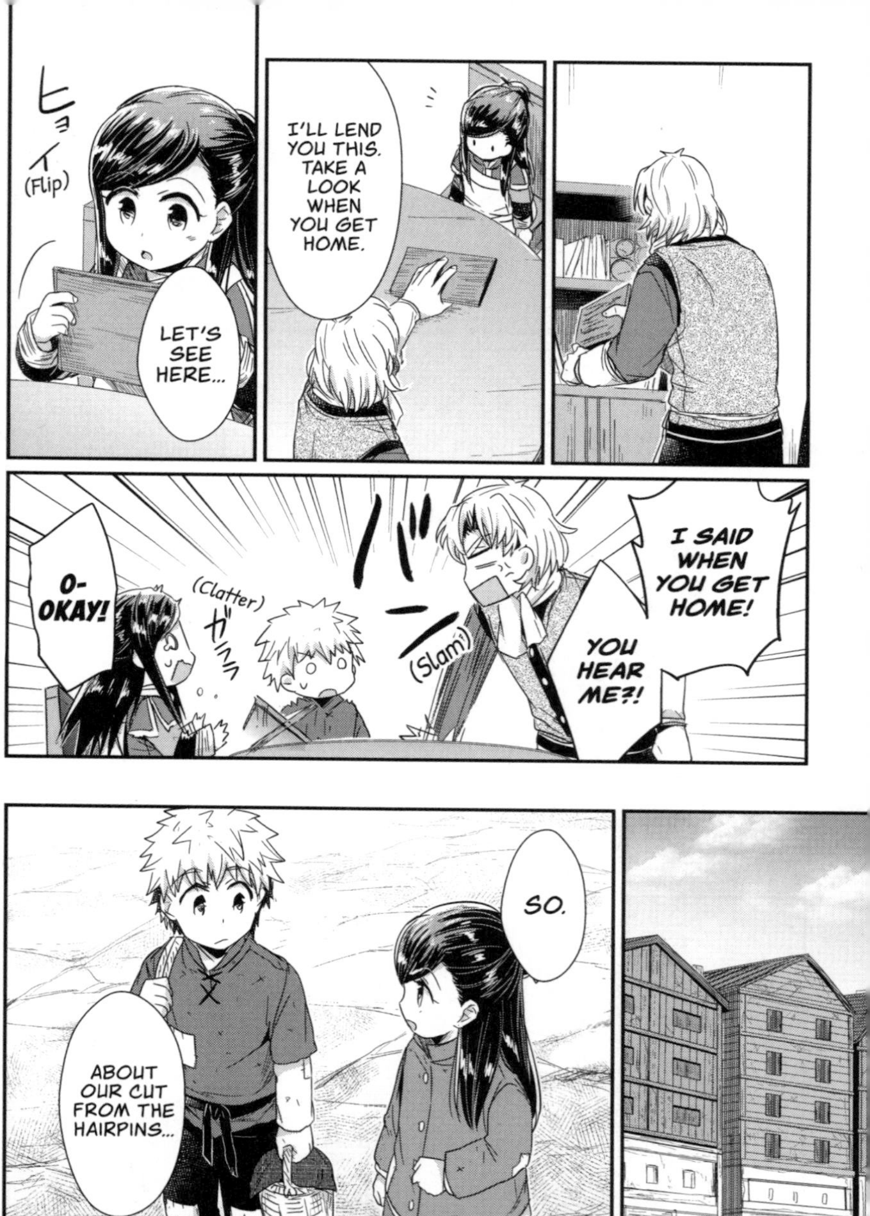
I'LL LEND YOU THIS. TAKE A LOOK WHEN YOU GET HOME.
ヒョイ
(Flip)
LET'S SEE HERE...
I SAID WHEN YOU GET HOME!
YOU HEAR ME?!
(Slam)
(Clatter)
O-OKAY!
SO.
ABOUT OUR CUT FROM THE HAIRPINS...

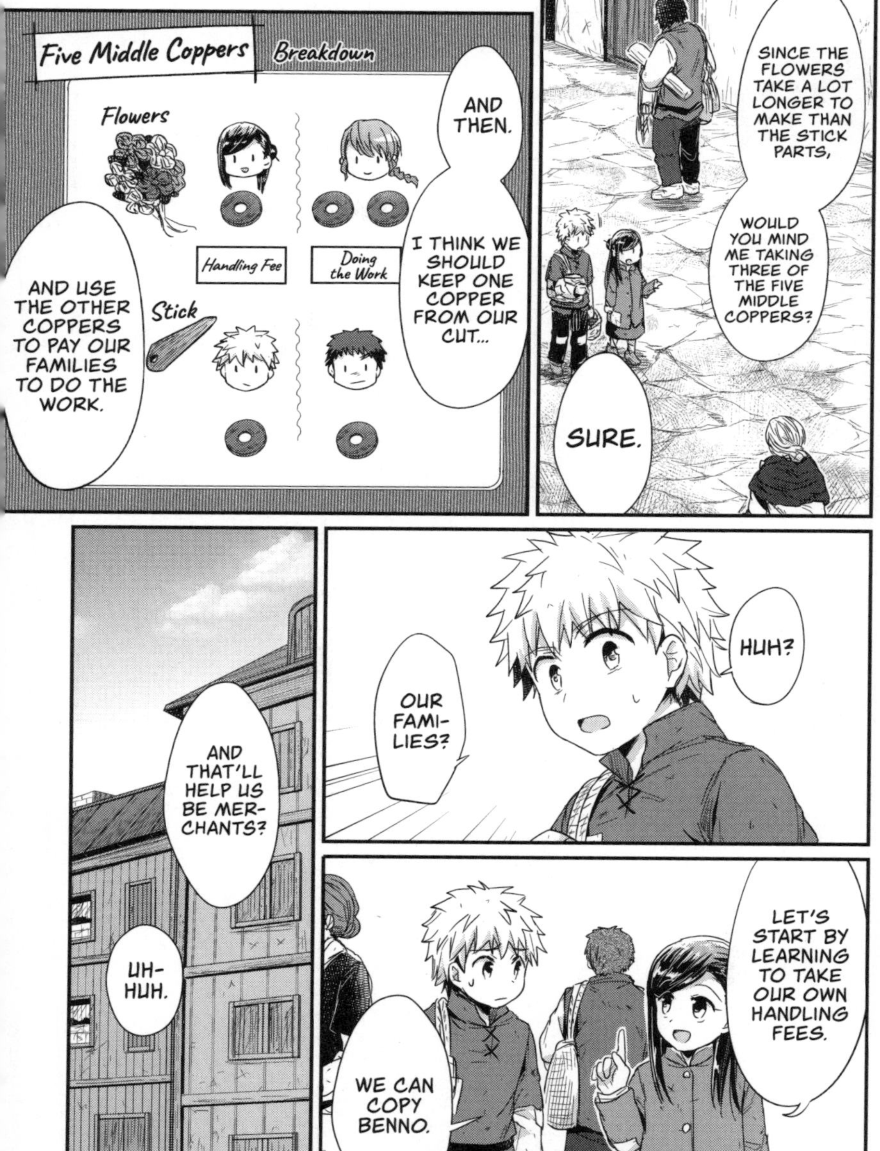
SINCE THE FLOWERS TAKE A LOT LONGER TO MAKE THAN THE STICK PARTS,
WOULD YOU MIND ME TAKING THREE OF THE FIVE MIDDLE COPPERS?
SURE.
AND THEN.
I THINK WE SHOULD KEEP ONE COPPER FROM OUR CUT...
Five Middle Coppers
Breakdown
Flowers
Handling Fee
Doing the Work
Stick
AND USE THE OTHER COPPERS TO PAY OUR FAMILIES TO DO THE WORK.
HUH?
OUR FAMI-LIES?
LET'S START BY LEARNING TO TAKE OUR OWN HANDLING FEES.
WE CAN COPY BENNO.
AND THAT'LL HELP US BE MER-CHANTS?
UH-HUH.

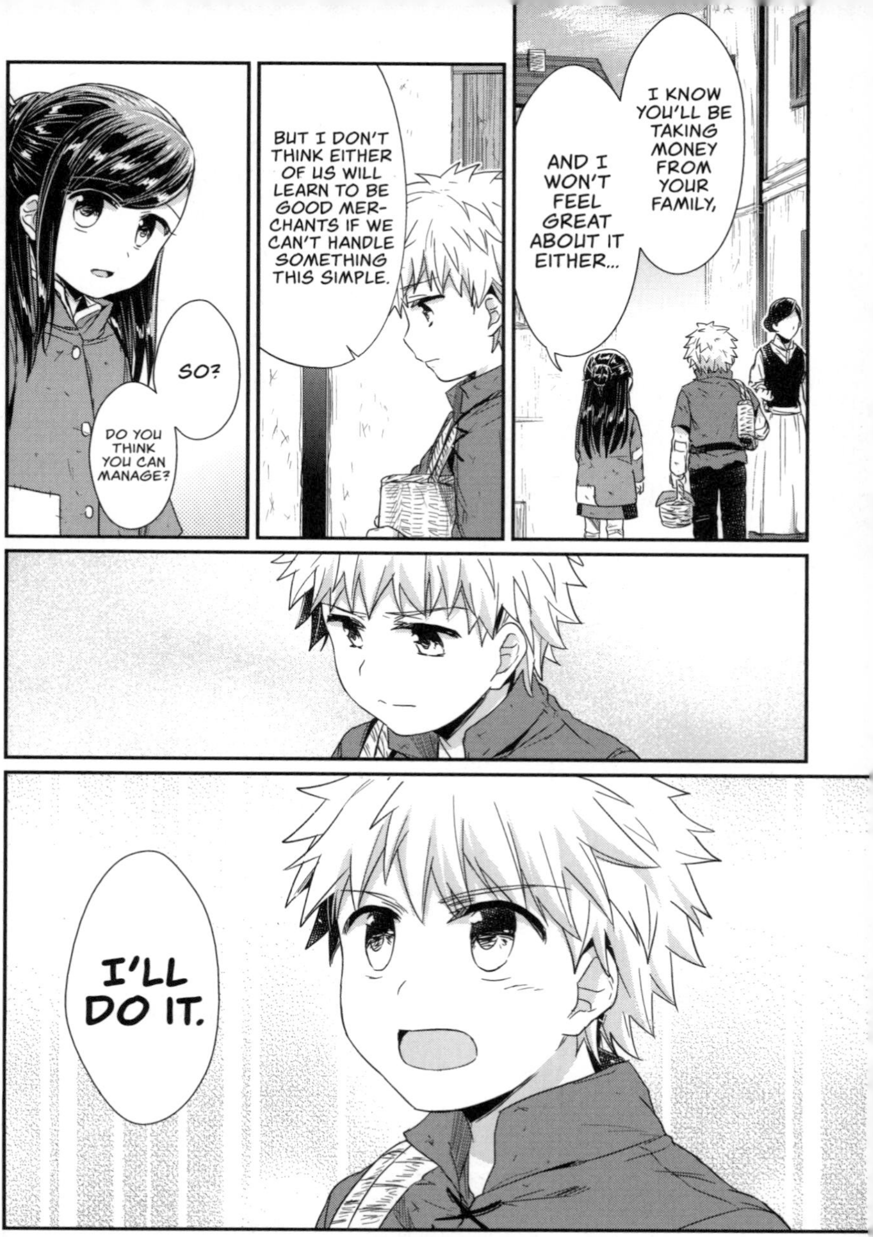
I KNOW YOU'LL BE TAKING MONEY FROM YOUR FAMILY,
AND I WON'T FEEL GREAT ABOUT IT EITHER...
BUT I DON'T THINK EITHER OF US WILL LEARN TO BE GOOD MER-CHANTS IF WE CAN'T HANDLE SOMETHING THIS SIMPLE.
SO?
DO YOU THINK YOU CAN MANAGE?
I'LL DO IT.

Ch.21: Freida's Hairpins End

ASCENDANCE
OF A
BOOKWORM

I'll do anything to become a librarian!

Part 1 **If there aren't any books, I'll just have to make some!**

What about me?!

Um...

Could you make some more sewing needles?

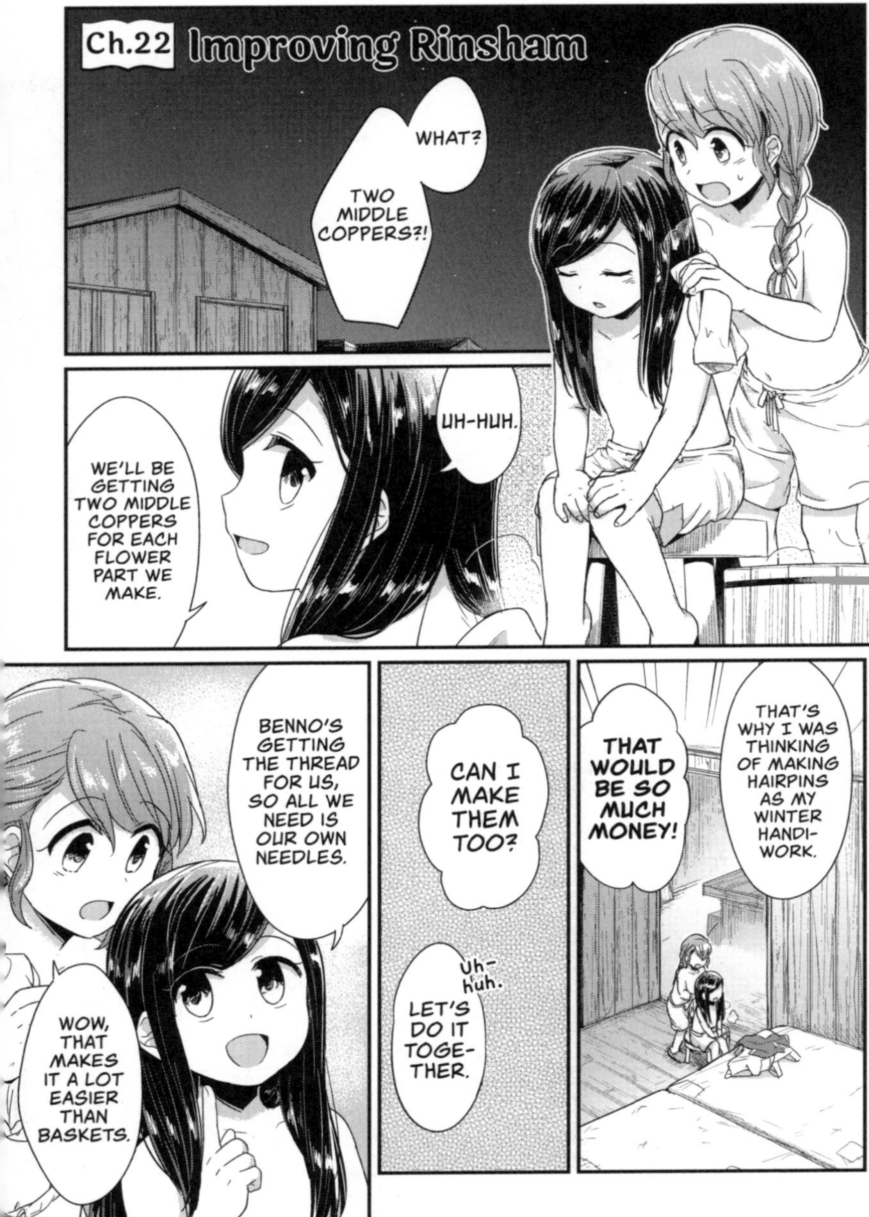
Ch.22 Improving Rinsham
WHAT?
TWO MIDDLE COPPERS?!
UH-HUH.
WE'LL BE GETTING TWO MIDDLE COPPERS FOR EACH FLOWER PART WE MAKE.
THAT'S WHY I WAS THINKING OF MAKING HAIRPINS AS MY WINTER HANDI-WORK.
THAT WOULD BE SO MUCH MONEY!
CAN I MAKE THEM TOO?
Uh-huh.
LET'S DO IT TOGE-THER.
BENNO'S GETTING THE THREAD FOR US, SO ALL WE NEED IS OUR OWN NEEDLES.
WOW, THAT MAKES IT A LOT EASIER THAN BASKETS.

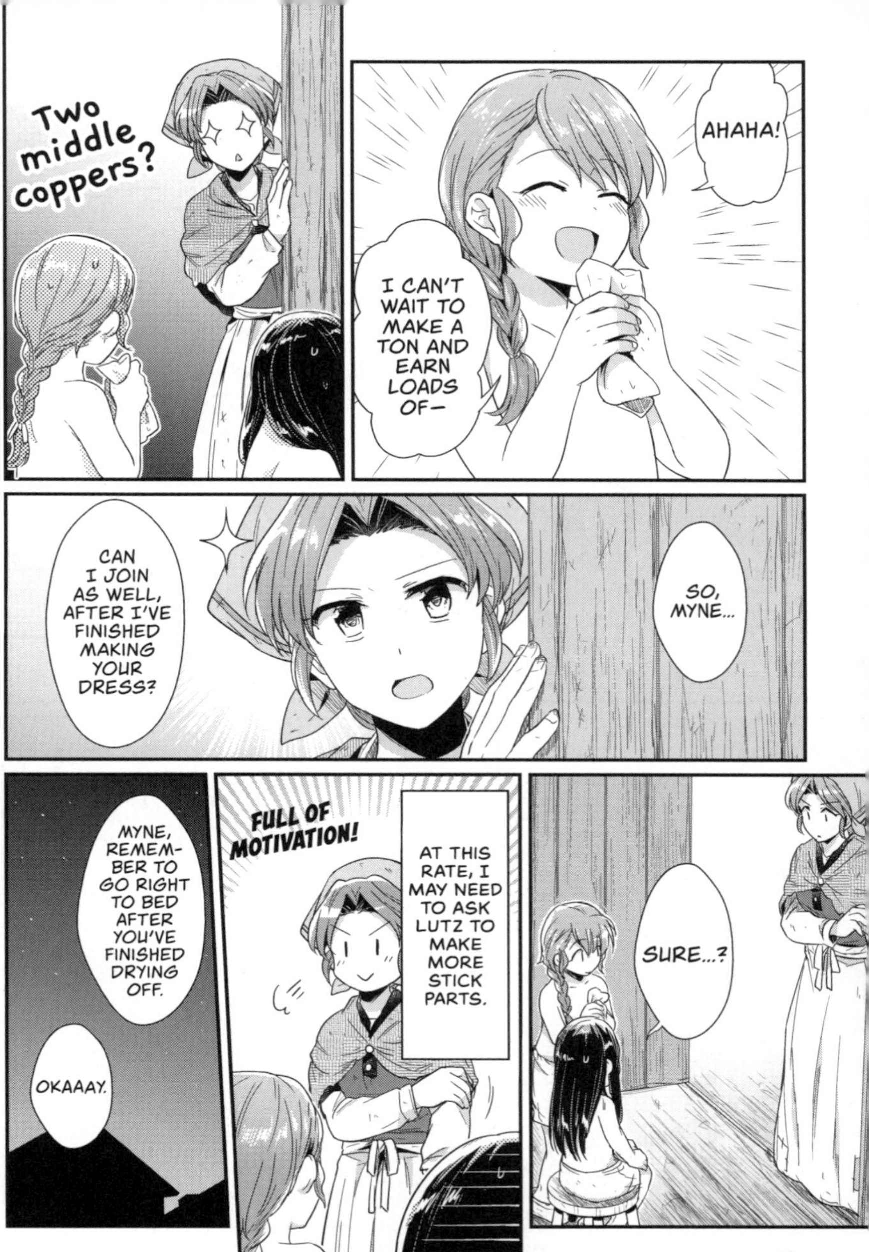
AHAHA!
I CAN'T WAIT TO MAKE A TON AND EARN LOADS OF—
Two middle coppers?
SO, MYNE...
CAN I JOIN AS WELL, AFTER I'VE FINISHED MAKING YOUR DRESS?
SURE...?
AT THIS RATE, I MAY NEED TO ASK LUTZ TO MAKE MORE STICK PARTS.
FULL OF MOTIVATION!
MYNE, REMEMBER TO GO RIGHT TO BED AFTER YOU'VE FINISHED DRYING OFF.
OKAAAY.

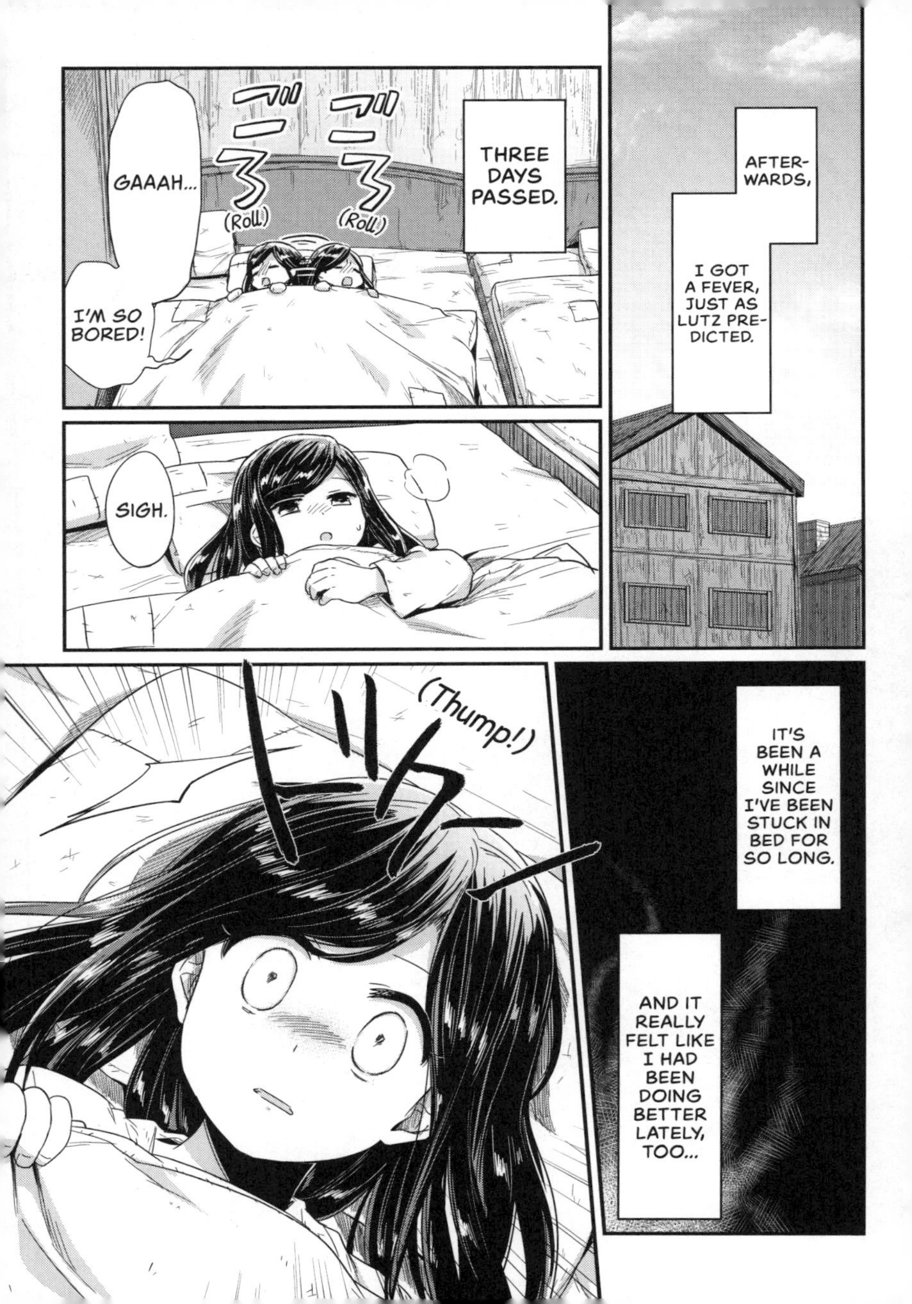
AFTER-WARDS,
I GOT A FEVER, JUST AS LUTZ PREDICTED.
THREE DAYS PASSED.
(Roll)
(Roll)
GAAAH...
I'M SO BORED!
SIGH.
IT'S BEEN A WHILE SINCE I'VE BEEN STUCK IN BED FOR SO LONG.
AND IT REALLY FELT LIKE I HAD BEEN DOING BETTER LATELY, TOO...
(Thump!)

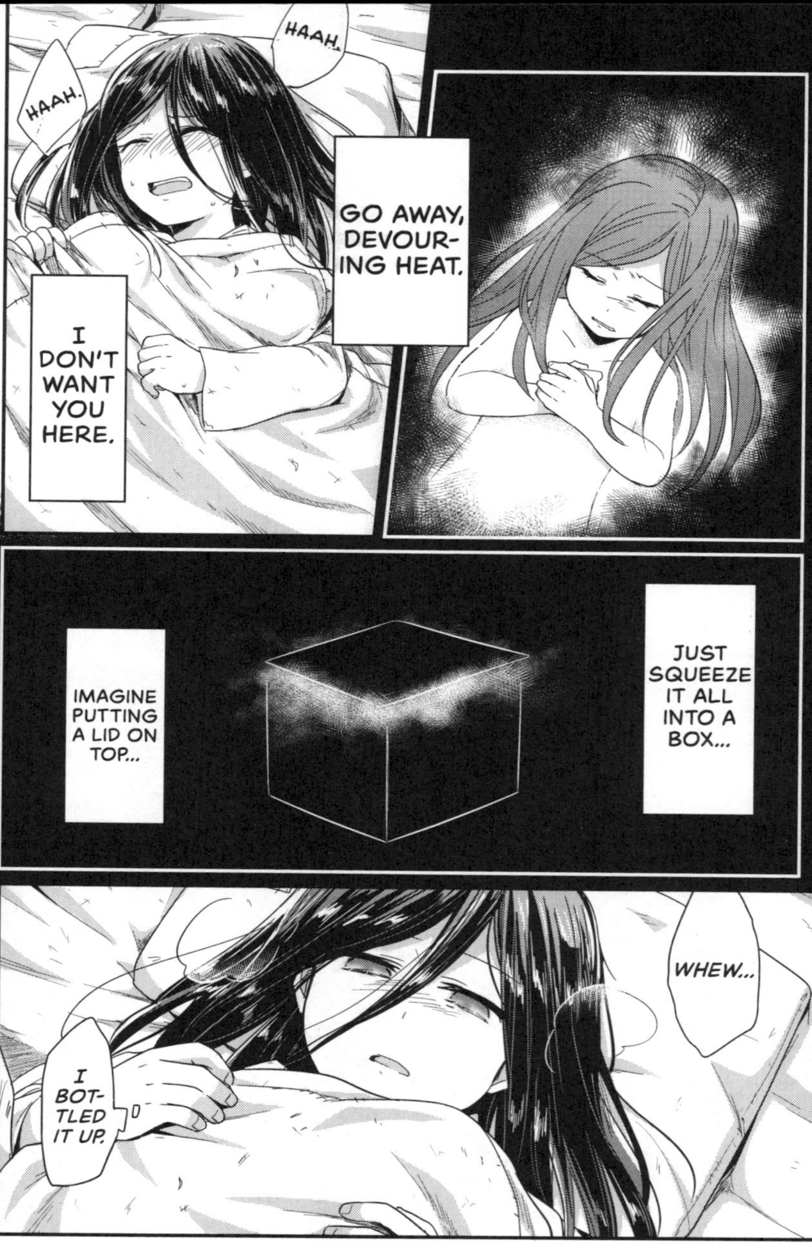

HAAH.
HAAH.
GO AWAY, DEVOUR-ING HEAT.
I DON'T WANT YOU HERE.
JUST SQUEEZE IT ALL INTO A BOX...
IMAGINE PUTTING A LID ON TOP...
WHEW...
I BOT-TLED IT UP.

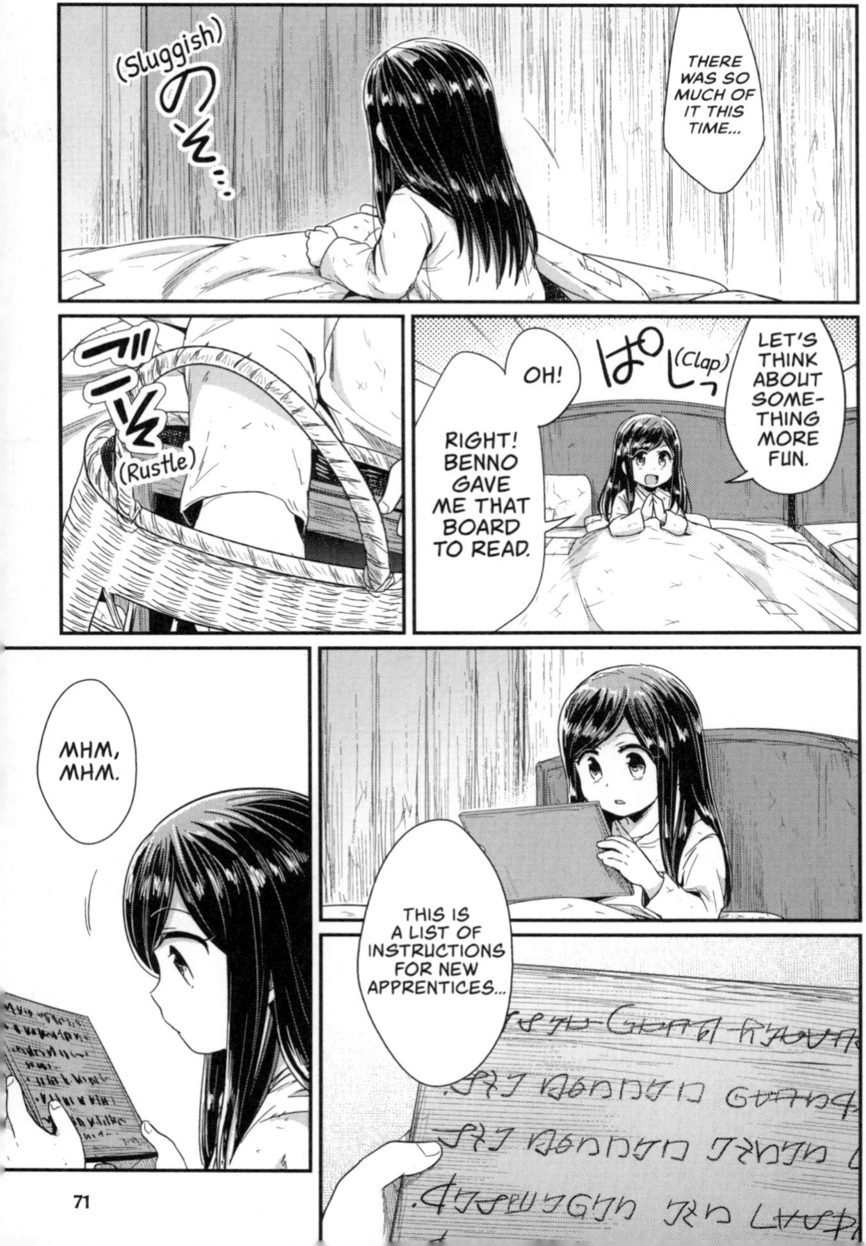
THERE WAS SO MUCH OF IT THIS TIME...
(Sluggish)
LET'S THINK ABOUT SOME-THING MORE FUN.
(Clap)
OH!
RIGHT! BENNO GAVE ME THAT BOARD TO READ.
(Rustle)
THIS IS A LIST OF INSTRUCTIONS FOR NEW APPRENTICES...
MHM, MHM.

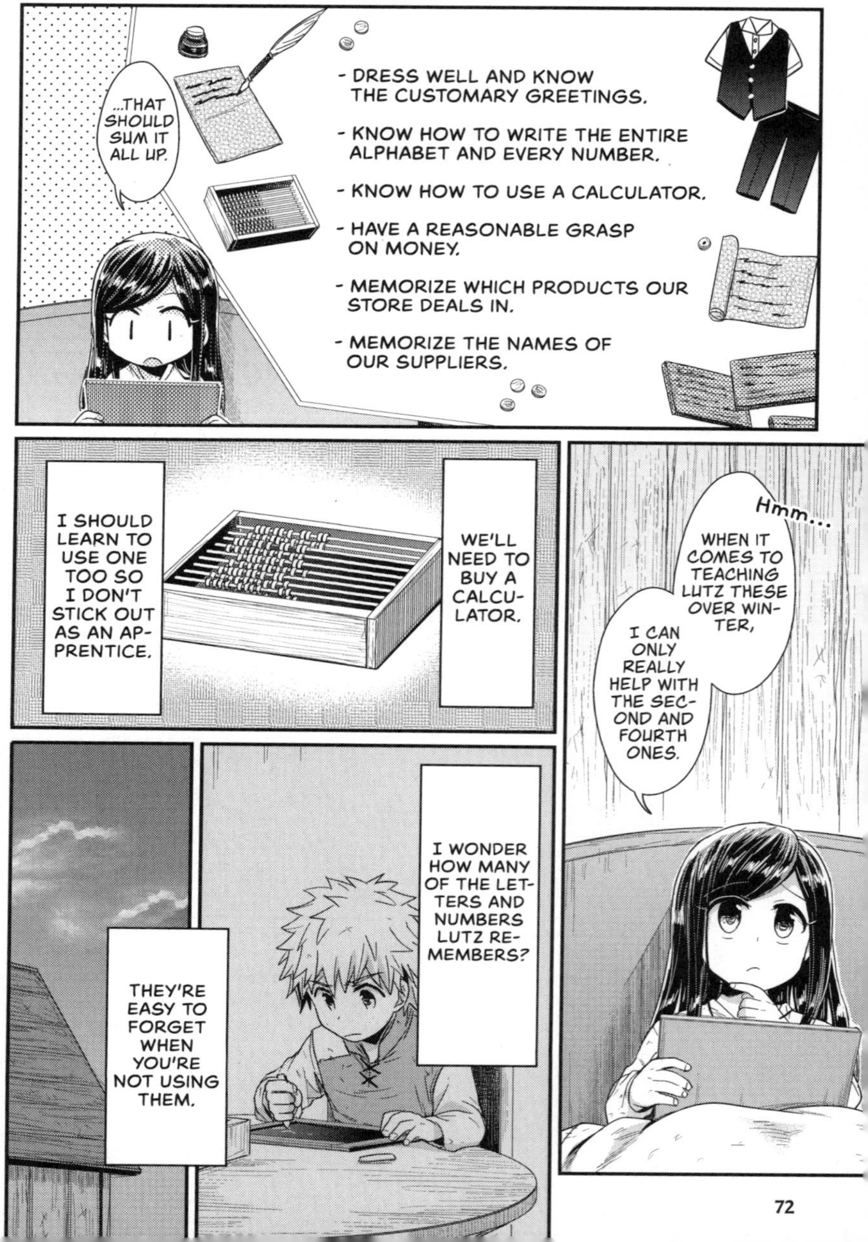

- DRESS WELL AND KNOW THE CUSTOMARY GREETINGS.
- KNOW HOW TO WRITE THE ENTIRE ALPHABET AND EVERY NUMBER.
- KNOW HOW TO USE A CALCULATOR.
- HAVE A REASONABLE GRASP ON MONEY.
- MEMORIZE WHICH PRODUCTS OUR STORE DEALS IN.
- MEMORIZE THE NAMES OF OUR SUPPLIERS.
...THAT SHOULD SUM IT ALL UP.
Hmm...
WHEN IT COMES TO TEACHING LUTZ THESE OVER WINTER,
I CAN ONLY REALLY HELP WITH THE SECOND AND FOURTH ONES.
WE'LL NEED TO BUY A CALCULATOR.
I SHOULD LEARN TO USE ONE TOO SO I DON'T STICK OUT AS AN APPRENTICE.
I WONDER HOW MANY OF THE LETTERS AND NUMBERS LUTZ REMEMBERS?
THEY'RE EASY TO FORGET WHEN YOU'RE NOT USING THEM.

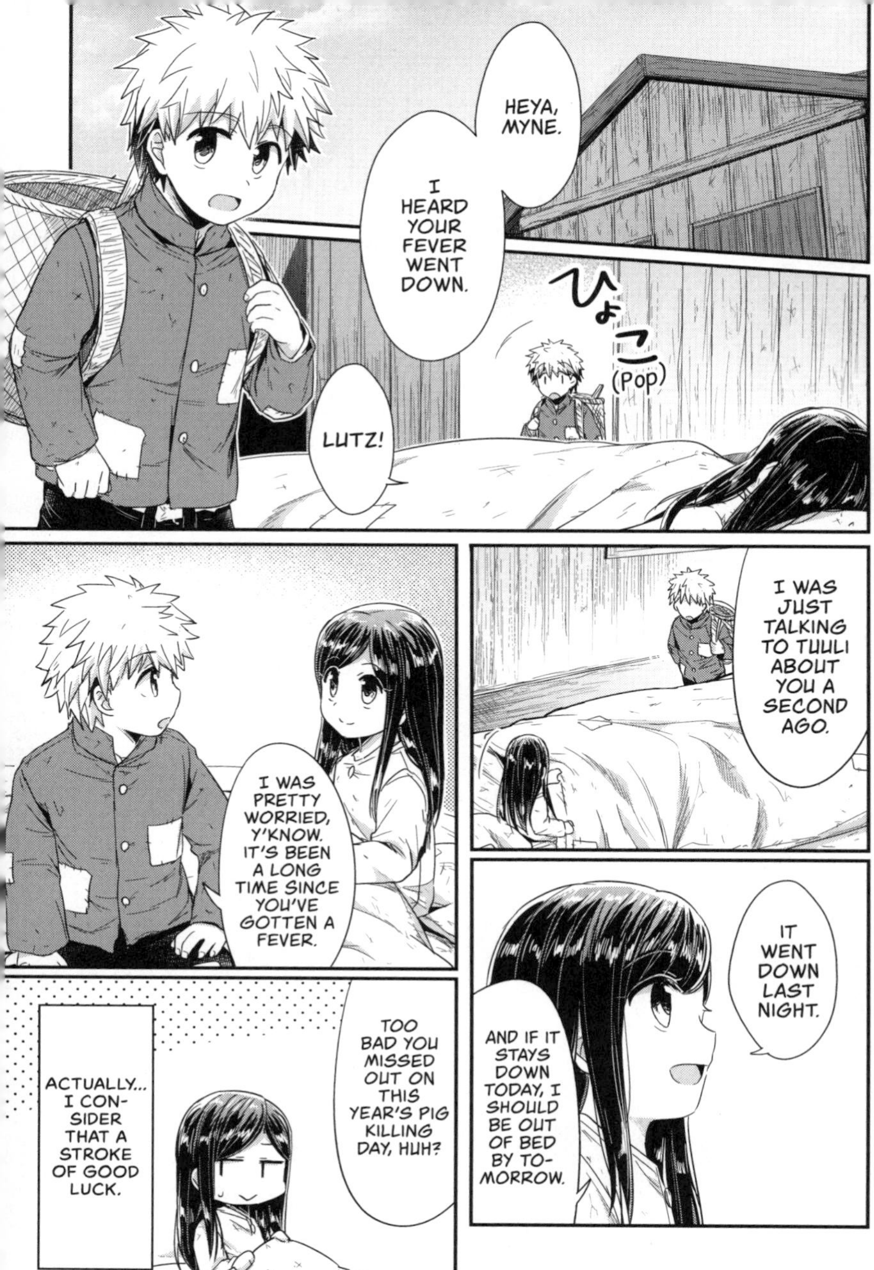
ひょこ
(Pop)
LUTZ!
HEYA, MYNE.
I HEARD YOUR FEVER WENT DOWN.
I WAS JUST TALKING TO TUULI ABOUT YOU A SECOND AGO.
I WAS PRETTY WORRIED, Y'KNOW. IT'S BEEN A LONG TIME SINCE YOU'VE GOTTEN A FEVER.
IT WENT DOWN LAST NIGHT.
AND IF IT STAYS DOWN TODAY, I SHOULD BE OUT OF BED BY TO-MORROW.
TOO BAD YOU MISSED OUT ON THIS YEAR'S PIG KILLING DAY, HUH?
ACTUALLY... I CON-SIDER THAT A STROKE OF GOOD LUCK.

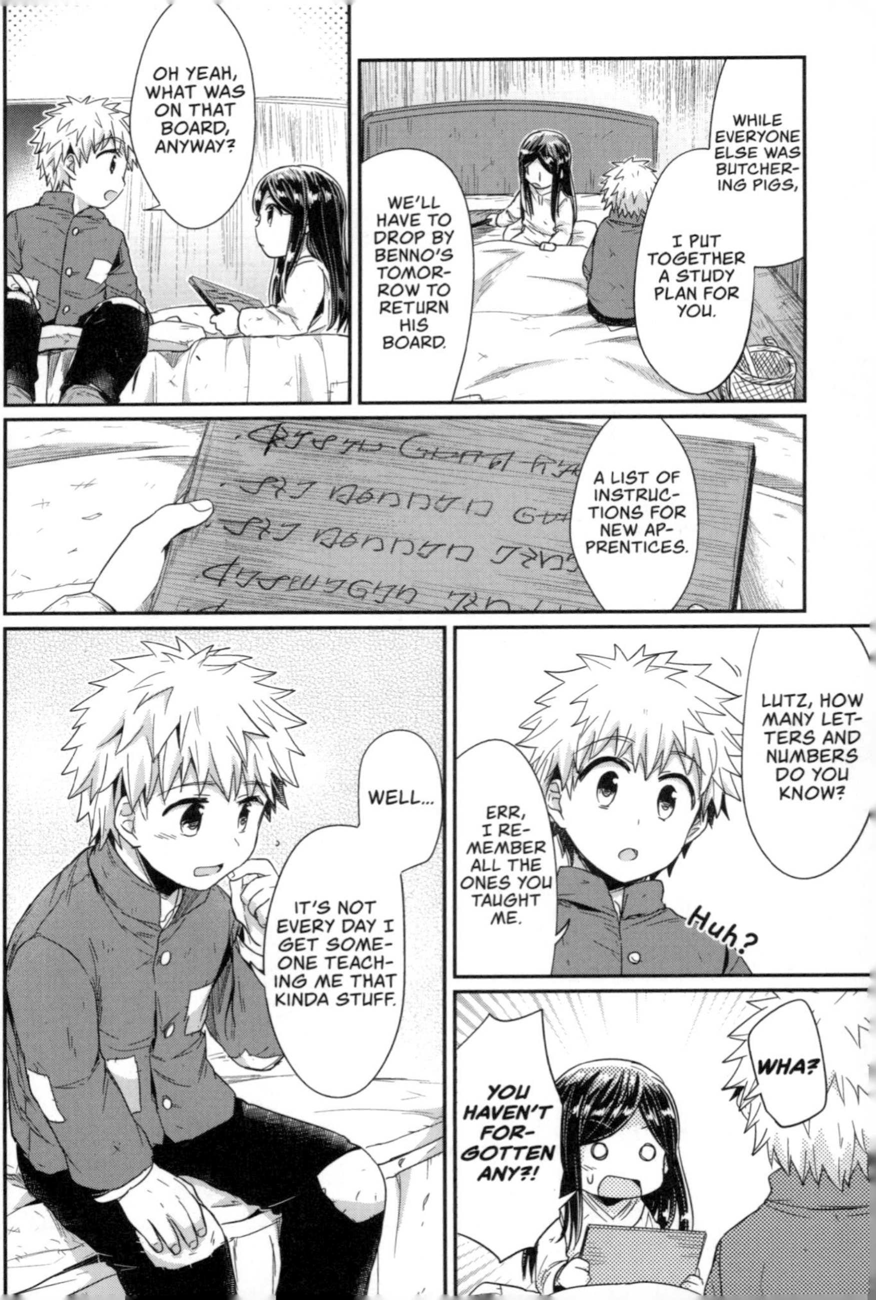
WHILE EVERYONE ELSE WAS BUTCHER-ING PIGS,
I PUT TOGETHER A STUDY PLAN FOR YOU.
WE'LL HAVE TO DROP BY BENNO'S TOMOR-ROW TO RETURN HIS BOARD.
OH YEAH, WHAT WAS ON THAT BOARD, ANYWAY?
A LIST OF INSTRUC-TIONS FOR NEW AP-PRENTICES.
LUTZ, HOW MANY LET-TERS AND NUMBERS DO YOU KNOW?
ERR, I RE-MEMBER ALL THE ONES YOU TAUGHT ME.
Huh?
WHA?
YOU HAVEN'T FOR-GOTTEN ANY?!
WELL...
IT'S NOT EVERY DAY I GET SOME-ONE TEACH-ING ME THAT KINDA STUFF.

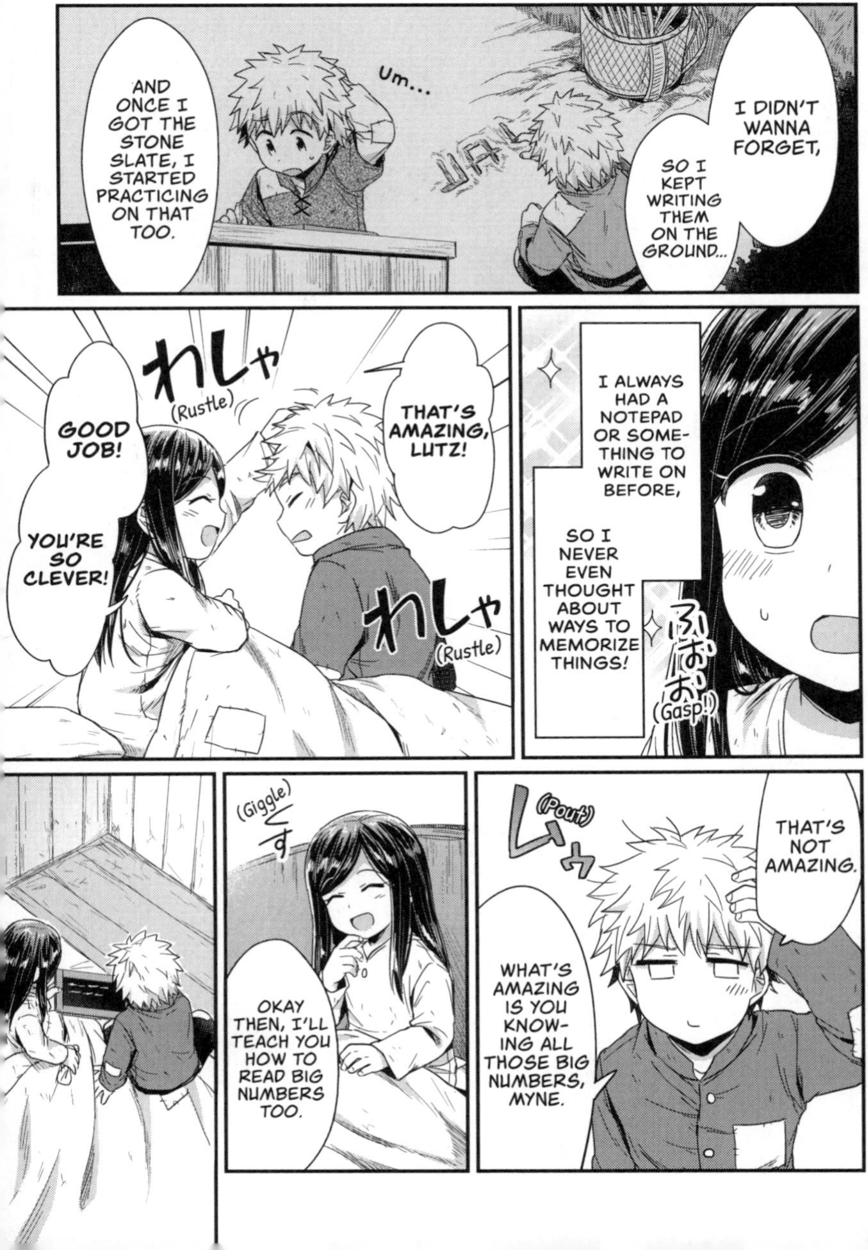
I DIDN'T WANNA FORGET,
SO I KEPT WRITING THEM ON THE GROUND...
Um...
AND ONCE I GOT THE STONE SLATE, I STARTED PRACTICING ON THAT TOO.
I ALWAYS HAD A NOTEPAD OR SOME-THING TO WRITE ON BEFORE,
SO I NEVER EVEN THOUGHT ABOUT WAYS TO MEMORIZE THINGS!
ふぉぉ (Gasp!)
THAT'S AMAZING, LUTZ!
わしゃ (Rustle)
GOOD JOB!
YOU'RE SO CLEVER!
わしゃ (Rustle)
THAT'S NOT AMAZING.
ムゥ (Pout)
WHAT'S AMAZING IS YOU KNOWING ALL THOSE BIG NUMBERS, MYNE.
くす (Giggle)
OKAY THEN, I'LL TEACH YOU HOW TO READ BIG NUMBERS TOO.

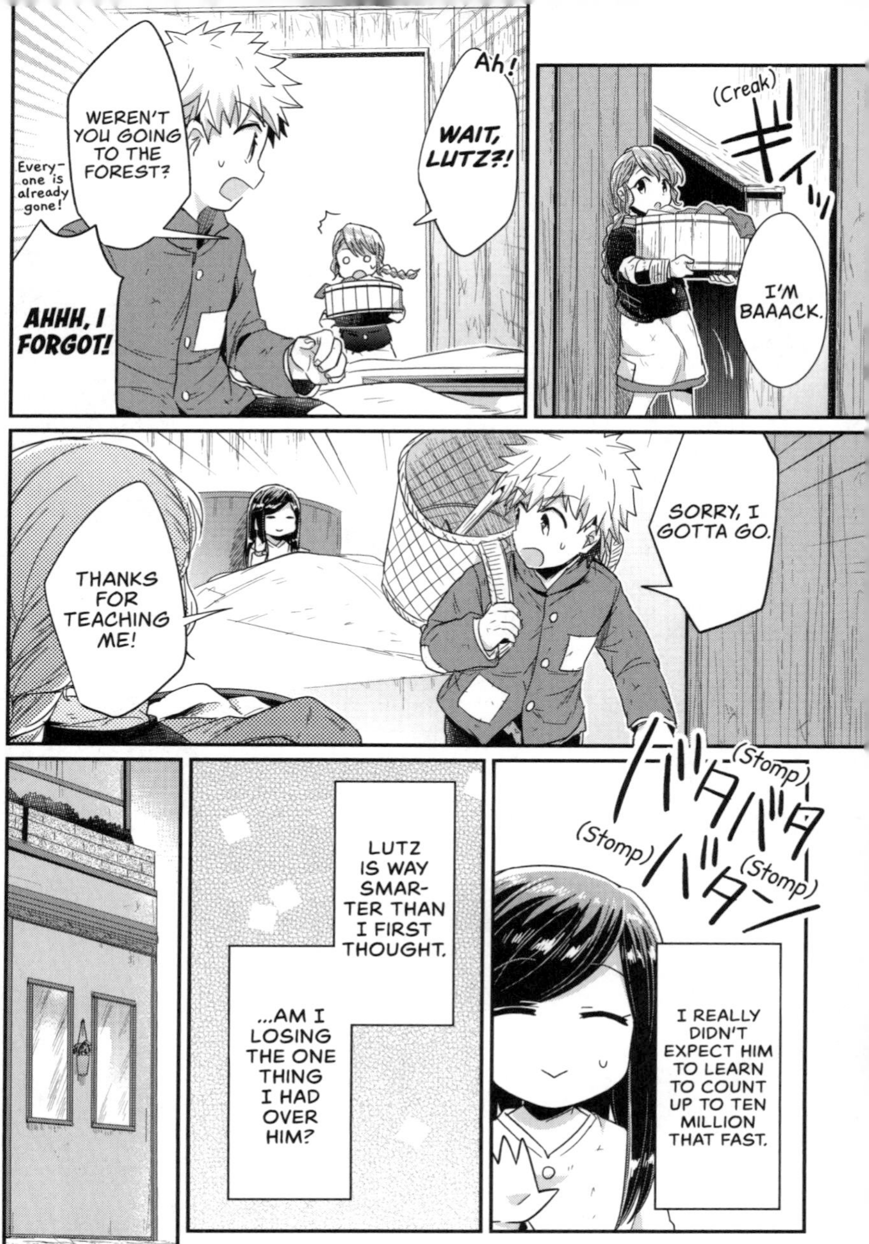
(Creak)
ギイッ
I'M BAAACK.
Ah!
WAIT, LUTZ?!
WEREN'T YOU GOING TO THE FOREST?
Every-one is already gone!
AHHH, I FORGOT!
SORRY, I GOTTA GO.
THANKS FOR TEACHING ME!
(Stomp)
バタバタ
(Stomp)
バターン
(Stomp)
I REALLY DIDN'T EXPECT HIM TO LEARN TO COUNT UP TO TEN MILLION THAT FAST.
LUTZ IS WAY SMARTER THAN I FIRST THOUGHT.
...AM I LOSING THE ONE THING I HAD OVER HIM?

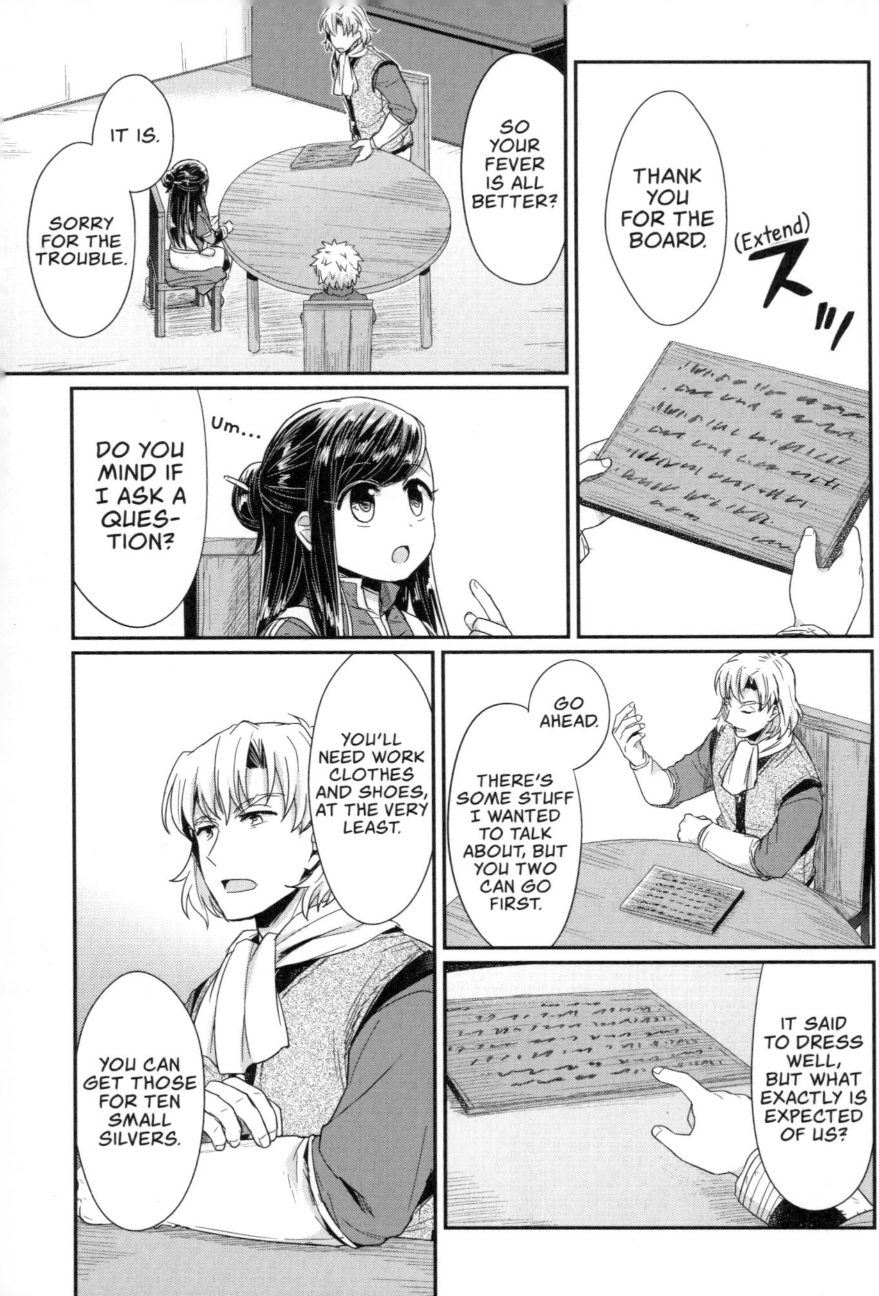
THANK YOU FOR THE BOARD.
(Extend)
スッ
SO YOUR FEVER IS ALL BETTER?
IT IS.
SORRY FOR THE TROUBLE.
Um...
DO YOU MIND IF I ASK A QUES-TION?
GO AHEAD.
THERE'S SOME STUFF I WANTED TO TALK ABOUT, BUT YOU TWO CAN GO FIRST.
IT SAID TO DRESS WELL, BUT WHAT EXACTLY IS EXPECTED OF US?
YOU'LL NEED WORK CLOTHES AND SHOES, AT THE VERY LEAST.
YOU CAN GET THOSE FOR TEN SMALL SILVERS.

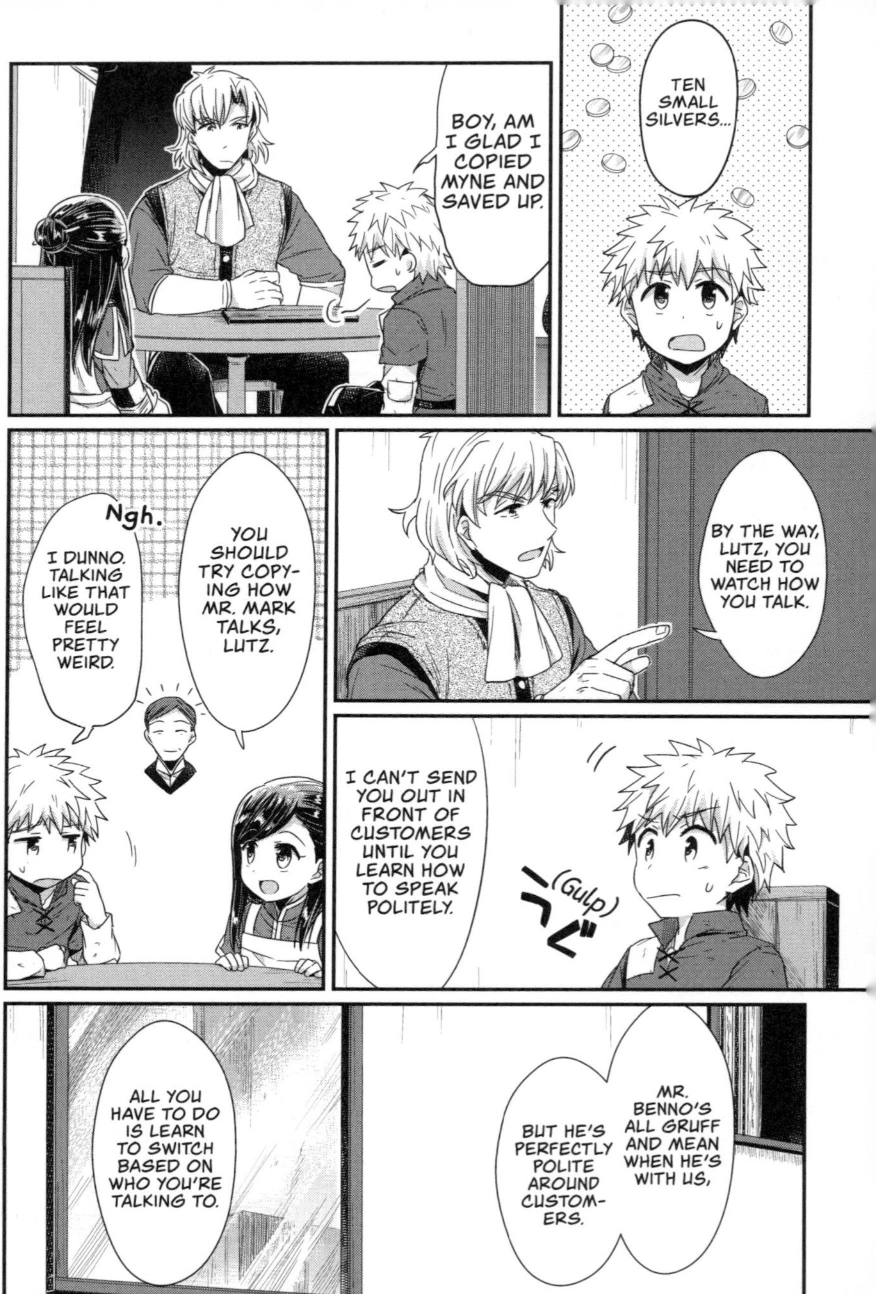
TEN SMALL SILVERS...
BOY, AM I GLAD I COPIED MYNE AND SAVED UP.
BY THE WAY, LUTZ, YOU NEED TO WATCH HOW YOU TALK.
I CAN'T SEND YOU OUT IN FRONT OF CUSTOMERS UNTIL YOU LEARN HOW TO SPEAK POLITELY.
(Gulp)
YOU SHOULD TRY COPYING HOW MR. MARK TALKS, LUTZ.
Ngh.
I DUNNO. TALKING LIKE THAT WOULD FEEL PRETTY WEIRD.
MR. BENNO'S ALL GRUFF AND MEAN WHEN HE'S WITH US,
BUT HE'S PERFECTLY POLITE AROUND CUSTOMERS.
ALL YOU HAVE TO DO IS LEARN TO SWITCH BASED ON WHO YOU'RE TALKING TO.

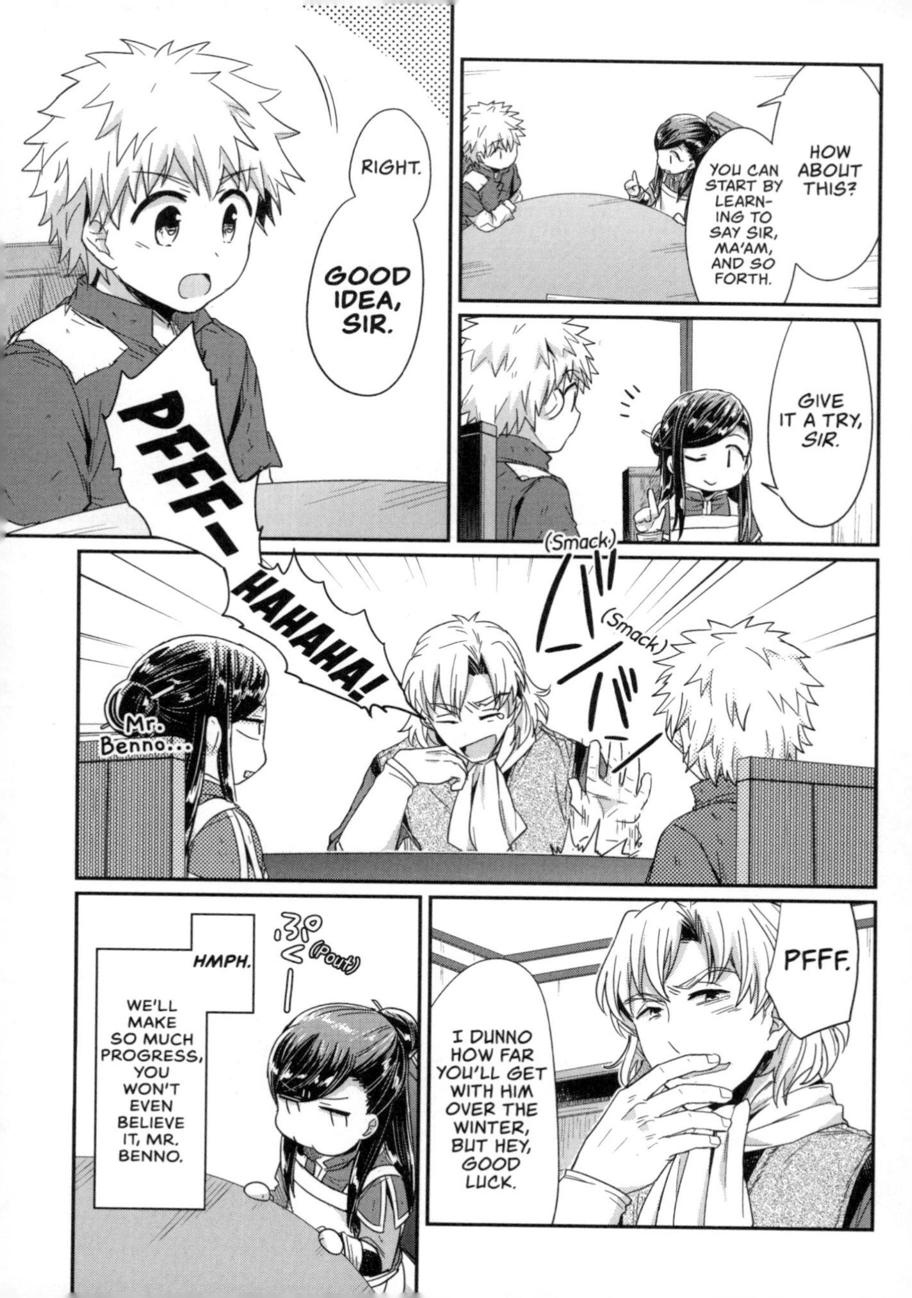
HOW ABOUT THIS?
YOU CAN START BY LEARN-ING TO SAY SIR, MA'AM, AND SO FORTH.
GIVE IT A TRY, SIR.
RIGHT.
GOOD IDEA, SIR.
PFFF-
HAHAHA!
(Smack)
(Smack)
Mr. Benno...
PFFF.
I DUNNO HOW FAR YOU'LL GET WITH HIM OVER THE WINTER, BUT HEY, GOOD LUCK.
(Pout)
HMPH.
WE'LL MAKE SO MUCH PROGRESS, YOU WON'T EVEN BELIEVE IT, MR. BENNO.

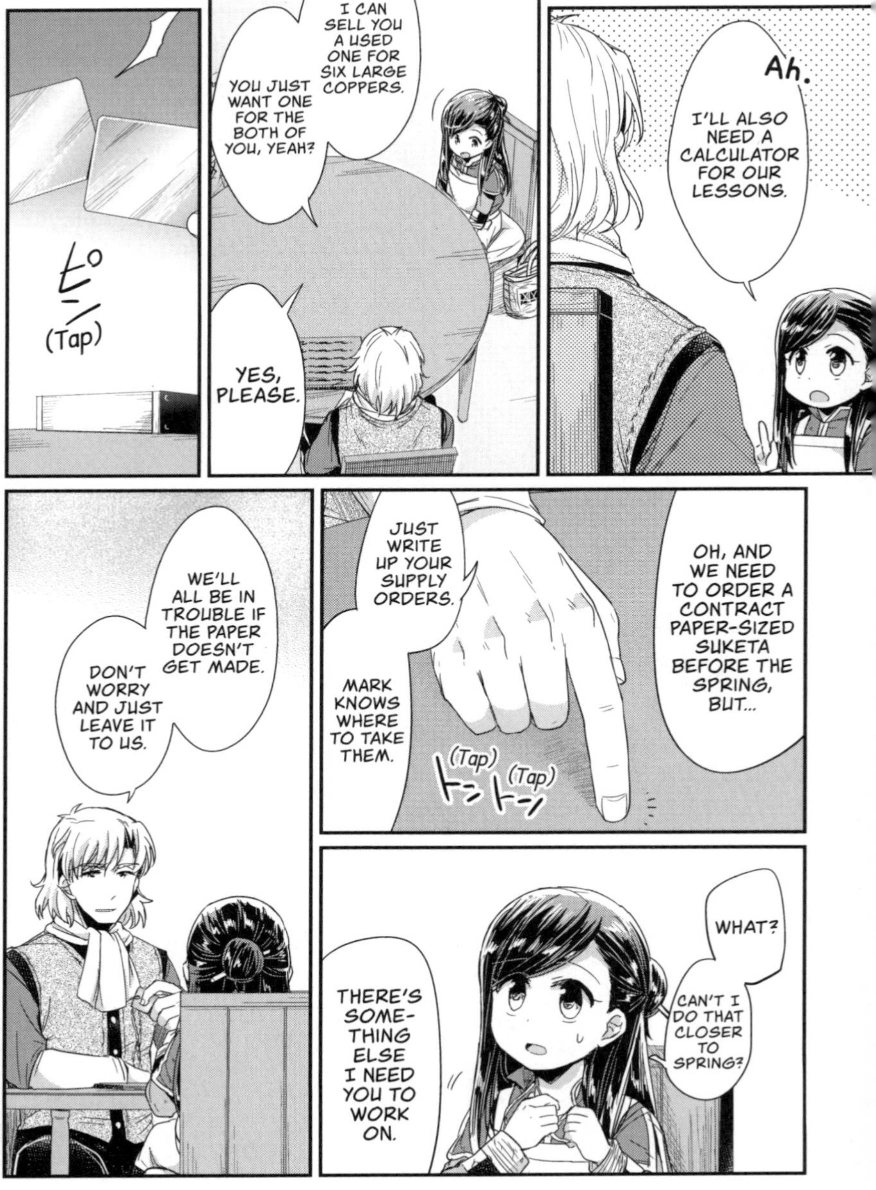
Ah.
I'LL ALSO NEED A CALCULATOR FOR OUR LESSONS.
I CAN SELL YOU A USED ONE FOR SIX LARGE COPPERS.
YOU JUST WANT ONE FOR THE BOTH OF YOU, YEAH?
YES, PLEASE.
ピン
(Tap)
OH, AND WE NEED TO ORDER A CONTRACT PAPER-SIZED SUKETA BEFORE THE SPRING, BUT...
JUST WRITE UP YOUR SUPPLY ORDERS.
MARK KNOWS WHERE TO TAKE THEM.
トン (Tap) トン (Tap)
WHAT?
CAN'T I DO THAT CLOSER TO SPRING?
THERE'S SOMETHING ELSE I NEED YOU TO WORK ON.
WE'LL ALL BE IN TROUBLE IF THE PAPER DOESN'T GET MADE.
DON'T WORRY AND JUST LEAVE IT TO US.

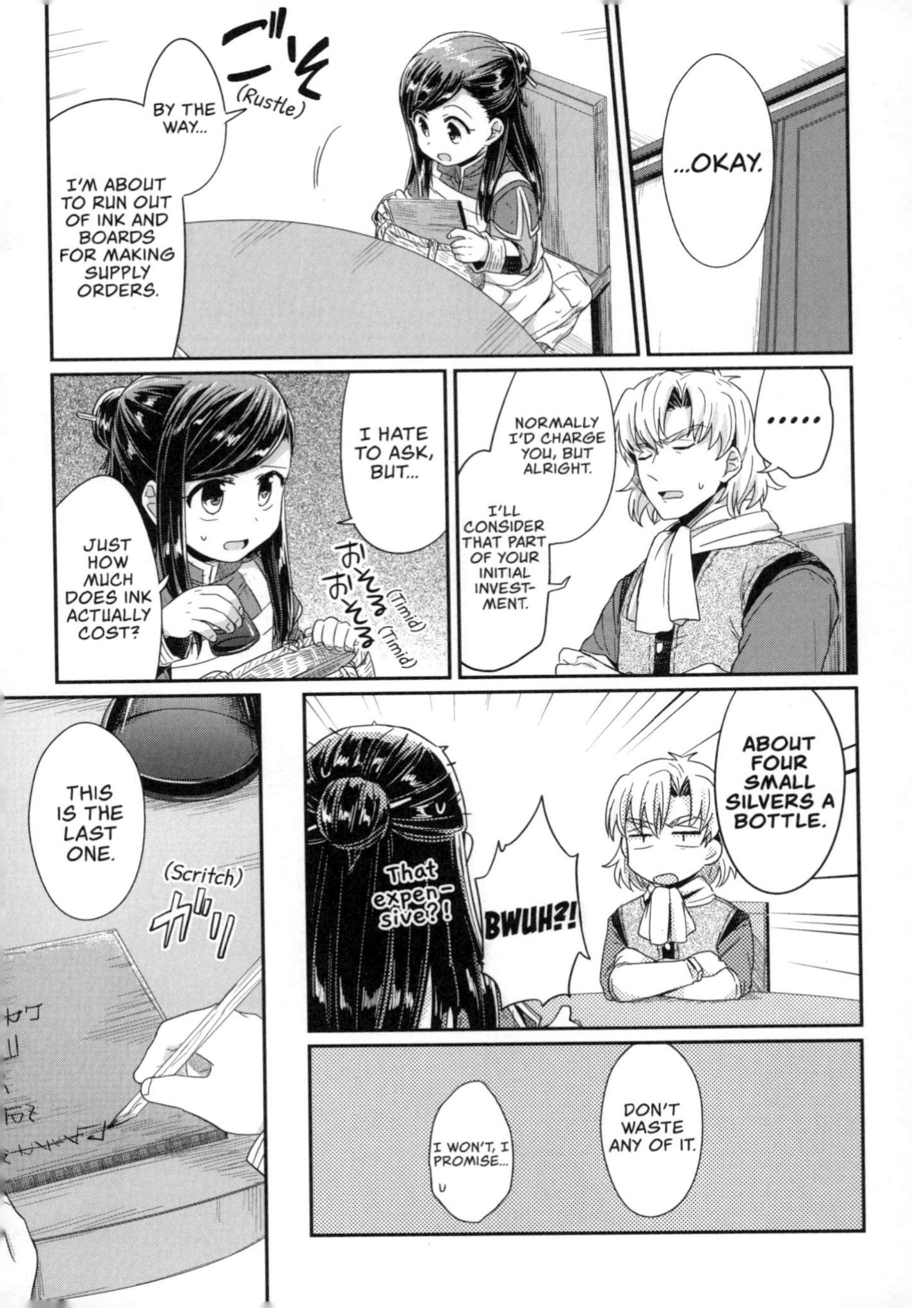
...OKAY.
ごそ
(Rustle)
BY THE WAY...
I'M ABOUT TO RUN OUT OF INK AND BOARDS FOR MAKING SUPPLY ORDERS.
.....
NORMALLY I'D CHARGE YOU, BUT ALRIGHT.
I'LL CONSIDER THAT PART OF YOUR INITIAL INVESTMENT.
I HATE TO ASK, BUT...
おそる おそる
(Timid) (Timid)
JUST HOW MUCH DOES INK ACTUALLY COST?
ABOUT FOUR SMALL SILVERS A BOTTLE.
BWUH?!
That expen-sive?!
DON'T WASTE ANY OF IT.
I WON'T, I PROMISE...
THIS IS THE LAST ONE.
(Scritch)
ガリ

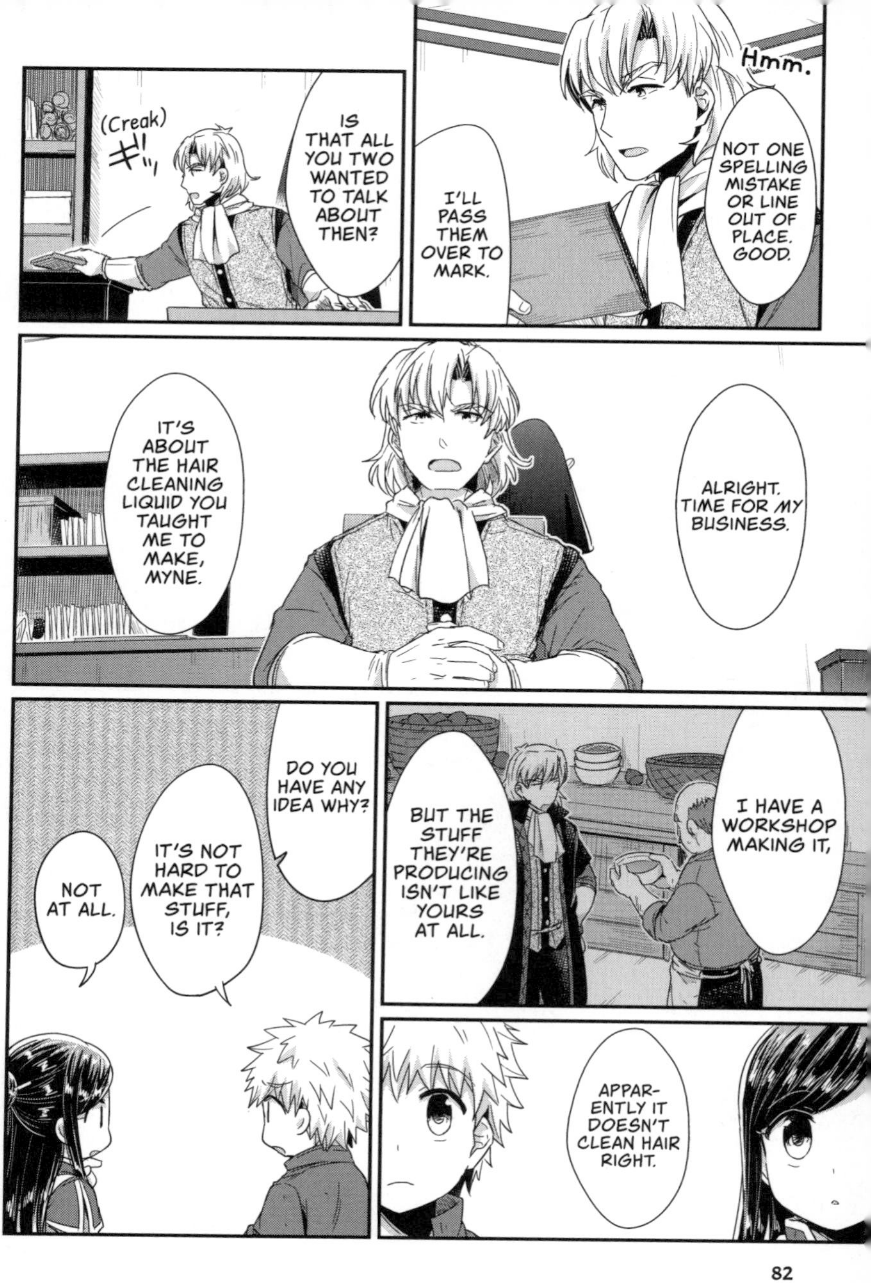
Hmm.
NOT ONE SPELLING MISTAKE OR LINE OUT OF PLACE. GOOD.
I'LL PASS THEM OVER TO MARK.
(Creak)
IS THAT ALL YOU TWO WANTED TO TALK ABOUT THEN?
ALRIGHT. TIME FOR MY BUSINESS.
IT'S ABOUT THE HAIR CLEANING LIQUID YOU TAUGHT ME TO MAKE, MYNE.
I HAVE A WORKSHOP MAKING IT,
BUT THE STUFF THEY'RE PRODUCING ISN'T LIKE YOURS AT ALL.
APPAR-ENTLY IT DOESN'T CLEAN HAIR RIGHT.
DO YOU HAVE ANY IDEA WHY?
IT'S NOT HARD TO MAKE THAT STUFF, IS IT?
NOT AT ALL.

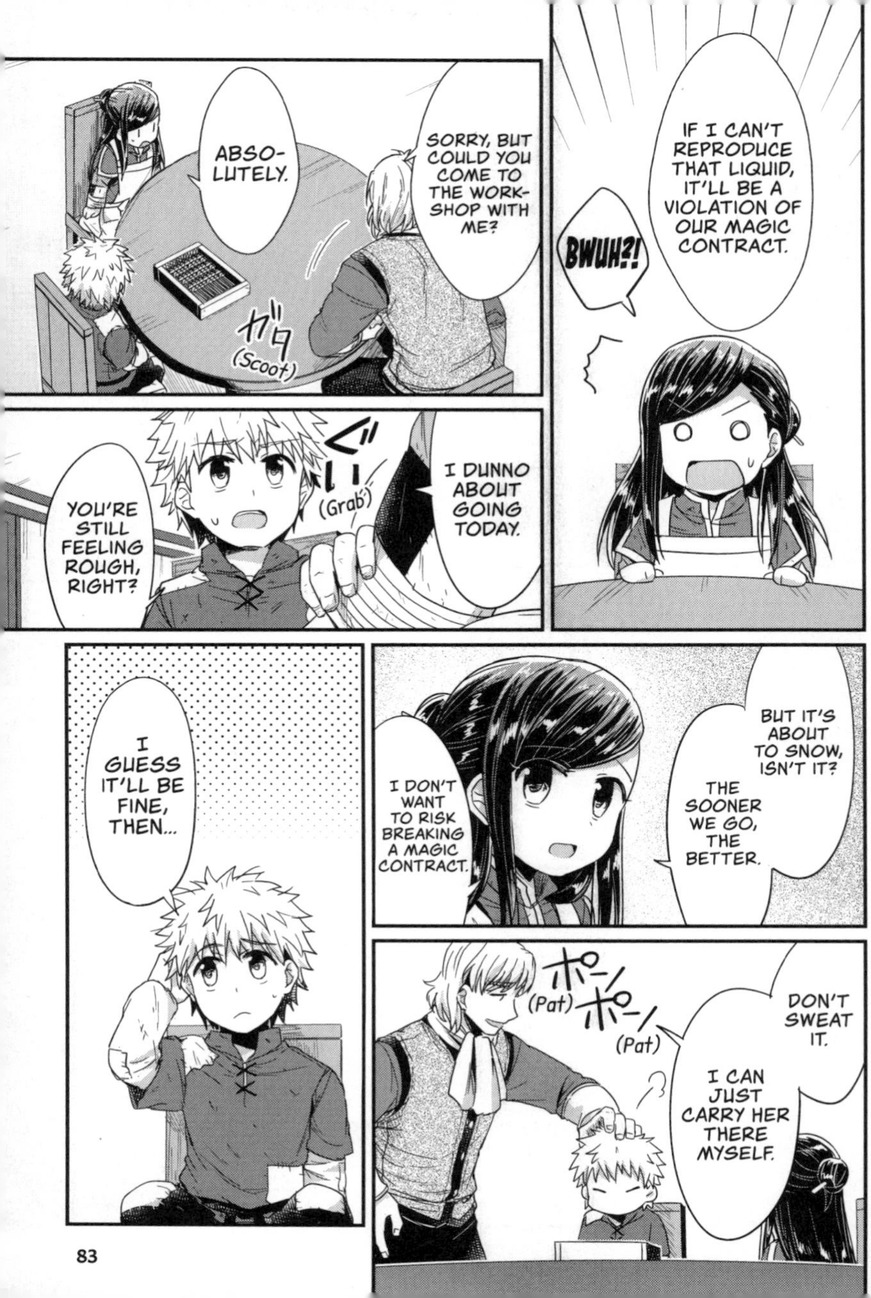
IF I CAN'T REPRODUCE THAT LIQUID, IT'LL BE A VIOLATION OF OUR MAGIC CONTRACT.
BWUH?!
SORRY, BUT COULD YOU COME TO THE WORK-SHOP WITH ME?
ABSO-LUTELY.
(Scoot)
I DUNNO ABOUT GOING TODAY.
(Grab)
YOU'RE STILL FEELING ROUGH, RIGHT?
BUT IT'S ABOUT TO SNOW, ISN'T IT?
THE SOONER WE GO, THE BETTER.
I DON'T WANT TO RISK BREAKING A MAGIC CONTRACT.
DON'T SWEAT IT.
I CAN JUST CARRY HER THERE MYSELF.
(Pat)
(Pat)
I GUESS IT'LL BE FINE, THEN...

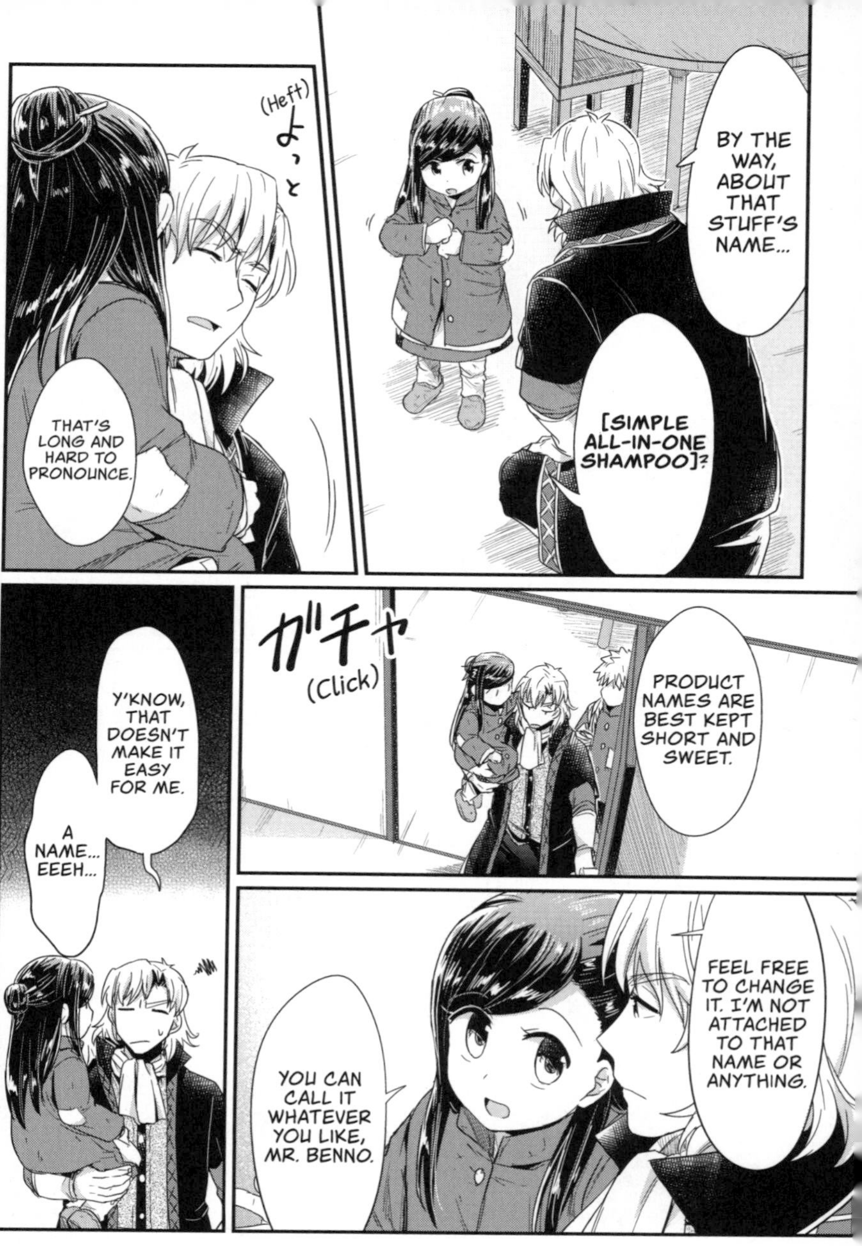

BY THE WAY, ABOUT THAT STUFF'S NAME...
[SIMPLE ALL-IN-ONE SHAMPOO]?
よっと
(Heft)
THAT'S LONG AND HARD TO PRONOUNCE.
ガチャ
(Click)
PRODUCT NAMES ARE BEST KEPT SHORT AND SWEET.
FEEL FREE TO CHANGE IT. I'M NOT ATTACHED TO THAT NAME OR ANYTHING.
YOU CAN CALL IT WHATEVER YOU LIKE, MR. BENNO.
Y'KNOW, THAT DOESN'T MAKE IT EASY FOR ME.
A NAME... EEEH...

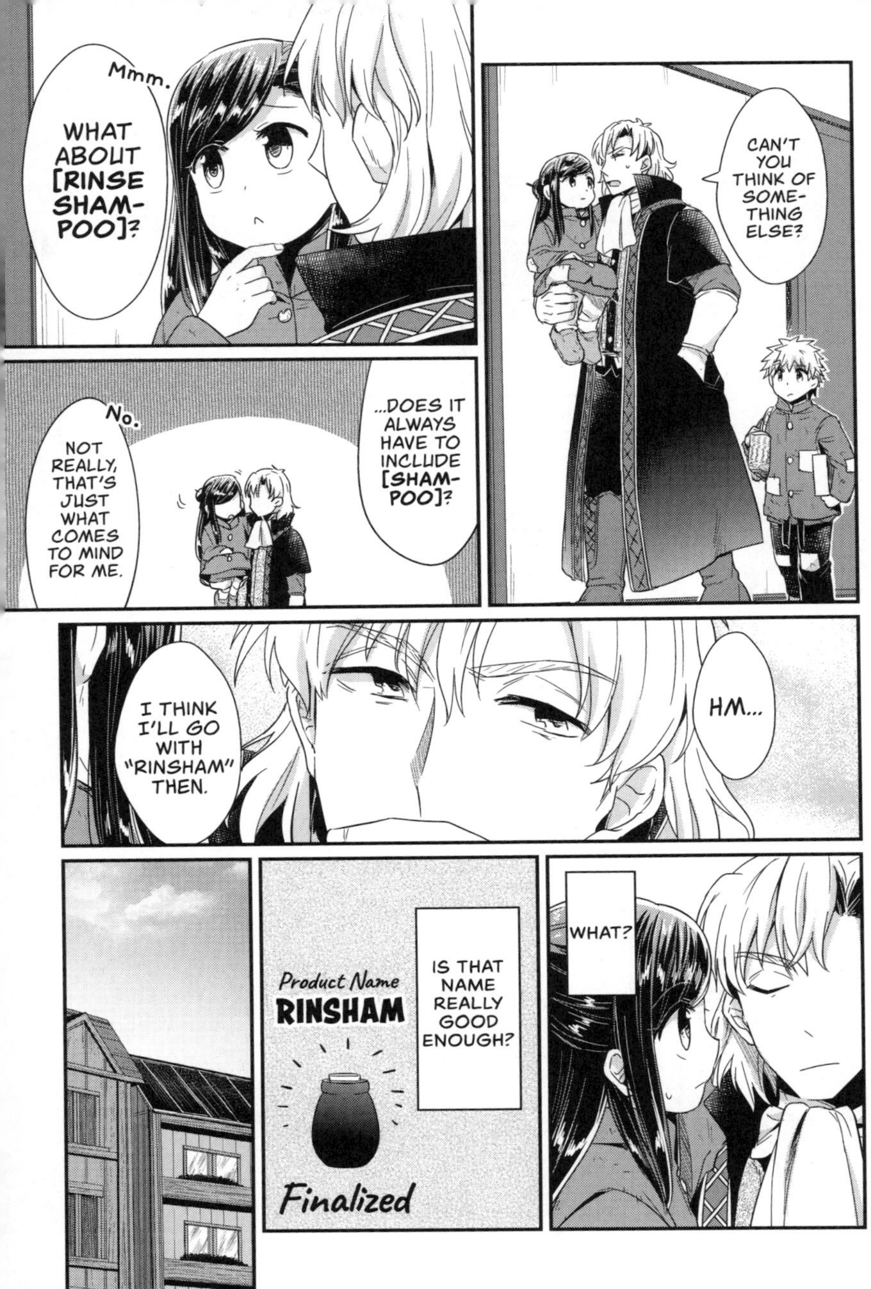
CAN'T YOU THINK OF SOME-THING ELSE?
Mmm.
WHAT ABOUT [RINSE SHAM-POO]?
...DOES IT ALWAYS HAVE TO INCLUDE [SHAM-POO]?
No.
NOT REALLY, THAT'S JUST WHAT COMES TO MIND FOR ME.
HM...
I THINK I'LL GO WITH "RINSHAM" THEN.
WHAT?
IS THAT NAME REALLY GOOD ENOUGH?
Product Name
RINSHAM
Finalized

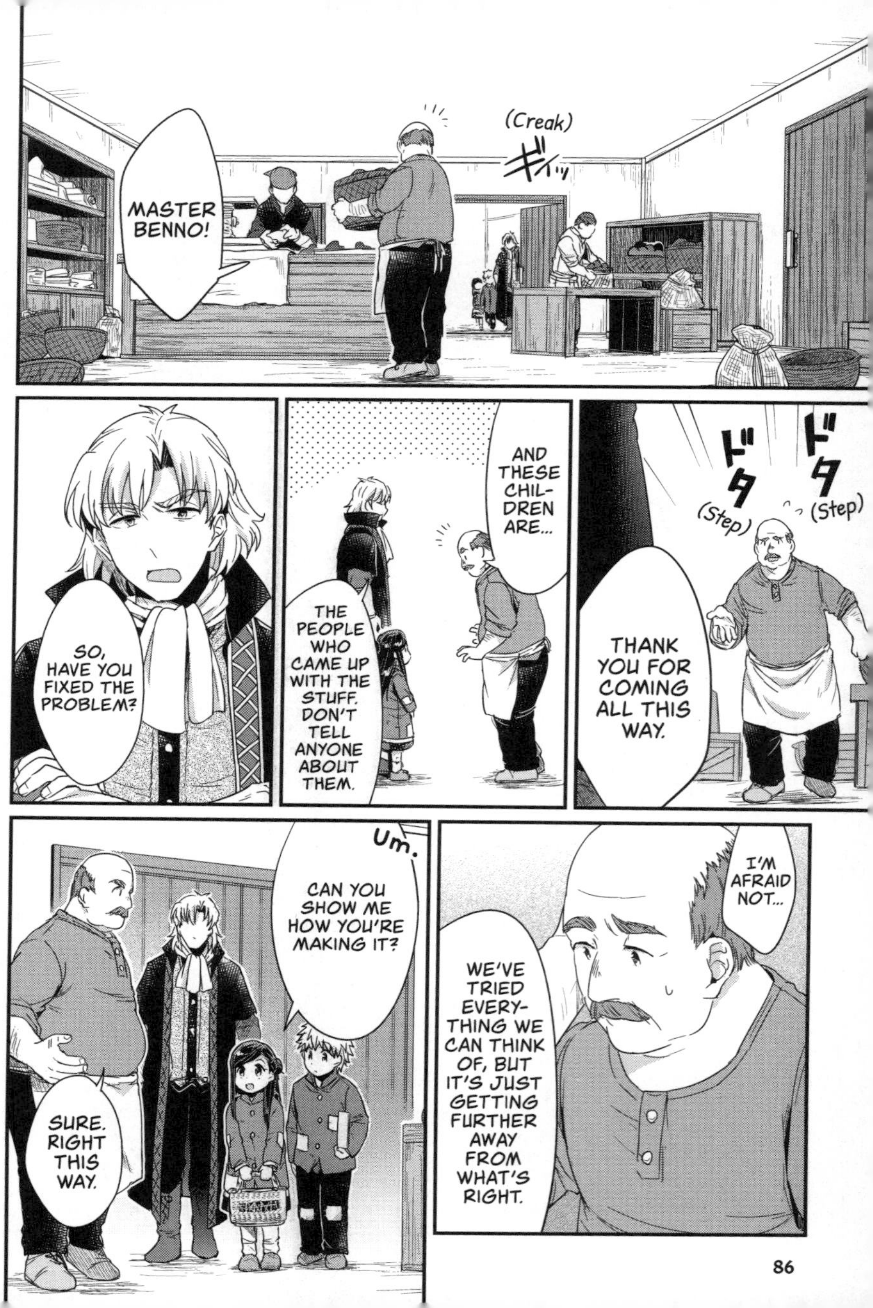
(Creak)
ギィッ
MASTER BENNO!
ドタ
ドタ
(Step)
(Step)
THANK YOU FOR COMING ALL THIS WAY.
AND THESE CHILDREN ARE...
THE PEOPLE WHO CAME UP WITH THE STUFF. DON'T TELL ANYONE ABOUT THEM.
SO, HAVE YOU FIXED THE PROBLEM?
I'M AFRAID NOT...
WE'VE TRIED EVERYTHING WE CAN THINK OF, BUT IT'S JUST GETTING FURTHER AWAY FROM WHAT'S RIGHT.
Um.
CAN YOU SHOW ME HOW YOU'RE MAKING IT?
SURE. RIGHT THIS WAY.

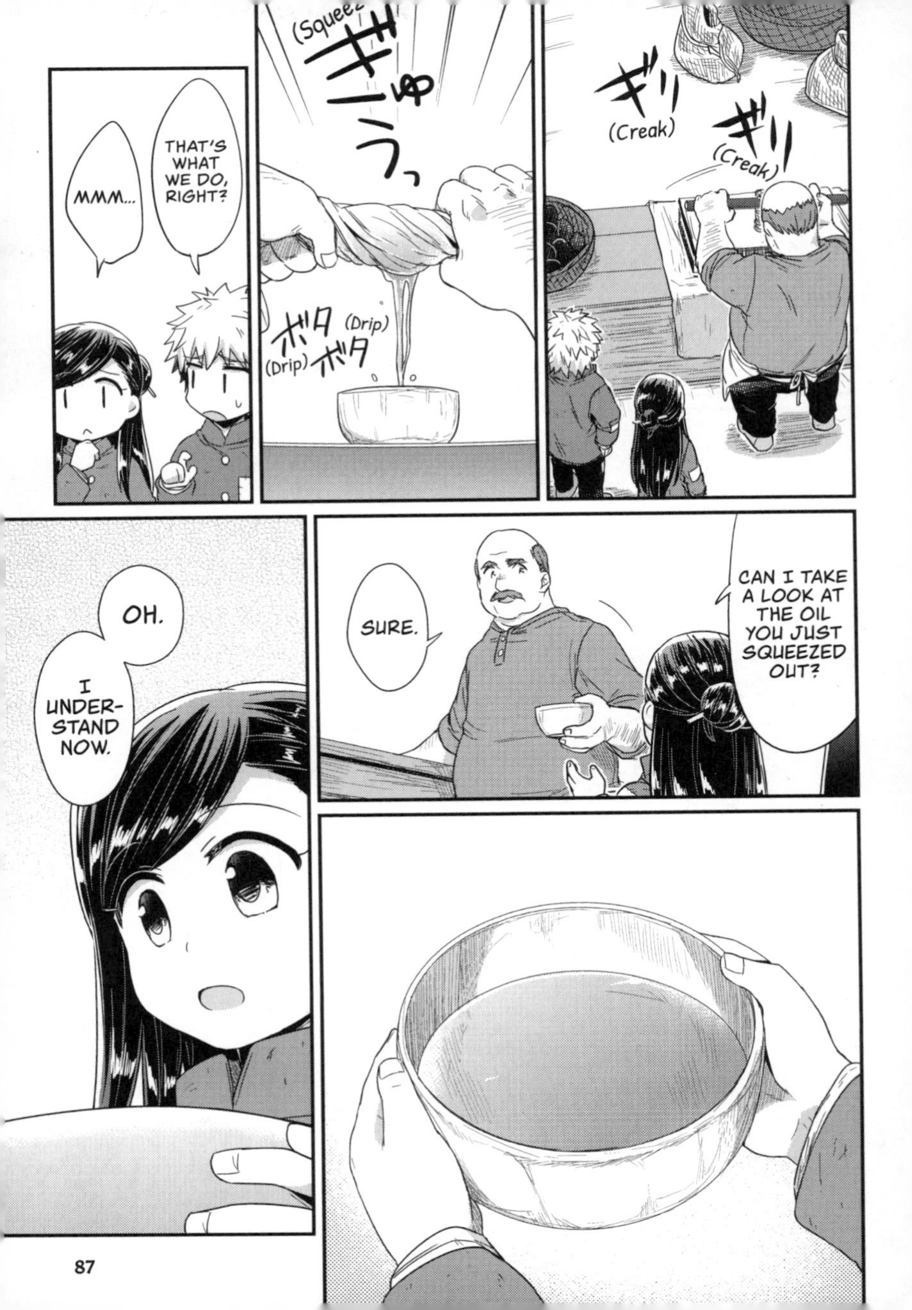
ギリ
(Creak)
ギリ
(Creak)
(Squeez
ぎゅうっ
ボタ
(Drip)
ボタ
(Drip)
THAT'S WHAT WE DO, RIGHT?
MMM...
CAN I TAKE A LOOK AT THE OIL YOU JUST SQUEEZED OUT?
SURE.
OH.
I UNDER-STAND NOW.

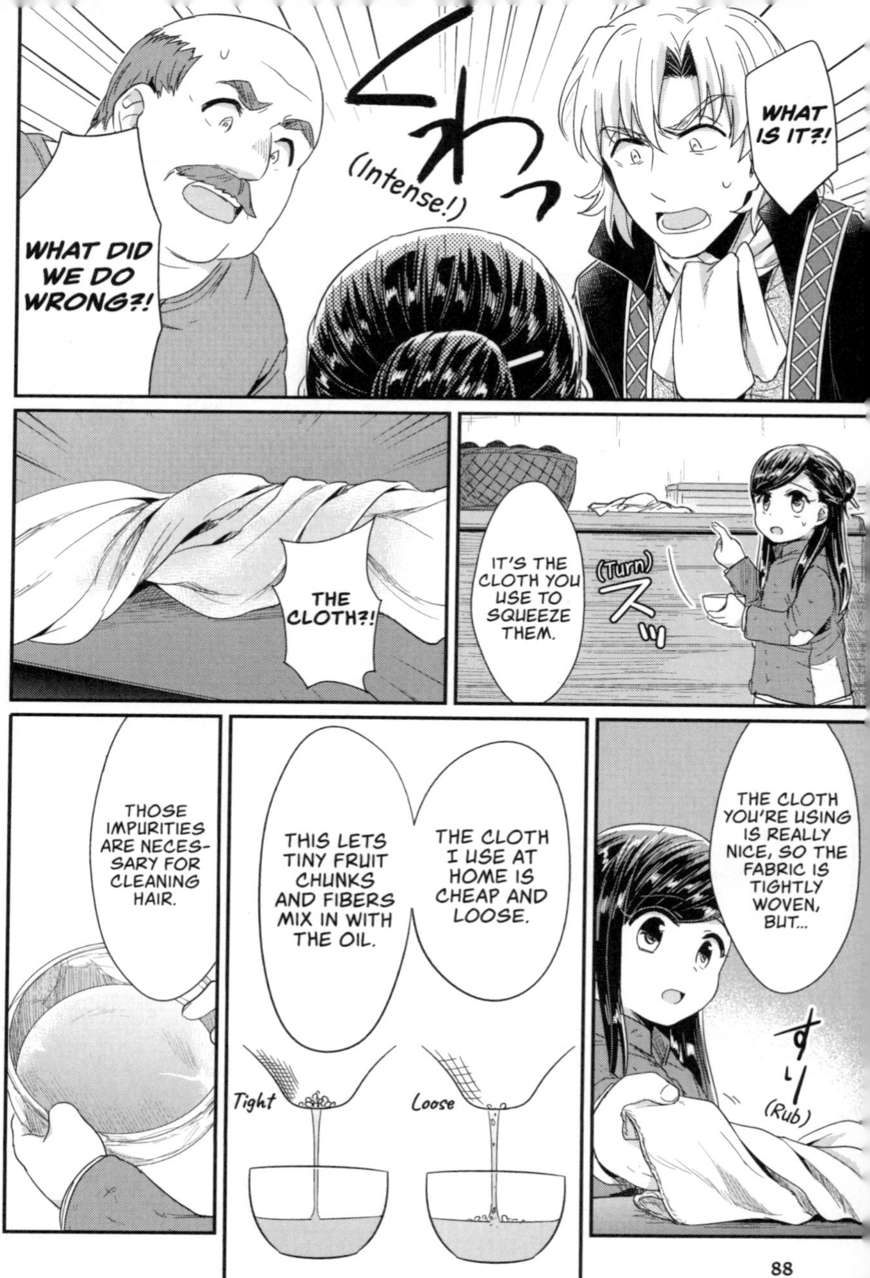
WHAT IS IT?!
くわっ
(Intense!)
WHAT DID WE DO WRONG?!
スッ
(Turn)
IT'S THE CLOTH YOU USE TO SQUEEZE THEM.
THE CLOTH?!
THE CLOTH YOU'RE USING IS REALLY NICE, SO THE FABRIC IS TIGHTLY WOVEN, BUT...
すー
(Rub)
THE CLOTH I USE AT HOME IS CHEAP AND LOOSE.
THIS LETS TINY FRUIT CHUNKS AND FIBERS MIX IN WITH THE OIL.
Tight
Loose
THOSE IMPURITIES ARE NECES-SARY FOR CLEANING HAIR.

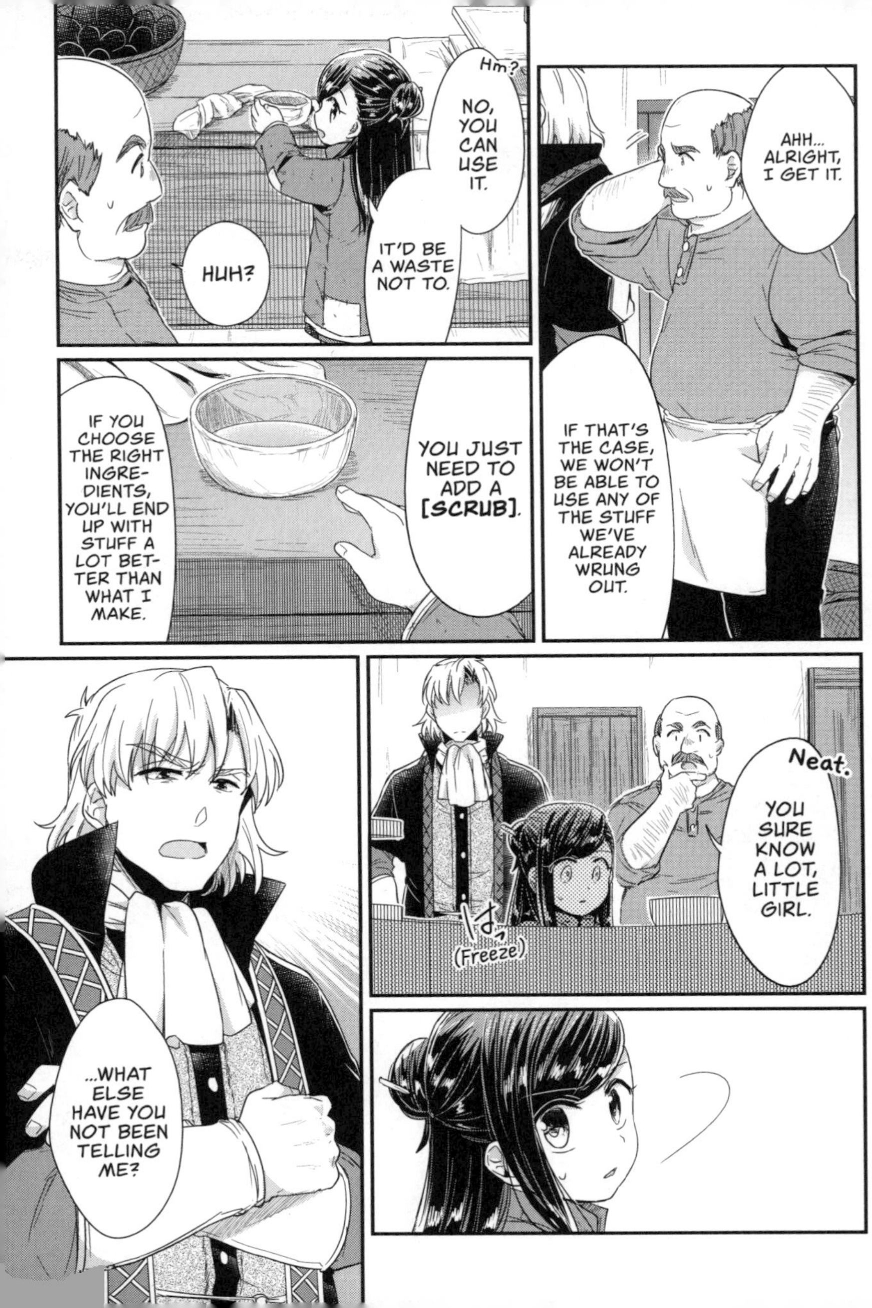
AHH... ALRIGHT, I GET IT.
IF THAT'S THE CASE, WE WON'T BE ABLE TO USE ANY OF THE STUFF WE'VE ALREADY WRUNG OUT.
Hm?
NO, YOU CAN USE IT.
IT'D BE A WASTE NOT TO.
HUH?
YOU JUST NEED TO ADD A [SCRUB].
IF YOU CHOOSE THE RIGHT INGRE-DIENTS, YOU'LL END UP WITH STUFF A LOT BET-TER THAN WHAT I MAKE.
Neat.
YOU SURE KNOW A LOT, LITTLE GIRL.
(Freeze)
...WHAT ELSE HAVE YOU NOT BEEN TELLING ME?

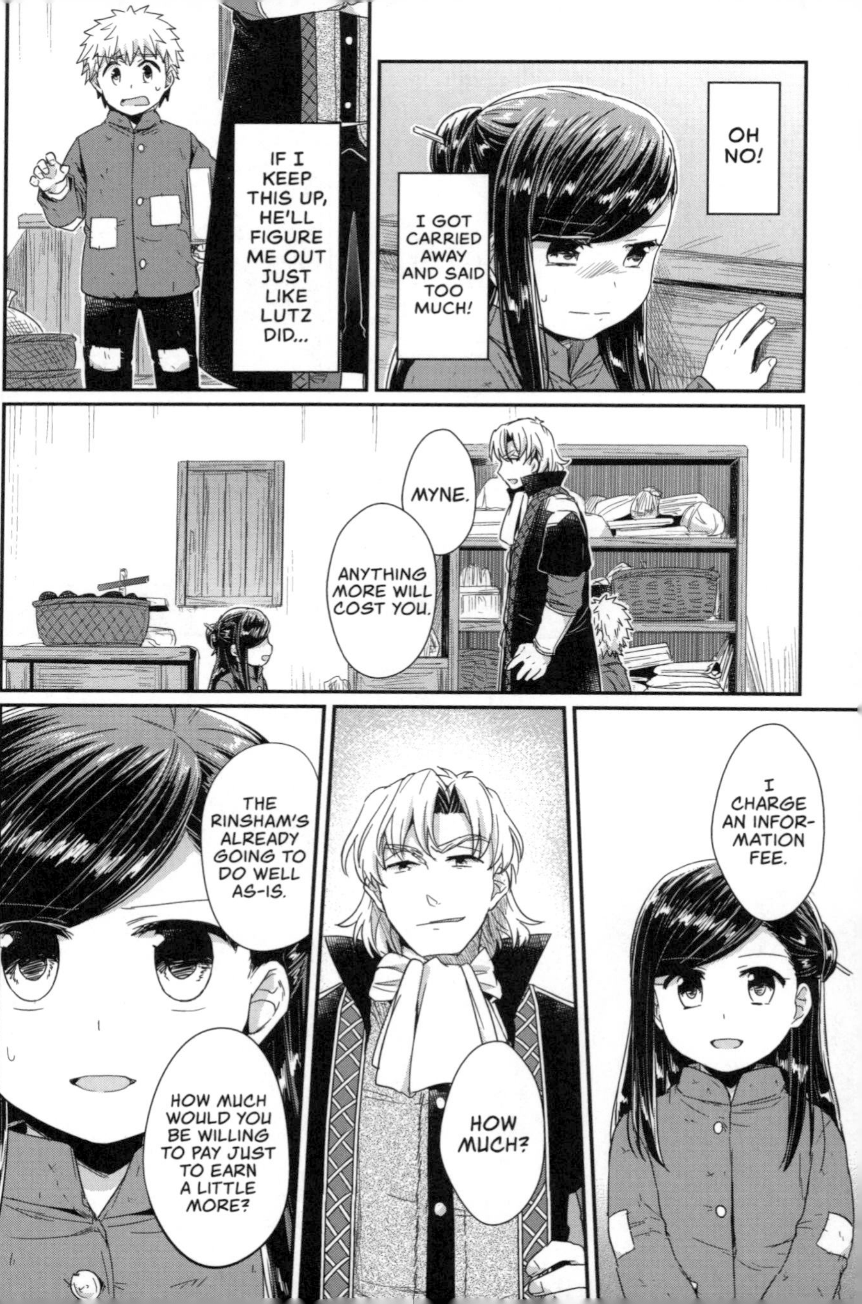
OH NO!
I GOT CARRIED AWAY AND SAID TOO MUCH!
IF I KEEP THIS UP, HE'LL FIGURE ME OUT JUST LIKE LUTZ DID...
MYNE.
ANYTHING MORE WILL COST YOU.
I CHARGE AN INFORMATION FEE.
HOW MUCH?
THE RINSHAM'S ALREADY GOING TO DO WELL AS-IS.
HOW MUCH WOULD YOU BE WILLING TO PAY JUST TO EARN A LITTLE MORE?

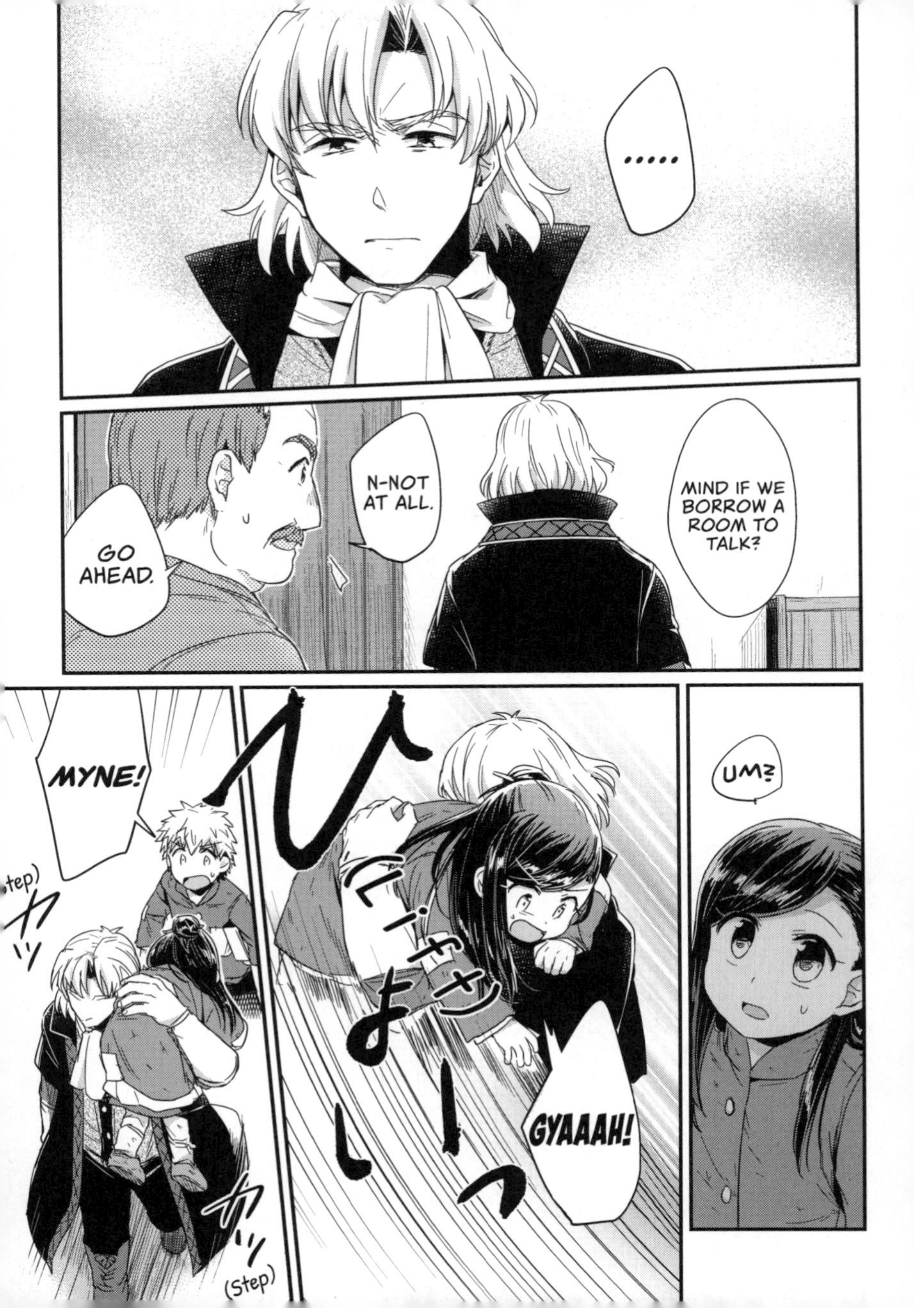
......
MIND IF WE BORROW A ROOM TO TALK?
N-NOT AT ALL.
GO AHEAD.
UM?
GYAAAH!
MYNE!
tep)
(Step)

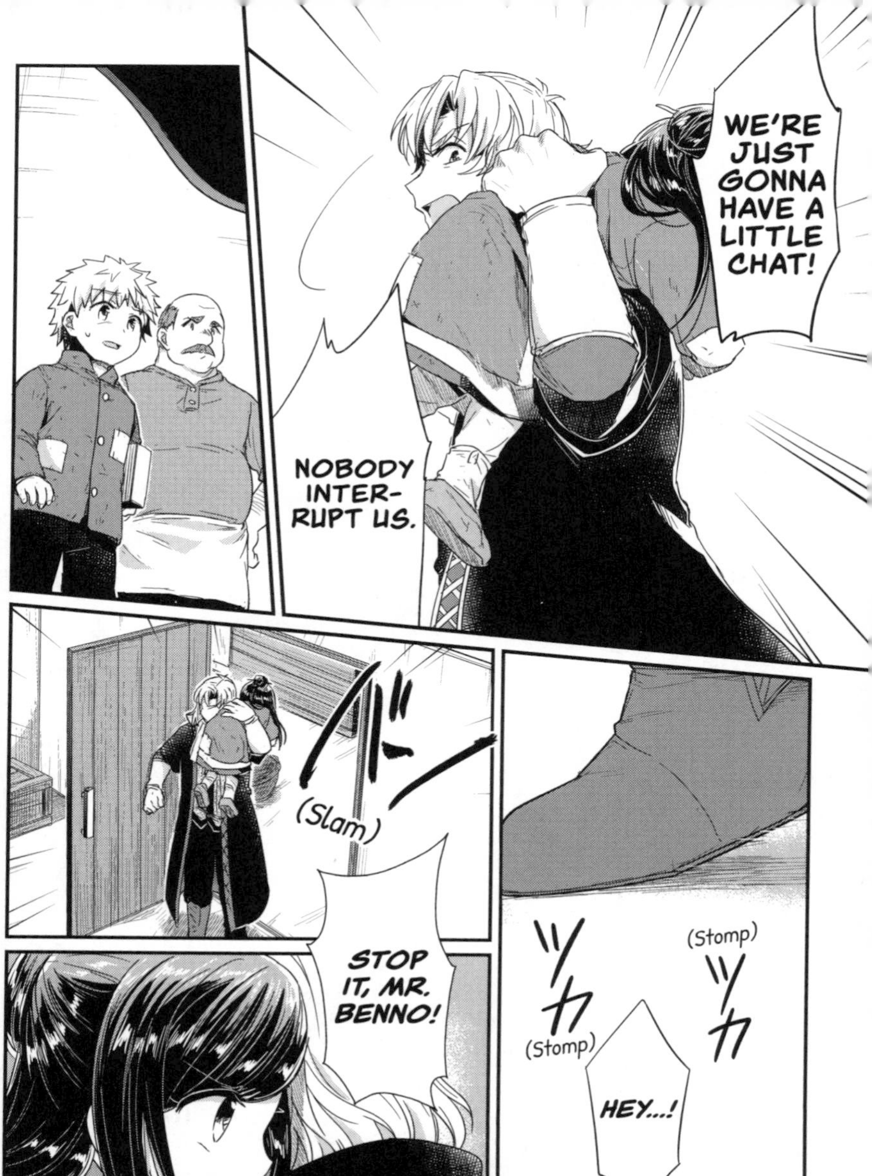
WE'RE JUST GONNA HAVE A LITTLE CHAT!
NOBODY INTER-RUPT US.
ツカ (Stomp)
ツカ (Stomp)
HEY...!
バ (Slam)
STOP IT, MR. BENNO!

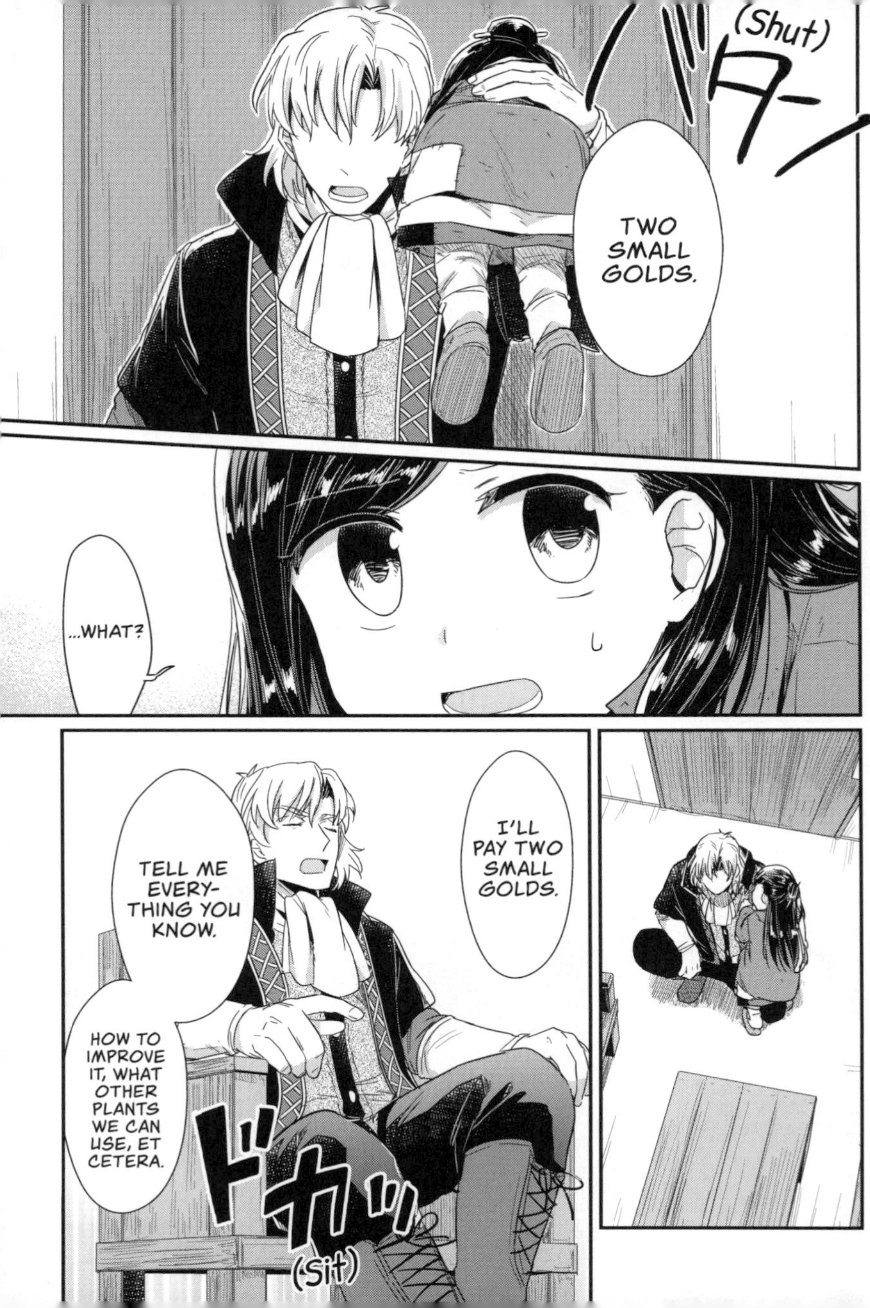
バターン
(Shut)
TWO SMALL GOLDS.
...WHAT?
I'LL PAY TWO SMALL GOLDS.
TELL ME EVERY-THING YOU KNOW.
HOW TO IMPROVE IT, WHAT OTHER PLANTS WE CAN USE, ET CETERA.
ドカッ
(Sit)

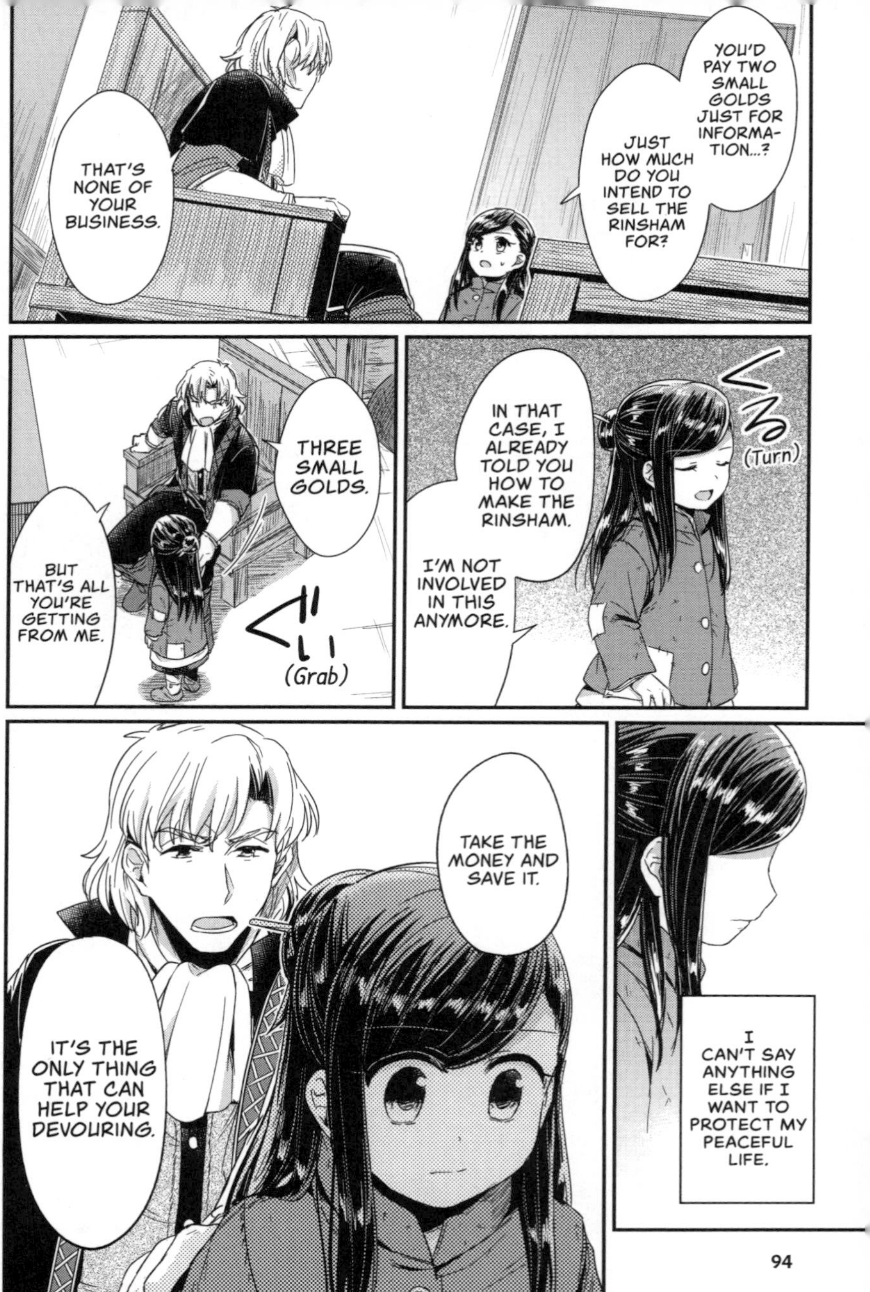
YOU'D PAY TWO SMALL GOLDS JUST FOR INFORMATION...?
JUST HOW MUCH DO YOU INTEND TO SELL THE RINSHAM FOR?
THAT'S NONE OF YOUR BUSINESS.
くる
(Turn)
IN THAT CASE, I ALREADY TOLD YOU HOW TO MAKE THE RINSHAM.
I'M NOT INVOLVED IN THIS ANYMORE.
THREE SMALL GOLDS.
BUT THAT'S ALL YOU'RE GETTING FROM ME.
ぐい
(Grab)
I CAN'T SAY ANYTHING ELSE IF I WANT TO PROTECT MY PEACEFUL LIFE.
TAKE THE MONEY AND SAVE IT.
IT'S THE ONLY THING THAT CAN HELP YOUR DEVOURING.

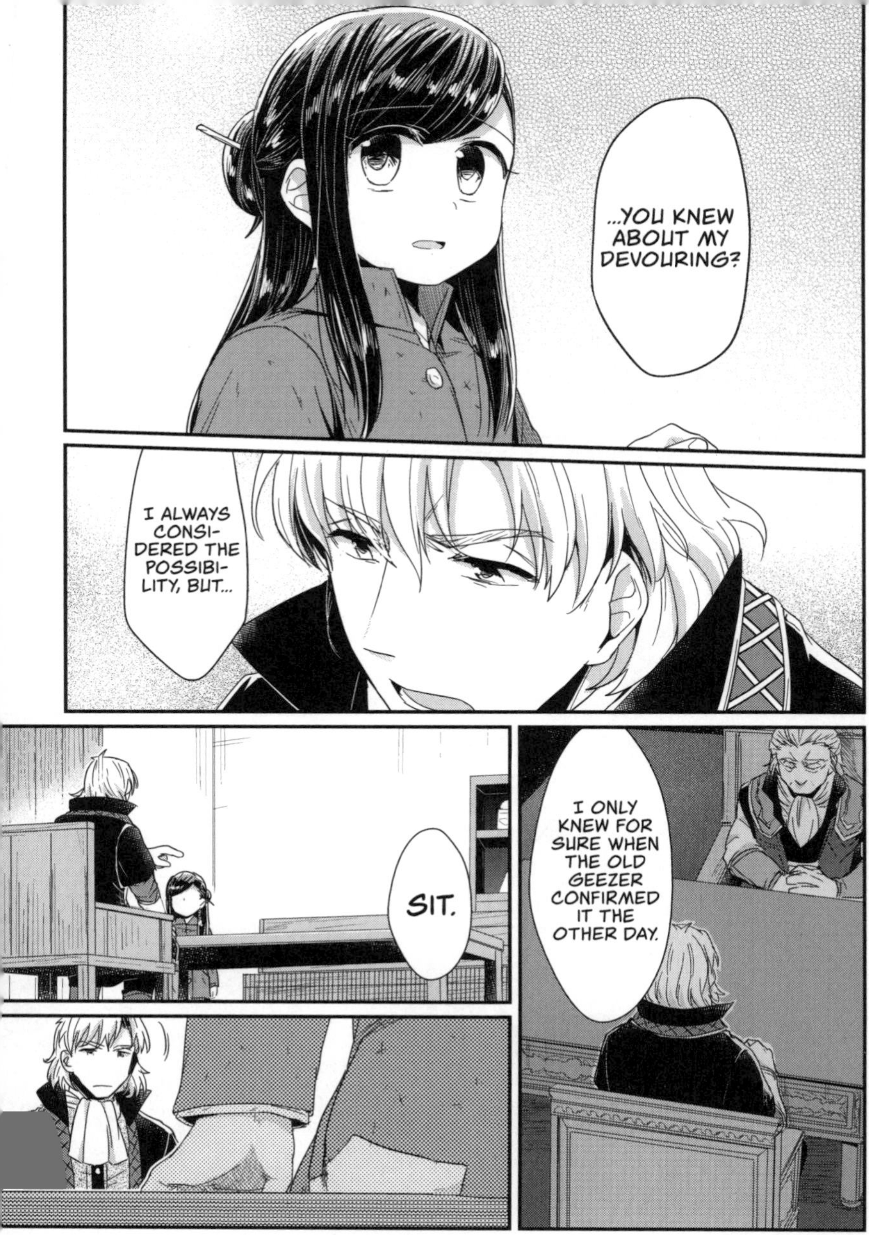
...YOU KNEW ABOUT MY DEVOURING?
I ALWAYS CONSI-DERED THE POSSIBI-LITY, BUT...
I ONLY KNEW FOR SURE WHEN THE OLD GEEZER CONFIRMED IT THE OTHER DAY.
SIT.

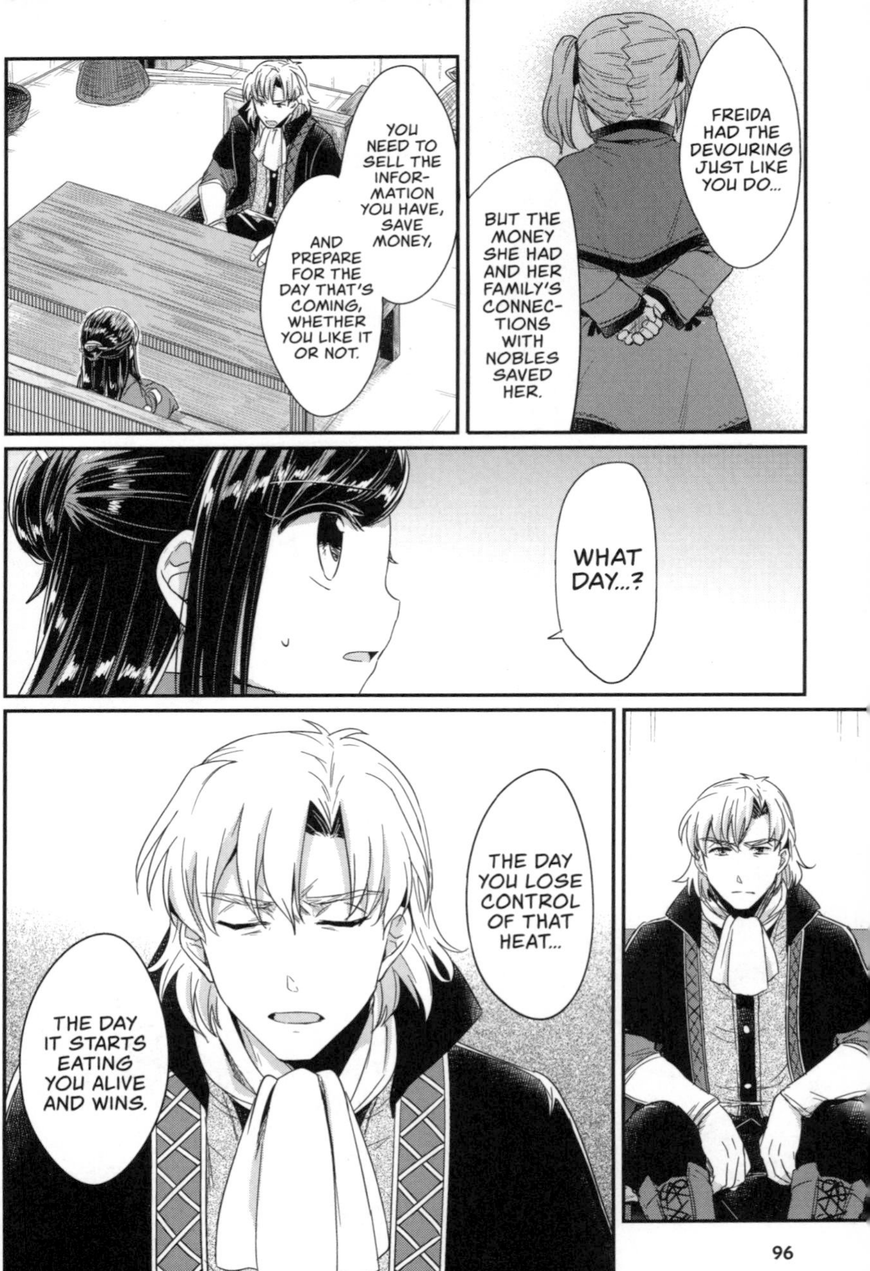
FREIDA HAD THE DEVOURING JUST LIKE YOU DO...
BUT THE MONEY SHE HAD AND HER FAMILY'S CONNECTIONS WITH NOBLES SAVED HER.
YOU NEED TO SELL THE INFORMATION YOU HAVE, SAVE MONEY,
AND PREPARE FOR THE DAY THAT'S COMING, WHETHER YOU LIKE IT OR NOT.
WHAT DAY...?
THE DAY YOU LOSE CONTROL OF THAT HEAT...
THE DAY IT STARTS EATING YOU ALIVE AND WINS.

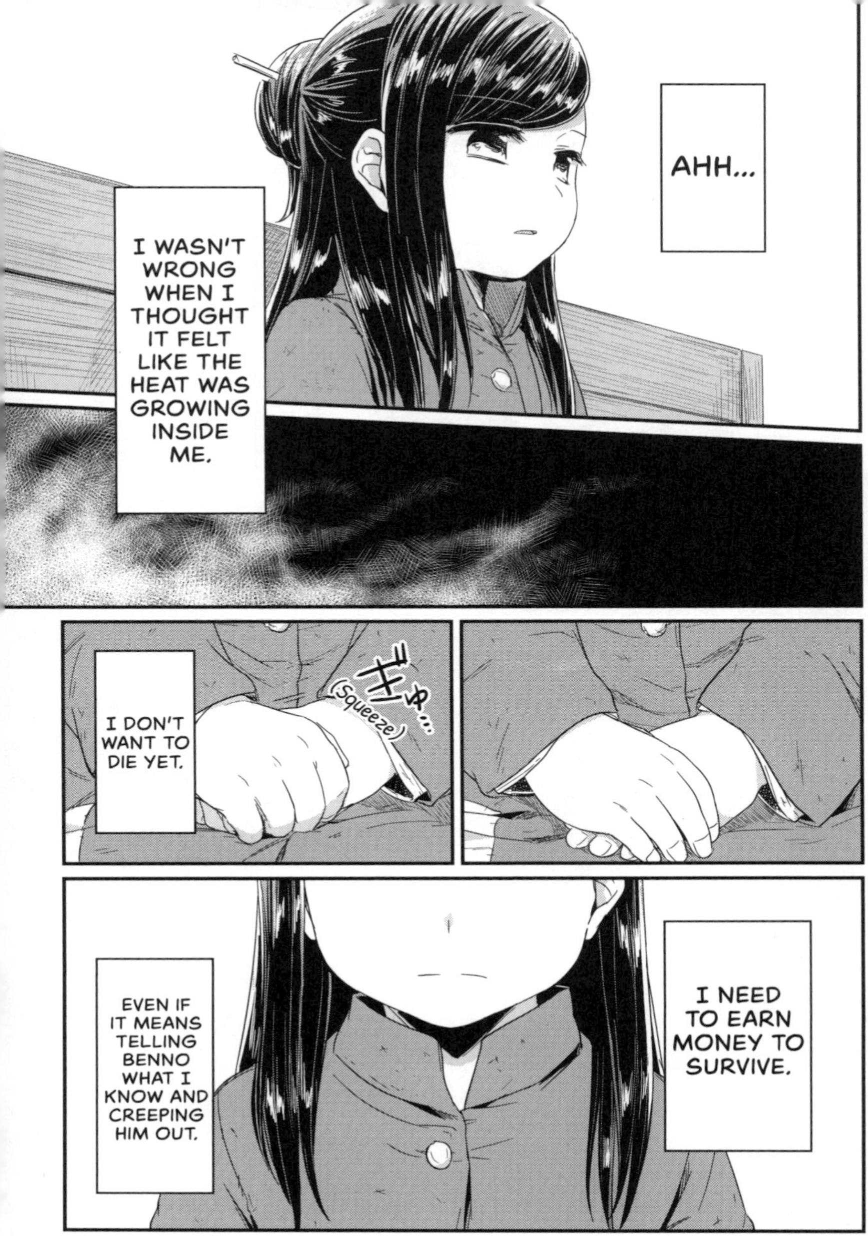
AHH...
I WASN'T WRONG WHEN I THOUGHT IT FELT LIKE THE HEAT WAS GROWING INSIDE ME.
ギュ…
(Squeeze)
I DON'T WANT TO DIE YET.
I NEED TO EARN MONEY TO SURVIVE.
EVEN IF IT MEANS TELLING BENNO WHAT I KNOW AND CREEPING HIM OUT.

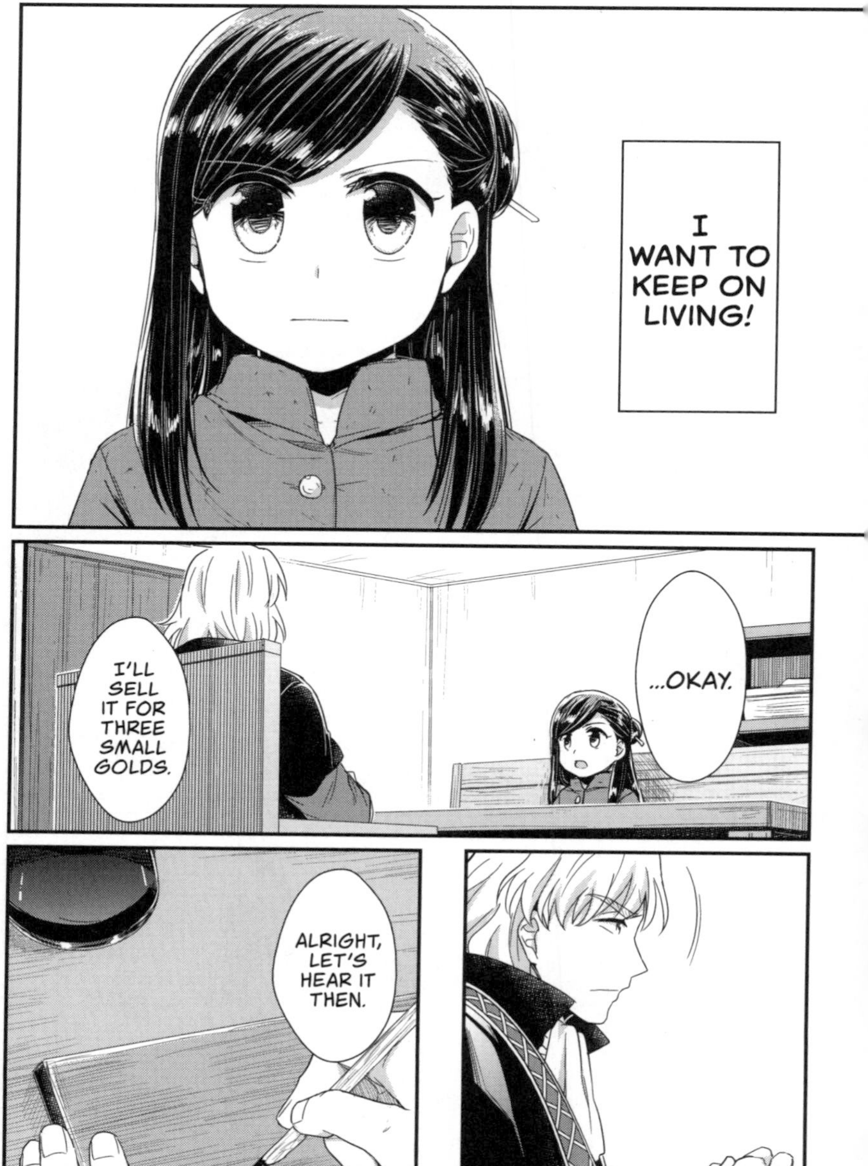
I WANT TO KEEP ON LIVING!
...OKAY.
I'LL SELL IT FOR THREE SMALL GOLDS.
ALRIGHT, LET'S HEAR IT THEN.

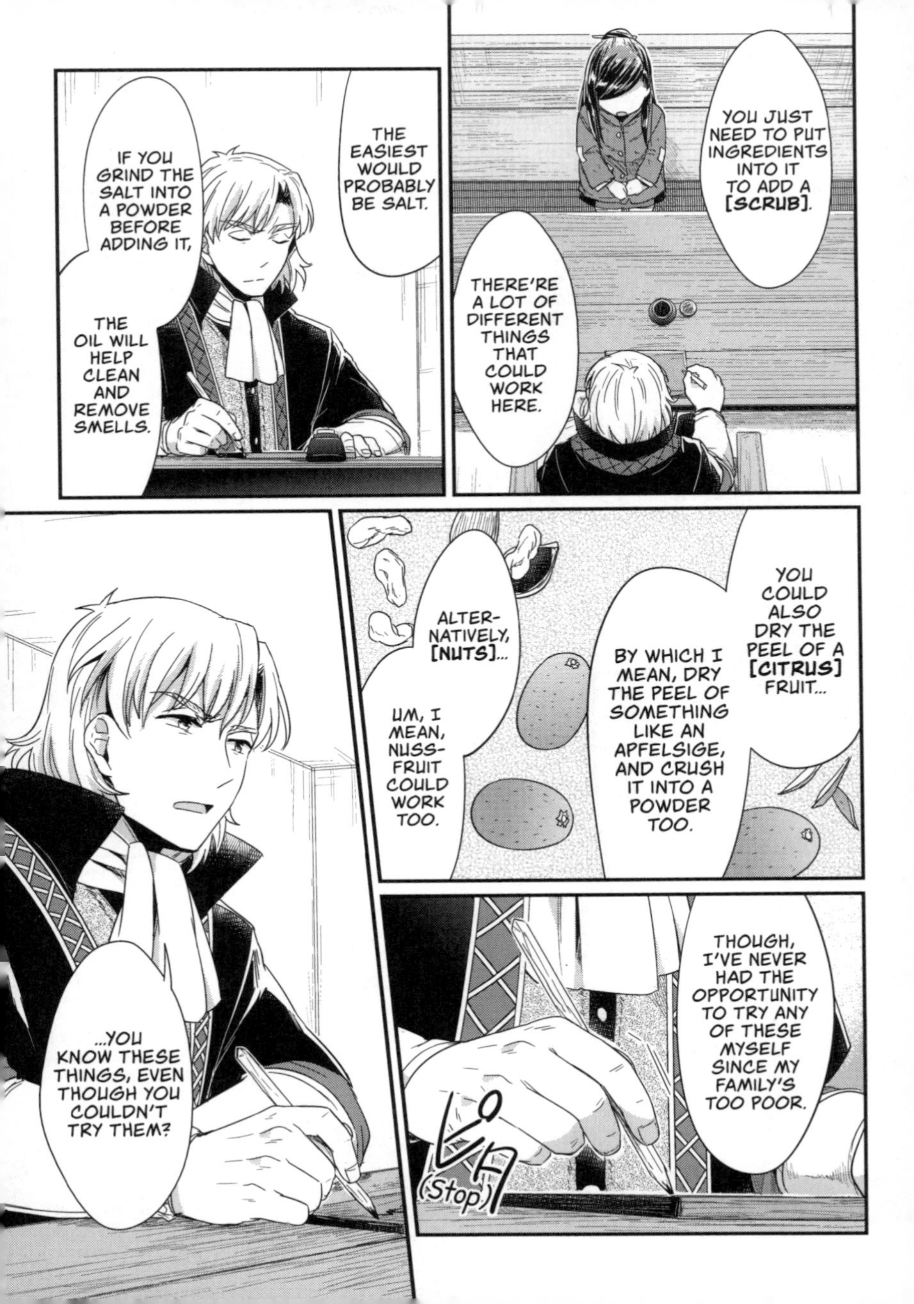
YOU JUST NEED TO PUT INGREDIENTS INTO IT TO ADD A [SCRUB].
THERE'RE A LOT OF DIFFERENT THINGS THAT COULD WORK HERE.
THE EASIEST WOULD PROBABLY BE SALT.
IF YOU GRIND THE SALT INTO A POWDER BEFORE ADDING IT,
THE OIL WILL HELP CLEAN AND REMOVE SMELLS.
YOU COULD ALSO DRY THE PEEL OF A [CITRUS] FRUIT...
BY WHICH I MEAN, DRY THE PEEL OF SOMETHING LIKE AN APFELSIGE, AND CRUSH IT INTO A POWDER TOO.
ALTER-NATIVELY, [NUTS]...
UM, I MEAN, NUSS-FRUIT COULD WORK TOO.
THOUGH, I'VE NEVER HAD THE OPPORTUNITY TO TRY ANY OF THESE MYSELF SINCE MY FAMILY'S TOO POOR.
ピタ
(Stop)
...YOU KNOW THESE THINGS, EVEN THOUGH YOU COULDN'T TRY THEM?

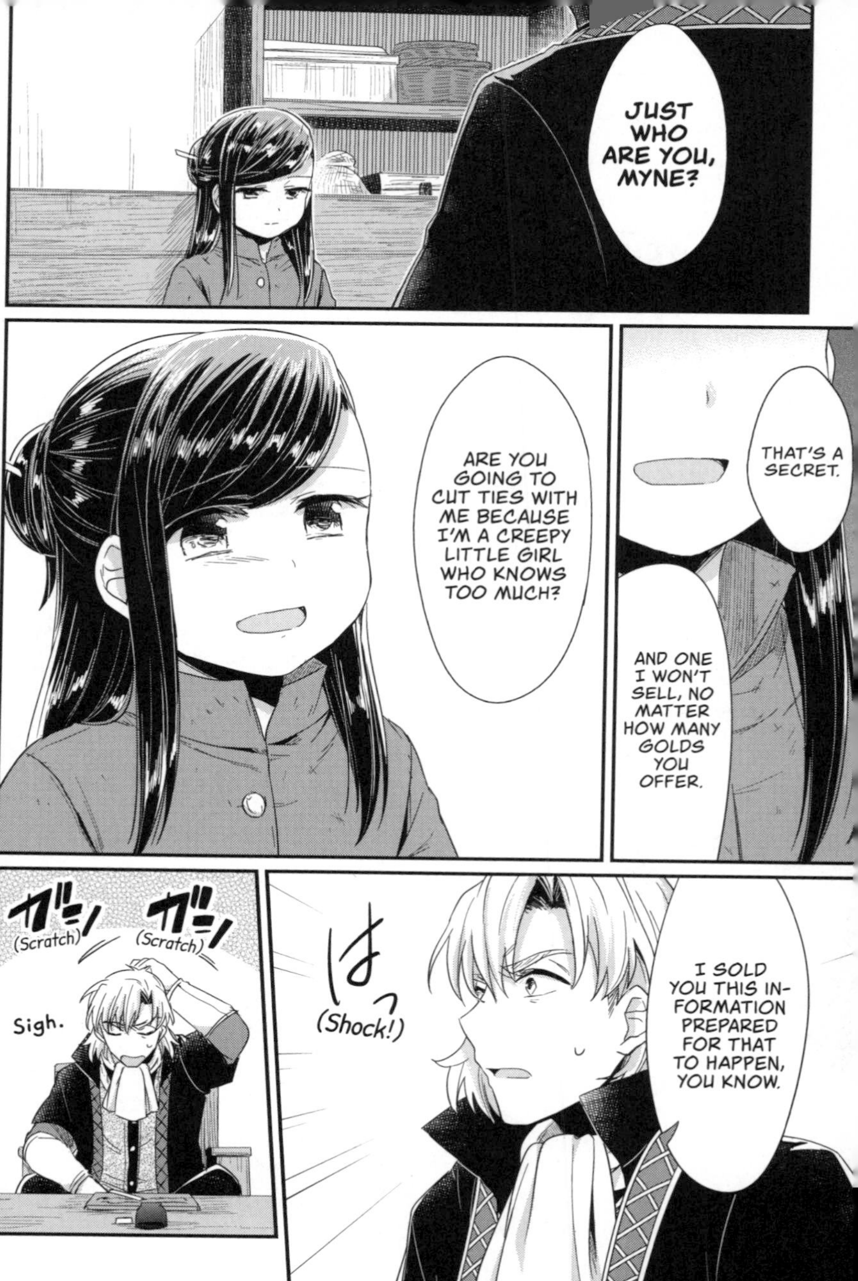
JUST WHO ARE YOU, MYNE?
THAT'S A SECRET.
AND ONE I WON'T SELL, NO MATTER HOW MANY GOLDS YOU OFFER.
ARE YOU GOING TO CUT TIES WITH ME BECAUSE I'M A CREEPY LITTLE GIRL WHO KNOWS TOO MUCH?
I SOLD YOU THIS INFORMATION PREPARED FOR THAT TO HAPPEN, YOU KNOW.
はっ
(Shock!)
(Scratch)
(Scratch)
Sigh.

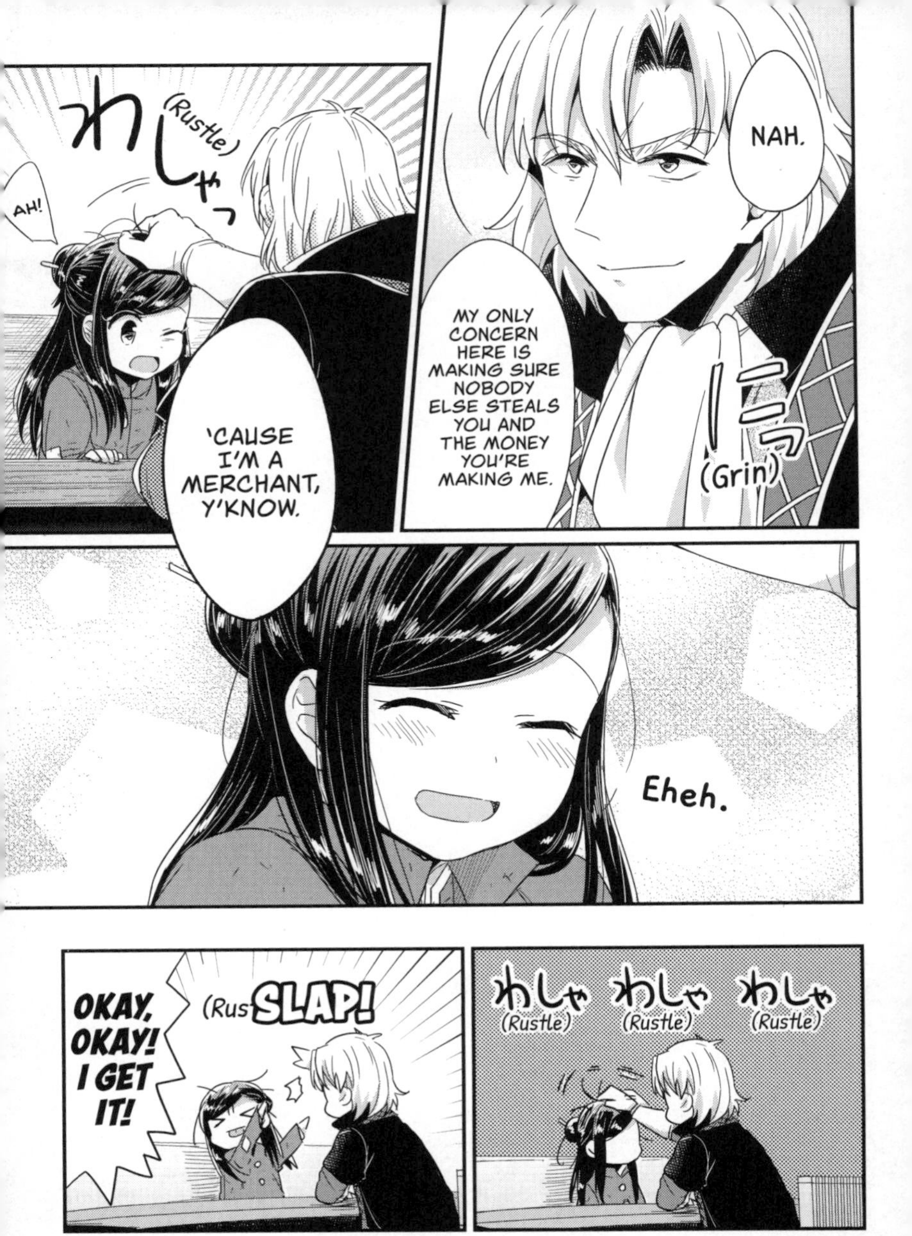
NAH.
MY ONLY CONCERN HERE IS MAKING SURE NOBODY ELSE STEALS YOU AND THE MONEY YOU'RE MAKING ME.
ニッ
(Grin)
'CAUSE I'M A MERCHANT, Y'KNOW.
わしゃっ
(Rustle)
AH!
Eheh.
わしゃ わしゃ わしゃ
(Rustle) (Rustle) (Rustle)
(Rus-SLAP!
OKAY, OKAY! I GET IT!

Ch.22: Improving Rinsham **End**

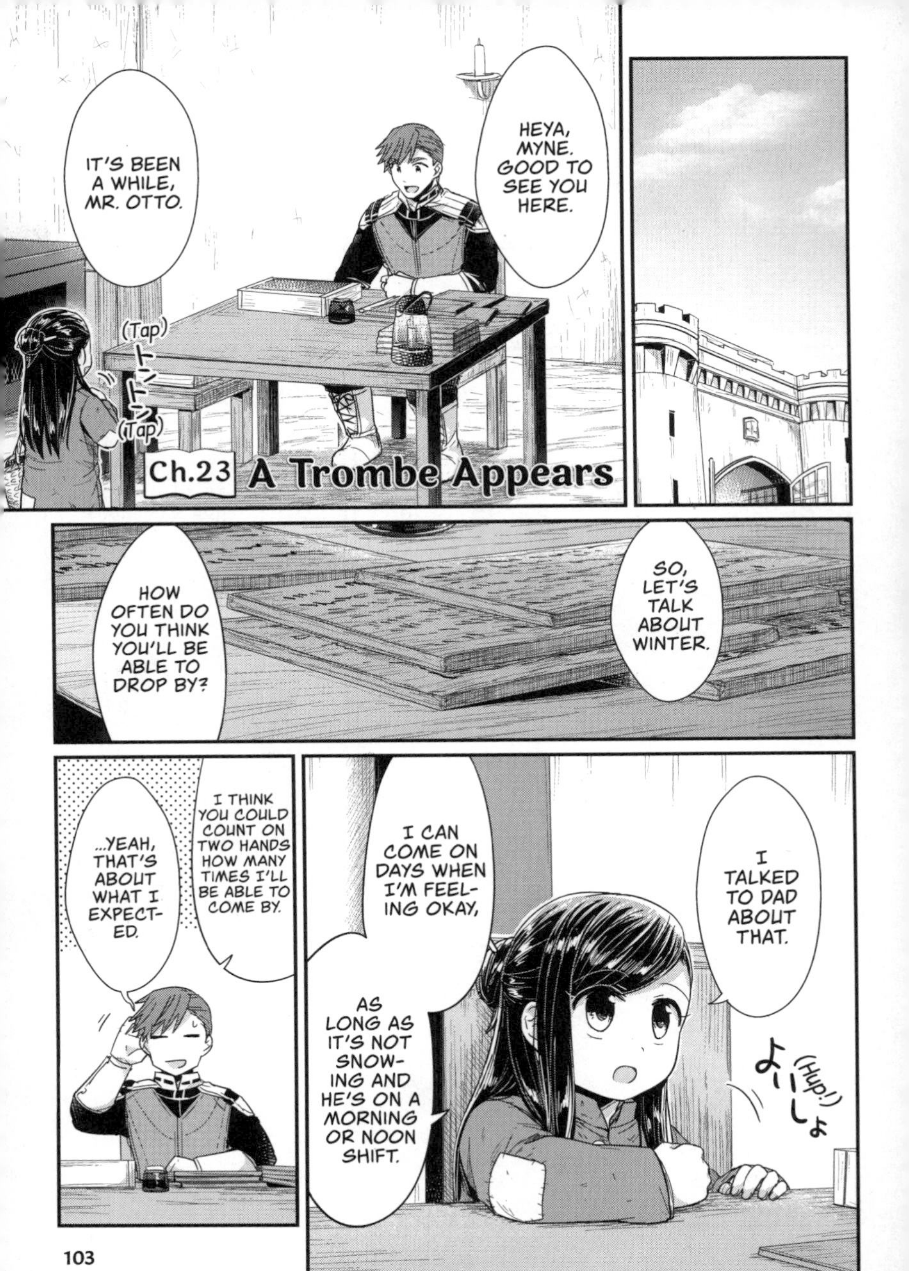
HEYA, MYNE. GOOD TO SEE YOU HERE.
IT'S BEEN A WHILE, MR. OTTO.
(Tap) トン
トン (Tap)
Ch.23 A Trombe Appears
SO, LET'S TALK ABOUT WINTER.
HOW OFTEN DO YOU THINK YOU'LL BE ABLE TO DROP BY?
I TALKED TO DAD ABOUT THAT.
よいしょ (Hup!)
I CAN COME ON DAYS WHEN I'M FEEL-ING OKAY,
AS LONG AS IT'S NOT SNOW-ING AND HE'S ON A MORNING OR NOON SHIFT.
I THINK YOU COULD COUNT ON TWO HANDS HOW MANY TIMES I'LL BE ABLE TO COME BY.
...YEAH, THAT'S ABOUT WHAT I EXPECT-ED.

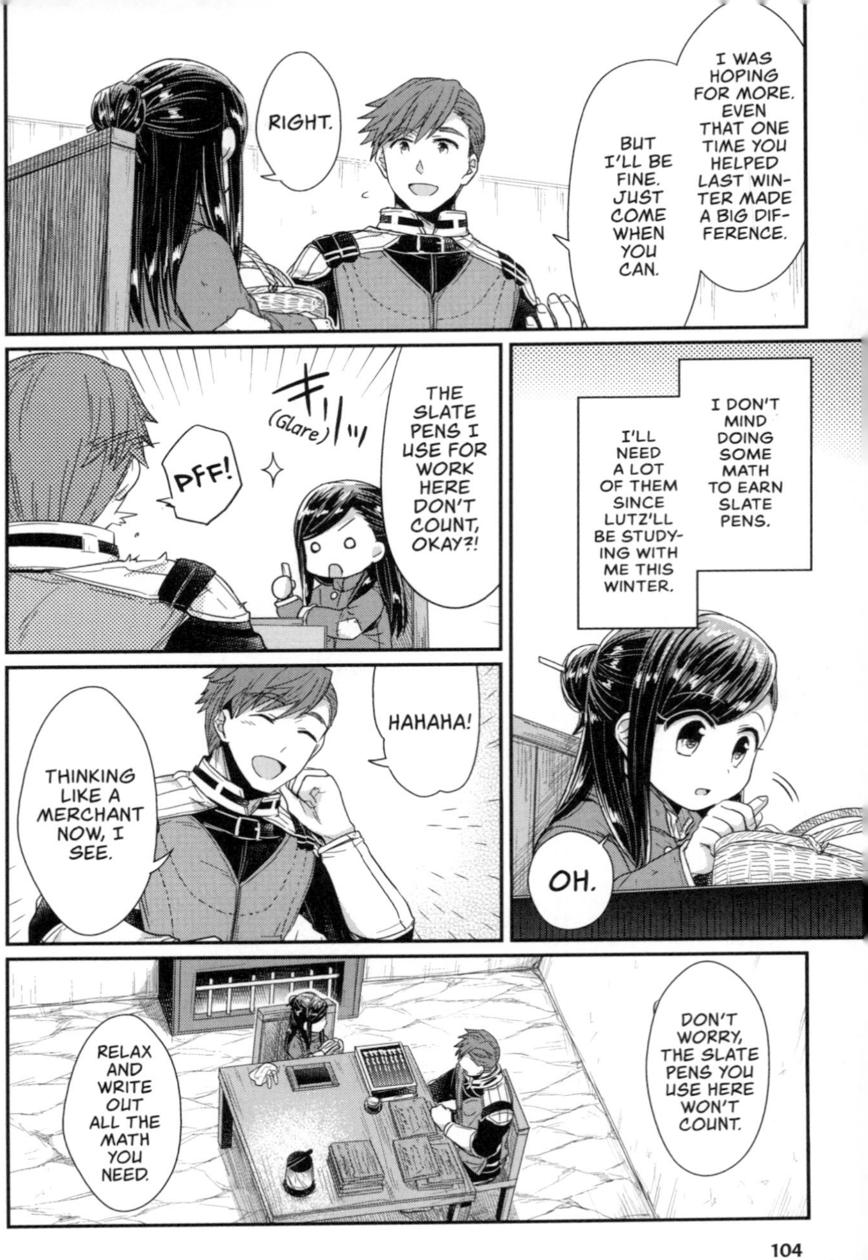
I WAS HOPING FOR MORE. EVEN THAT ONE TIME YOU HELPED LAST WINTER MADE A BIG DIFFERENCE.
BUT I'LL BE FINE. JUST COME WHEN YOU CAN.
RIGHT.
I DON'T MIND DOING SOME MATH TO EARN SLATE PENS.
I'LL NEED A LOT OF THEM SINCE LUTZ'LL BE STUDYING WITH ME THIS WINTER.
OH.
THE SLATE PENS I USE FOR WORK HERE DON'T COUNT, OKAY?!
(Glare)
PFF!
HAHAHA!
THINKING LIKE A MERCHANT NOW, I SEE.
DON'T WORRY, THE SLATE PENS YOU USE HERE WON'T COUNT.
RELAX AND WRITE OUT ALL THE MATH YOU NEED.

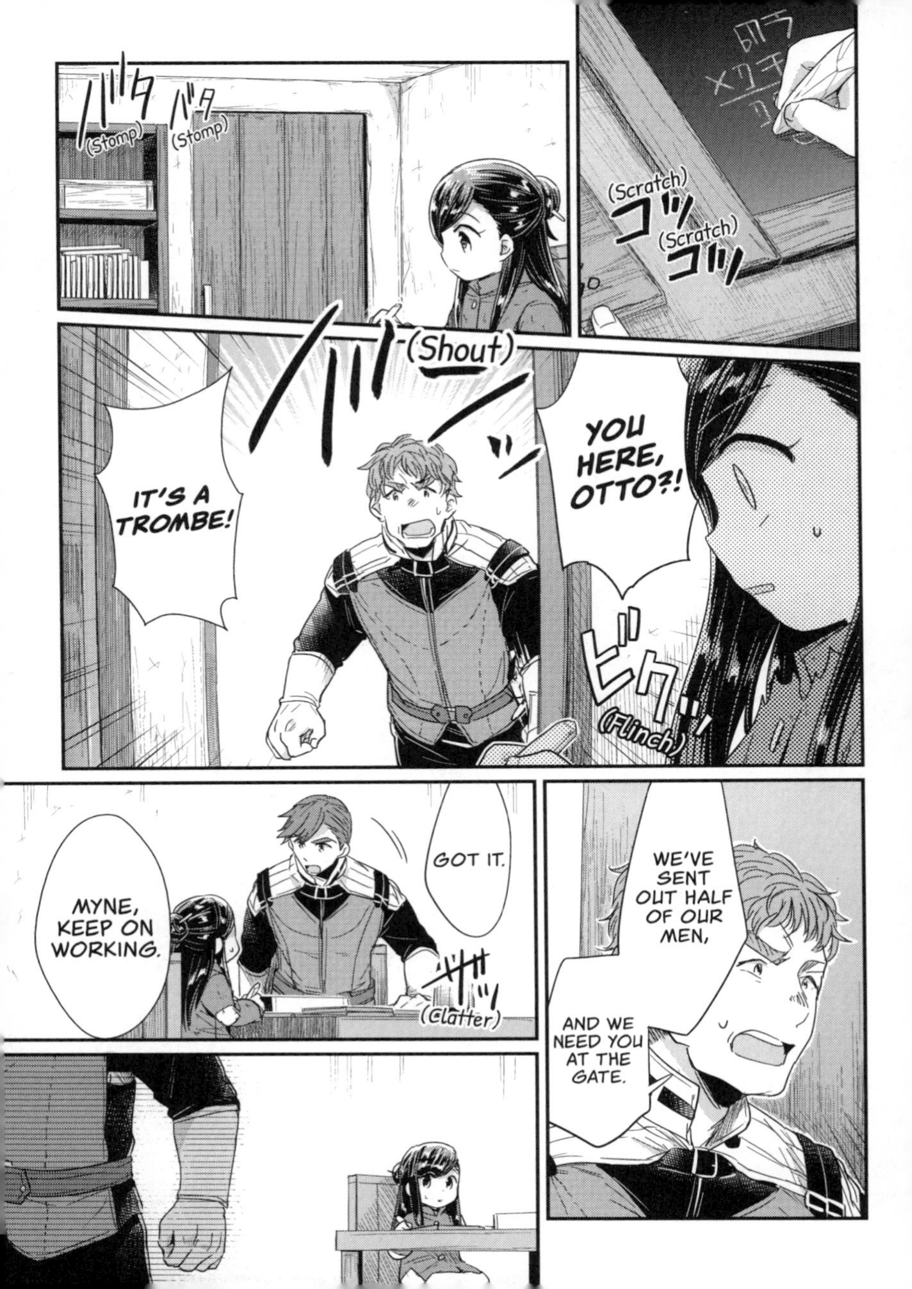
(Scratch)
コッ
(Scratch)
コッ
バタ
(Stomp)
バタ
(Stomp)
YOU HERE, OTTO?!
(Flinch)
(Shout)
IT'S A TROMBE!
WE'VE SENT OUT HALF OF OUR MEN,
AND WE NEED YOU AT THE GATE.
GOT IT.
(Clatter)
MYNE, KEEP ON WORKING.

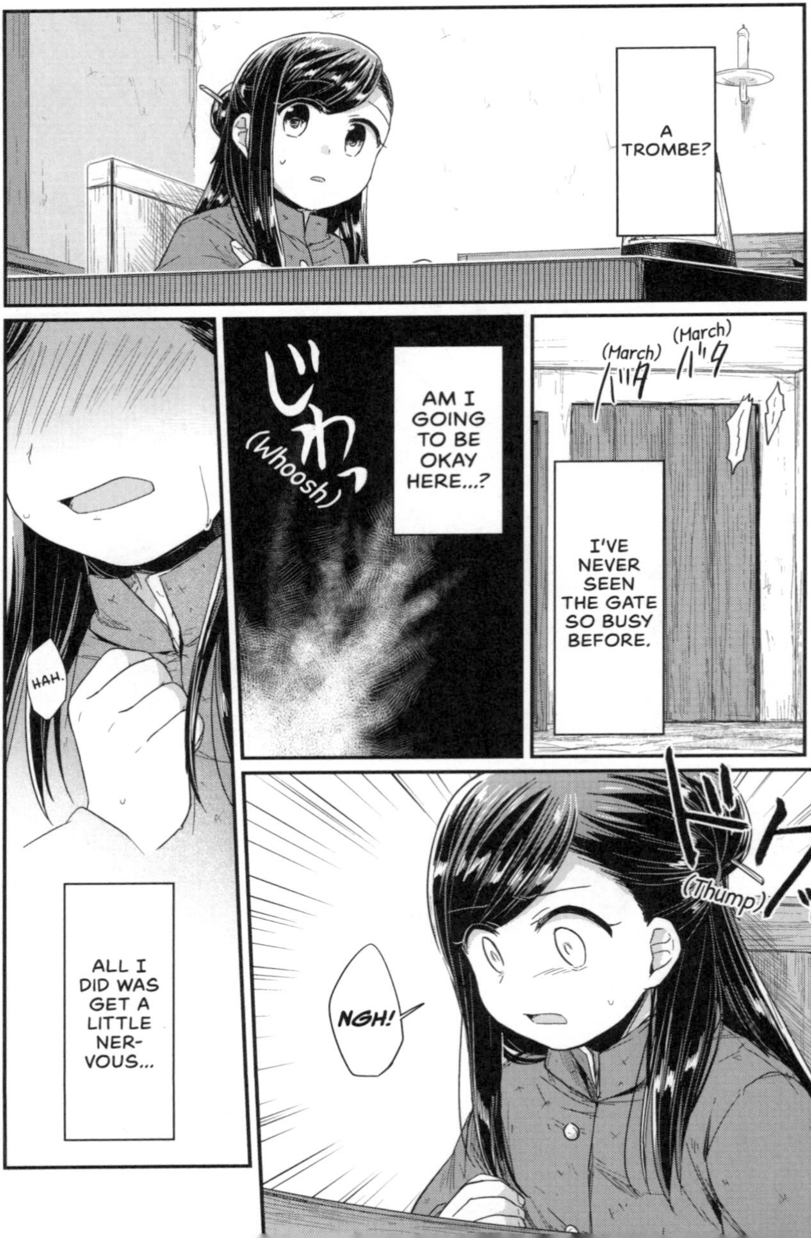
A TROMBE?
(March) バタ
(March) バタ
I'VE NEVER SEEN THE GATE SO BUSY BEFORE.
じわっ (Whoosh)
AM I GOING TO BE OKAY HERE...?
ドクッ (Thump)
NGH!
HAH.
ALL I DID WAS GET A LITTLE NER-VOUS...

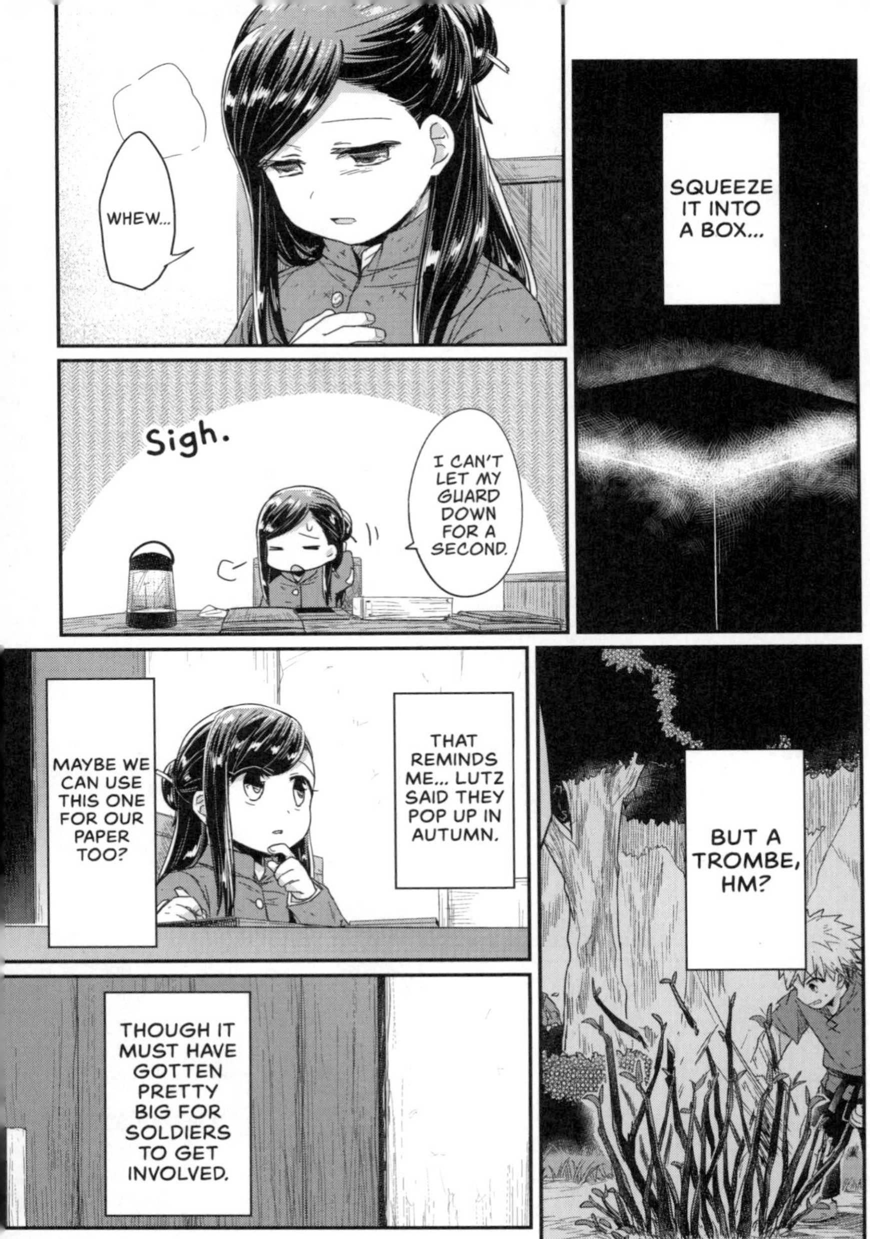
SQUEEZE IT INTO A BOX...
WHEW...
Sigh.
I CAN'T LET MY GUARD DOWN FOR A SECOND.
BUT A TROMBE, HM?
THAT REMINDS ME... LUTZ SAID THEY POP UP IN AUTUMN.
MAYBE WE CAN USE THIS ONE FOR OUR PAPER TOO?
THOUGH IT MUST HAVE GOTTEN PRETTY BIG FOR SOLDIERS TO GET INVOLVED.

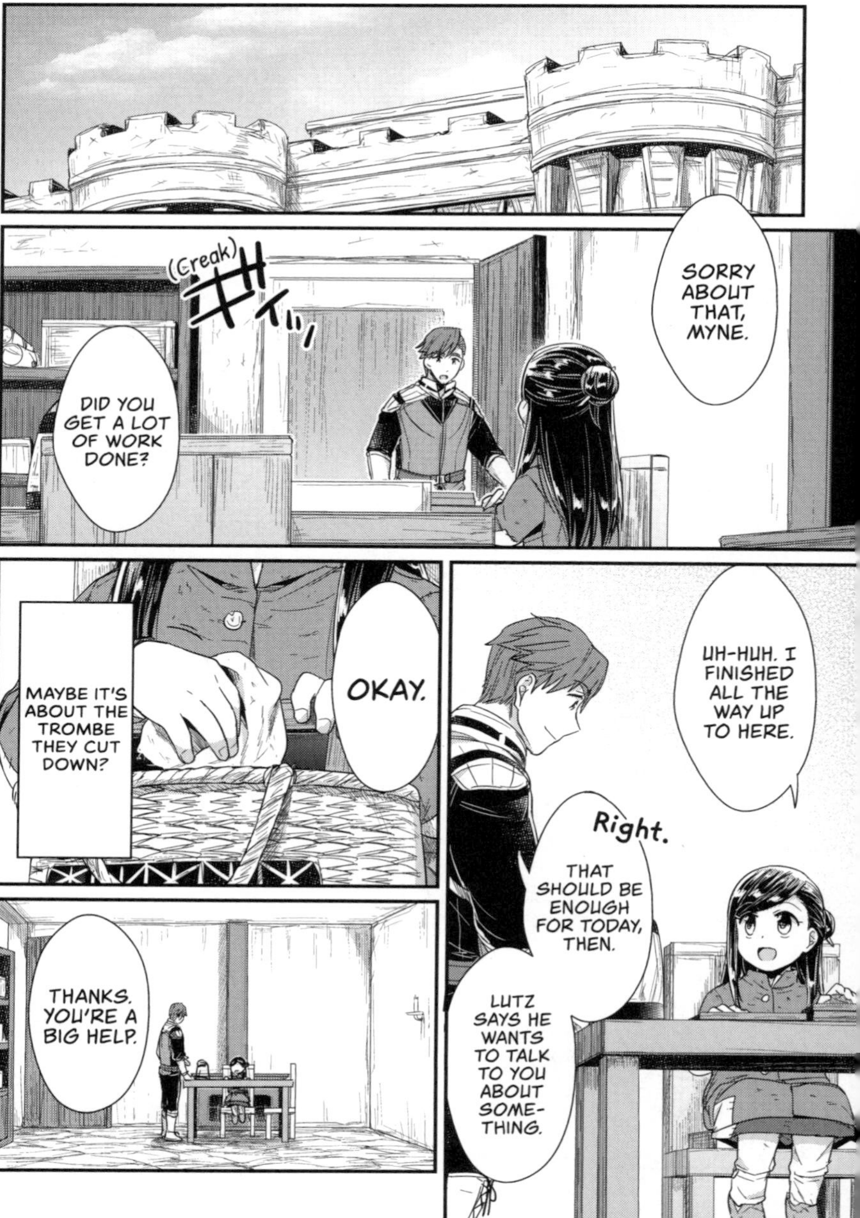
SORRY ABOUT THAT, MYNE.
(Creak)
DID YOU GET A LOT OF WORK DONE?
UH-HUH. I FINISHED ALL THE WAY UP TO HERE.
Right.
THAT SHOULD BE ENOUGH FOR TODAY, THEN.
LUTZ SAYS HE WANTS TO TALK TO YOU ABOUT SOME-THING.
OKAY.
MAYBE IT'S ABOUT THE TROMBE THEY CUT DOWN?
THANKS. YOU'RE A BIG HELP.

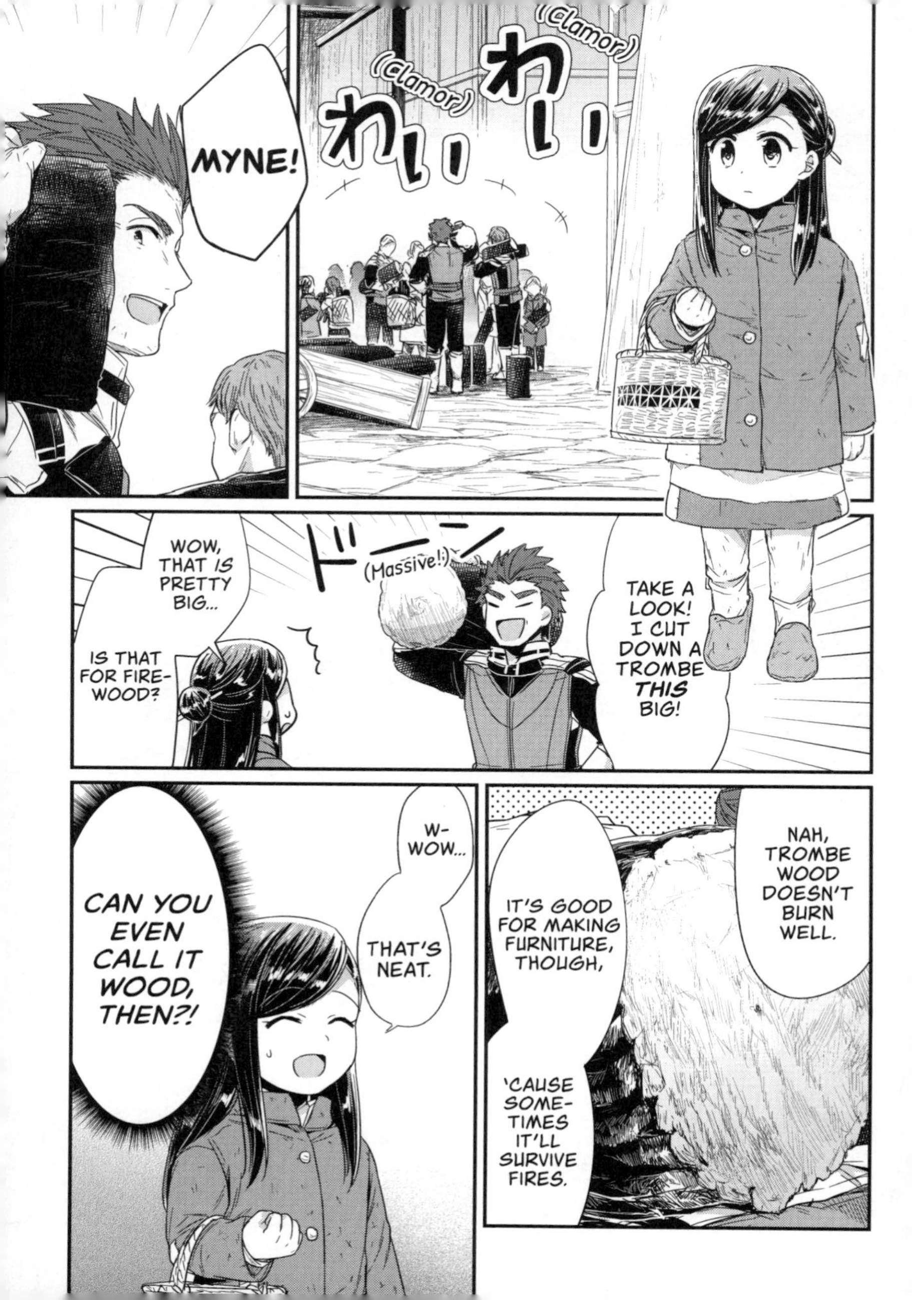
わい (Clamor)
わい (Clamor)
MYNE!
TAKE A LOOK! I CUT DOWN A TROMBE THIS BIG!
ドーン (Massive!)
WOW, THAT IS PRETTY BIG...
IS THAT FOR FIRE-WOOD?
NAH, TROMBE WOOD DOESN'T BURN WELL.
IT'S GOOD FOR MAKING FURNITURE, THOUGH,
'CAUSE SOME-TIMES IT'LL SURVIVE FIRES.
W-WOW...
THAT'S NEAT.
CAN YOU EVEN CALL IT WOOD, THEN?!

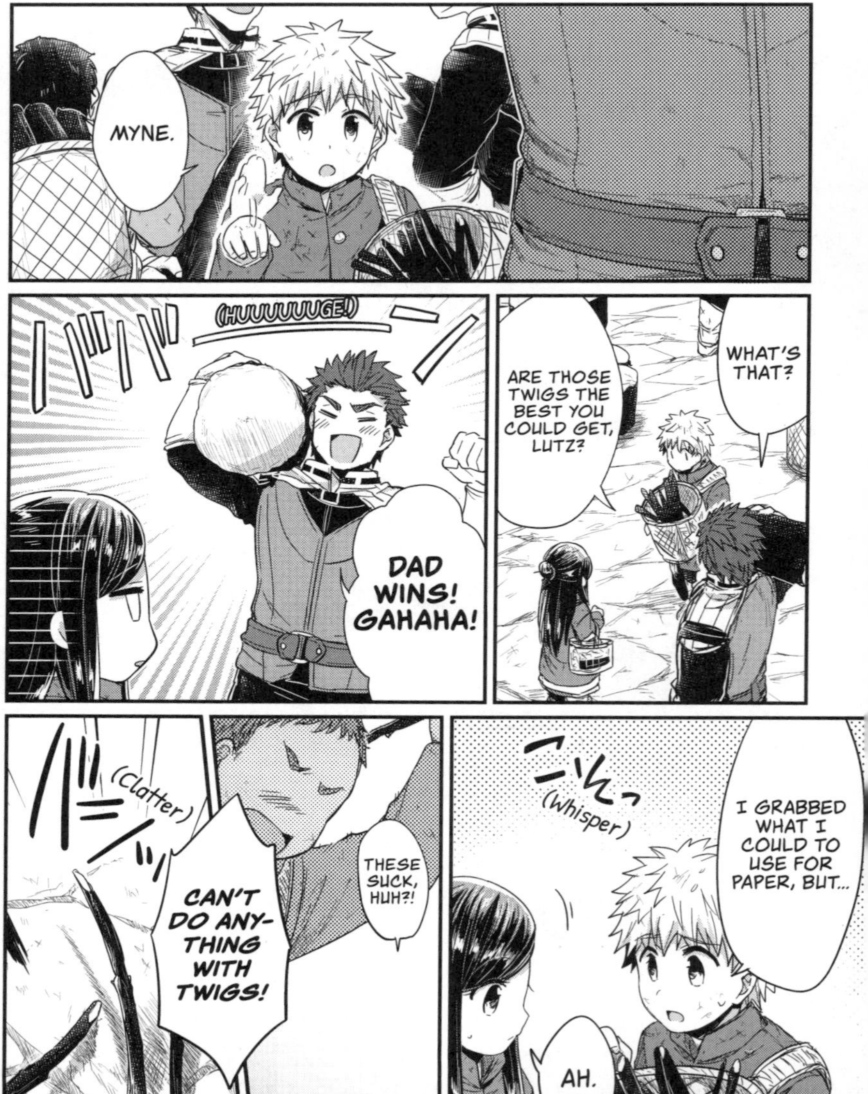
MYNE.
WHAT'S THAT?
ARE THOSE TWIGS THE BEST YOU COULD GET, LUTZ?
(HUUUUUUGE!)
DAD WINS! GAHAHA!
I GRABBED WHAT I COULD TO USE FOR PAPER, BUT...
(Whisper)
AH.
THESE SUCK, HUH?!
(Clatter)
CAN'T DO ANY-THING WITH TWIGS!

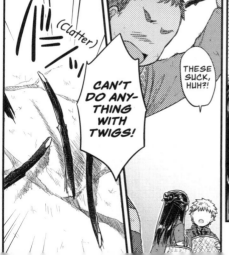

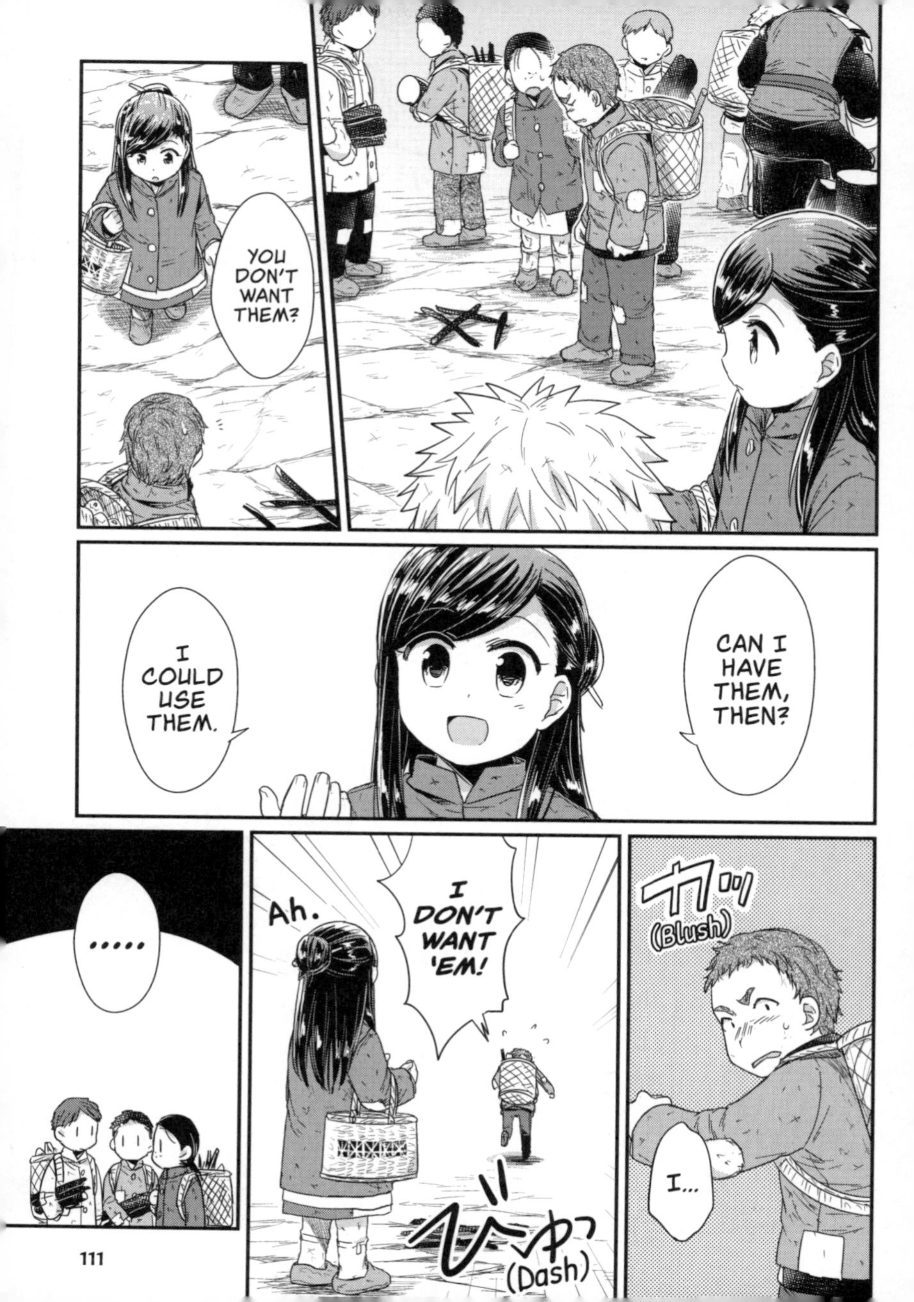
YOU DON'T WANT THEM?
CAN I HAVE THEM, THEN?
I COULD USE THEM.
カッ
(Blush)
I...
I DON'T WANT 'EM!
Ah.
びゅっ
(Dash)
......

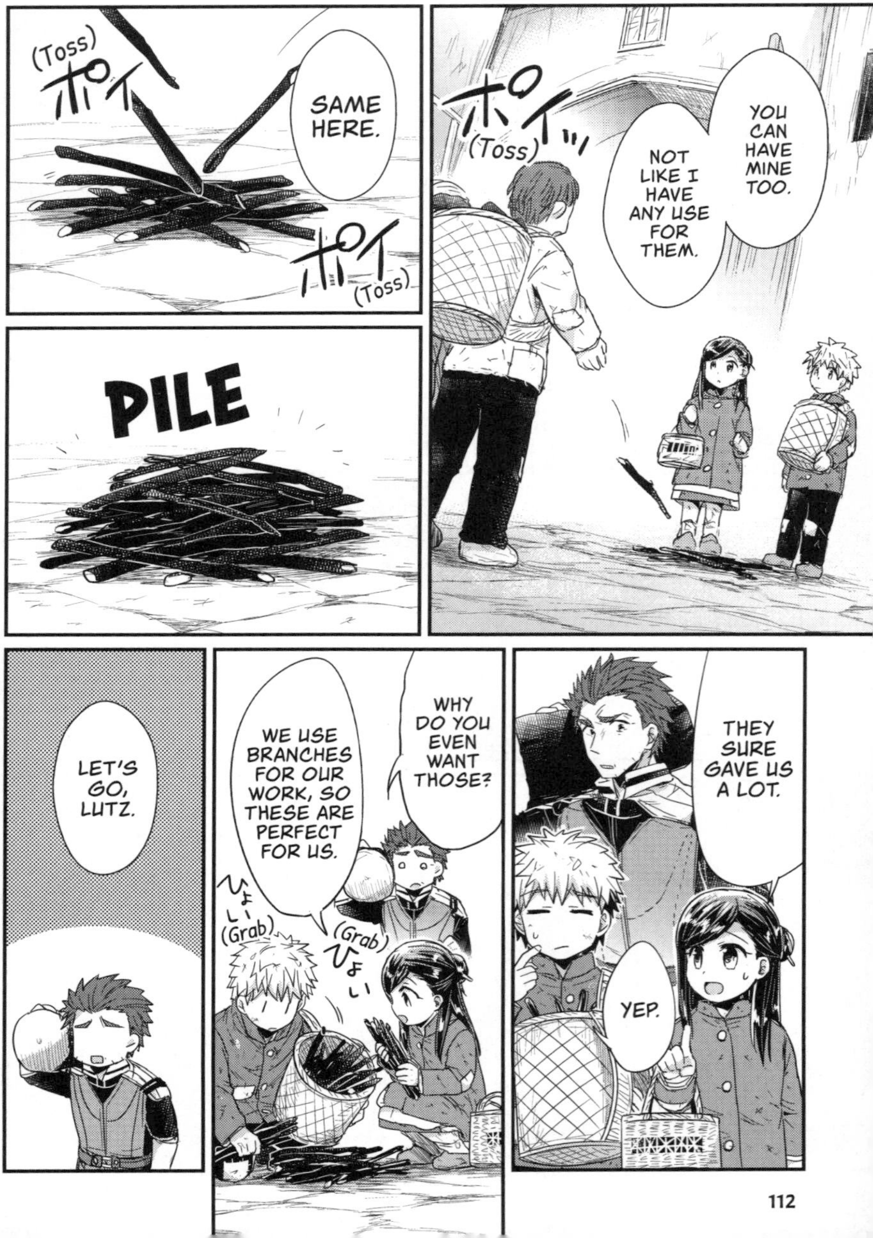
ポイッ
(Toss)
YOU CAN HAVE MINE TOO.
NOT LIKE I HAVE ANY USE FOR THEM.
(Toss)
ポイ
SAME HERE.
ポイ
(Toss)
PILE
THEY SURE GAVE US A LOT.
YEP.
WHY DO YOU EVEN WANT THOSE?
WE USE BRANCHES FOR OUR WORK, SO THESE ARE PERFECT FOR US.
ひょい
(Grab)
ひょい
(Grab)
LET'S GO, LUTZ.

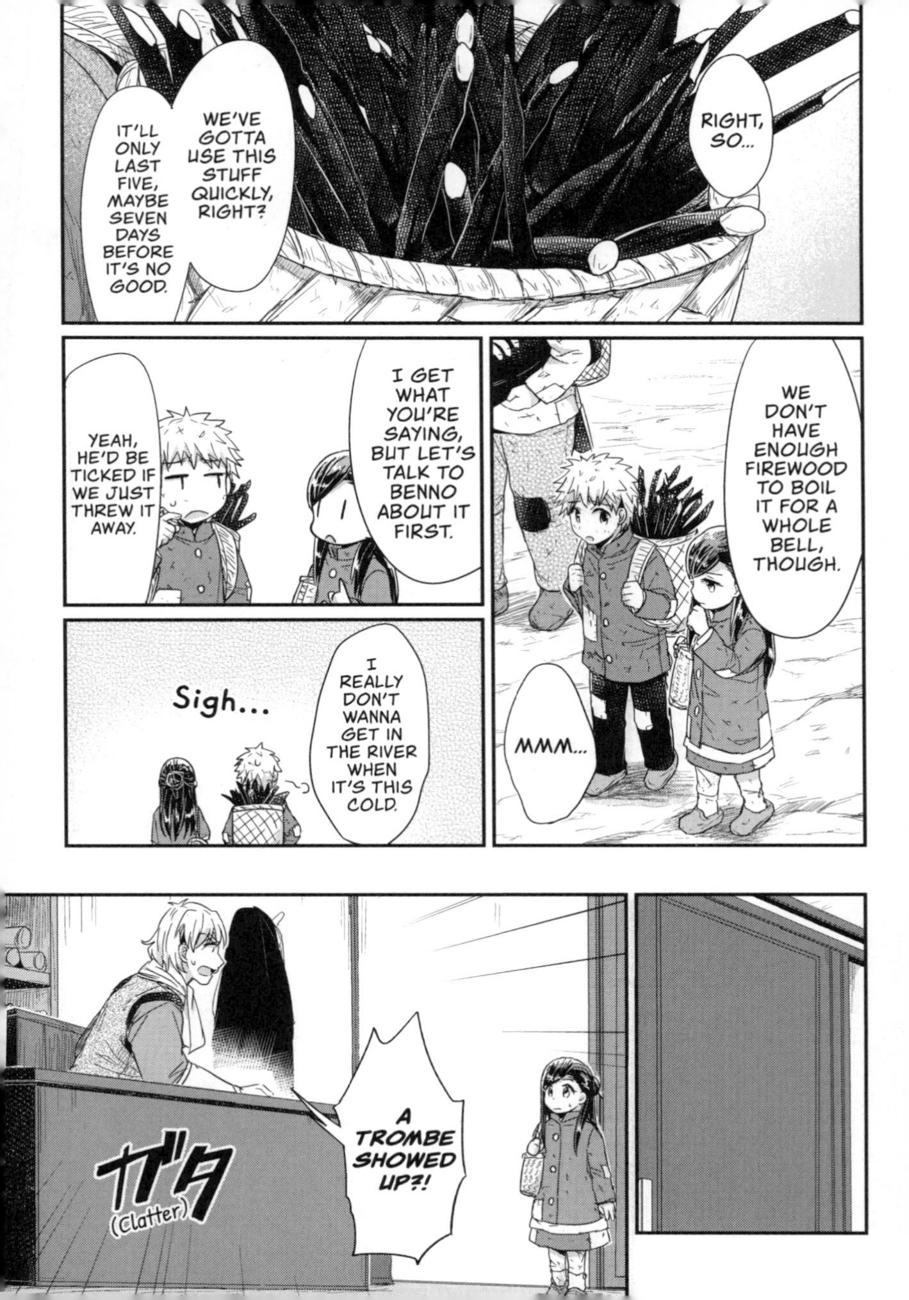
RIGHT, SO...
WE'VE GOTTA USE THIS STUFF QUICKLY, RIGHT?
IT'LL ONLY LAST FIVE, MAYBE SEVEN DAYS BEFORE IT'S NO GOOD.
WE DON'T HAVE ENOUGH FIREWOOD TO BOIL IT FOR A WHOLE BELL, THOUGH.
MMM...
I GET WHAT YOU'RE SAYING, BUT LET'S TALK TO BENNO ABOUT IT FIRST.
YEAH, HE'D BE TICKED IF WE JUST THREW IT AWAY.
I REALLY DON'T WANNA GET IN THE RIVER WHEN IT'S THIS COLD.
Sigh...
A TROMBE SHOWED UP?!
ガタ
(Clatter)

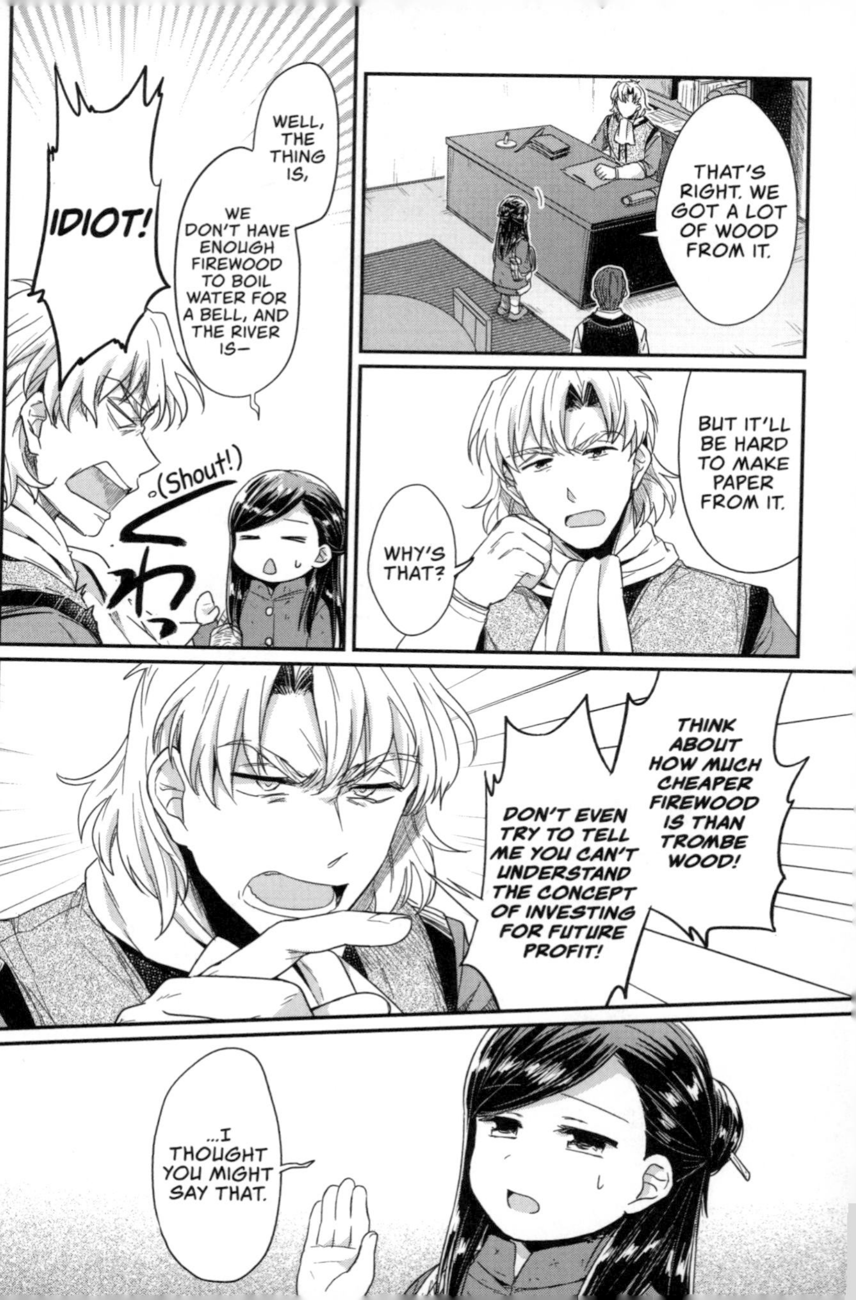
THAT'S RIGHT. WE GOT A LOT OF WOOD FROM IT.
BUT IT'LL BE HARD TO MAKE PAPER FROM IT.
WHY'S THAT?
WELL, THE THING IS,
WE DON'T HAVE ENOUGH FIREWOOD TO BOIL WATER FOR A BELL, AND THE RIVER IS—
IDIOT!
(Shout!)
THINK ABOUT HOW MUCH CHEAPER FIREWOOD IS THAN TROMBE WOOD!
DON'T EVEN TRY TO TELL ME YOU CAN'T UNDERSTAND THE CONCEPT OF INVESTING FOR FUTURE PROFIT!
...I THOUGHT YOU MIGHT SAY THAT.

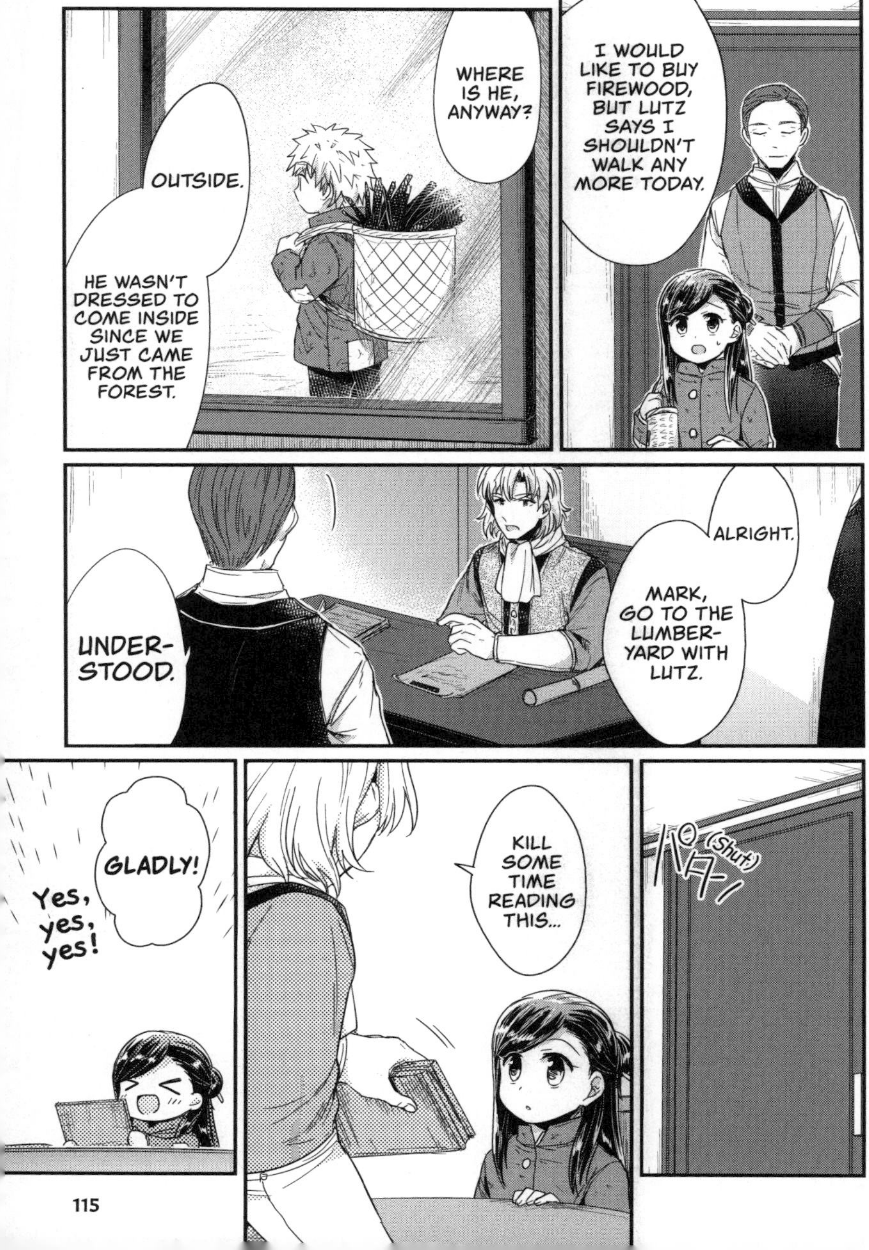
I WOULD LIKE TO BUY FIREWOOD, BUT LUTZ SAYS I SHOULDN'T WALK ANY MORE TODAY.
WHERE IS HE, ANYWAY?
OUTSIDE.
HE WASN'T DRESSED TO COME INSIDE SINCE WE JUST CAME FROM THE FOREST.
ALRIGHT.
MARK, GO TO THE LUMBER-YARD WITH LUTZ.
UNDER-STOOD.
パタン
(Shut)
KILL SOME TIME READING THIS...
GLADLY!
Yes, yes, yes!

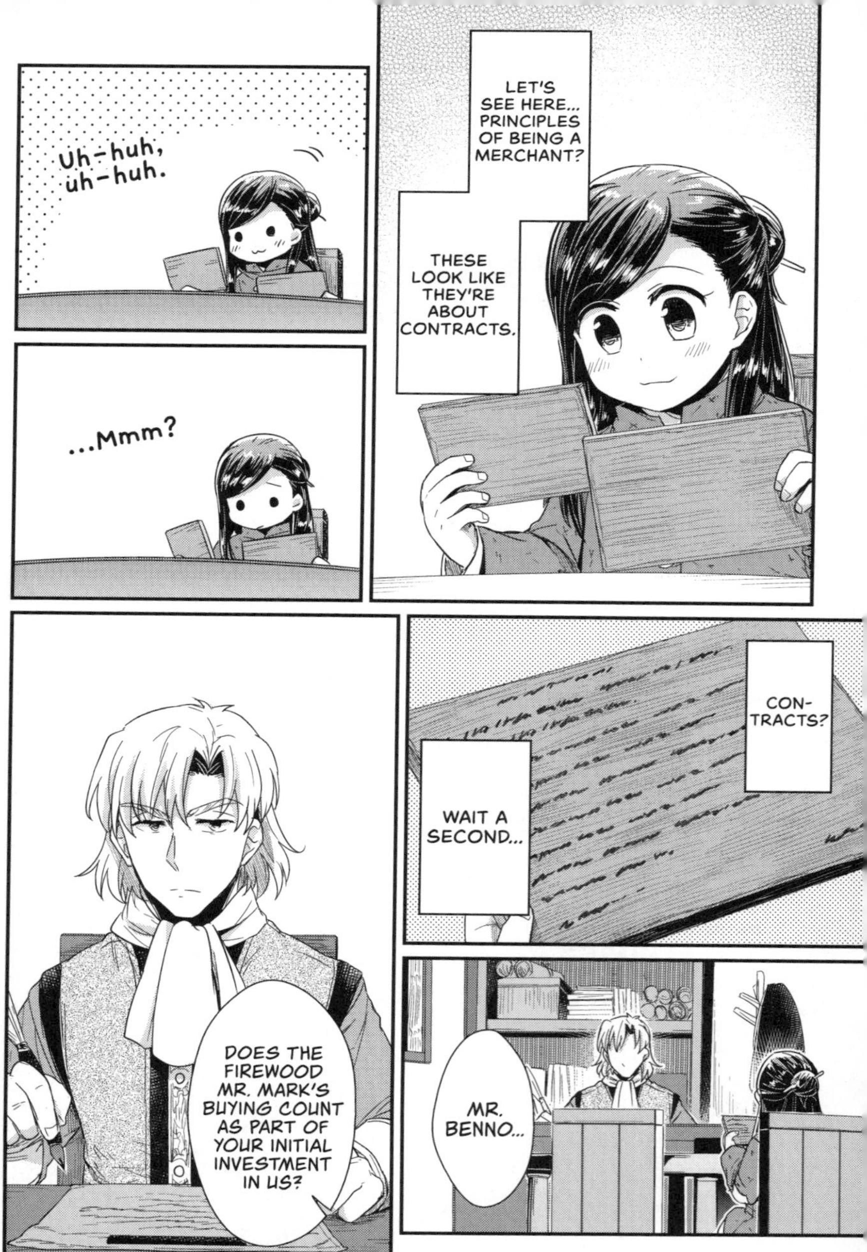
LET'S SEE HERE... PRINCIPLES OF BEING A MERCHANT?
THESE LOOK LIKE THEY'RE ABOUT CONTRACTS.
Uh-huh, uh-huh.
...Mmm?
CON-TRACTS?
WAIT A SECOND...
MR. BENNO...
DOES THE FIREWOOD MR. MARK'S BUYING COUNT AS PART OF YOUR INITIAL INVESTMENT IN US?

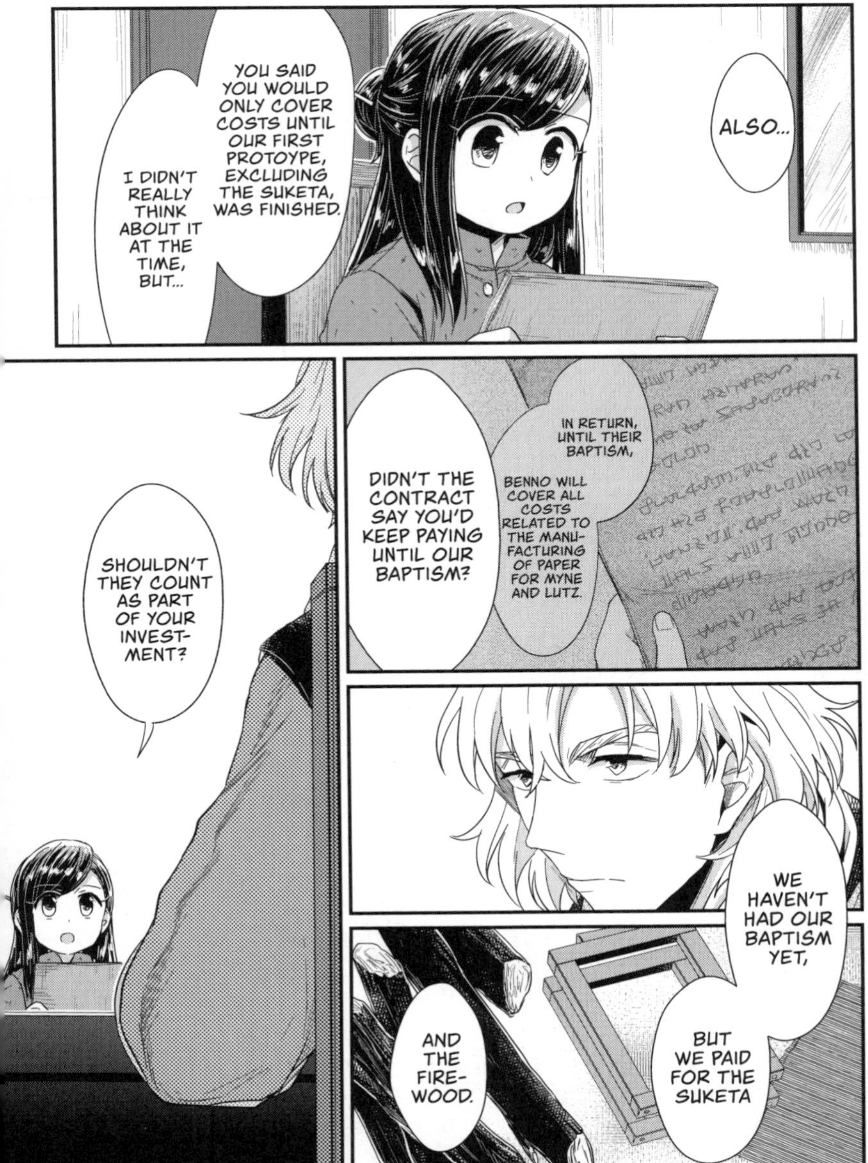
ALSO...
YOU SAID YOU WOULD ONLY COVER COSTS UNTIL OUR FIRST PROTOYPE, EXCLUDING THE SUKETA, WAS FINISHED.
I DIDN'T REALLY THINK ABOUT IT AT THE TIME, BUT...
IN RETURN, UNTIL THEIR BAPTISM,
BENNO WILL COVER ALL COSTS RELATED TO THE MANUFACTURING OF PAPER FOR MYNE AND LUTZ.
DIDN'T THE CONTRACT SAY YOU'D KEEP PAYING UNTIL OUR BAPTISM?
WE HAVEN'T HAD OUR BAPTISM YET,
BUT WE PAID FOR THE SUKETA
AND THE FIREWOOD.
SHOULDN'T THEY COUNT AS PART OF YOUR INVESTMENT?

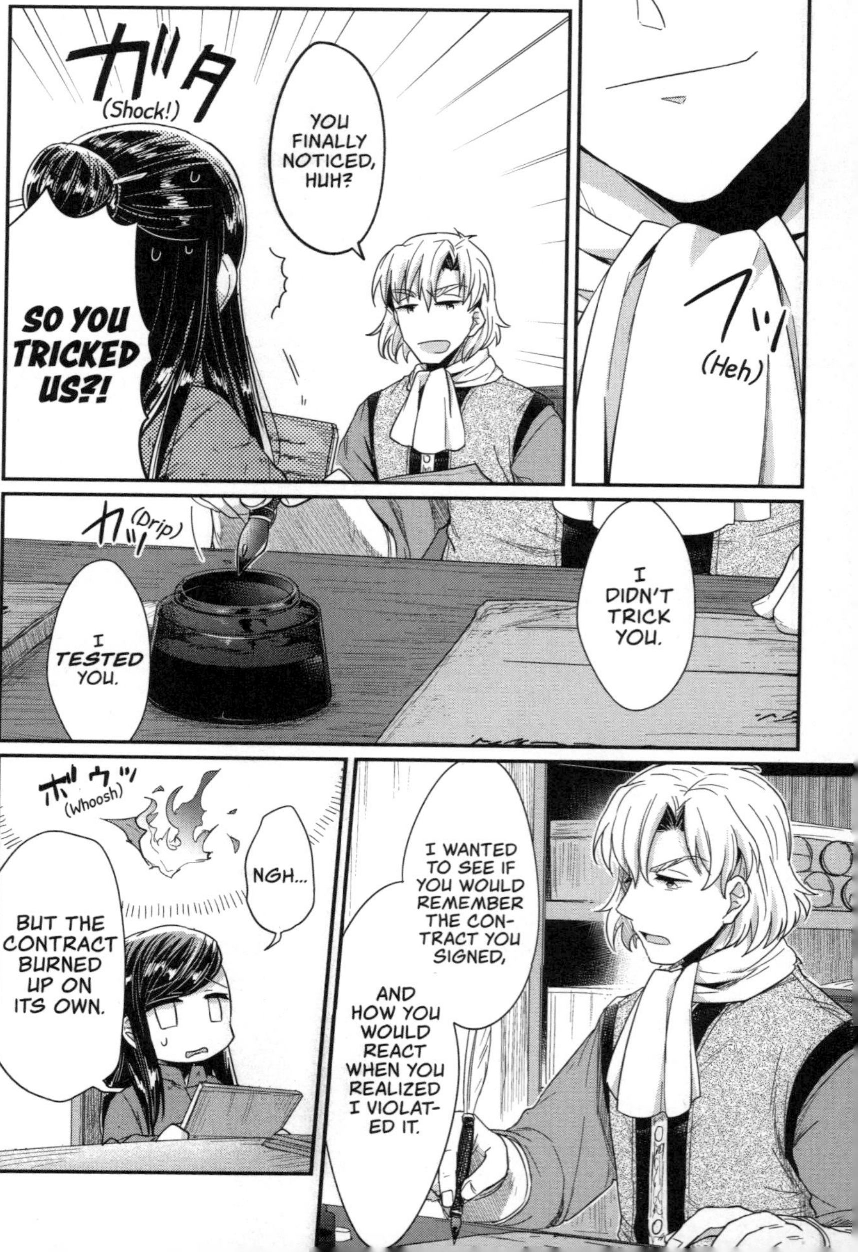
ヘッ
(Heh)
YOU FINALLY NOTICED, HUH?
ガタ
(Shock!)
SO YOU TRICKED US?!
I DIDN'T TRICK YOU.
ガッ
(Drip)
I TESTED YOU.
I WANTED TO SEE IF YOU WOULD REMEMBER THE CONTRACT YOU SIGNED,
AND HOW YOU WOULD REACT WHEN YOU REALIZED I VIOLATED IT.
NGH...
ボウッ
(Whoosh)
BUT THE CONTRACT BURNED UP ON ITS OWN.

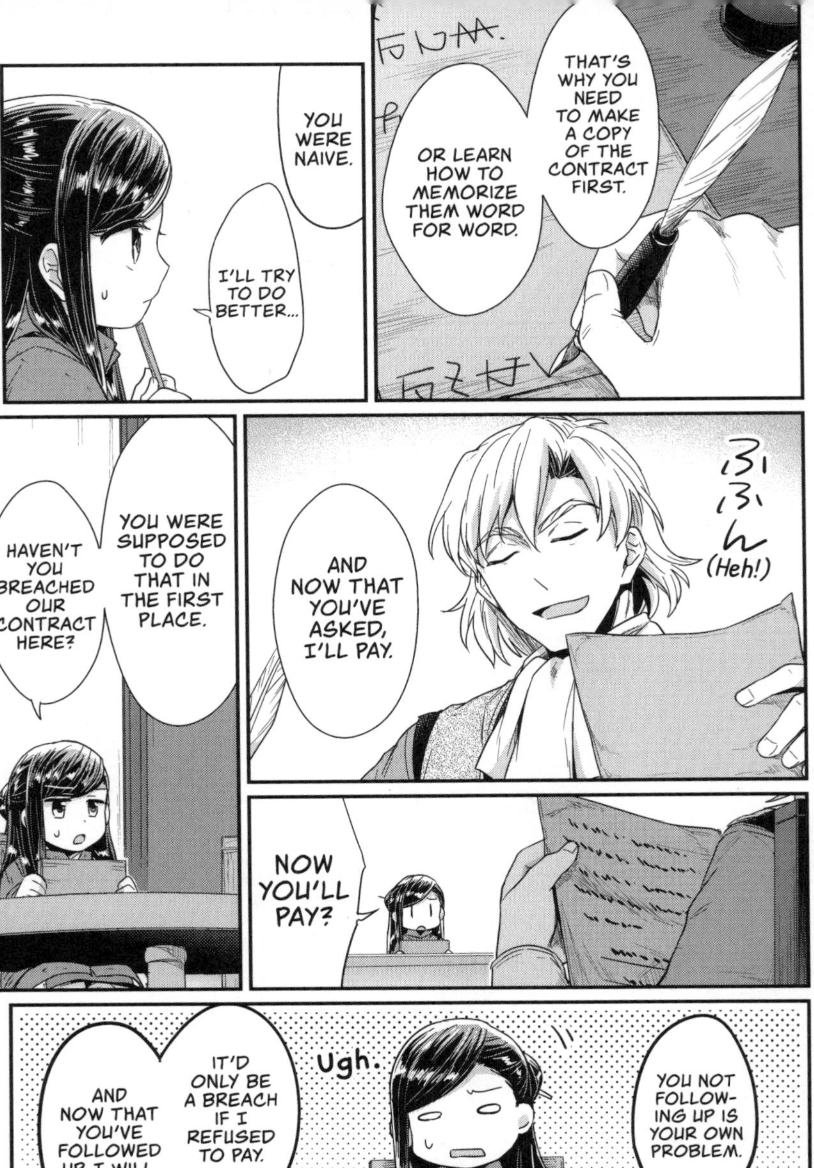
THAT'S WHY YOU NEED TO MAKE A COPY OF THE CONTRACT FIRST.
OR LEARN HOW TO MEMORIZE THEM WORD FOR WORD.
YOU WERE NAIVE.
I'LL TRY TO DO BETTER...
ふふん (Heh!)
AND NOW THAT YOU'VE ASKED, I'LL PAY.
NOW YOU'LL PAY?
YOU WERE SUPPOSED TO DO THAT IN THE FIRST PLACE.
HAVEN'T YOU BREACHED OUR CONTRACT HERE?
YOU NOT FOLLOWING UP IS YOUR OWN PROBLEM.
Ugh.
IT'D ONLY BE A BREACH IF I REFUSED TO PAY.
AND NOW THAT YOU'VE FOLLOWED UP, I WILL.

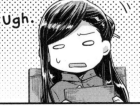

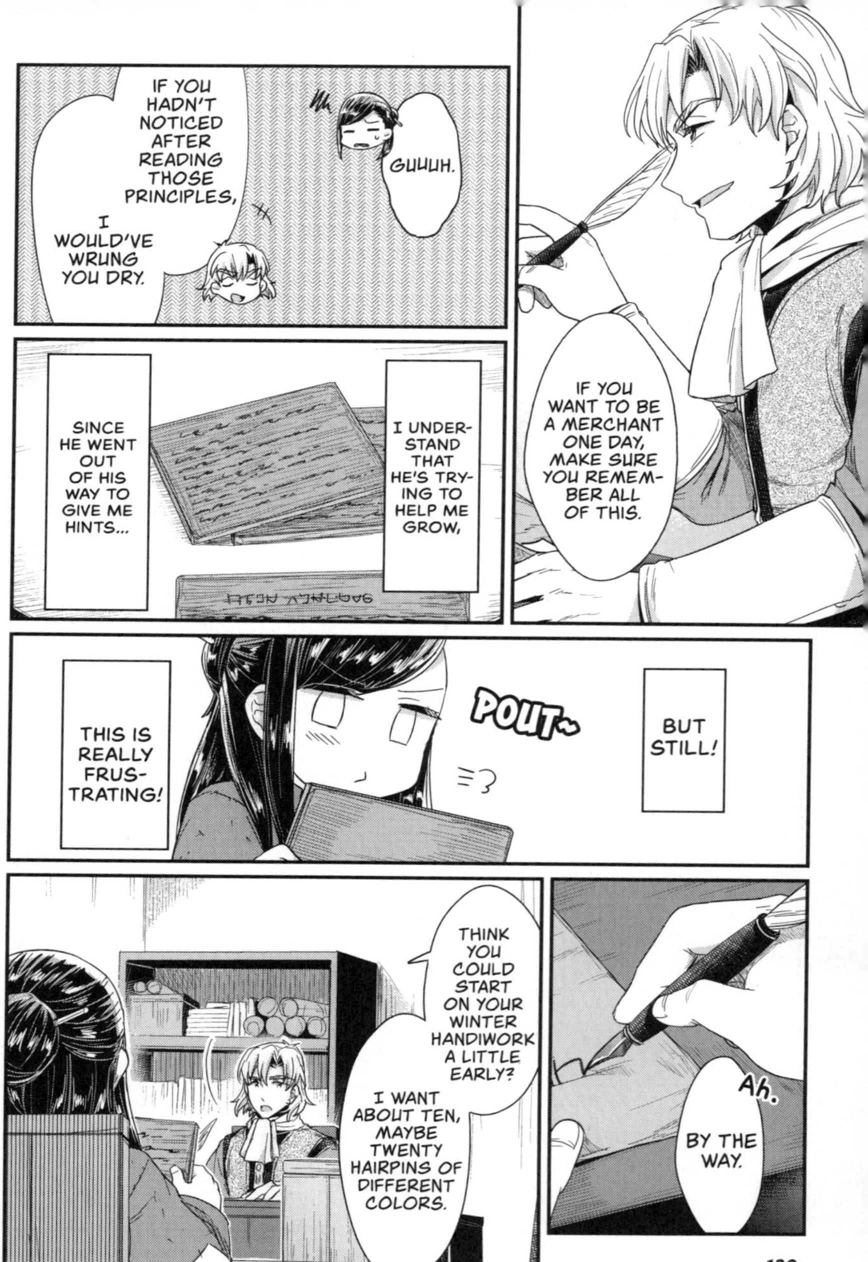
IF YOU WANT TO BE A MERCHANT ONE DAY, MAKE SURE YOU REMEMBER ALL OF THIS.
IF YOU HADN'T NOTICED AFTER READING THOSE PRINCIPLES, I WOULD'VE WRUNG YOU DRY.
GUUUH.
I UNDER-STAND THAT HE'S TRY-ING TO HELP ME GROW,
SINCE HE WENT OUT OF HIS WAY TO GIVE ME HINTS...
BUT STILL!
POUT~
THIS IS REALLY FRUS-TRATING!
Ah.
BY THE WAY.
THINK YOU COULD START ON YOUR WINTER HANDIWORK A LITTLE EARLY?
I WANT ABOUT TEN, MAYBE TWENTY HAIRPINS OF DIFFERENT COLORS.

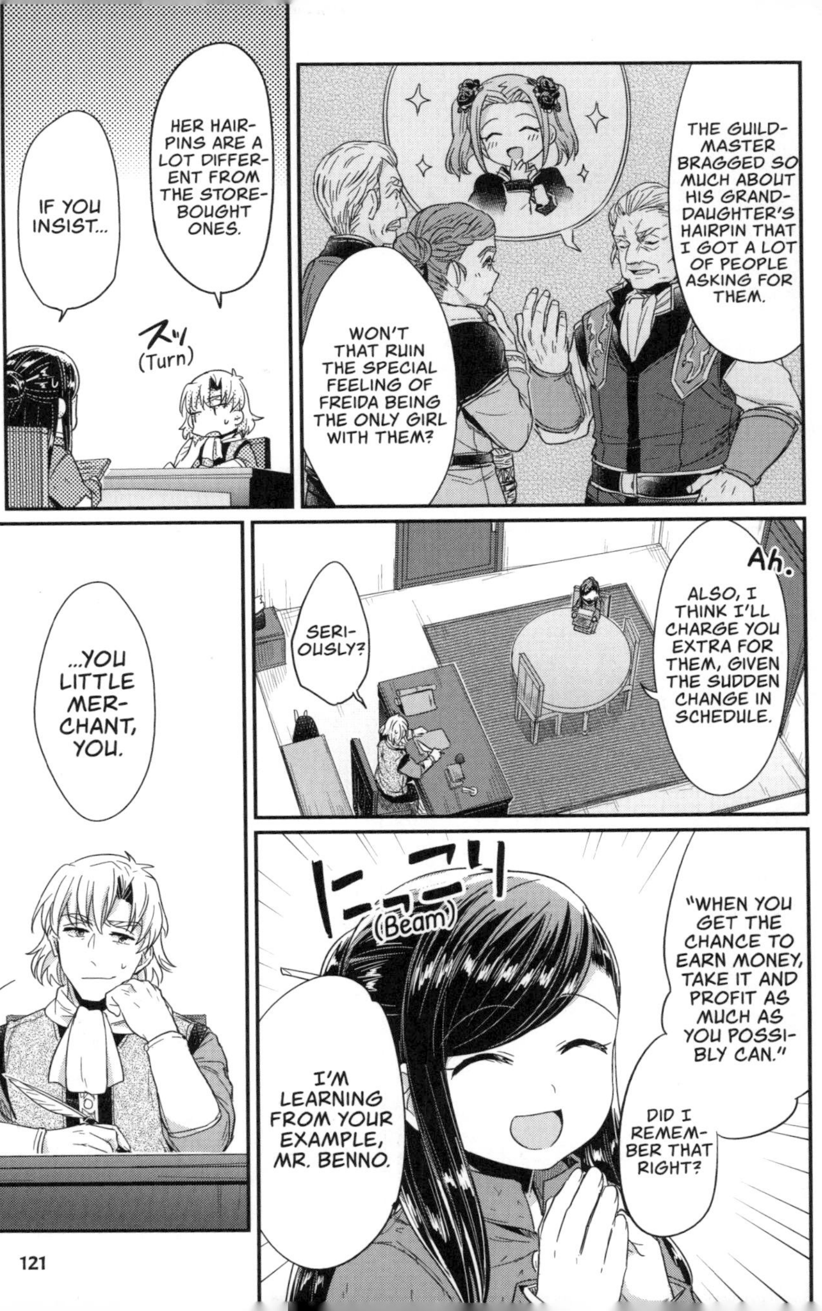
THE GUILD-MASTER BRAGGED SO MUCH ABOUT HIS GRAND-DAUGHTER'S HAIRPIN THAT I GOT A LOT OF PEOPLE ASKING FOR THEM.
WON'T THAT RUIN THE SPECIAL FEELING OF FREIDA BEING THE ONLY GIRL WITH THEM?
HER HAIR-PINS ARE A LOT DIFFER-ENT FROM THE STORE-BOUGHT ONES.
IF YOU INSIST...
ズッ
(Turn)
Ah.
ALSO, I THINK I'LL CHARGE YOU EXTRA FOR THEM, GIVEN THE SUDDEN CHANGE IN SCHEDULE.
SERI-OUSLY?
...YOU LITTLE MER-CHANT, YOU.
にっこり
(Beam)
"WHEN YOU GET THE CHANCE TO EARN MONEY, TAKE IT AND PROFIT AS MUCH AS YOU POSSI-BLY CAN."
DID I REMEM-BER THAT RIGHT?
I'M LEARNING FROM YOUR EXAMPLE, MR. BENNO.

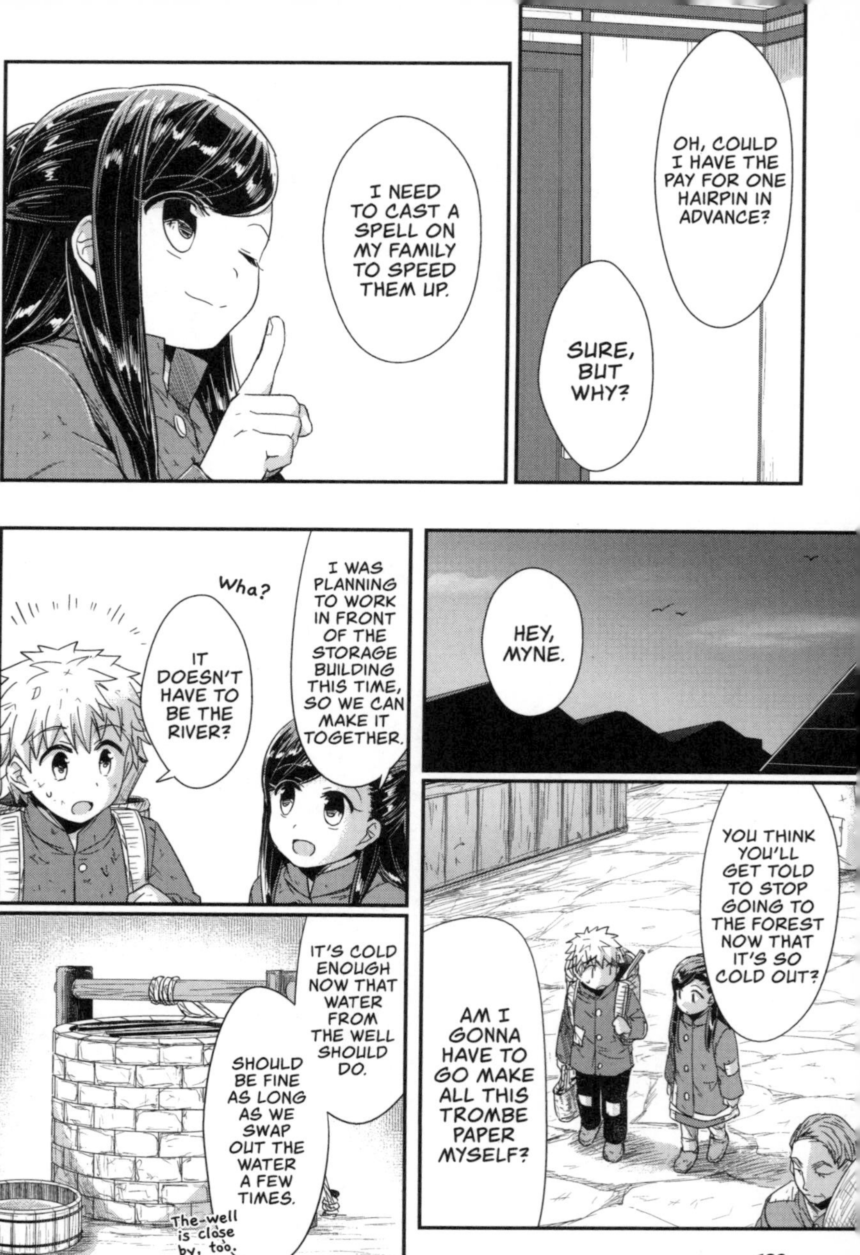
OH, COULD I HAVE THE PAY FOR ONE HAIRPIN IN ADVANCE?
SURE, BUT WHY?
I NEED TO CAST A SPELL ON MY FAMILY TO SPEED THEM UP.
HEY, MYNE.
YOU THINK YOU'LL GET TOLD TO STOP GOING TO THE FOREST NOW THAT IT'S SO COLD OUT?
AM I GONNA HAVE TO GO MAKE ALL THIS TROMBE PAPER MYSELF?
I WAS PLANNING TO WORK IN FRONT OF THE STORAGE BUILDING THIS TIME, SO WE CAN MAKE IT TOGETHER.
Wha?
IT DOESN'T HAVE TO BE THE RIVER?
IT'S COLD ENOUGH NOW THAT WATER FROM THE WELL SHOULD DO.
SHOULD BE FINE AS LONG AS WE SWAP OUT THE WATER A FEW TIMES.
The well is close by, too.

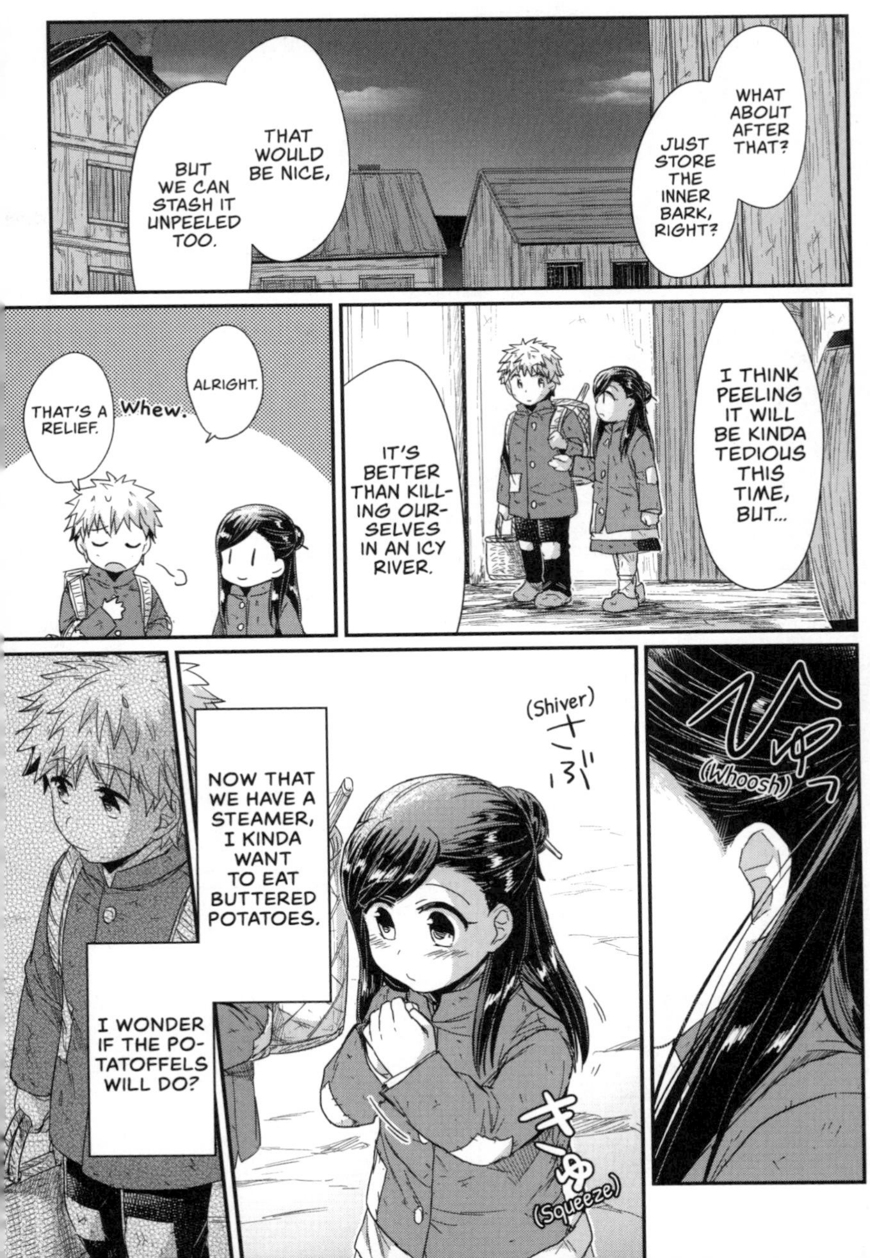
WHAT ABOUT AFTER THAT?
JUST STORE THE INNER BARK, RIGHT?
THAT WOULD BE NICE,
BUT WE CAN STASH IT UNPEELED TOO.
I THINK PEELING IT WILL BE KINDA TEDIOUS THIS TIME, BUT...
IT'S BETTER THAN KILLING OURSELVES IN AN ICY RIVER.
ALRIGHT.
Whew.
THAT'S A RELIEF.
(Whoosh)
(Shiver)
NOW THAT WE HAVE A STEAMER, I KINDA WANT TO EAT BUTTERED POTATOES.
I WONDER IF THE POTATOFFELS WILL DO?
(Squeeze)

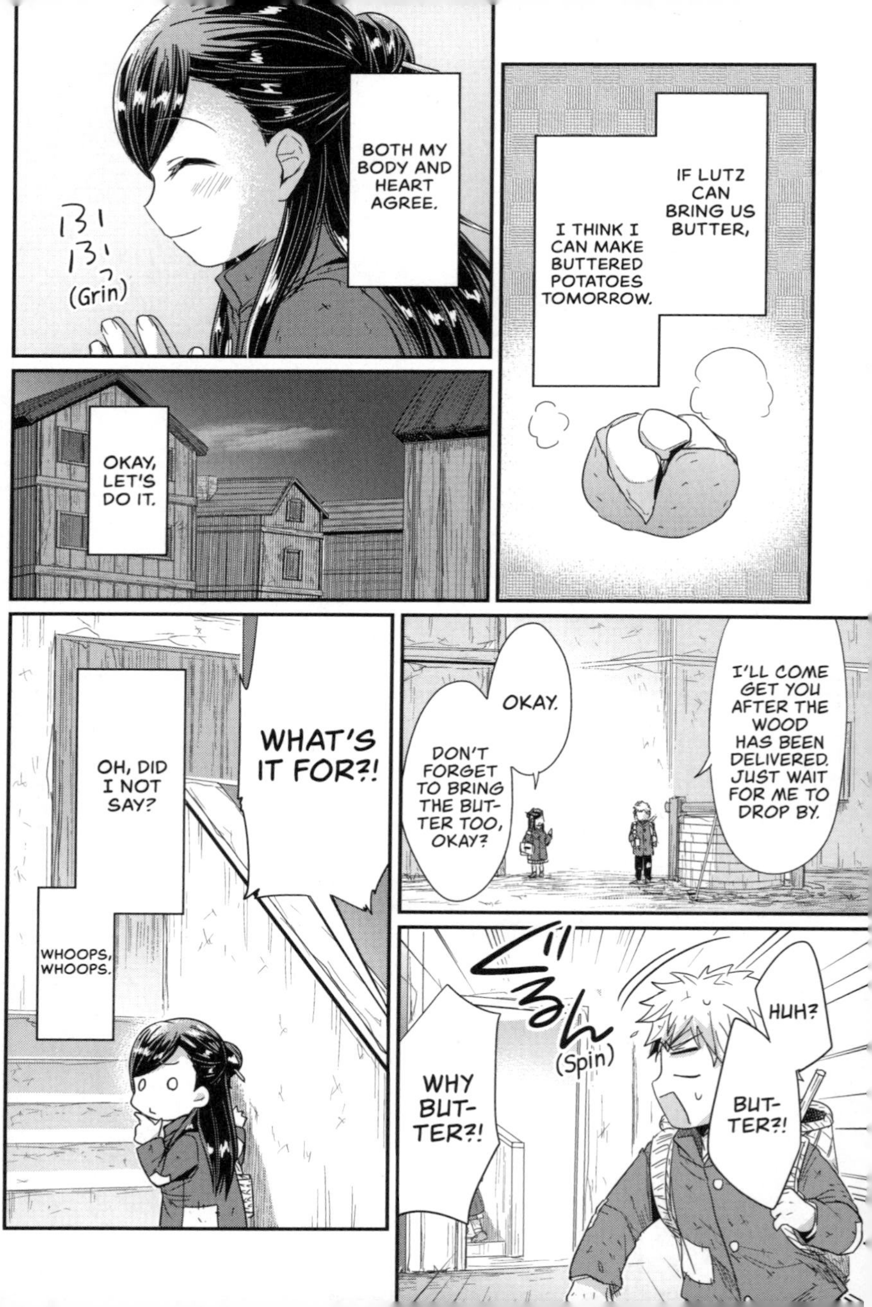
IF LUTZ CAN BRING US BUTTER,
I THINK I CAN MAKE BUTTERED POTATOES TOMORROW.
BOTH MY BODY AND HEART AGREE.
ふふっ
(Grin)
OKAY, LET'S DO IT.
I'LL COME GET YOU AFTER THE WOOD HAS BEEN DELIVERED. JUST WAIT FOR ME TO DROP BY.
OKAY.
DON'T FORGET TO BRING THE BUT-TER TOO, OKAY?
ぐるん
(Spin)
HUH?
BUT-TER?!
WHY BUT-TER?!
WHAT'S IT FOR?!
OH, DID I NOT SAY?
WHOOPS, WHOOPS.

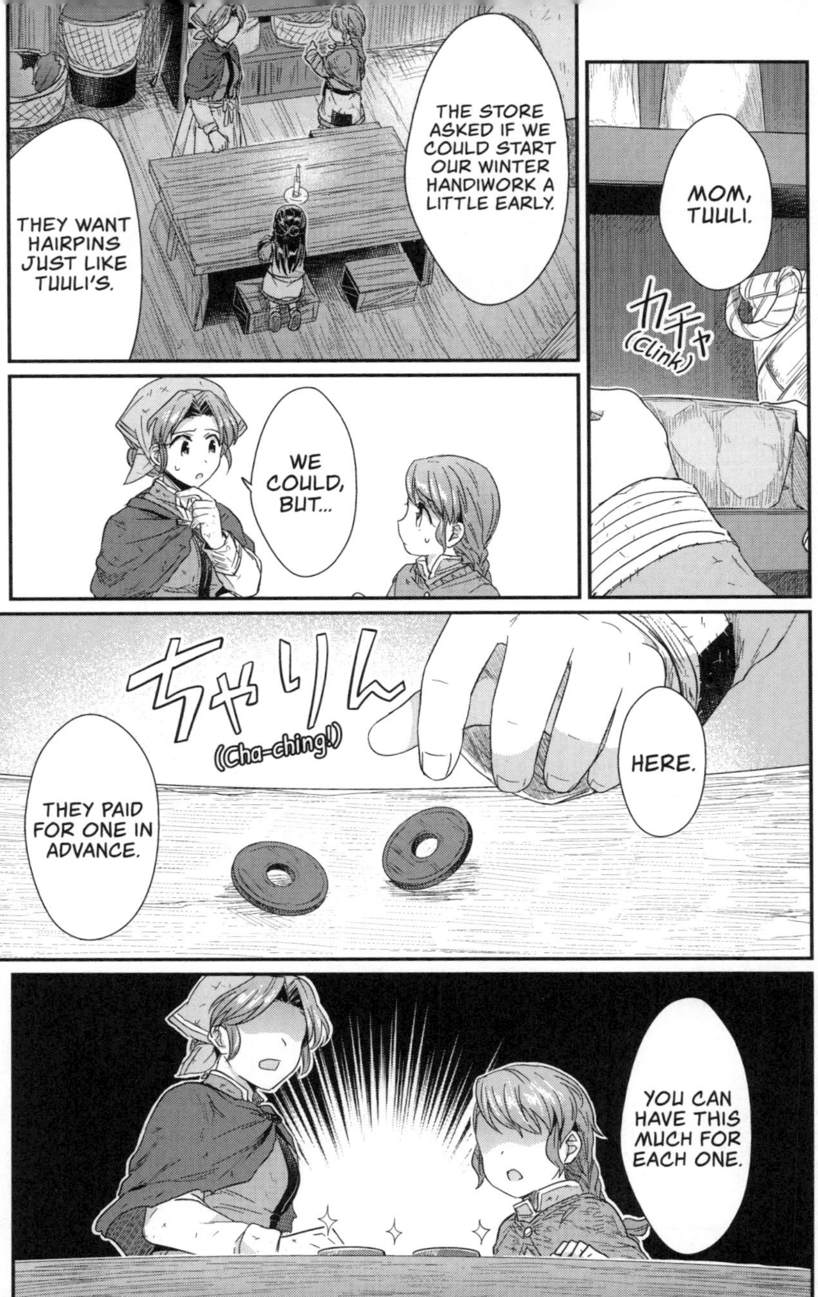
MOM, TUULI.
カチャ
(Clink)
THE STORE ASKED IF WE COULD START OUR WINTER HANDIWORK A LITTLE EARLY.
THEY WANT HAIRPINS JUST LIKE TUULI'S.
WE COULD, BUT...
HERE.
ちゃりん
(Cha-ching!)
THEY PAID FOR ONE IN ADVANCE.
YOU CAN HAVE THIS MUCH FOR EACH ONE.

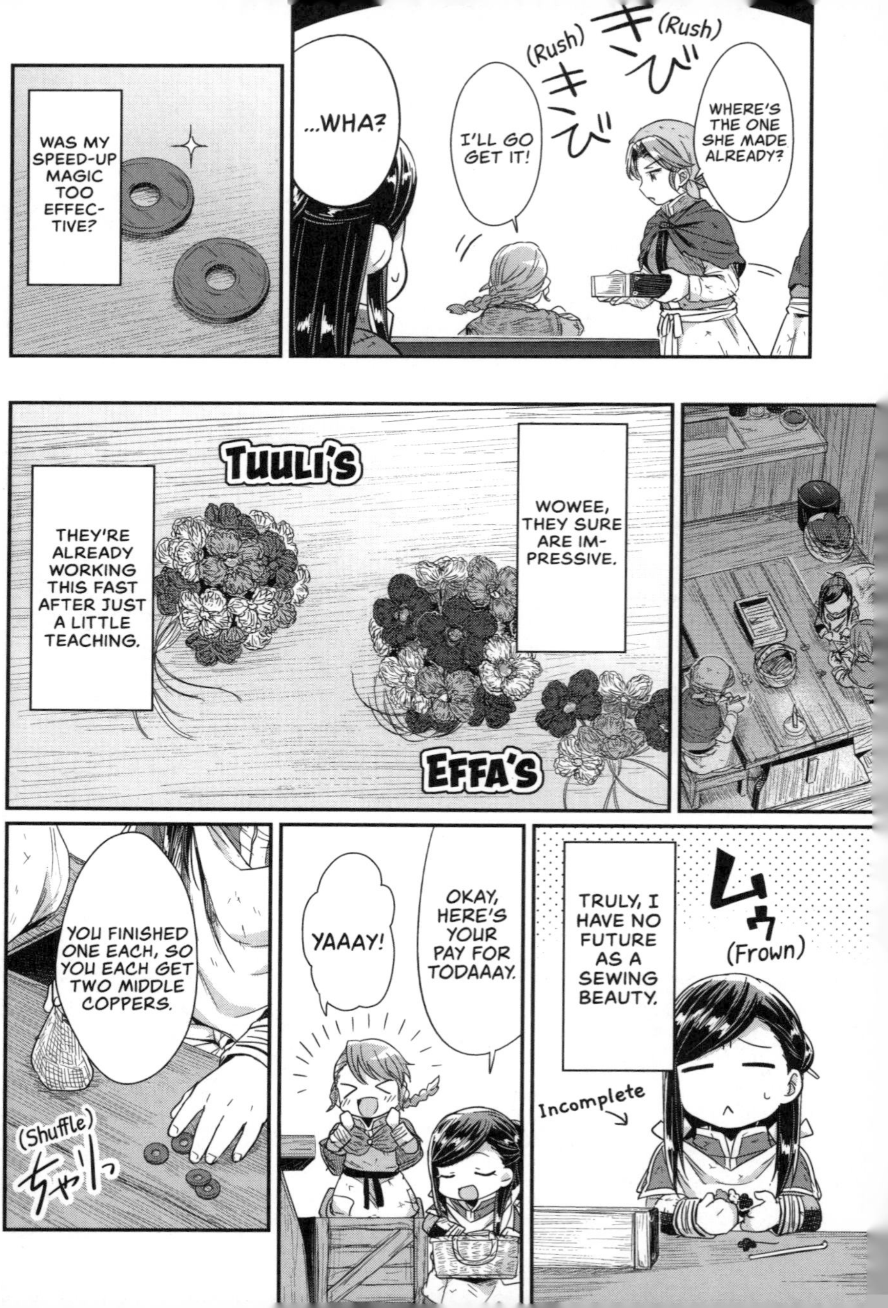
(Rush)
きびきび
(Rush)
WHERE'S THE ONE SHE MADE ALREADY?
I'LL GO GET IT!
...WHA?
WAS MY SPEED-UP MAGIC TOO EFFECTIVE?
WOWEE, THEY SURE ARE IMPRESSIVE.
Tuuli's
Effa's
THEY'RE ALREADY WORKING THIS FAST AFTER JUST A LITTLE TEACHING.
TRULY, I HAVE NO FUTURE AS A SEWING BEAUTY.
ムゥ
(Frown)
Incomplete
OKAY, HERE'S YOUR PAY FOR TODAAAY.
YAAAY!
YOU FINISHED ONE EACH, SO YOU EACH GET TWO MIDDLE COPPERS.
(Shuffle)
ちゃりっ

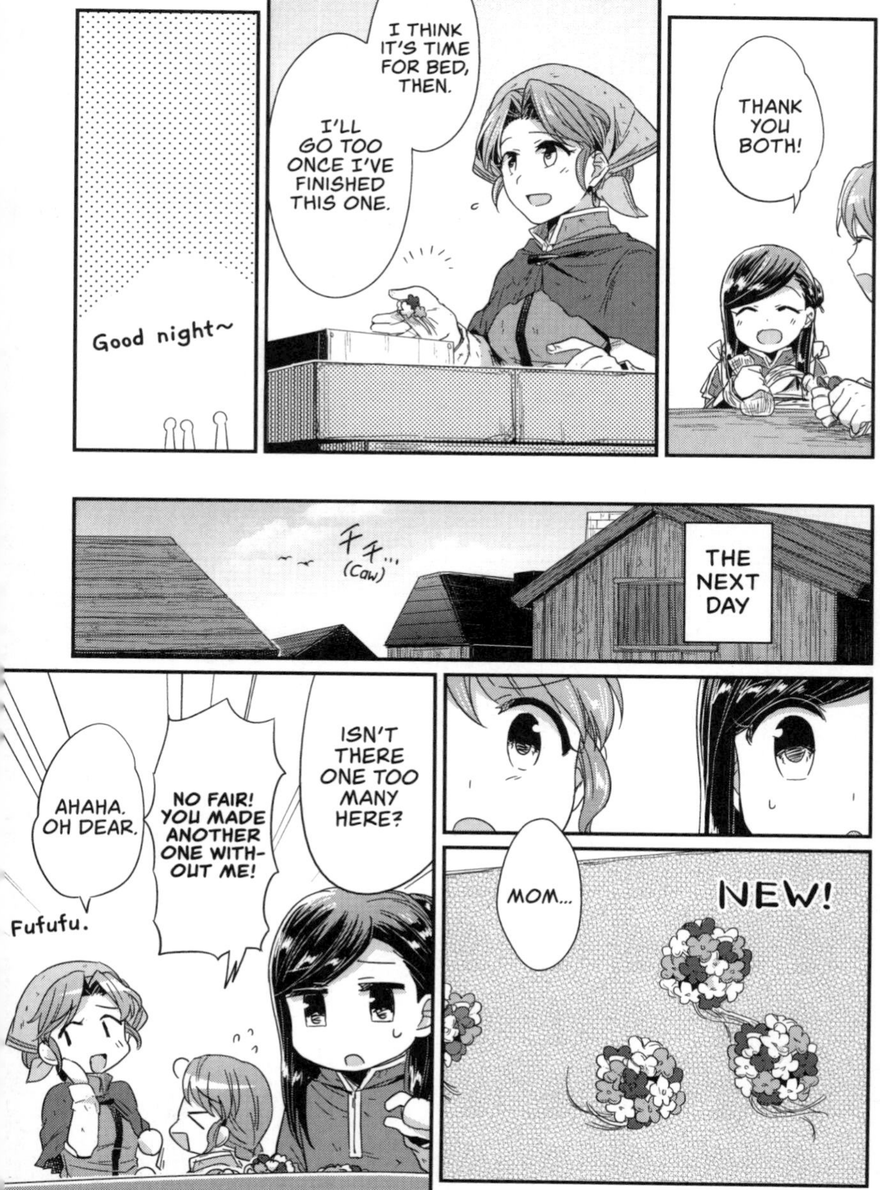
THANK YOU BOTH!
I THINK IT'S TIME FOR BED, THEN.
I'LL GO TOO ONCE I'VE FINISHED THIS ONE.
Good night~
THE NEXT DAY
チチ... (Caw)
MOM...
NEW!
ISN'T THERE ONE TOO MANY HERE?
NO FAIR! YOU MADE ANOTHER ONE WITH-OUT ME!
AHAHA. OH DEAR.
Fufufu.

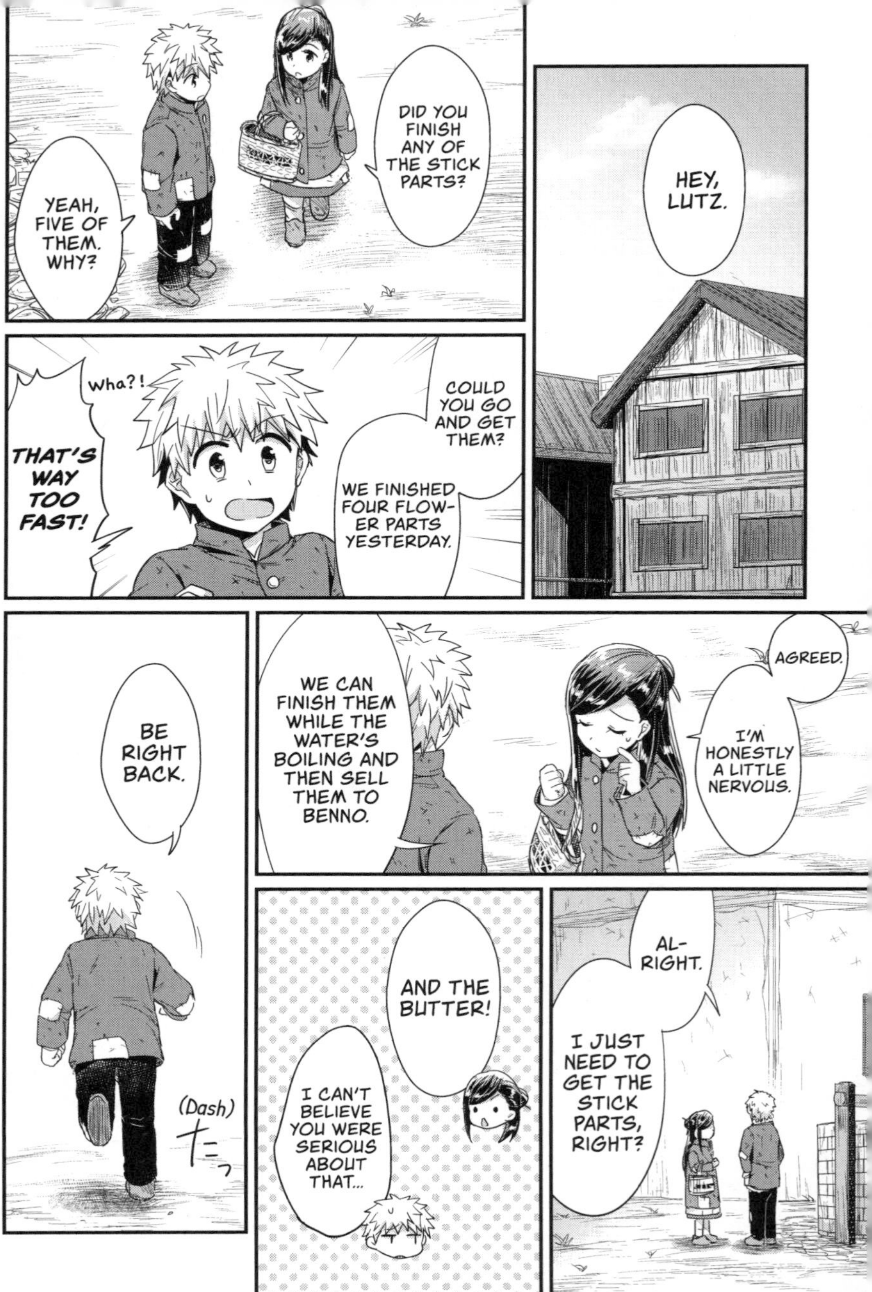
HEY, LUTZ.
DID YOU FINISH ANY OF THE STICK PARTS?
YEAH, FIVE OF THEM. WHY?
WE FINISHED FOUR FLOWER PARTS YESTERDAY.
COULD YOU GO AND GET THEM?
Wha?!
THAT'S WAY TOO FAST!
AGREED.
I'M HONESTLY A LITTLE NERVOUS.
WE CAN FINISH THEM WHILE THE WATER'S BOILING AND THEN SELL THEM TO BENNO.
AL-RIGHT.
I JUST NEED TO GET THE STICK PARTS, RIGHT?
AND THE BUTTER!
I CAN'T BELIEVE YOU WERE SERIOUS ABOUT THAT...
BE RIGHT BACK.
(Dash)

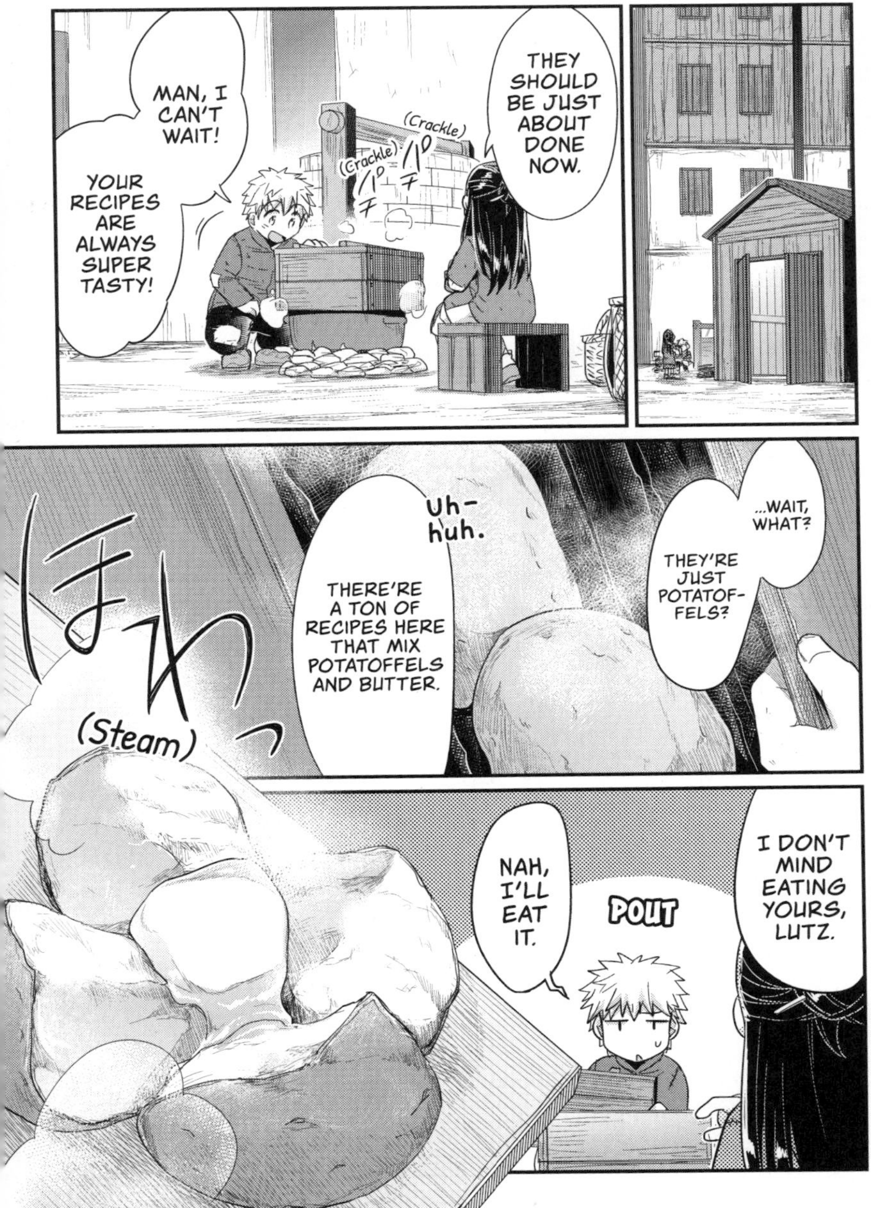
THEY SHOULD BE JUST ABOUT DONE NOW.
(Crackle)
(Crackle)
MAN, I CAN'T WAIT!
YOUR RECIPES ARE ALWAYS SUPER TASTY!
...WAIT, WHAT?
THEY'RE JUST POTATOFFELS?
Uh-huh.
THERE'RE A TON OF RECIPES HERE THAT MIX POTATOFFELS AND BUTTER.
I DON'T MIND EATING YOURS, LUTZ.
POUT
NAH, I'LL EAT IT.
ほわっ
(Steam)

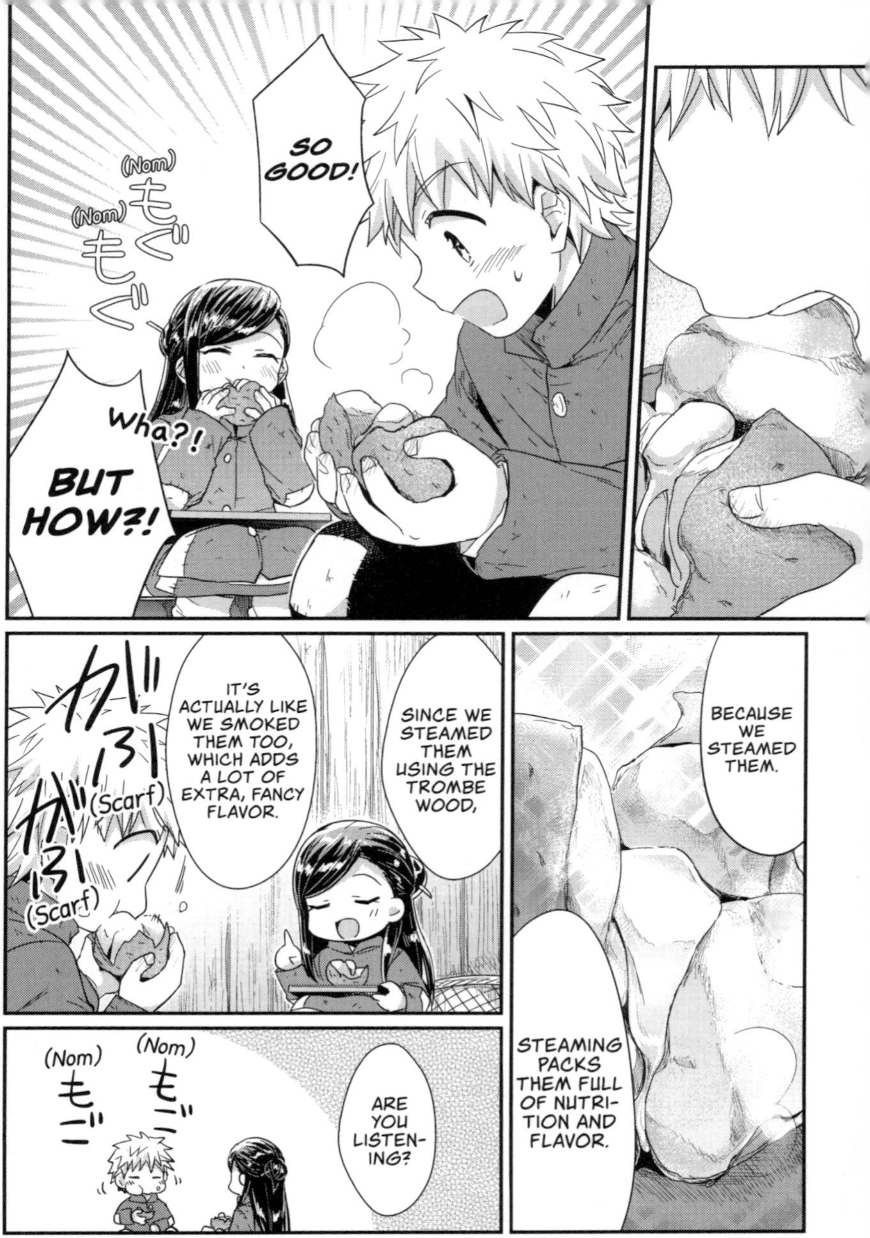
SO GOOD!
(Nom) もぐ
(Nom) もぐ
Wha?!
BUT HOW?!
BECAUSE WE STEAMED THEM.
STEAMING PACKS THEM FULL OF NUTRI-TION AND FLAVOR.
SINCE WE STEAMED THEM USING THE TROMBE WOOD,
IT'S ACTUALLY LIKE WE SMOKED THEM TOO, WHICH ADDS A LOT OF EXTRA, FANCY FLAVOR.
がぶ (Scarf)
がぶ (Scarf)
ARE YOU LISTEN-ING?
(Nom) もご
(Nom) もご

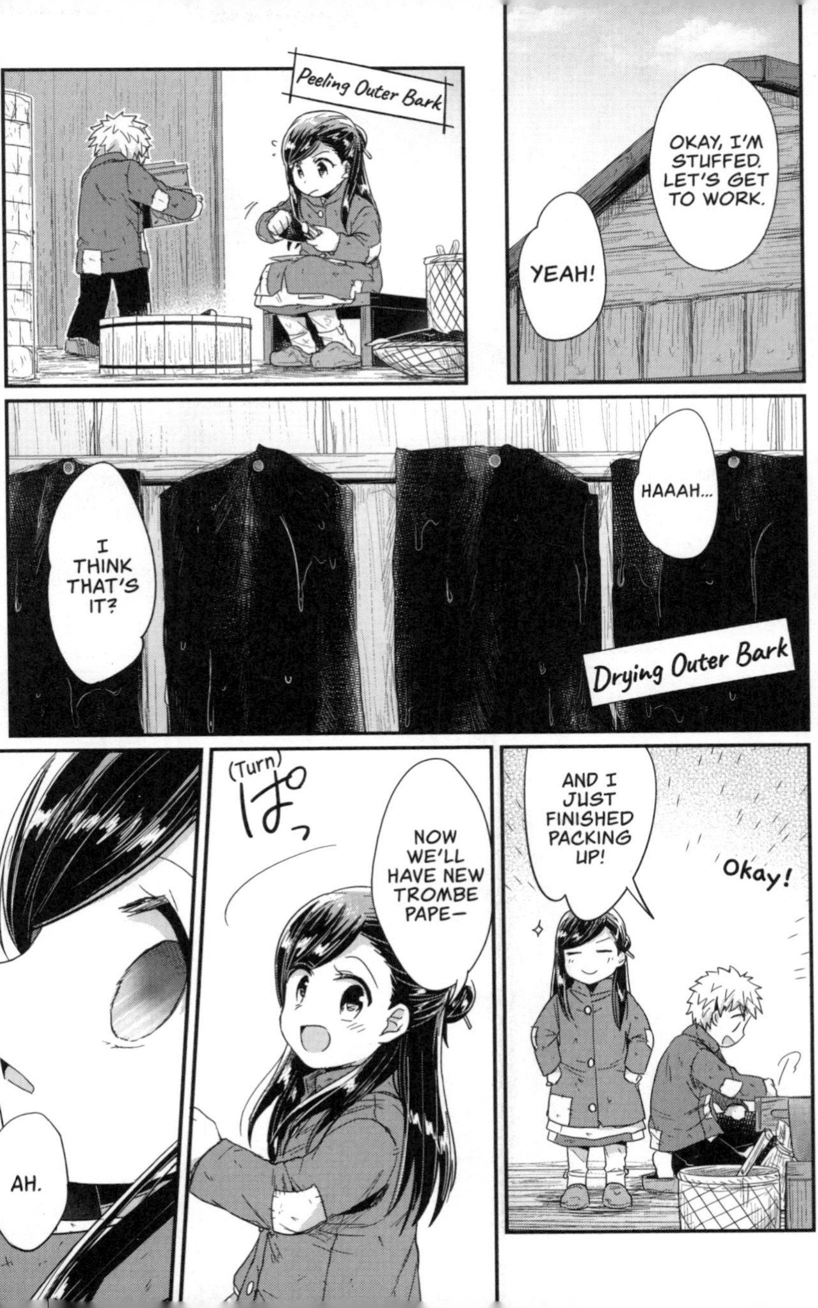
OKAY, I'M STUFFED. LET'S GET TO WORK.
YEAH!
Peeling Outer Bark
HAAAH...
Drying Outer Bark
I THINK THAT'S IT?
AND I JUST FINISHED PACKING UP!
Okay!
NOW WE'LL HAVE NEW TROMBE PAPE—
(Turn)
ぱっ
AH.

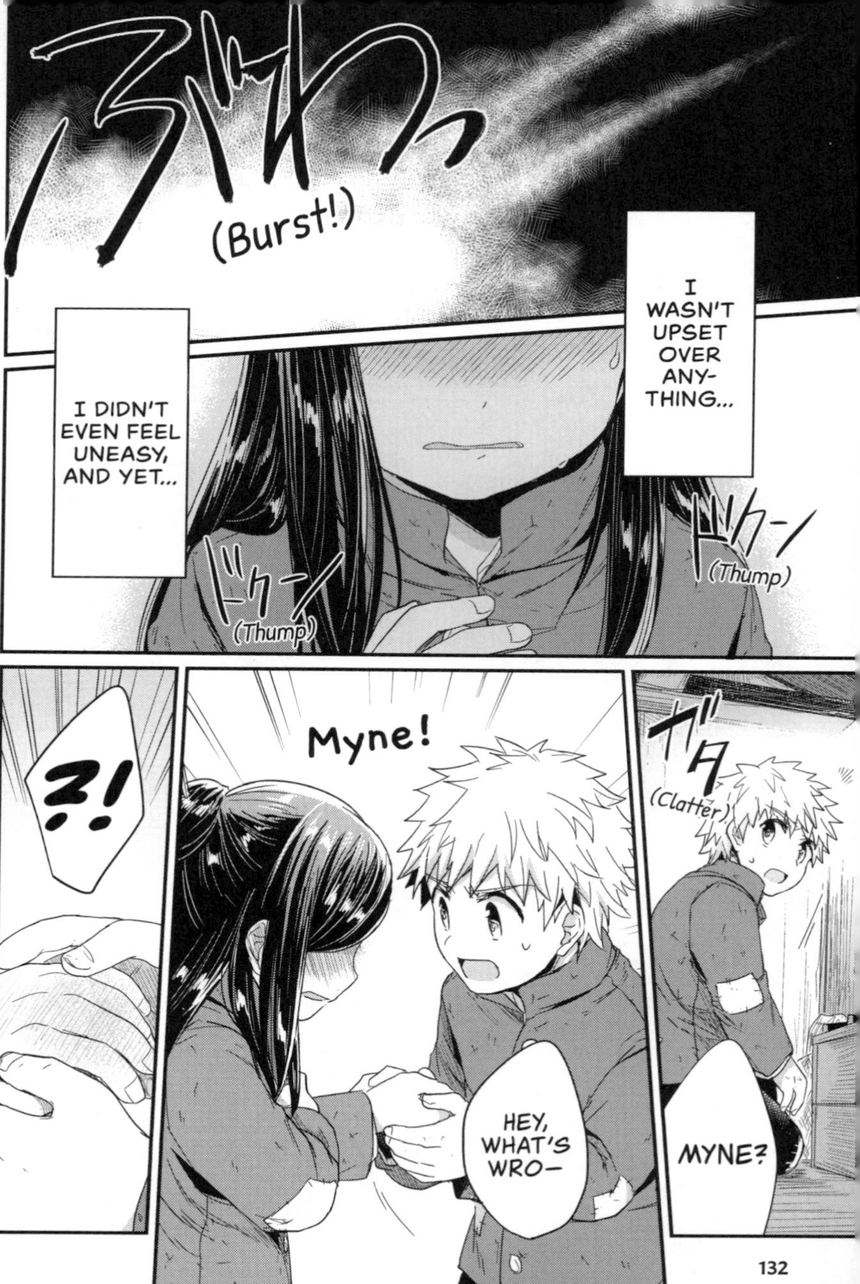

(Burst!)
I WASN'T UPSET OVER ANY-THING...
I DIDN'T EVEN FEEL UNEASY, AND YET...
(Thump)
(Thump)
(Clatter)
MYNE?
Myne!
HEY, WHAT'S WRO-
?!

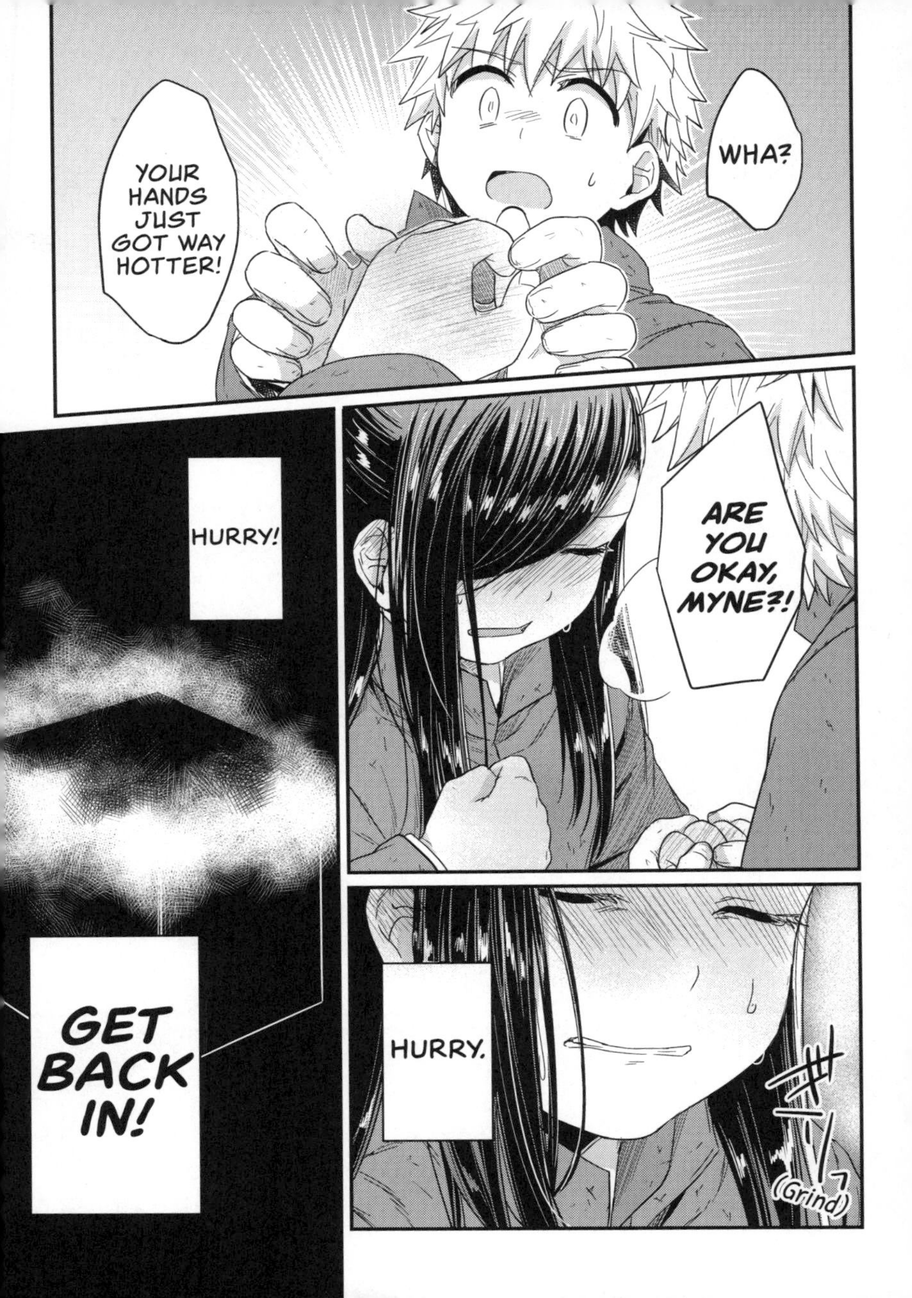
WHA?
YOUR HANDS JUST GOT WAY HOTTER!
ARE YOU OKAY, MYNE?!
HURRY.
(Grind)
HURRY!
GET BACK IN!

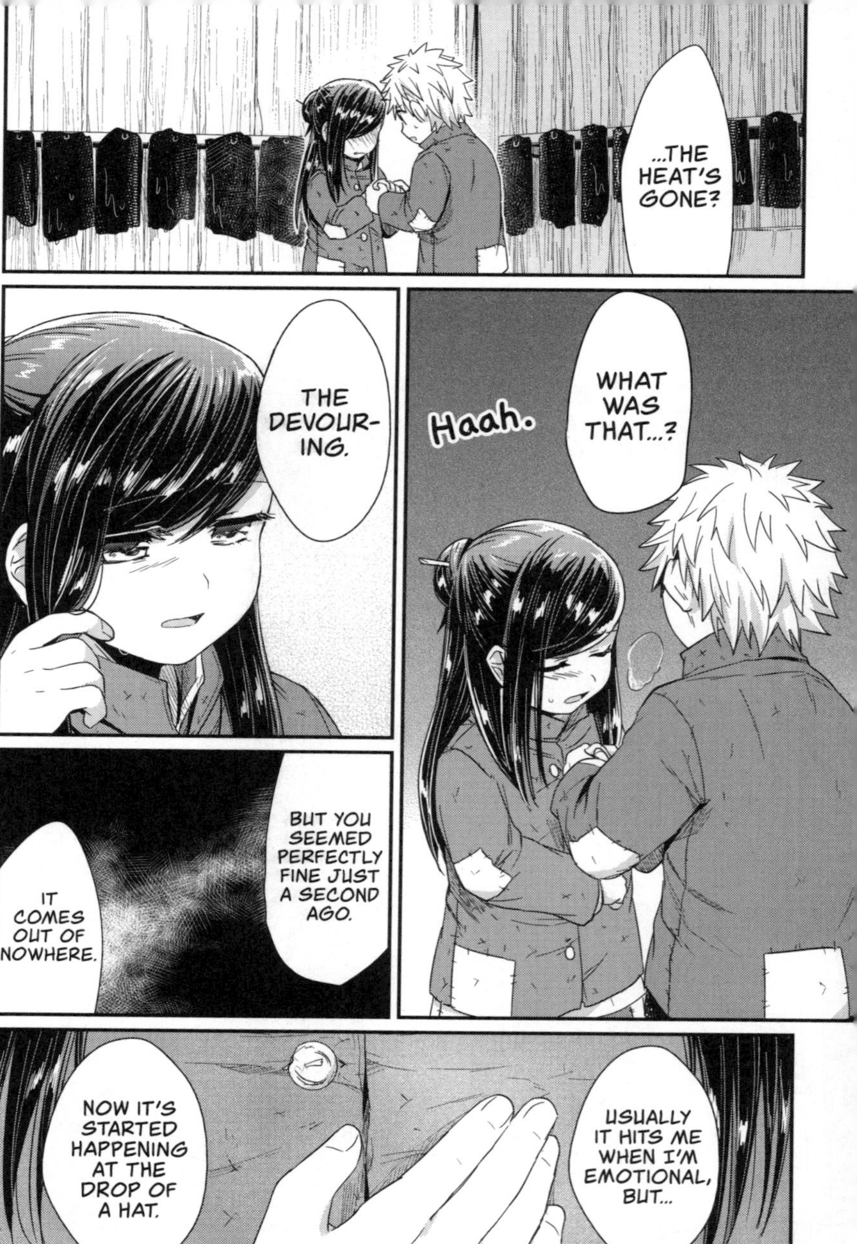
...THE HEAT'S GONE?
Haah.
WHAT WAS THAT...?
THE DEVOUR-ING.
BUT YOU SEEMED PERFECTLY FINE JUST A SECOND AGO.
IT COMES OUT OF NOWHERE.
USUALLY IT HITS ME WHEN I'M EMOTIONAL, BUT...
NOW IT'S STARTED HAPPENING AT THE DROP OF A HAT.

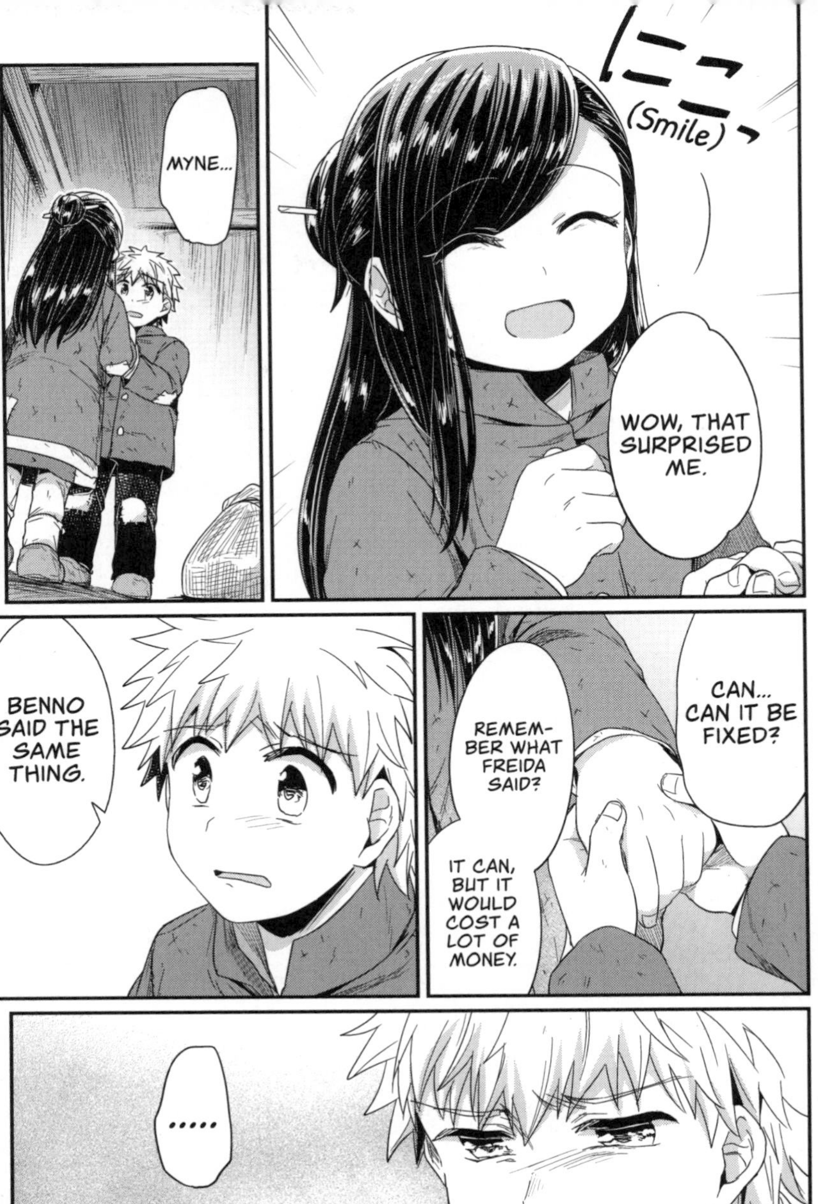
(Smile)
WOW, THAT SURPRISED ME.
MYNE...
CAN... CAN IT BE FIXED?
REMEMBER WHAT FREIDA SAID?
IT CAN, BUT IT WOULD COST A LOT OF MONEY.
BENNO SAID THE SAME THING.
......

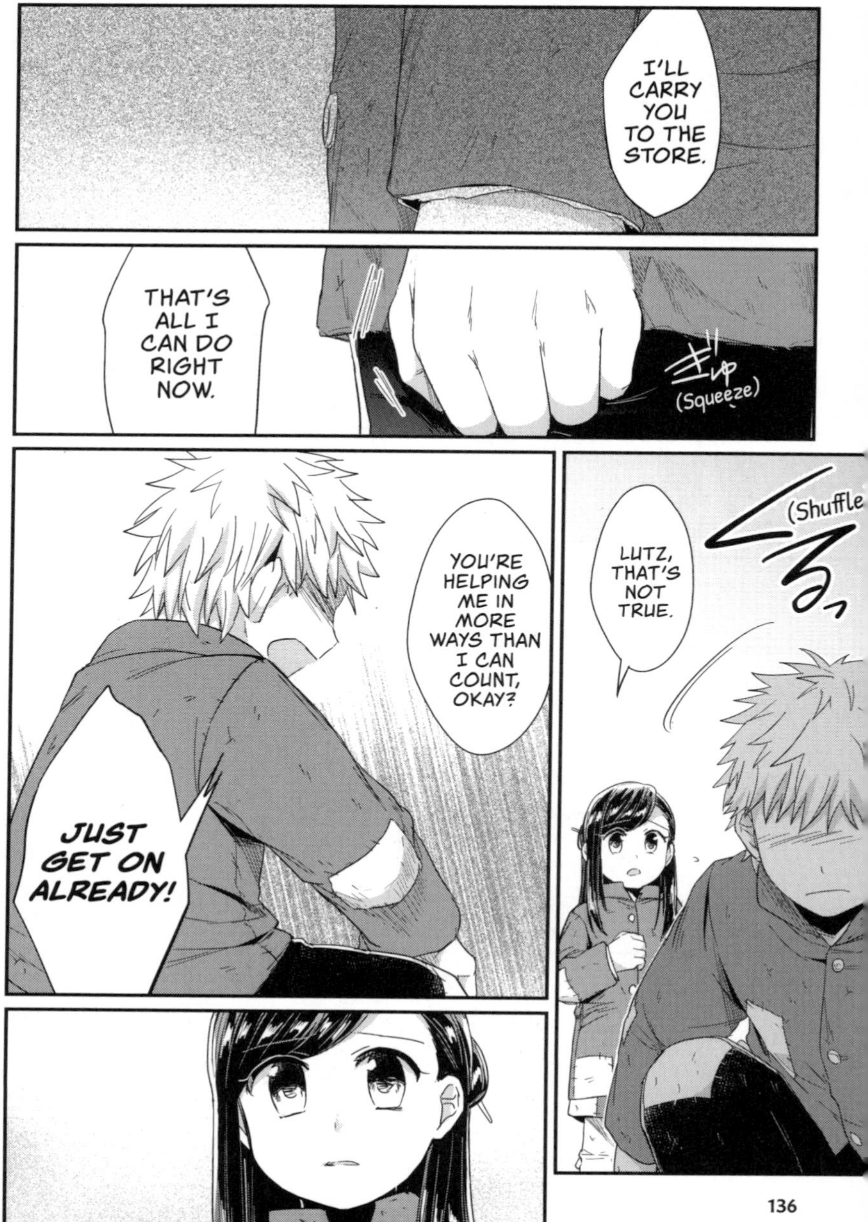
I'LL CARRY YOU TO THE STORE.
(Squeeze)
THAT'S ALL I CAN DO RIGHT NOW.
(Shuffle
LUTZ, THAT'S NOT TRUE.
YOU'RE HELPING ME IN MORE WAYS THAN I CAN COUNT, OKAY?
JUST GET ON ALREADY!

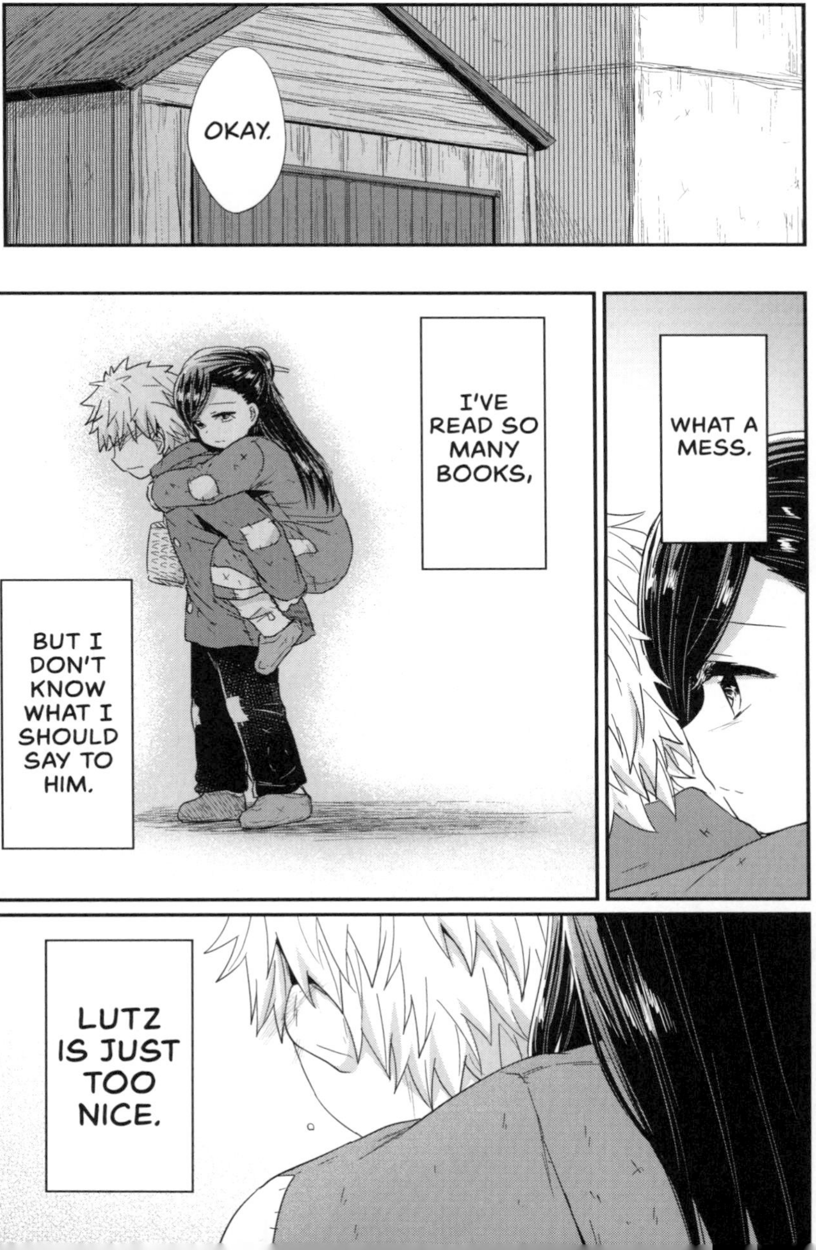
OKAY.
WHAT A MESS.
I'VE READ SO MANY BOOKS,
BUT I DON'T KNOW WHAT I SHOULD SAY TO HIM.
LUTZ IS JUST TOO NICE.

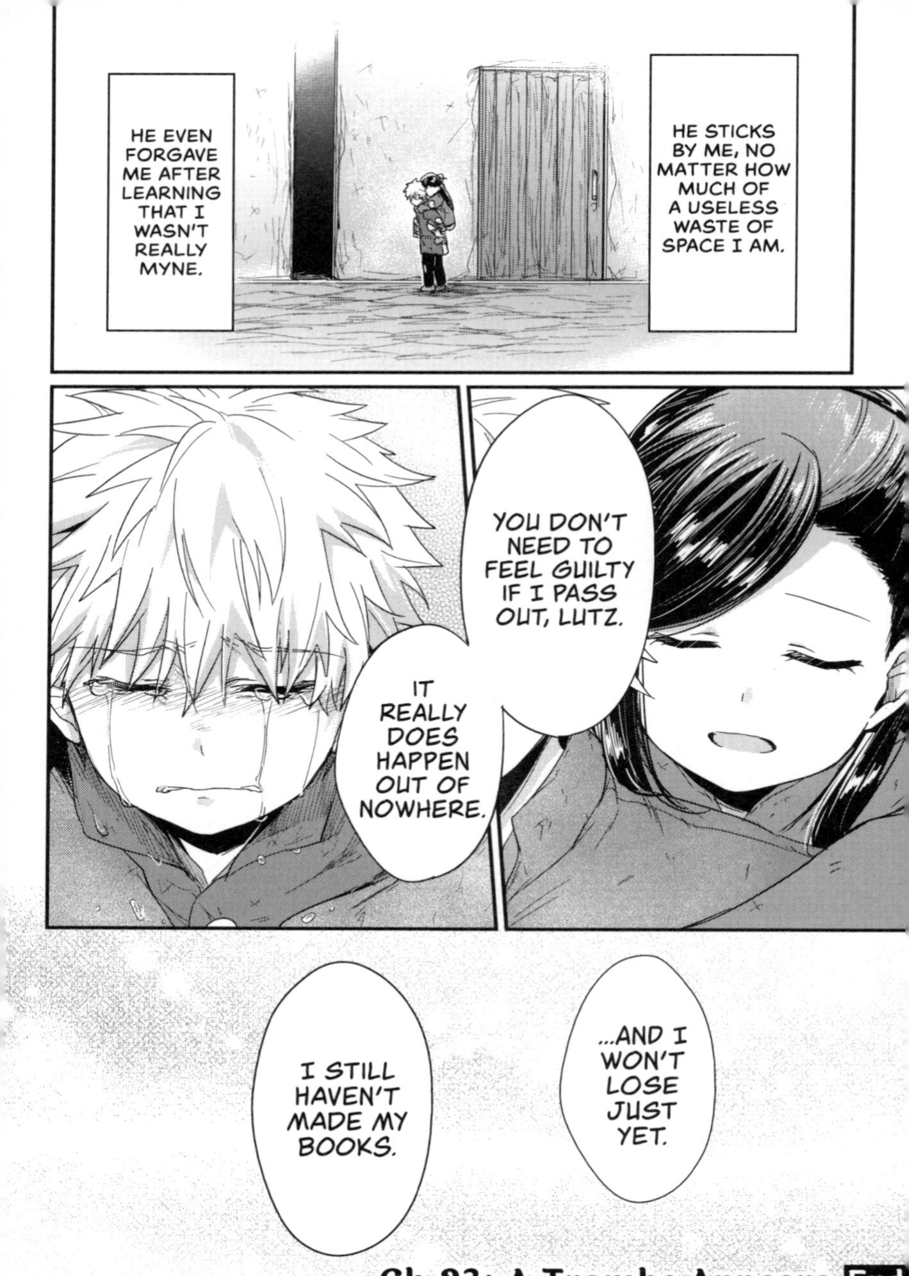
HE STICKS BY ME, NO MATTER HOW MUCH OF A USELESS WASTE OF SPACE I AM.
HE EVEN FORGAVE ME AFTER LEARNING THAT I WASN'T REALLY MYNE.
YOU DON'T NEED TO FEEL GUILTY IF I PASS OUT, LUTZ.
IT REALLY DOES HAPPEN OUT OF NOWHERE.
I STILL HAVEN'T MADE MY BOOKS.
...AND I WON'T LOSE JUST YET.

Ch.23: A Trombe Appears End

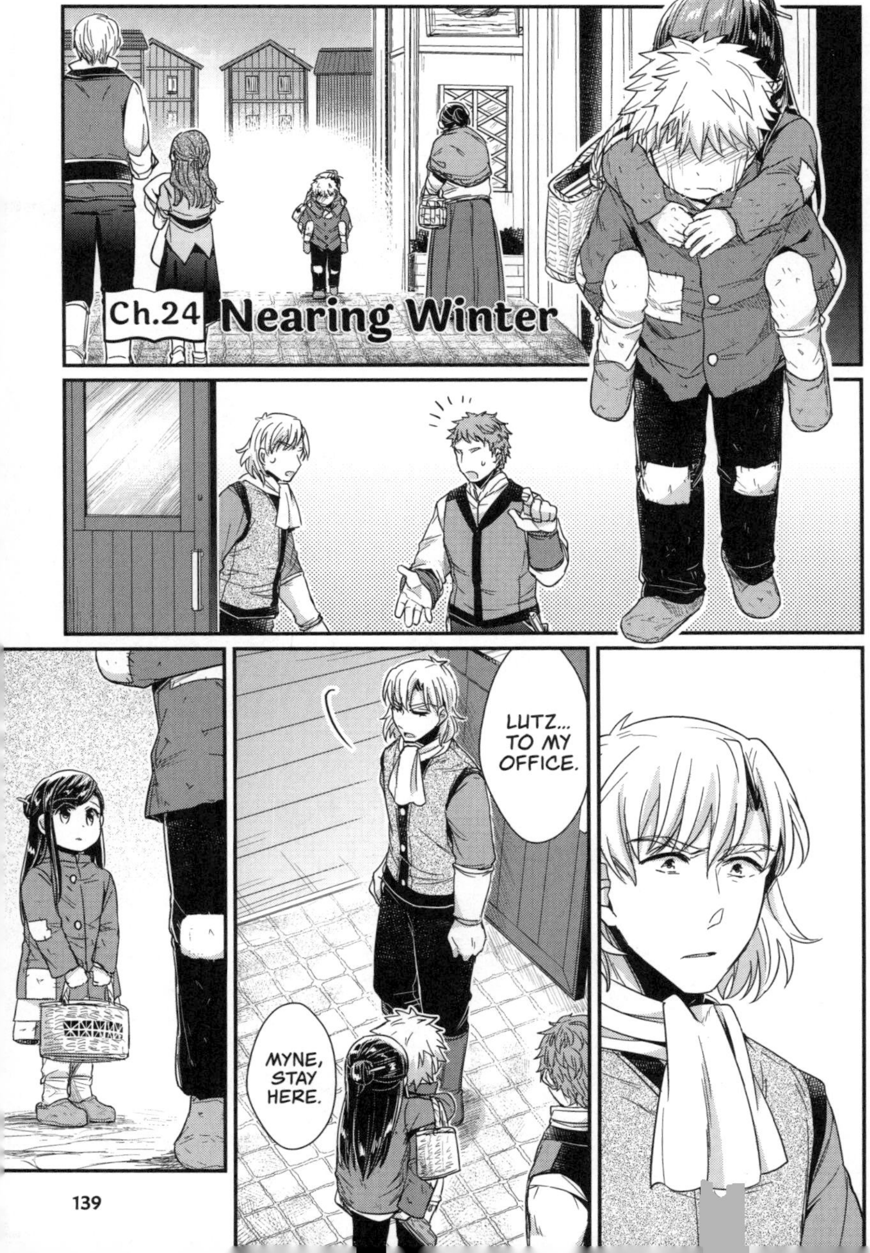
Ch.24 Nearing Winter
LUTZ... TO MY OFFICE.
MYNE, STAY HERE.

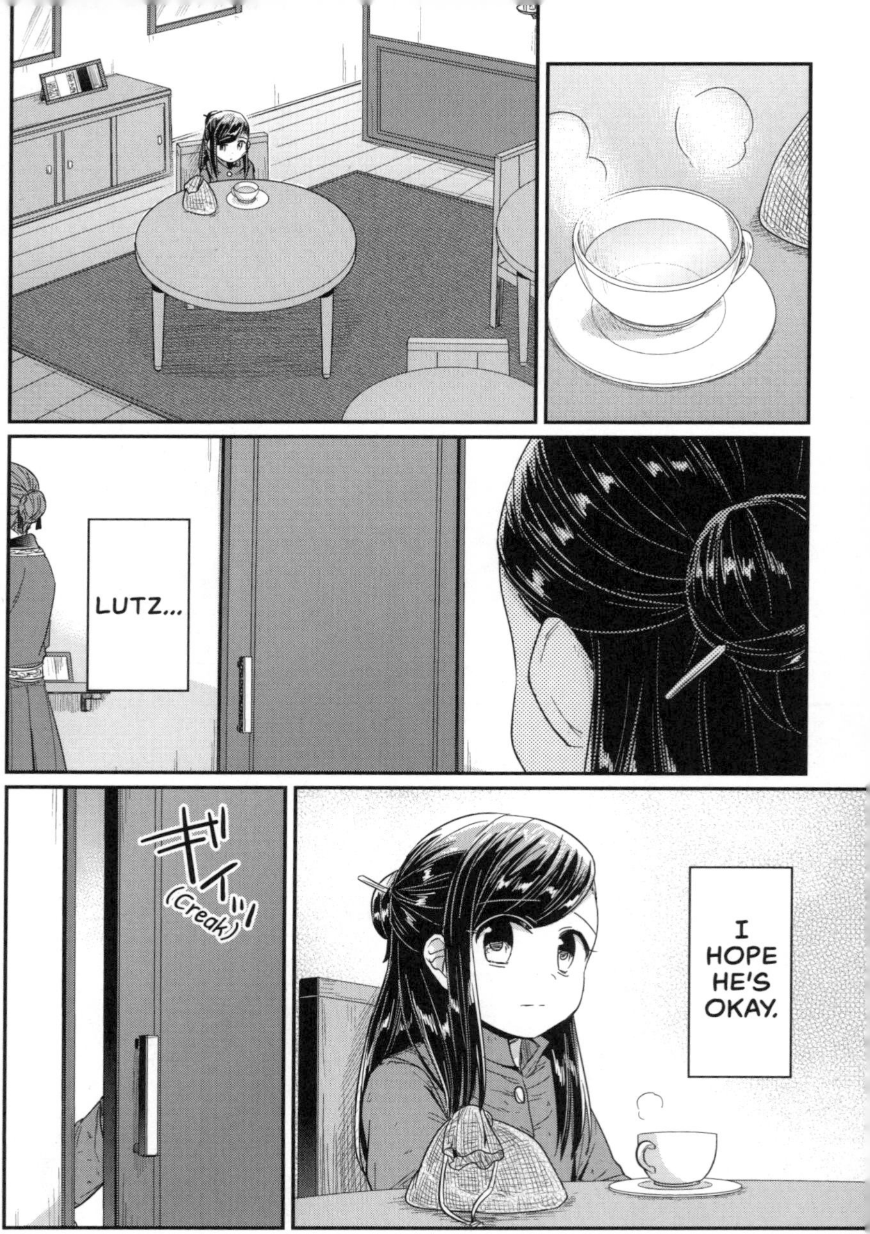
LUTZ...
I HOPE HE'S OKAY.
ギイッ
(Creak)

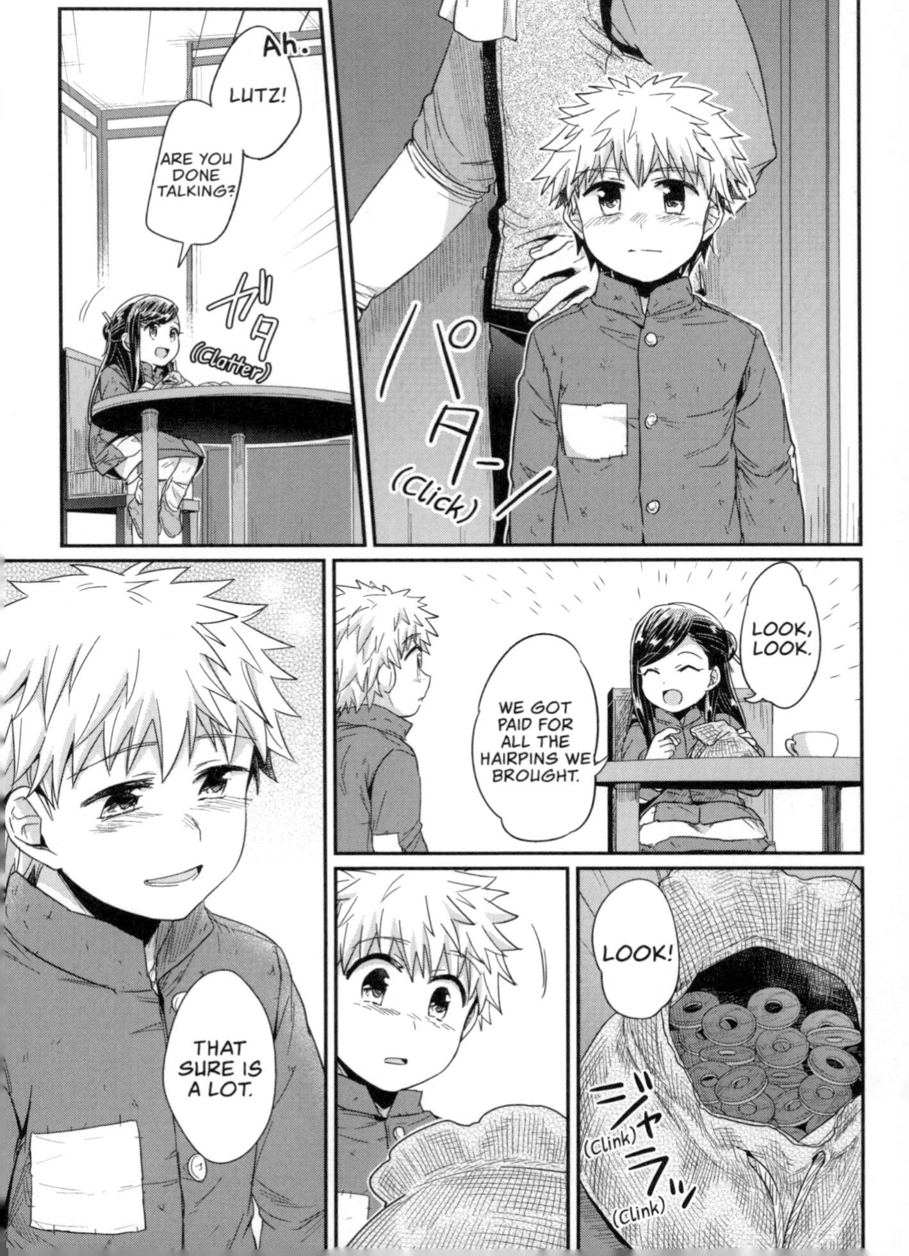
パターン
(Click)
Ah.
LUTZ!
ARE YOU DONE TALKING?
ガタ
(Clatter)
LOOK, LOOK.
WE GOT PAID FOR ALL THE HAIRPINS WE BROUGHT.
LOOK!
ジャラッ
(Clink)
(Clink)
THAT SURE IS A LOT.

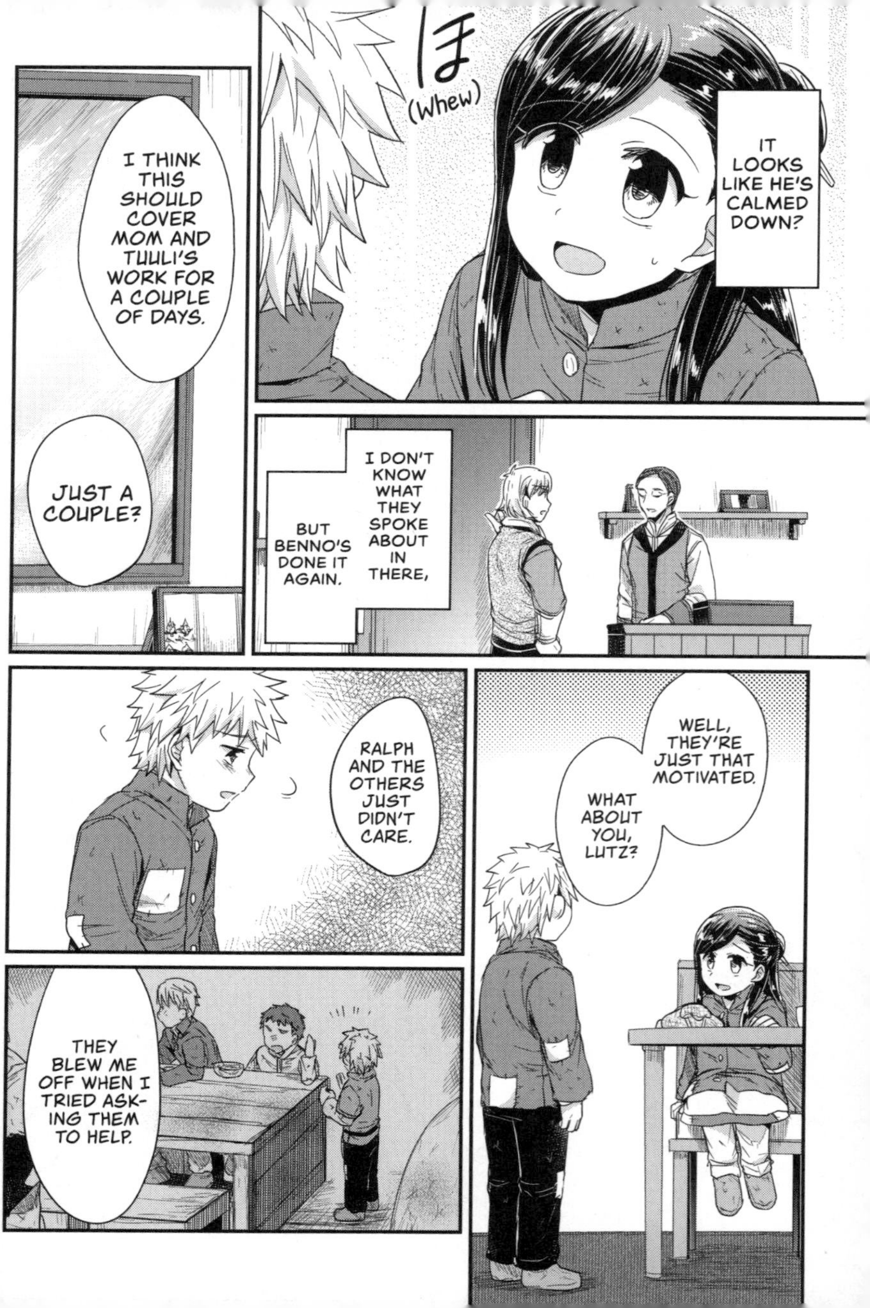
ほ
(Whew)
IT LOOKS LIKE HE'S CALMED DOWN?
I DON'T KNOW WHAT THEY SPOKE ABOUT IN THERE,
BUT BENNO'S DONE IT AGAIN.
I THINK THIS SHOULD COVER MOM AND TUULI'S WORK FOR A COUPLE OF DAYS.
JUST A COUPLE?
WELL, THEY'RE JUST THAT MOTIVATED.
WHAT ABOUT YOU, LUTZ?
RALPH AND THE OTHERS JUST DIDN'T CARE.
THEY BLEW ME OFF WHEN I TRIED ASK-ING THEM TO HELP.

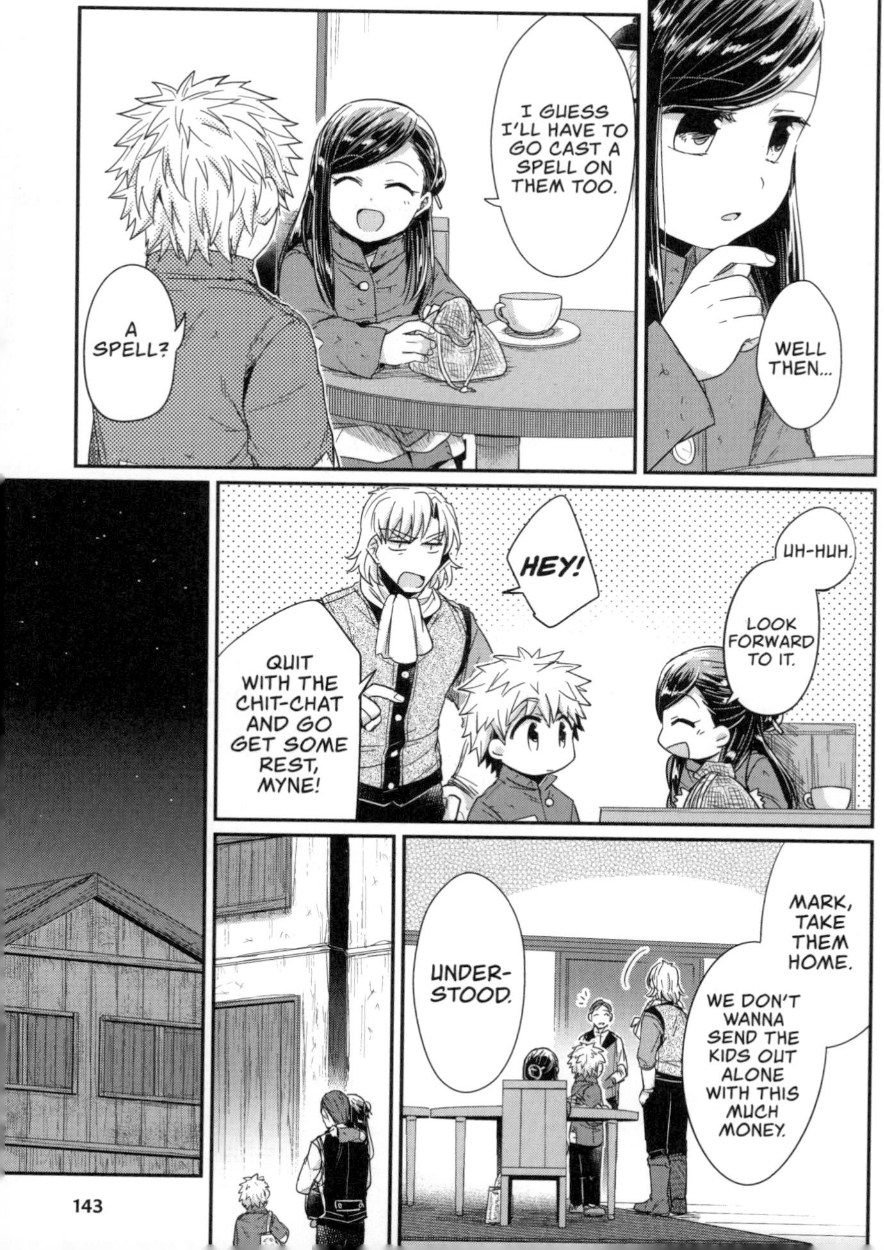
WELL THEN...
I GUESS I'LL HAVE TO GO CAST A SPELL ON THEM TOO.
A SPELL?
UH-HUH.
LOOK FORWARD TO IT.
HEY!
QUIT WITH THE CHIT-CHAT AND GO GET SOME REST, MYNE!
MARK, TAKE THEM HOME.
WE DON'T WANNA SEND THE KIDS OUT ALONE WITH THIS MUCH MONEY.
UNDER-STOOD.

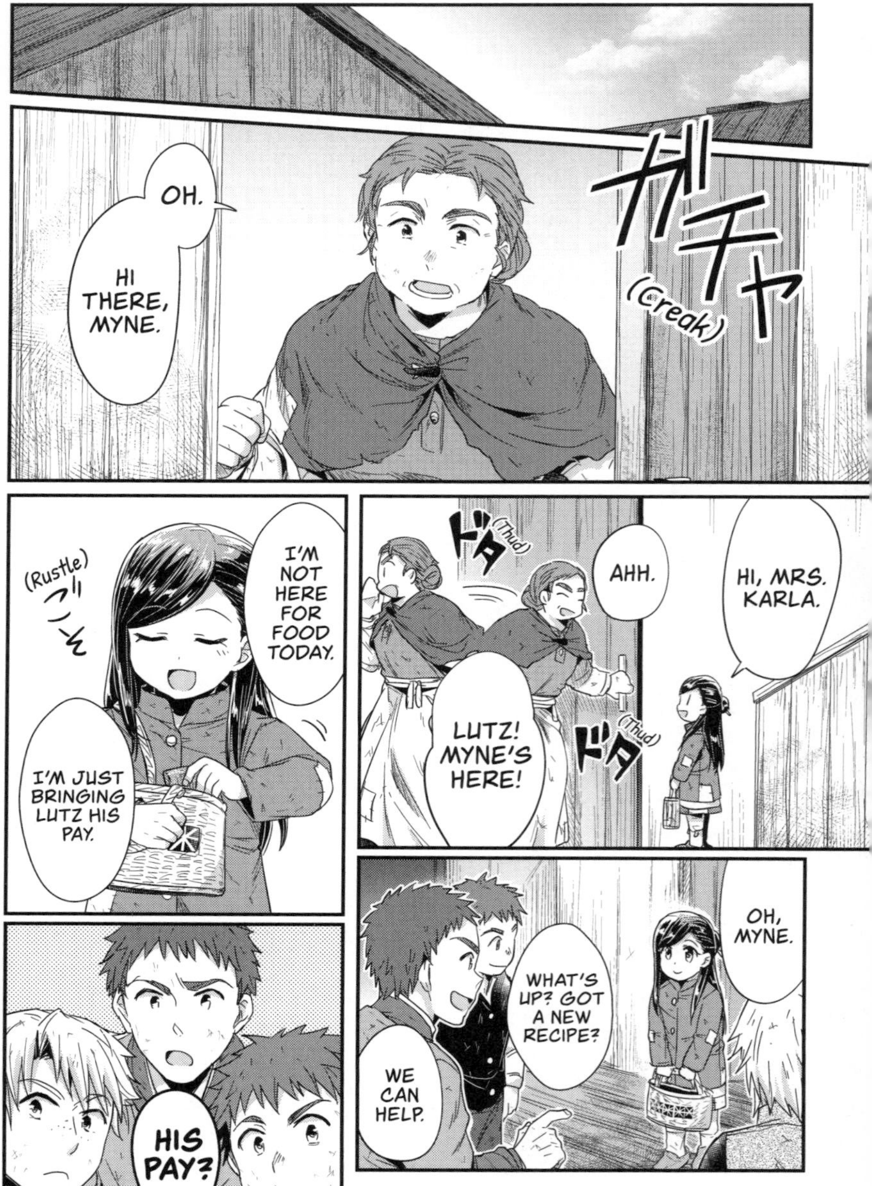
ガチャ
(Creak)
OH.
HI THERE, MYNE.
HI, MRS. KARLA.
AHH.
ドタ
(Thud)
ドタ
(Thud)
LUTZ! MYNE'S HERE!
(Rustle)
I'M NOT HERE FOR FOOD TODAY.
I'M JUST BRINGING LUTZ HIS PAY.
OH, MYNE.
WHAT'S UP? GOT A NEW RECIPE?
WE CAN HELP.
HIS PAY?

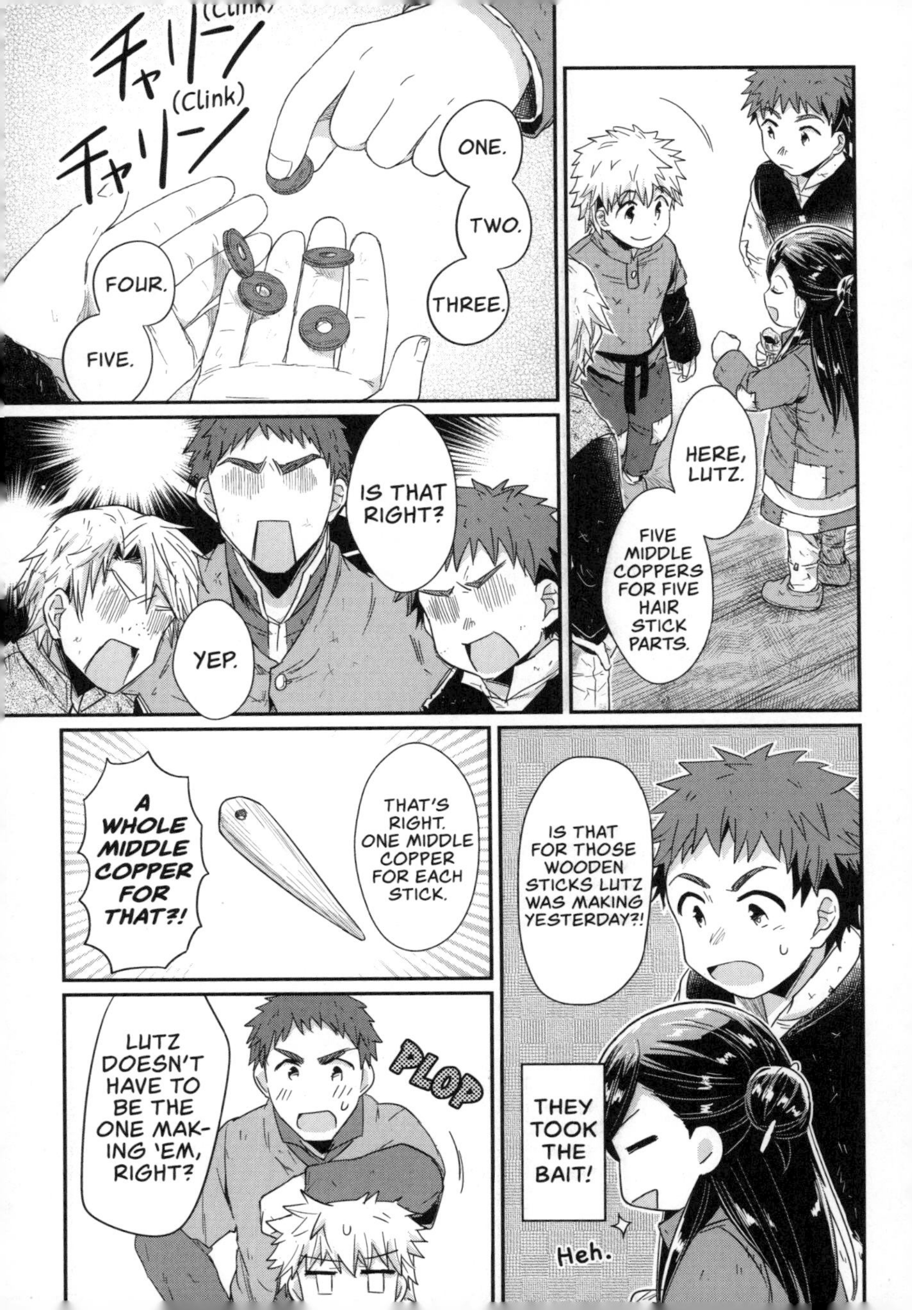
HERE, LUTZ.
FIVE MIDDLE COPPERS FOR FIVE HAIR STICK PARTS.
(Clink)
チャリーン
(Clink)
チャリーン
ONE.
TWO.
THREE.
FOUR.
FIVE.
IS THAT RIGHT?
YEP.
IS THAT FOR THOSE WOODEN STICKS LUTZ WAS MAKING YESTERDAY?!
THEY TOOK THE BAIT!
Heh.
THAT'S RIGHT. ONE MIDDLE COPPER FOR EACH STICK.
A WHOLE MIDDLE COPPER FOR THAT?!
PLOP
LUTZ DOESN'T HAVE TO BE THE ONE MAK-ING 'EM, RIGHT?

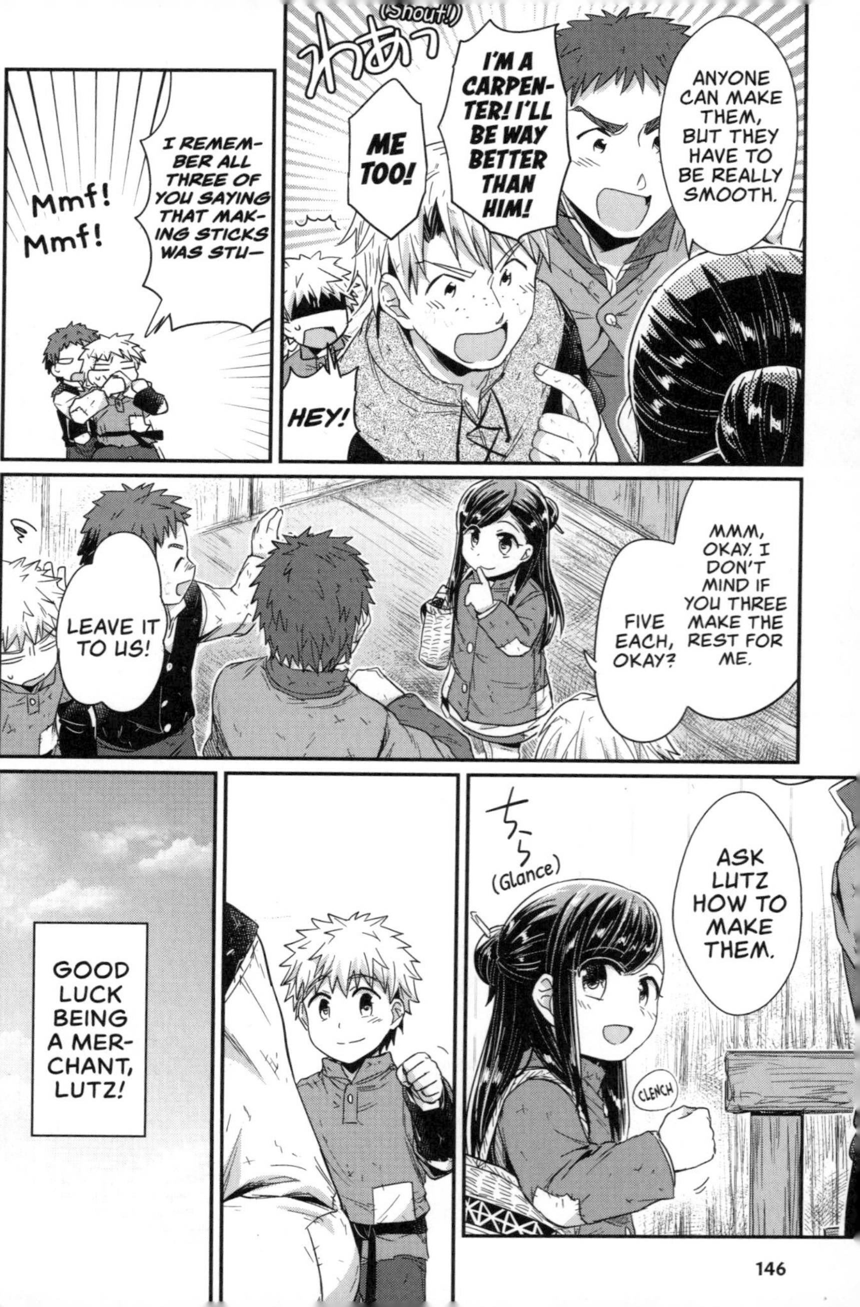
わあっ
(Shout!)
ANYONE CAN MAKE THEM, BUT THEY HAVE TO BE REALLY SMOOTH.
I'M A CARPENTER! I'LL BE WAY BETTER THAN HIM!
ME TOO!
HEY!
I REMEMBER ALL THREE OF YOU SAYING THAT MAKING STICKS WAS STU—
Mmf! Mmf!
MMM, OKAY. I DON'T MIND IF YOU THREE MAKE THE REST FOR ME.
FIVE EACH, OKAY?
LEAVE IT TO US!
ちら
(Glance)
ASK LUTZ HOW TO MAKE THEM.
CLENCH
GOOD LUCK BEING A MERCHANT, LUTZ!

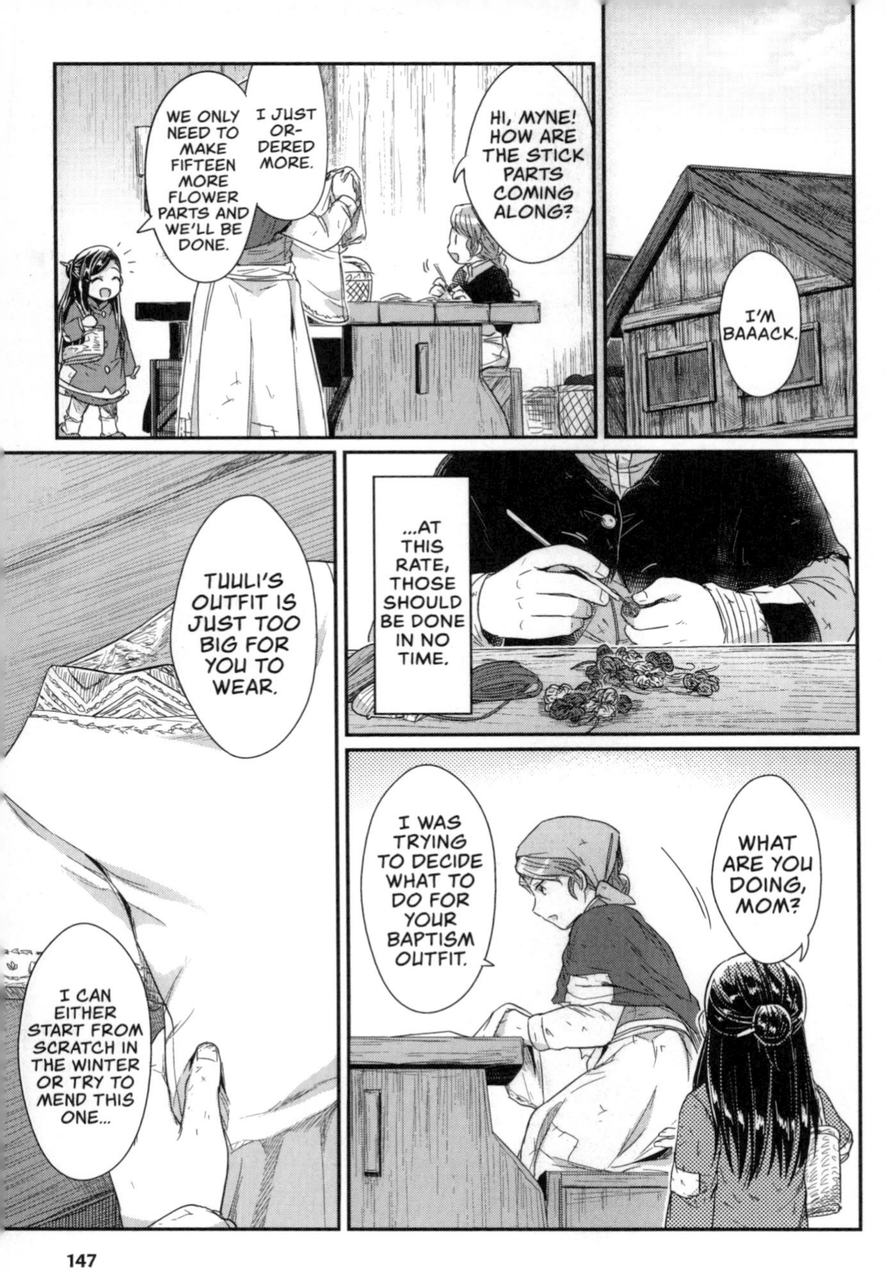

I'M BAAACK.
HI, MYNE! HOW ARE THE STICK PARTS COMING ALONG?
I JUST OR-DERED MORE.
WE ONLY NEED TO MAKE FIFTEEN MORE FLOWER PARTS AND WE'LL BE DONE.
...AT THIS RATE, THOSE SHOULD BE DONE IN NO TIME.
WHAT ARE YOU DOING, MOM?
I WAS TRYING TO DECIDE WHAT TO DO FOR YOUR BAPTISM OUTFIT.
TUULI'S OUTFIT IS JUST TOO BIG FOR YOU TO WEAR.
I CAN EITHER START FROM SCRATCH IN THE WINTER OR TRY TO MEND THIS ONE...

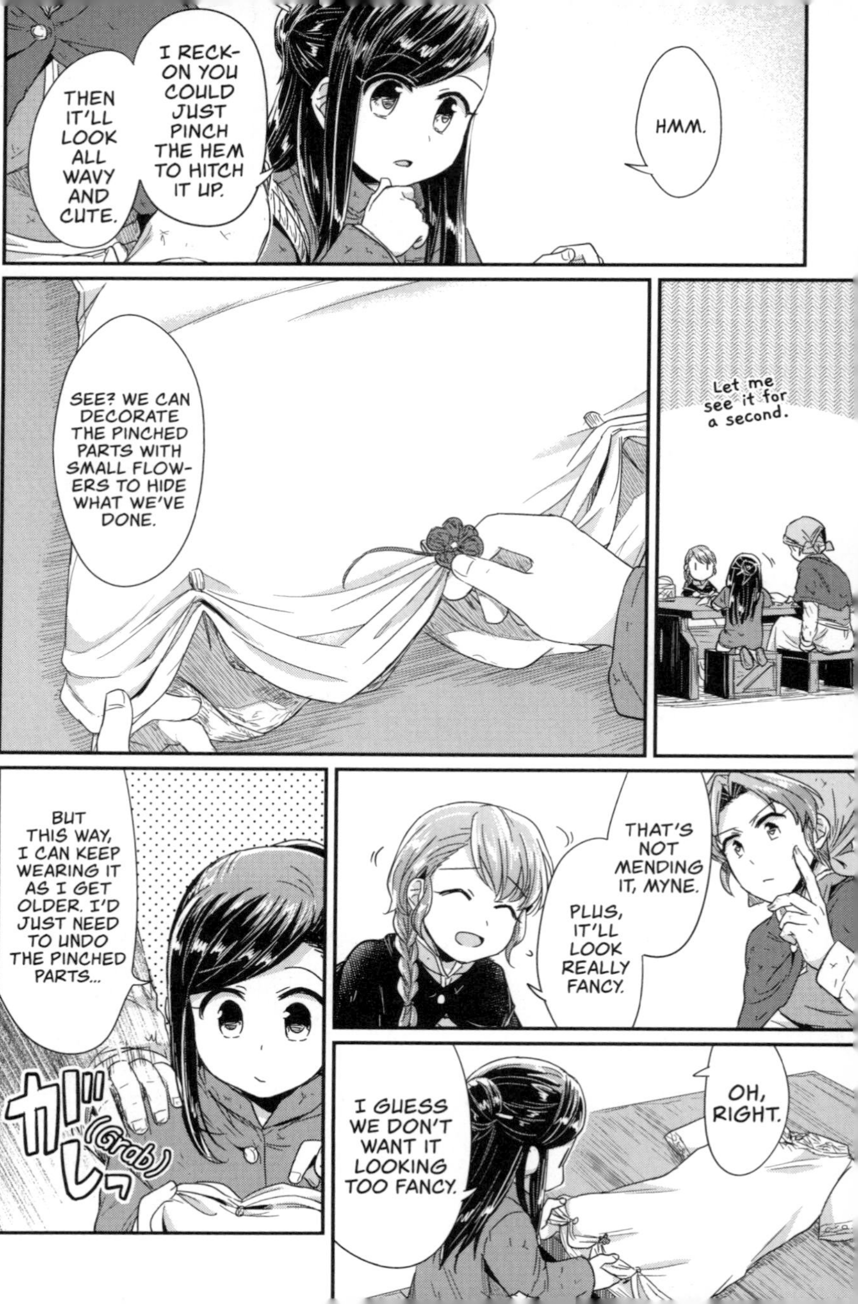
HMM.
I RECK-ON YOU COULD JUST PINCH THE HEM TO HITCH IT UP.
THEN IT'LL LOOK ALL WAVY AND CUTE.
Let me see it for a second.
SEE? WE CAN DECORATE THE PINCHED PARTS WITH SMALL FLOW-ERS TO HIDE WHAT WE'VE DONE.
THAT'S NOT MENDING IT, MYNE.
PLUS, IT'LL LOOK REALLY FANCY.
OH, RIGHT.
I GUESS WE DON'T WANT IT LOOKING TOO FANCY.
BUT THIS WAY, I CAN KEEP WEARING IT AS I GET OLDER. I'D JUST NEED TO UNDO THE PINCHED PARTS...
(Grab)

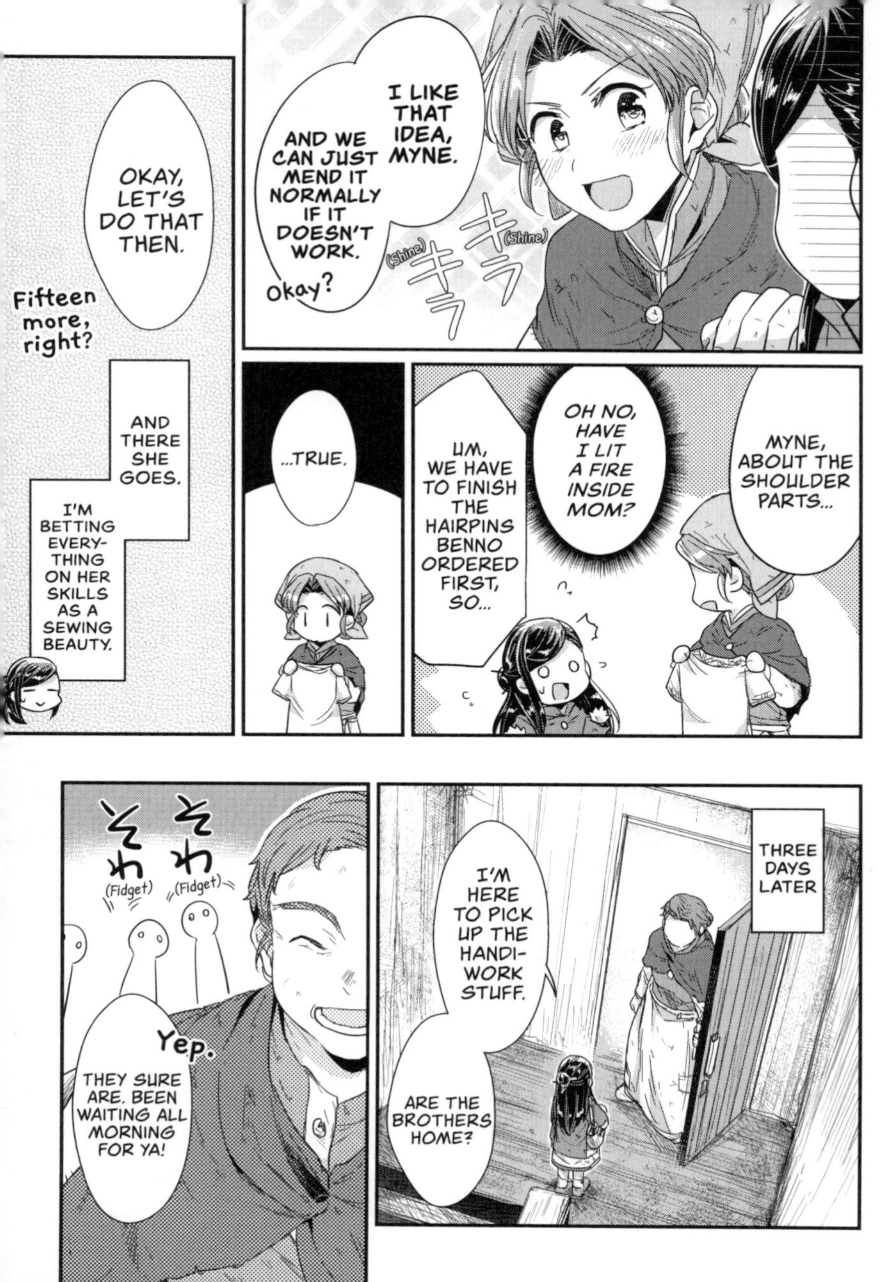
I LIKE THAT IDEA, MYNE.
AND WE CAN JUST MEND IT NORMALLY IF IT DOESN'T WORK.
Okay?
キラ (Shine) キラ (Shine)
MYNE, ABOUT THE SHOULDER PARTS...
OH NO, HAVE I LIT A FIRE INSIDE MOM?
UM, WE HAVE TO FINISH THE HAIRPINS BENNO ORDERED FIRST, SO...
...TRUE.
OKAY, LET'S DO THAT THEN.
Fifteen more, right?
AND THERE SHE GOES.
I'M BETTING EVERY-THING ON HER SKILLS AS A SEWING BEAUTY.
THREE DAYS LATER
I'M HERE TO PICK UP THE HANDI-WORK STUFF.
ARE THE BROTHERS HOME?
そわ (Fidget) そわ (Fidget)
Yep.
THEY SURE ARE. BEEN WAITING ALL MORNING FOR YA!

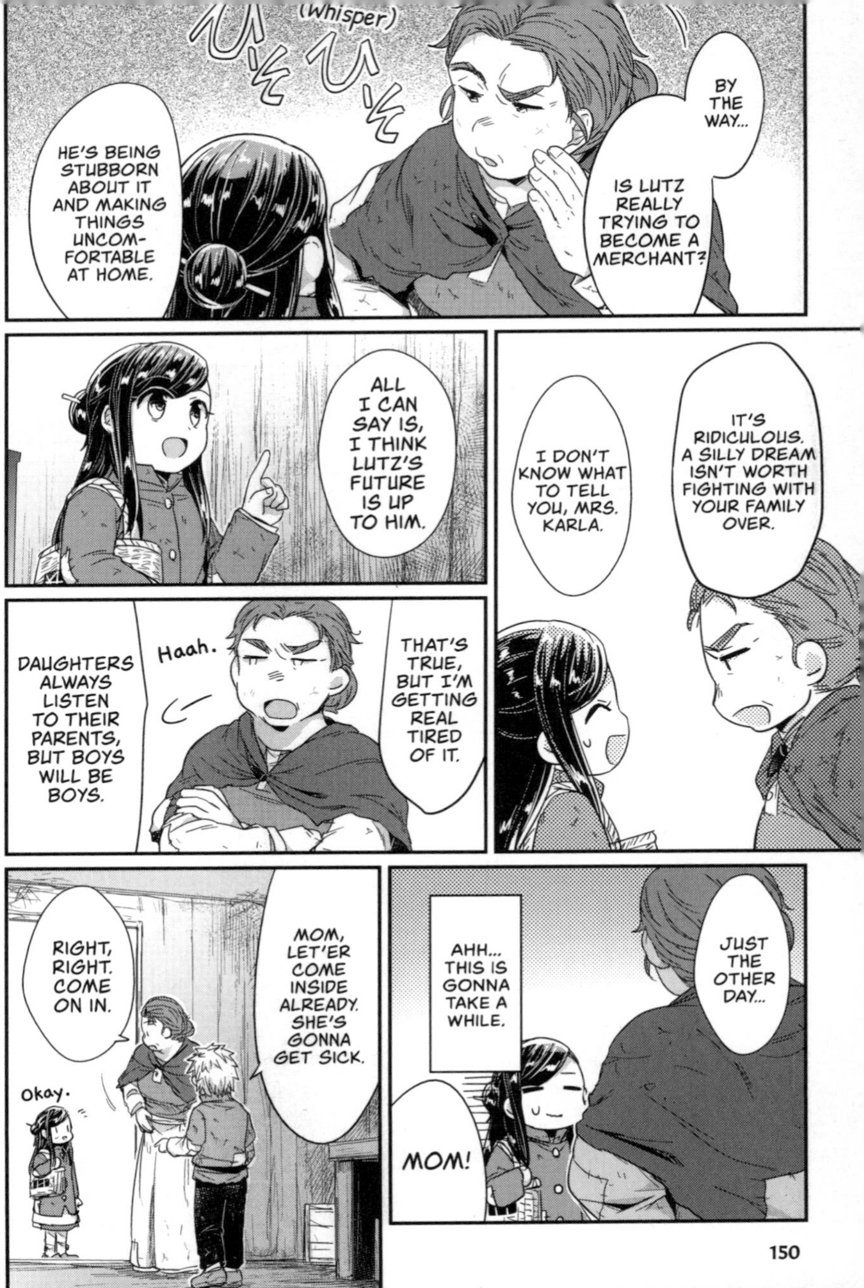
(whisper)
BY THE WAY...
IS LUTZ REALLY TRYING TO BECOME A MERCHANT?
HE'S BEING STUBBORN ABOUT IT AND MAKING THINGS UNCOM-FORTABLE AT HOME.
IT'S RIDICULOUS. A SILLY DREAM ISN'T WORTH FIGHTING WITH YOUR FAMILY OVER.
I DON'T KNOW WHAT TO TELL YOU, MRS. KARLA.
ALL I CAN SAY IS, I THINK LUTZ'S FUTURE IS UP TO HIM.
THAT'S TRUE, BUT I'M GETTING REAL TIRED OF IT.
Haah.
DAUGHTERS ALWAYS LISTEN TO THEIR PARENTS, BUT BOYS WILL BE BOYS.
JUST THE OTHER DAY...
AHH... THIS IS GONNA TAKE A WHILE.
MOM!
MOM, LET'ER COME INSIDE ALREADY. SHE'S GONNA GET SICK.
RIGHT, RIGHT. COME ON IN.
Okay.

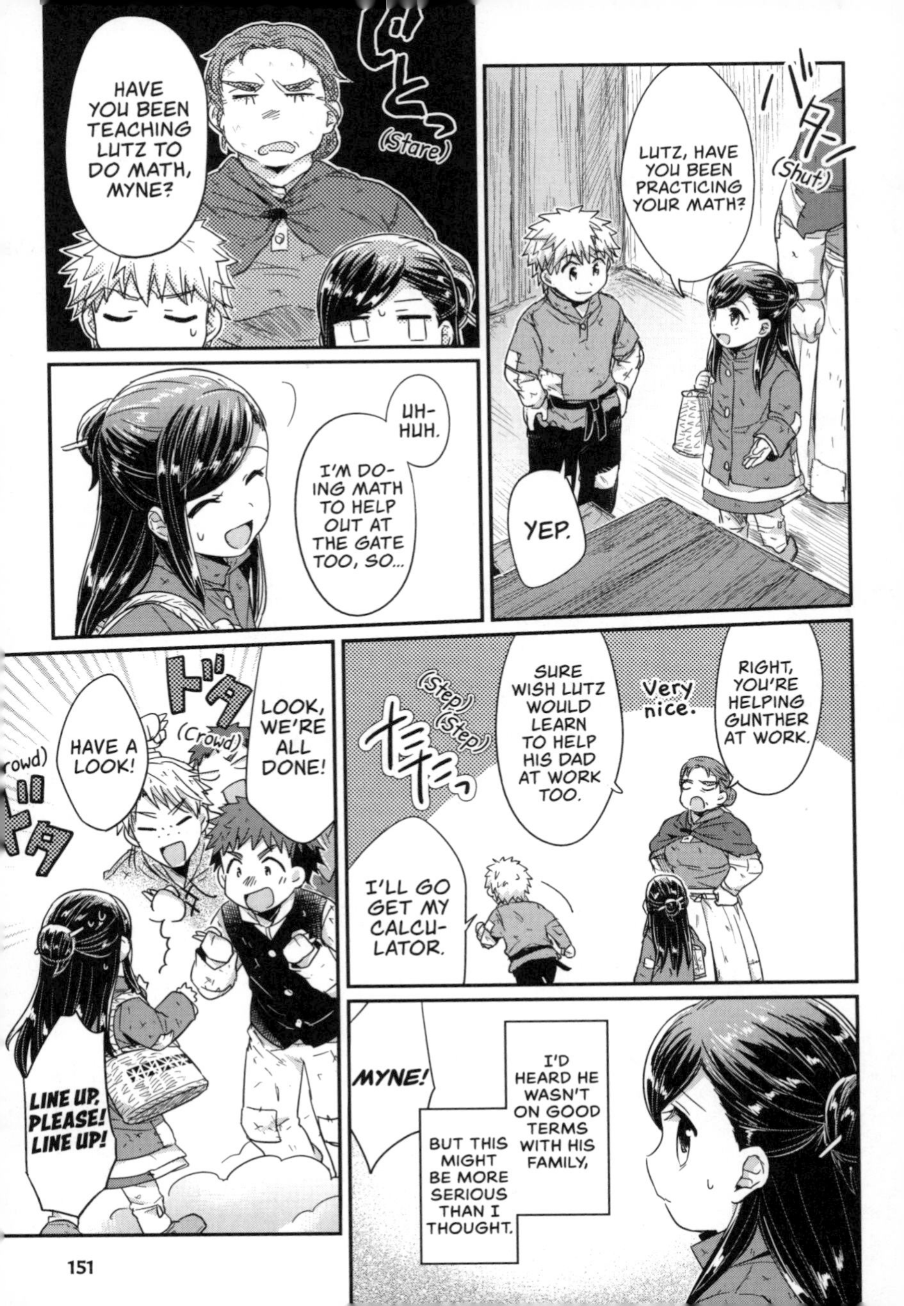

(Shut)
LUTZ, HAVE YOU BEEN PRACTICING YOUR MATH?
YEP.
(Stare)
HAVE YOU BEEN TEACHING LUTZ TO DO MATH, MYNE?
UH-HUH.
I'M DOING MATH TO HELP OUT AT THE GATE TOO, SO...
RIGHT, YOU'RE HELPING GUNTHER AT WORK.
Very nice.
SURE WISH LUTZ WOULD LEARN TO HELP HIS DAD AT WORK TOO.
(Step) (Step)
I'LL GO GET MY CALCULATOR.
I'D HEARD HE WASN'T ON GOOD TERMS WITH HIS FAMILY,
BUT THIS MIGHT BE MORE SERIOUS THAN I THOUGHT.
MYNE!
LOOK, WE'RE ALL DONE!
(Crowd)
HAVE A LOOK!
LINE UP, PLEASE! LINE UP!

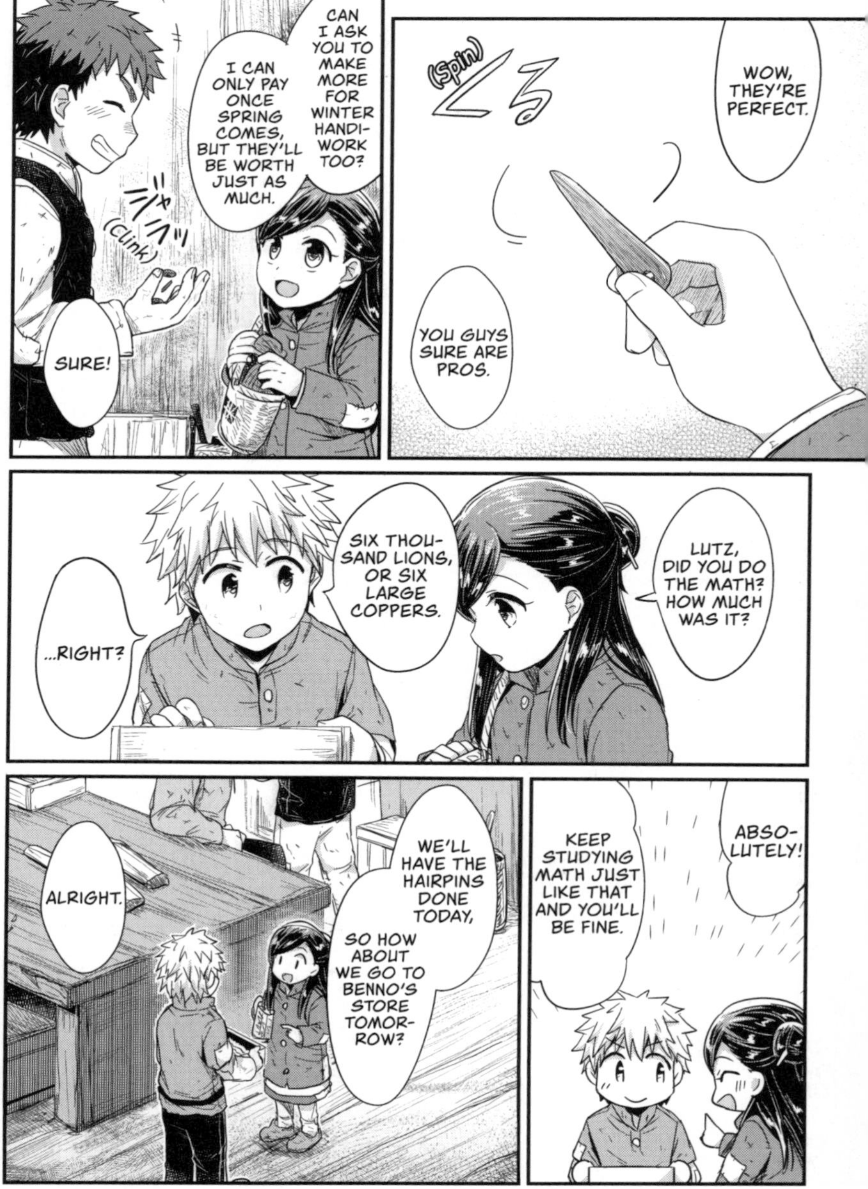
(Spin)
WOW, THEY'RE PERFECT.
YOU GUYS SURE ARE PROS.
CAN I ASK YOU TO MAKE MORE FOR WINTER HANDI-WORK TOO?
I CAN ONLY PAY ONCE SPRING COMES, BUT THEY'LL BE WORTH JUST AS MUCH.
(Clink)
SURE!
LUTZ, DID YOU DO THE MATH? HOW MUCH WAS IT?
SIX THOU-SAND LIONS, OR SIX LARGE COPPERS.
...RIGHT?
ABSO-LUTELY!
KEEP STUDYING MATH JUST LIKE THAT AND YOU'LL BE FINE.
WE'LL HAVE THE HAIRPINS DONE TODAY,
SO HOW ABOUT WE GO TO BENNO'S STORE TOMOR-ROW?
ALRIGHT.

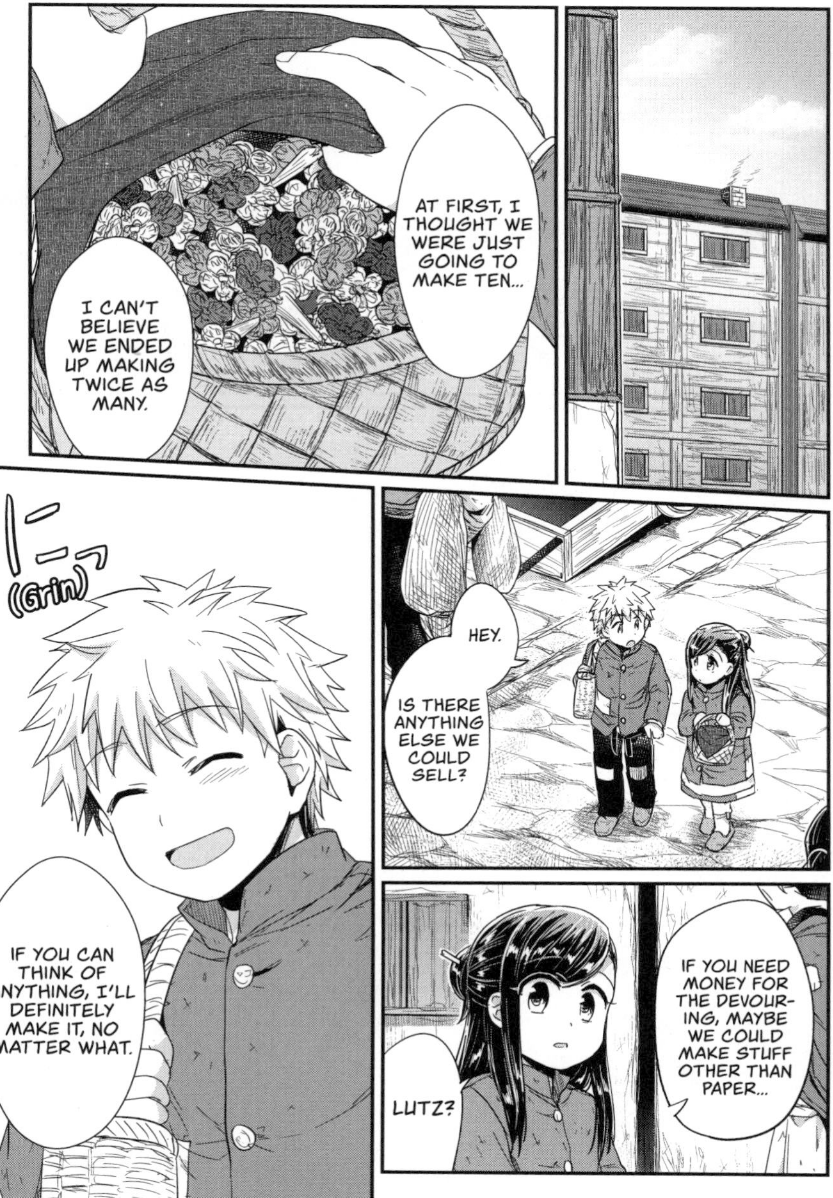
AT FIRST, I THOUGHT WE WERE JUST GOING TO MAKE TEN...
I CAN'T BELIEVE WE ENDED UP MAKING TWICE AS MANY.
HEY.
IS THERE ANYTHING ELSE WE COULD SELL?
IF YOU NEED MONEY FOR THE DEVOURING, MAYBE WE COULD MAKE STUFF OTHER THAN PAPER...
LUTZ?
(Grin)
IF YOU CAN THINK OF ANYTHING, I'LL DEFINITELY MAKE IT, NO MATTER WHAT.

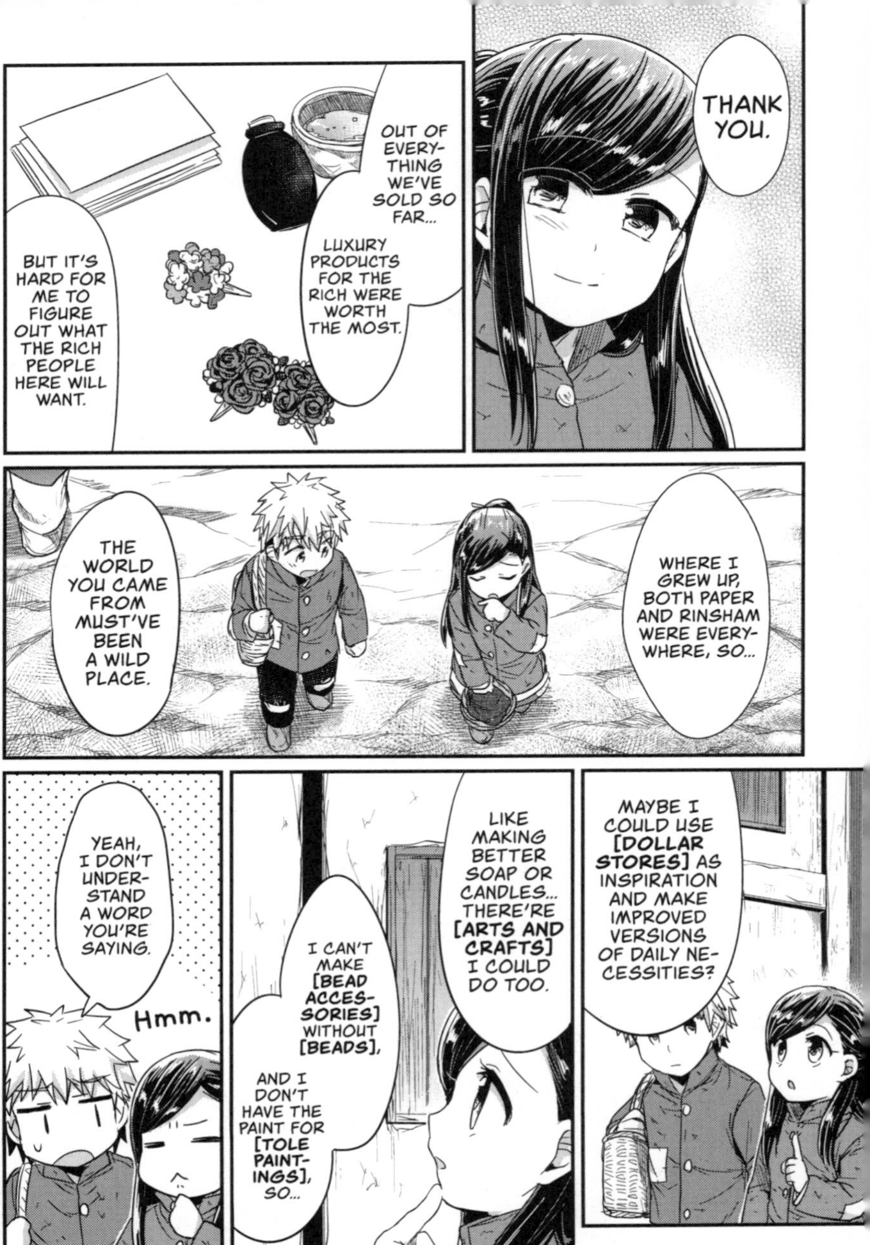
THANK YOU.
OUT OF EVERYTHING WE'VE SOLD SO FAR...
LUXURY PRODUCTS FOR THE RICH WERE WORTH THE MOST.
BUT IT'S HARD FOR ME TO FIGURE OUT WHAT THE RICH PEOPLE HERE WILL WANT.
WHERE I GREW UP, BOTH PAPER AND RINSHAM WERE EVERYWHERE, SO...
THE WORLD YOU CAME FROM MUST'VE BEEN A WILD PLACE.
MAYBE I COULD USE [DOLLAR STORES] AS INSPIRATION AND MAKE IMPROVED VERSIONS OF DAILY NECESSITIES?
LIKE MAKING BETTER SOAP OR CANDLES... THERE'RE [ARTS AND CRAFTS] I COULD DO TOO.
I CAN'T MAKE [BEAD ACCESSORIES] WITHOUT [BEADS],
AND I DON'T HAVE THE PAINT FOR [TOLE PAINTINGS], SO...
YEAH, I DON'T UNDERSTAND A WORD YOU'RE SAYING.
Hmm.

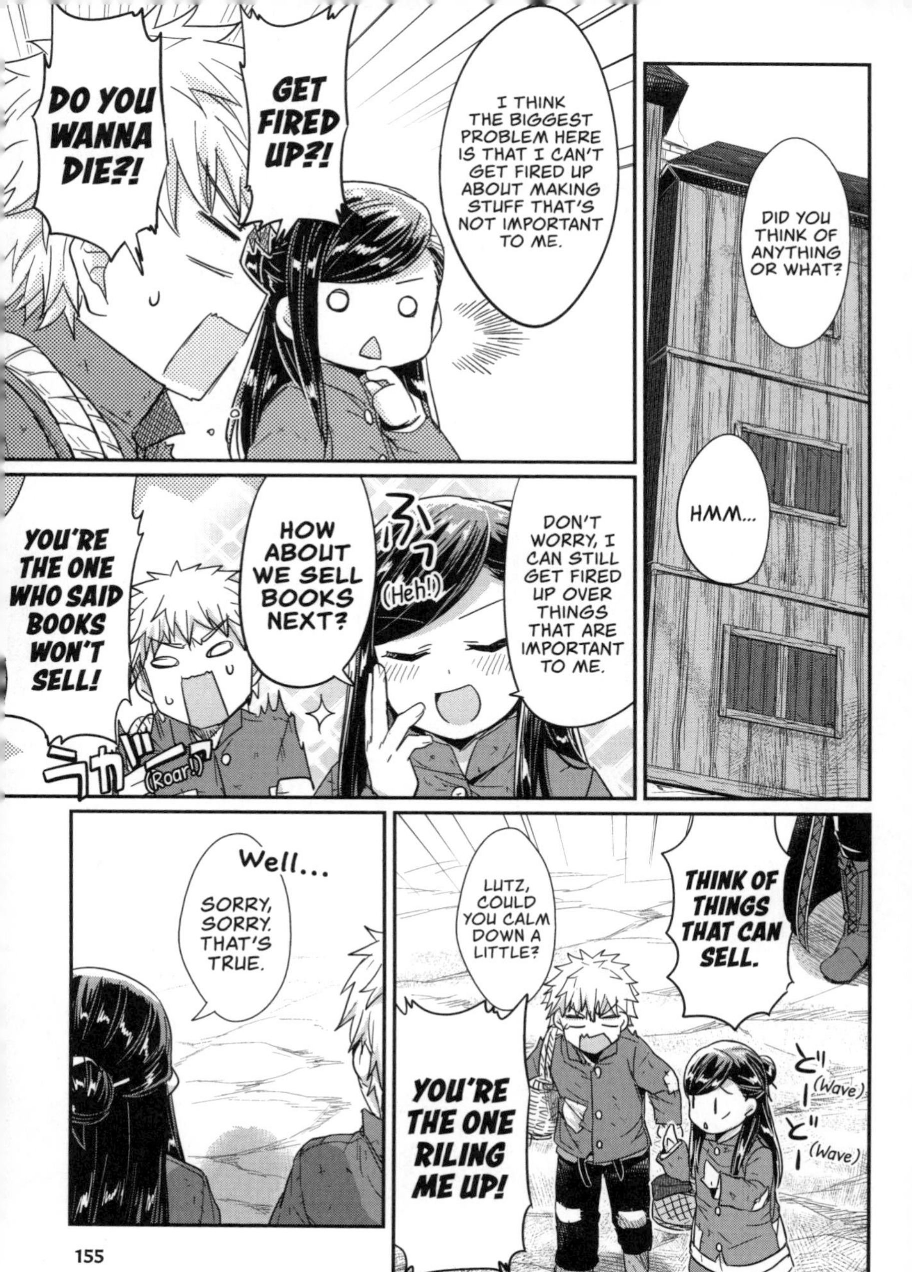
DID YOU THINK OF ANYTHING OR WHAT?
HMM...
I THINK THE BIGGEST PROBLEM HERE IS THAT I CAN'T GET FIRED UP ABOUT MAKING STUFF THAT'S NOT IMPORTANT TO ME.
GET FIRED UP?!
DO YOU WANNA DIE?!
DON'T WORRY, I CAN STILL GET FIRED UP OVER THINGS THAT ARE IMPORTANT TO ME.
ふっ
(Heh!)
HOW ABOUT WE SELL BOOKS NEXT?
YOU'RE THE ONE WHO SAID BOOKS WON'T SELL!
うがーっ
(Roar!)
THINK OF THINGS THAT CAN SELL.
LUTZ, COULD YOU CALM DOWN A LITTLE?
YOU'RE THE ONE RILING ME UP!
どーどー
(Wave)
(Wave)
Well...
SORRY, SORRY. THAT'S TRUE.

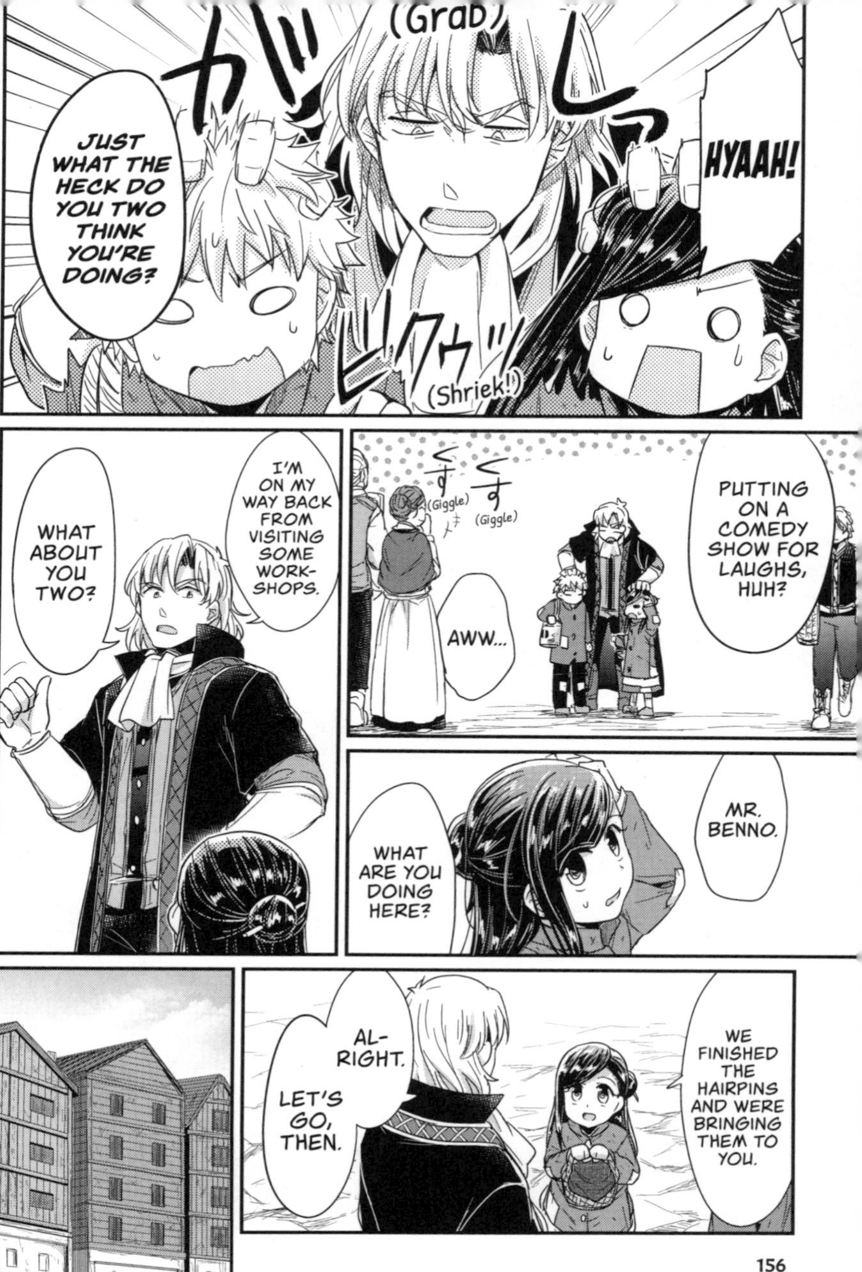
(Grab)
HYAAH!
JUST WHAT THE HECK DO YOU TWO THINK YOU'RE DOING?
(Shriek!)
PUTTING ON A COMEDY SHOW FOR LAUGHS, HUH?
(Giggle)
(Giggle)
AWW...
MR. BENNO.
WHAT ARE YOU DOING HERE?
I'M ON MY WAY BACK FROM VISITING SOME WORK-SHOPS.
WHAT ABOUT YOU TWO?
WE FINISHED THE HAIRPINS AND WERE BRINGING THEM TO YOU.
AL-RIGHT.
LET'S GO, THEN.

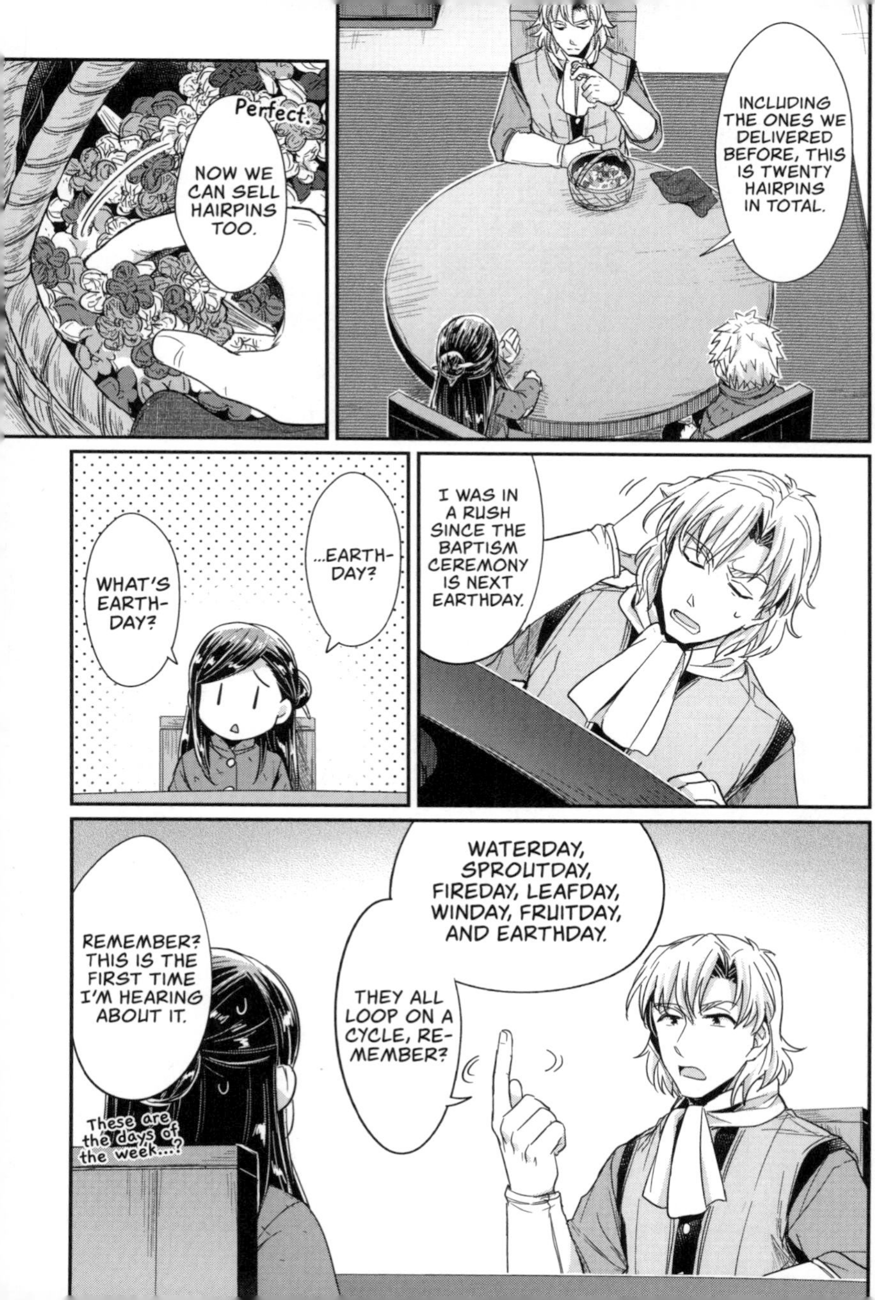
INCLUDING THE ONES WE DELIVERED BEFORE, THIS IS TWENTY HAIRPINS IN TOTAL.
Perfect.
NOW WE CAN SELL HAIRPINS TOO.
I WAS IN A RUSH SINCE THE BAPTISM CEREMONY IS NEXT EARTHDAY.
...EARTH-DAY?
WHAT'S EARTH-DAY?
WATERDAY, SPROUTDAY, FIREDAY, LEAFDAY, WINDAY, FRUITDAY, AND EARTHDAY.
THEY ALL LOOP ON A CYCLE, RE-MEMBER?
REMEMBER? THIS IS THE FIRST TIME I'M HEARING ABOUT IT.
These are the days of the week...?

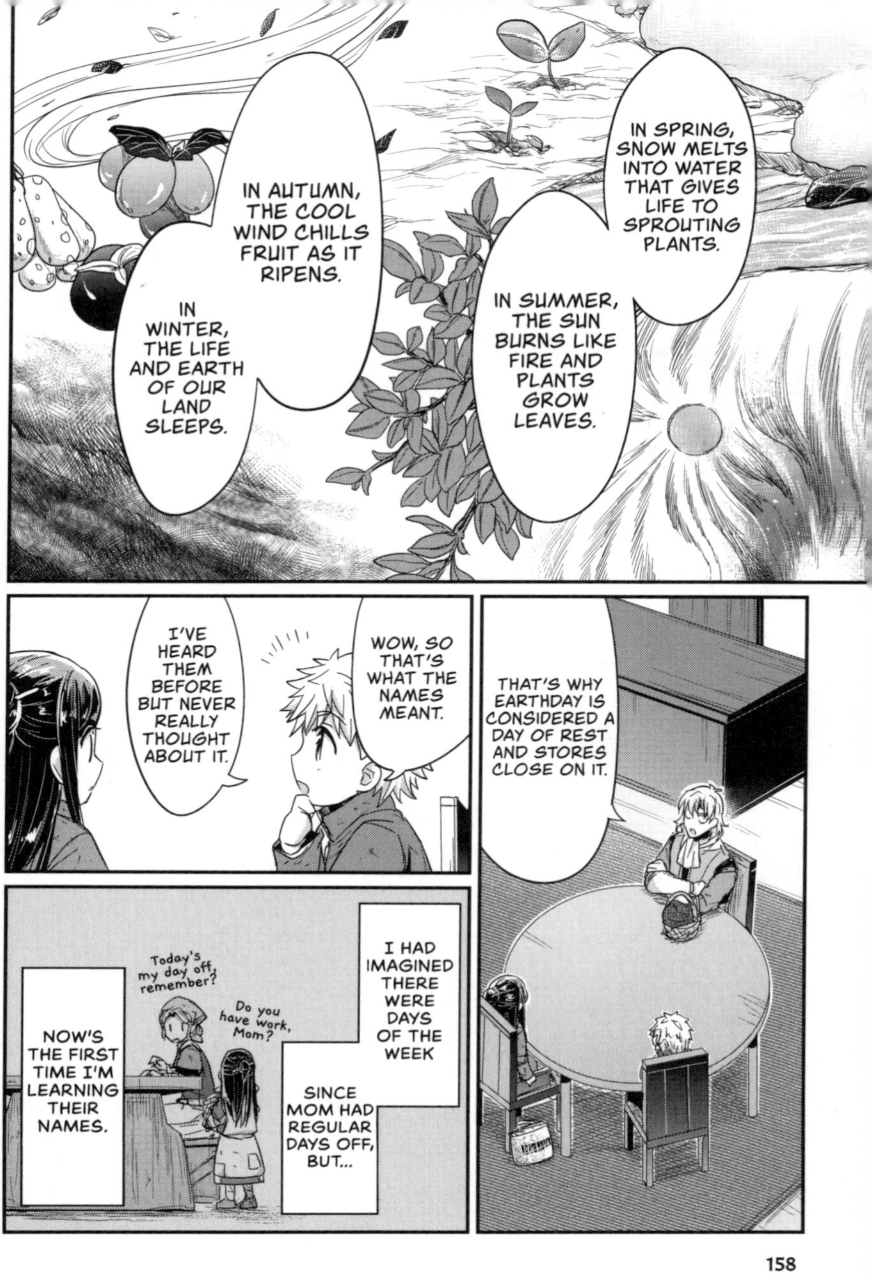
IN SPRING, SNOW MELTS INTO WATER THAT GIVES LIFE TO SPROUTING PLANTS.
IN SUMMER, THE SUN BURNS LIKE FIRE AND PLANTS GROW LEAVES.
IN AUTUMN, THE COOL WIND CHILLS FRUIT AS IT RIPENS.
IN WINTER, THE LIFE AND EARTH OF OUR LAND SLEEPS.
THAT'S WHY EARTHDAY IS CONSIDERED A DAY OF REST AND STORES CLOSE ON IT.
WOW, SO THAT'S WHAT THE NAMES MEANT.
I'VE HEARD THEM BEFORE BUT NEVER REALLY THOUGHT ABOUT IT.
I HAD IMAGINED THERE WERE DAYS OF THE WEEK
SINCE MOM HAD REGULAR DAYS OFF, BUT...
Do you have work, Mom?
Today's my day off, remember?
NOW'S THE FIRST TIME I'M LEARNING THEIR NAMES.

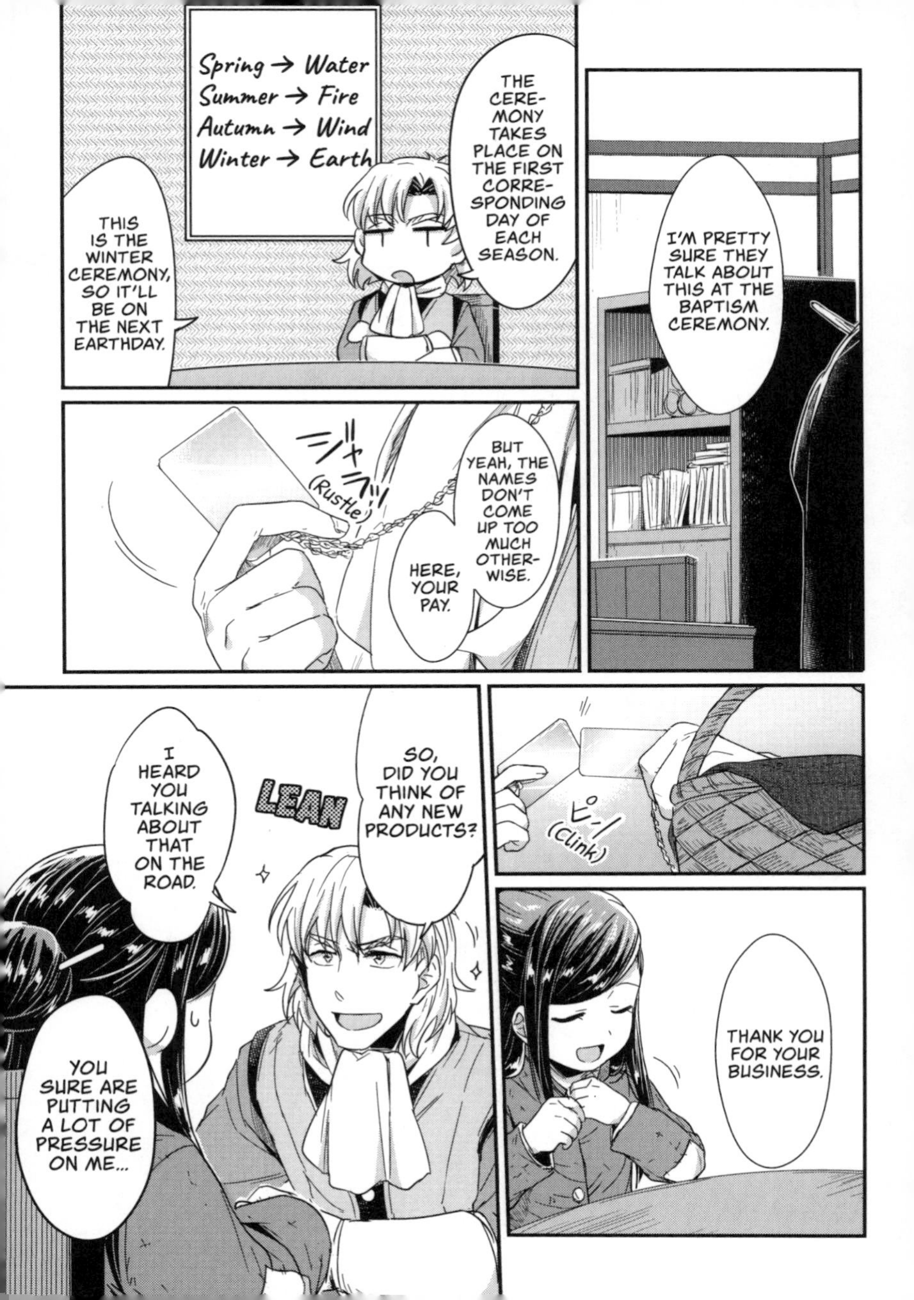
Spring → Water
Summer → Fire
Autumn → Wind
Winter → Earth
THE CEREMONY TAKES PLACE ON THE FIRST CORRESPONDING DAY OF EACH SEASON.
THIS IS THE WINTER CEREMONY, SO IT'LL BE ON THE NEXT EARTHDAY.
I'M PRETTY SURE THEY TALK ABOUT THIS AT THE BAPTISM CEREMONY.
BUT YEAH, THE NAMES DON'T COME UP TOO MUCH OTHERWISE.
(Rustle)
HERE, YOUR PAY.
(Clink)
THANK YOU FOR YOUR BUSINESS.
SO, DID YOU THINK OF ANY NEW PRODUCTS?
LEAN
I HEARD YOU TALKING ABOUT THAT ON THE ROAD.
YOU SURE ARE PUTTING A LOT OF PRESSURE ON ME...

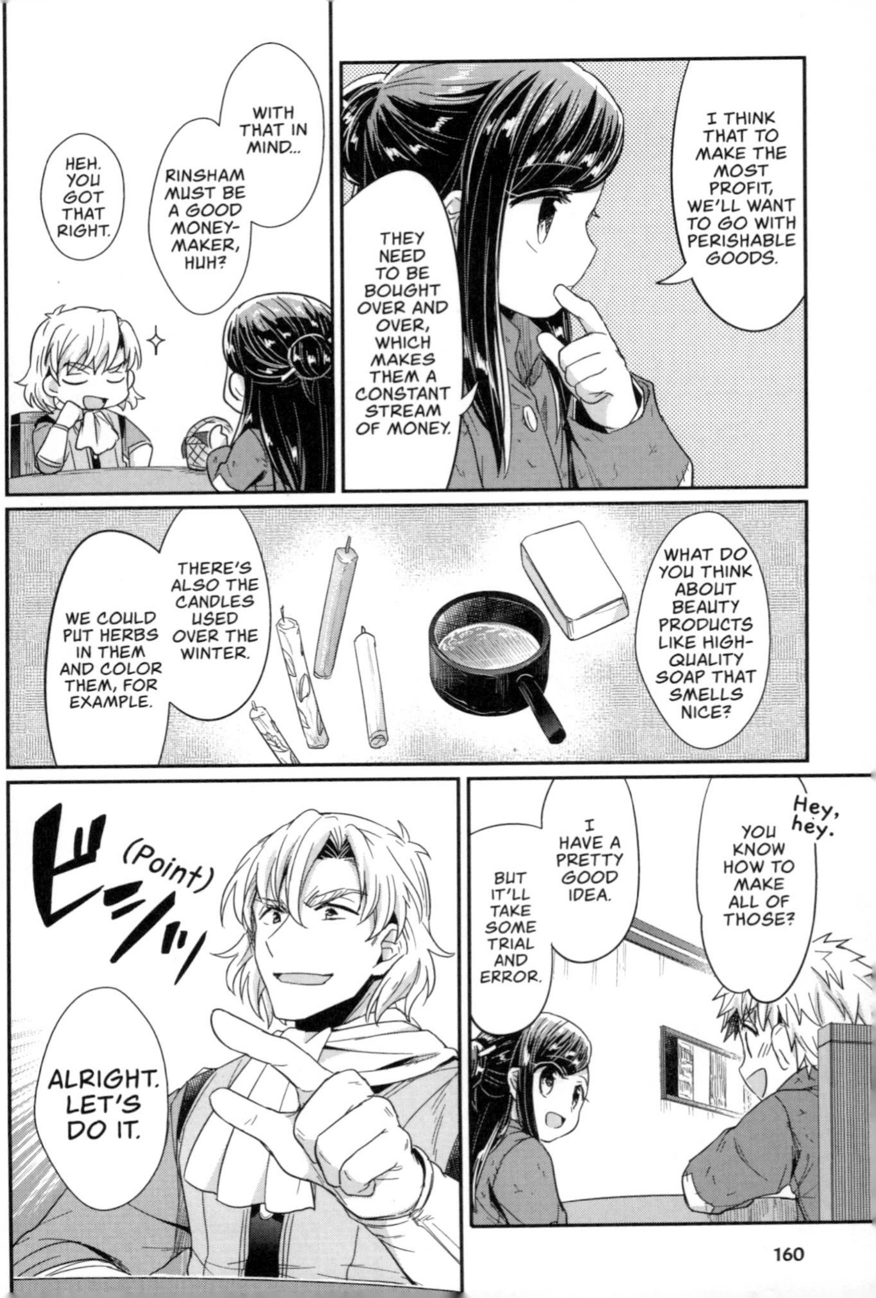
I THINK THAT TO MAKE THE MOST PROFIT, WE'LL WANT TO GO WITH PERISHABLE GOODS.
THEY NEED TO BE BOUGHT OVER AND OVER, WHICH MAKES THEM A CONSTANT STREAM OF MONEY.
WITH THAT IN MIND...
RINSHAM MUST BE A GOOD MONEY-MAKER, HUH?
HEH. YOU GOT THAT RIGHT.
WHAT DO YOU THINK ABOUT BEAUTY PRODUCTS LIKE HIGH-QUALITY SOAP THAT SMELLS NICE?
THERE'S ALSO THE CANDLES USED OVER THE WINTER.
WE COULD PUT HERBS IN THEM AND COLOR THEM, FOR EXAMPLE.
Hey, hey.
YOU KNOW HOW TO MAKE ALL OF THOSE?
I HAVE A PRETTY GOOD IDEA.
BUT IT'LL TAKE SOME TRIAL AND ERROR.
ビシッ
(Point)
ALRIGHT. LET'S DO IT.

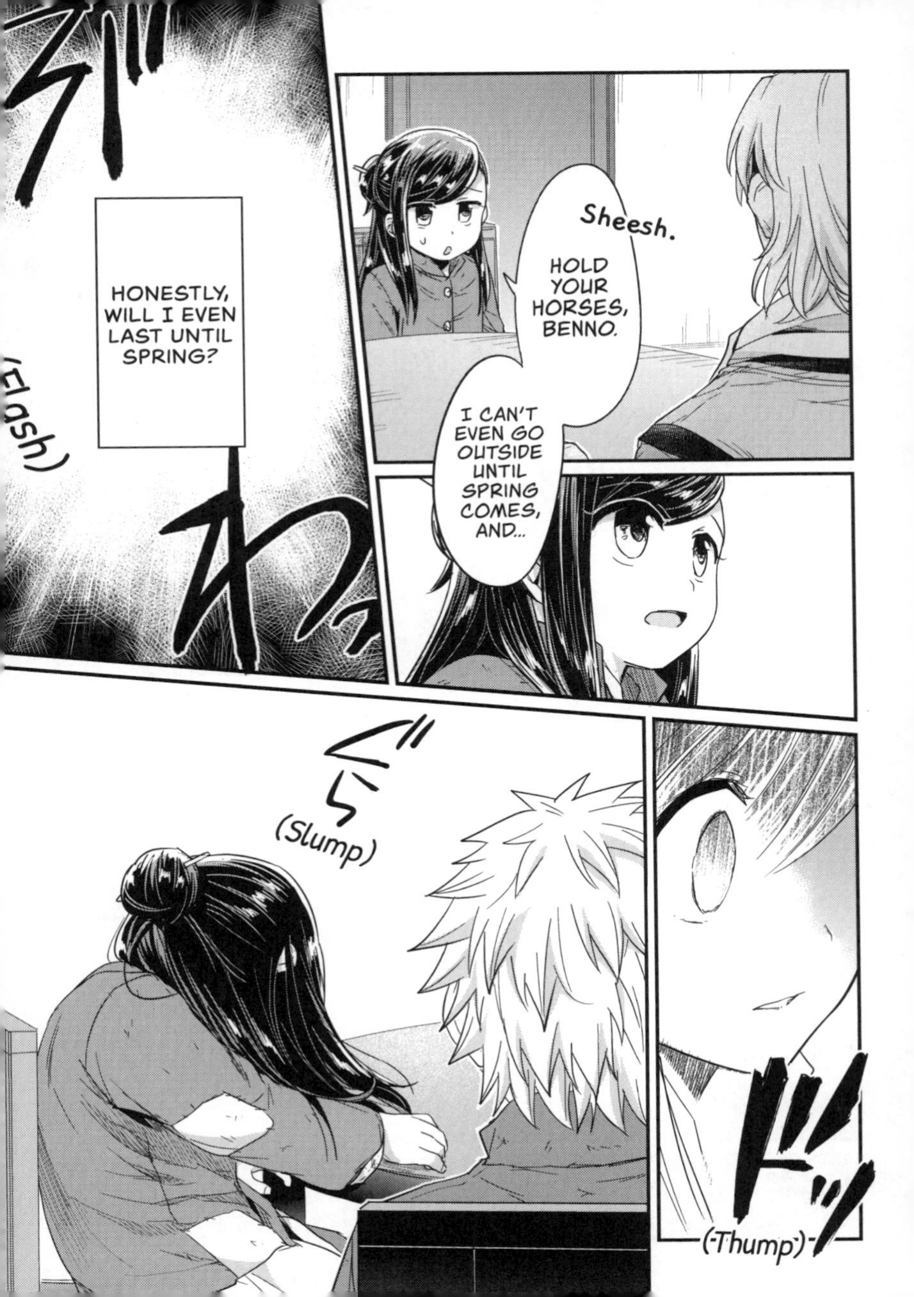

Sheesh.
HOLD YOUR HORSES, BENNO.
I CAN'T EVEN GO OUTSIDE UNTIL SPRING COMES, AND...
HONESTLY, WILL I EVEN LAST UNTIL SPRING?
(Flash)
(Thump)
(Slump)

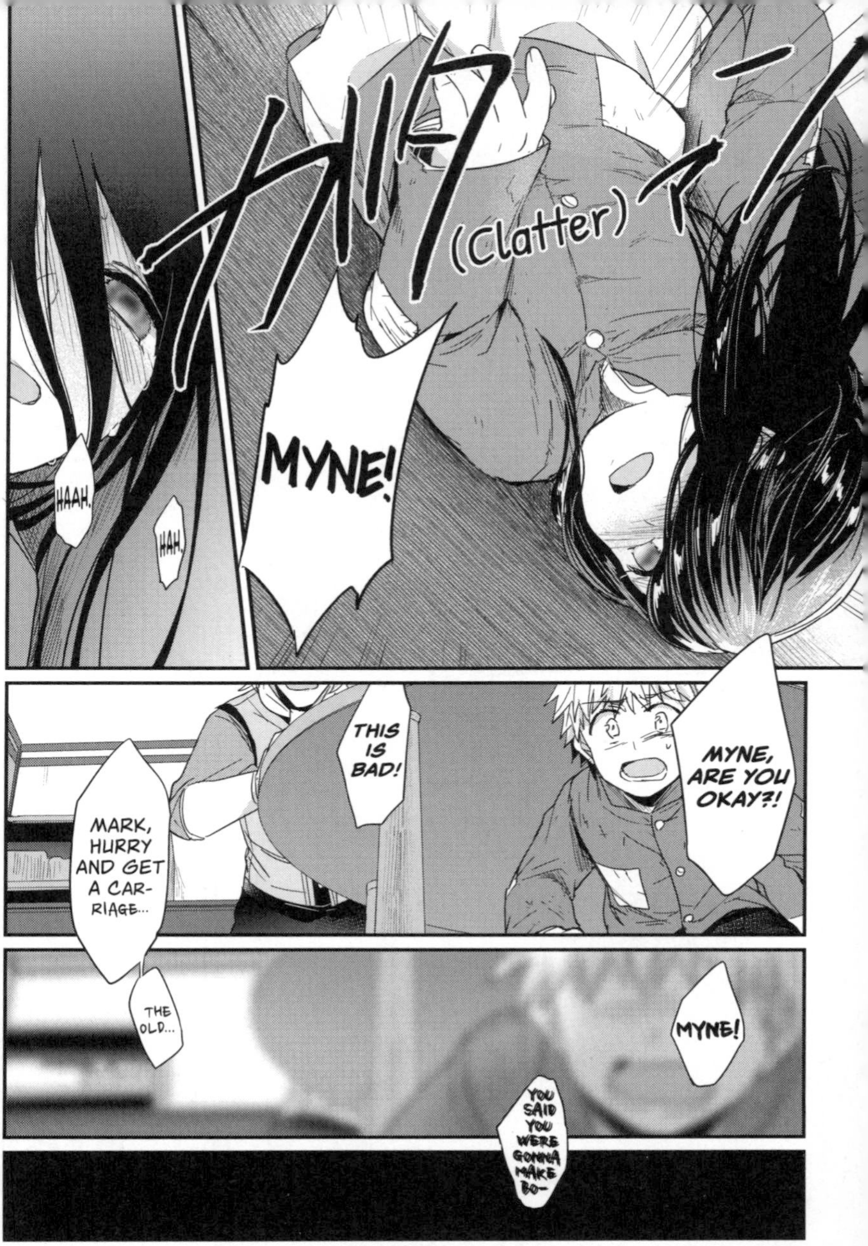
(Clatter)
MYNE!
HAH,
HAAH,
MYNE, ARE YOU OKAY?!
THIS IS BAD!
MARK, HURRY AND GET A CARRIAGE...
THE OLD...
MYNE!
YOU SAID YOU WERE GONNA MAKE BO-

Ch.24: Nearing Winter End

ASCENDANCE
OF A
BOOKWORM

I'll do anything to
become a librarian!

Part 1 **If there aren't any
books, I'll just have
to make some!**

Extra The Power of Money

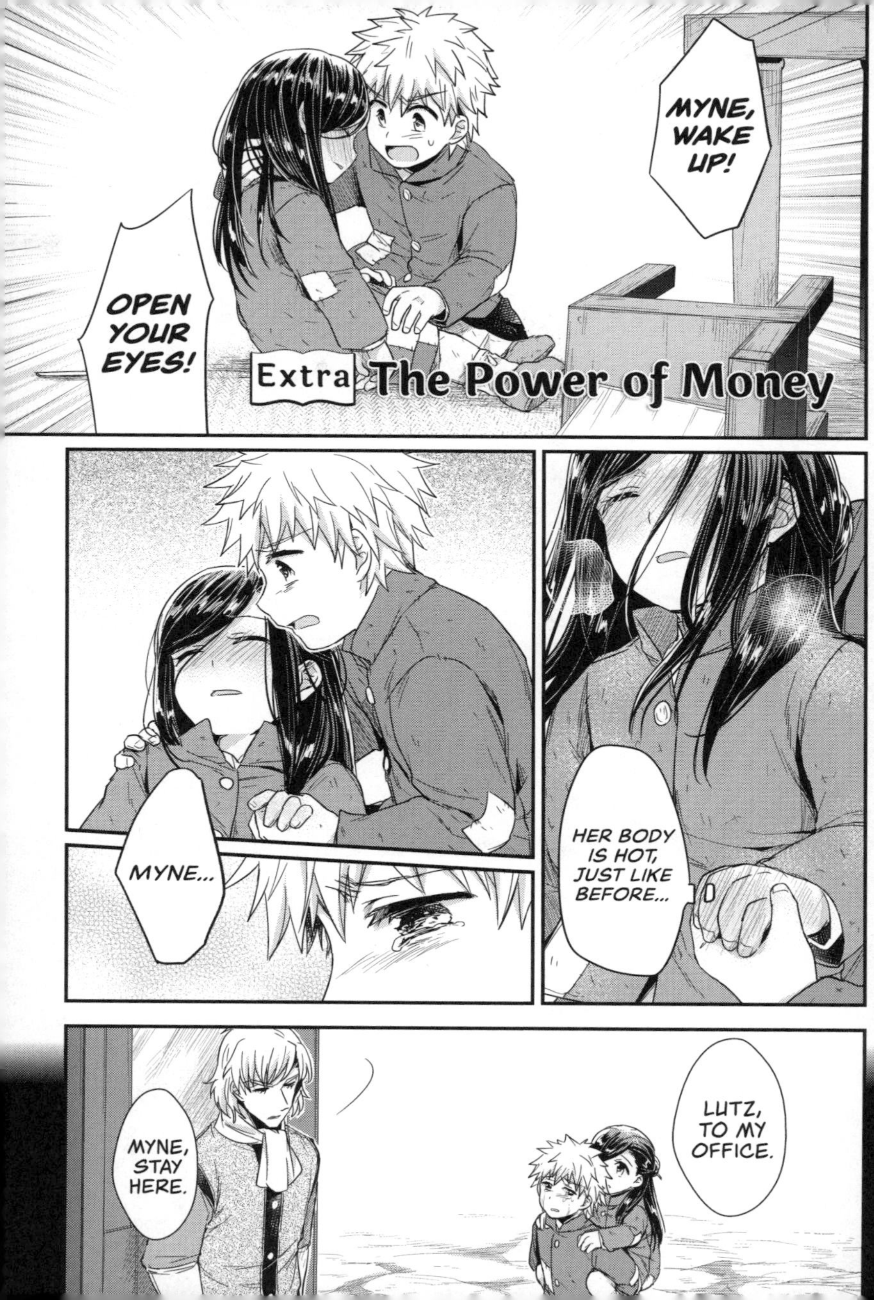
MYNE, WAKE UP!
OPEN YOUR EYES!
HER BODY IS HOT, JUST LIKE BEFORE...
MYNE...
LUTZ, TO MY OFFICE.
MYNE, STAY HERE.

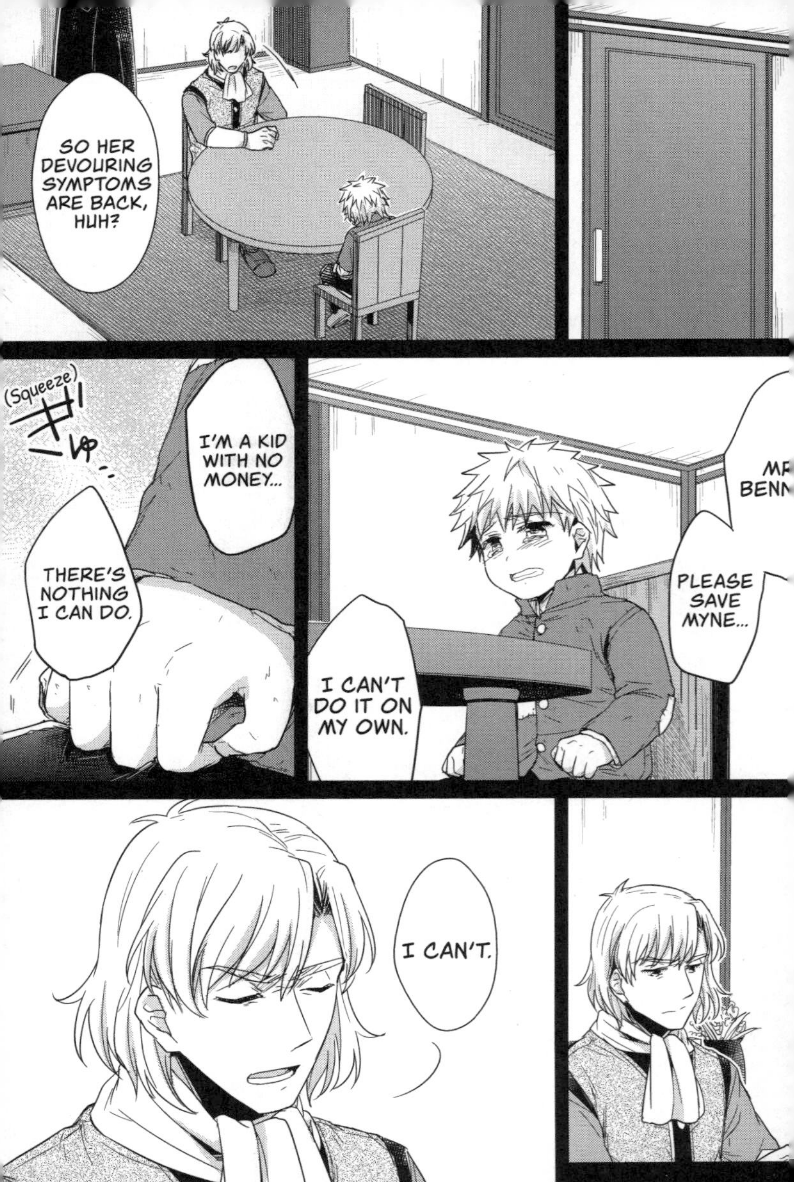
SO HER DEVOURING SYMPTOMS ARE BACK, HUH?
MR BENN
PLEASE SAVE MYNE...
I CAN'T DO IT ON MY OWN.
I'M A KID WITH NO MONEY...
THERE'S NOTHING I CAN DO.
(Squeeze)
I CAN'T.

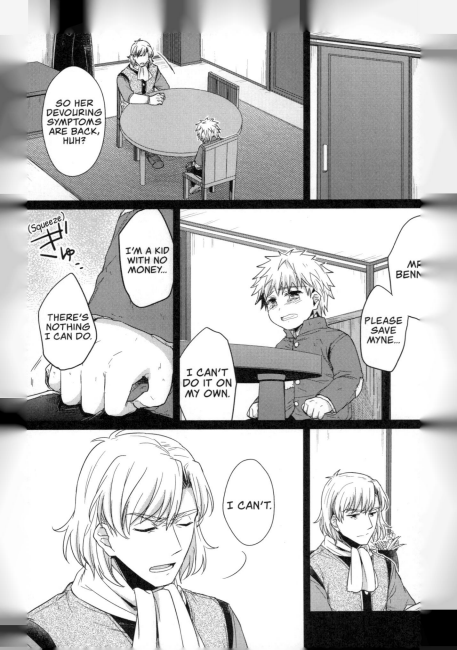

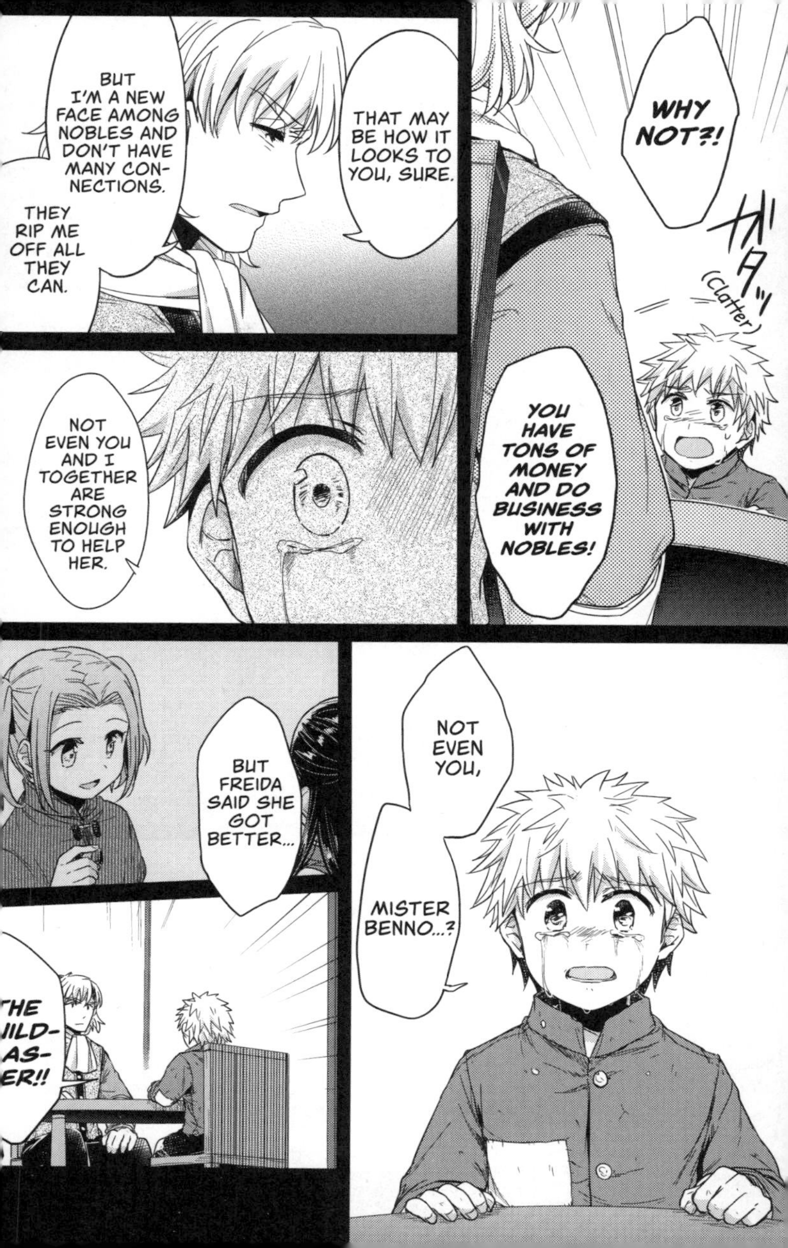
WHY NOT?!
(Clatter)
YOU HAVE TONS OF MONEY AND DO BUSINESS WITH NOBLES!
THAT MAY BE HOW IT LOOKS TO YOU, SURE.
BUT I'M A NEW FACE AMONG NOBLES AND DON'T HAVE MANY CON-NECTIONS.
THEY RIP ME OFF ALL THEY CAN.
NOT EVEN YOU AND I TOGETHER ARE STRONG ENOUGH TO HELP HER.
NOT EVEN YOU,
MISTER BENNO...?
BUT FREIDA SAID SHE GOT BETTER...
THE ILD- AS- ER!!

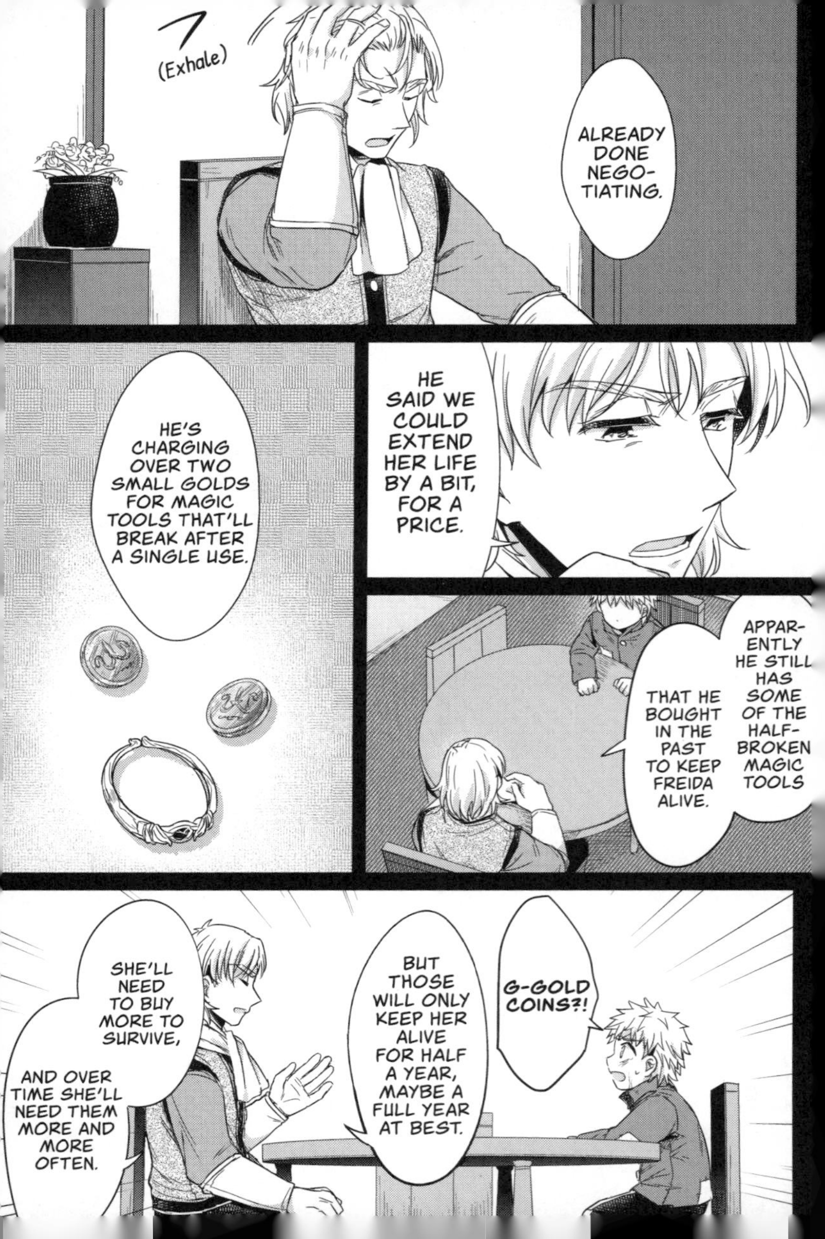
ALREADY DONE NEGO-TIATING.
(Exhale)
HE SAID WE COULD EXTEND HER LIFE BY A BIT, FOR A PRICE.
APPARENTLY HE STILL HAS SOME OF THE HALF-BROKEN MAGIC TOOLS
THAT HE BOUGHT IN THE PAST TO KEEP FREIDA ALIVE.
HE'S CHARGING OVER TWO SMALL GOLDS FOR MAGIC TOOLS THAT'LL BREAK AFTER A SINGLE USE.
G-GOLD COINS?!
BUT THOSE WILL ONLY KEEP HER ALIVE FOR HALF A YEAR, MAYBE A FULL YEAR AT BEST.
SHE'LL NEED TO BUY MORE TO SURVIVE,
AND OVER TIME SHE'LL NEED THEM MORE AND MORE OFTEN.

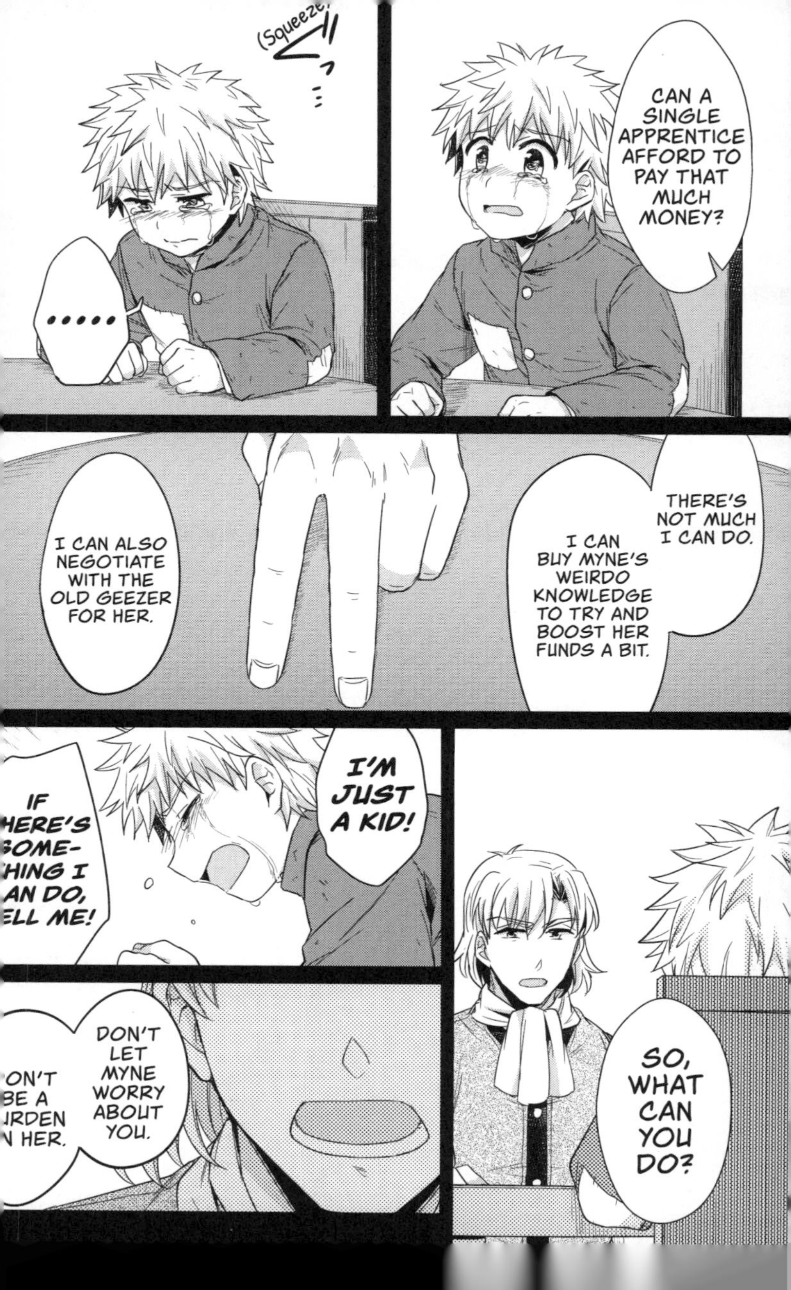
CAN A SINGLE APPRENTICE AFFORD TO PAY THAT MUCH MONEY?
(Squeeze)
.....
THERE'S NOT MUCH I CAN DO.
I CAN BUY MYNE'S WEIRDO KNOWLEDGE TO TRY AND BOOST HER FUNDS A BIT.
I CAN ALSO NEGOTIATE WITH THE OLD GEEZER FOR HER.
SO, WHAT CAN YOU DO?
I'M JUST A KID!
IF HERE'S SOME- HING I AN DO, ELL ME!
DON'T LET MYNE WORRY ABOUT YOU.
ON'T BE A RDEN N HER.

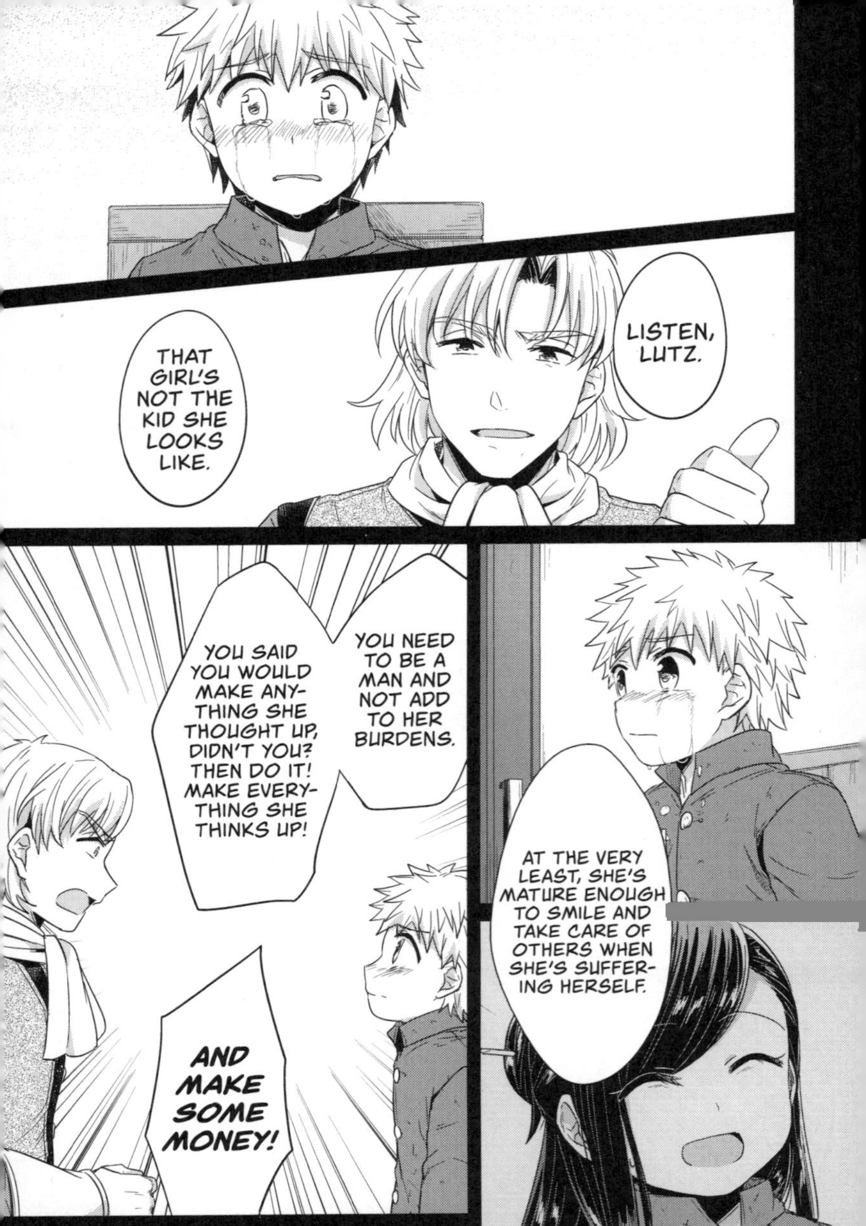
LISTEN, LUTZ.
THAT GIRL'S NOT THE KID SHE LOOKS LIKE.
AT THE VERY LEAST, SHE'S MATURE ENOUGH TO SMILE AND TAKE CARE OF OTHERS WHEN SHE'S SUFFERING HERSELF.
YOU NEED TO BE A MAN AND NOT ADD TO HER BURDENS.
YOU SAID YOU WOULD MAKE ANYTHING SHE THOUGHT UP, DIDN'T YOU? THEN DO IT! MAKE EVERYTHING SHE THINKS UP!
AND MAKE SOME MONEY!

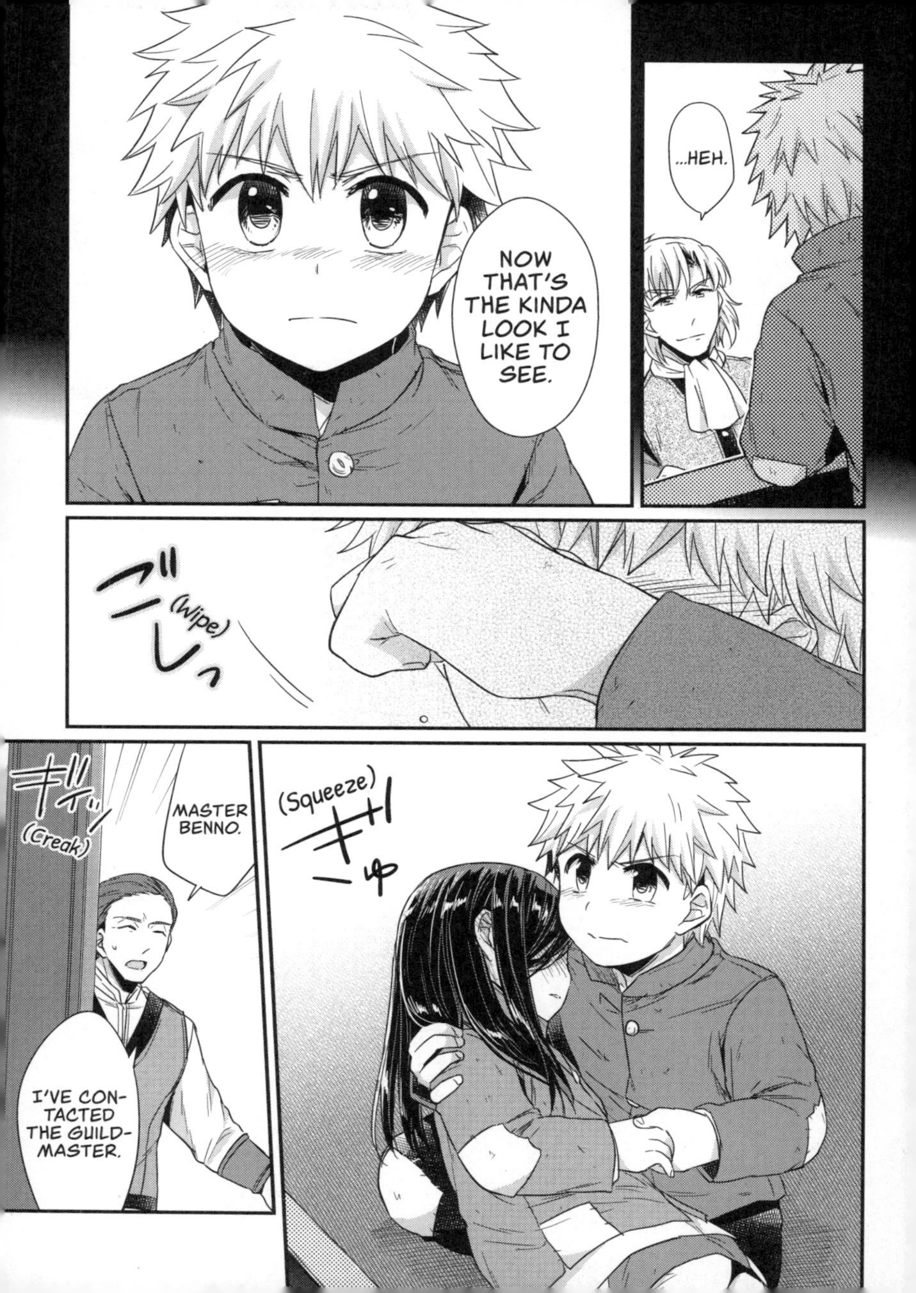
...HEH.
NOW THAT'S THE KINDA LOOK I LIKE TO SEE.
ごしっ
(wipe)
ぎゅ
(Squeeze)
ギィッ
(Creak)
MASTER BENNO.
I'VE CON-TACTED THE GUILD-MASTER.

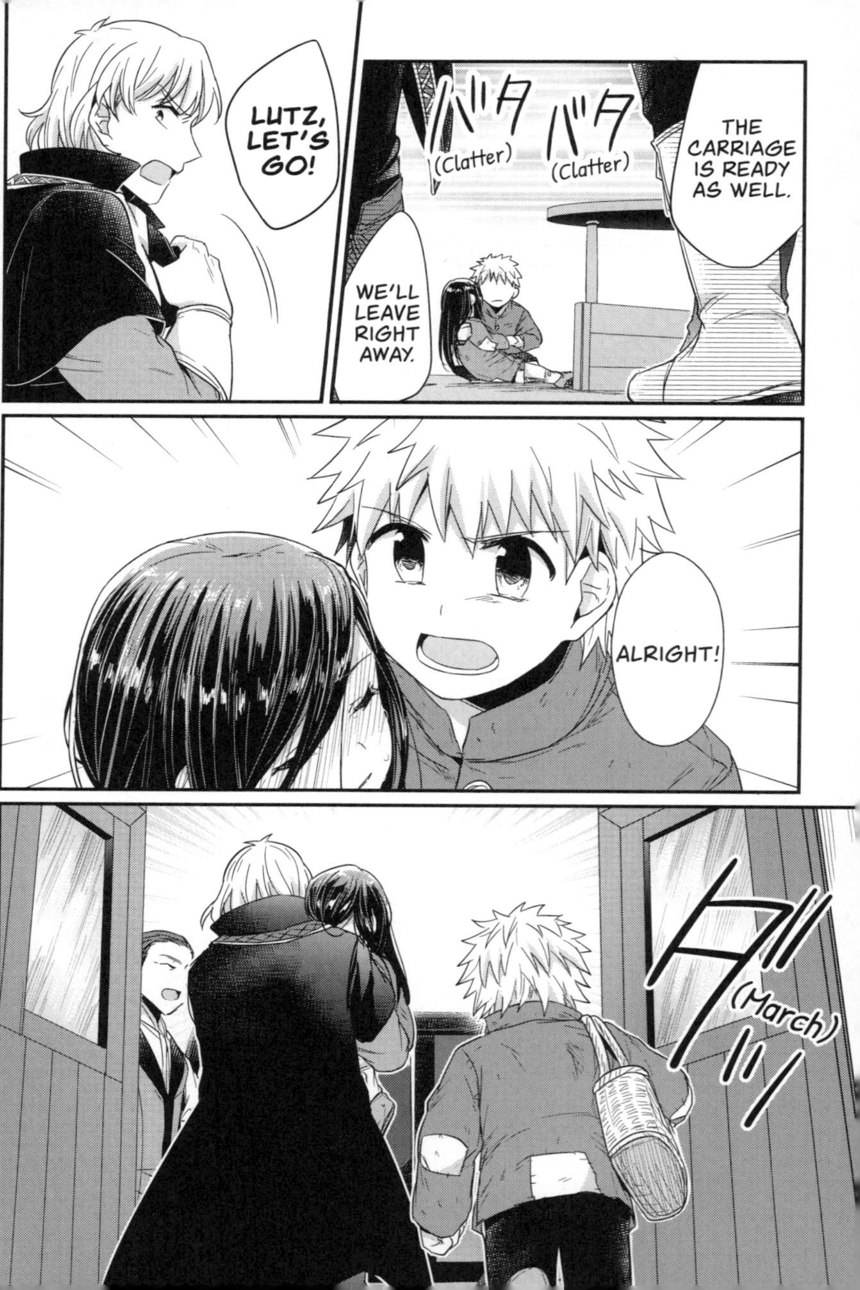
THE CARRIAGE IS READY AS WELL.
バタ (Clatter) バタ (Clatter)
WE'LL LEAVE RIGHT AWAY.
LUTZ, LET'S GO!
ALRIGHT!
(March)

Hairpins and the Meeting of Stores

Hairpins and the Meeting of Stores

A meeting of the largest stores in Ehrenfest was being held in the meeting room on the third floor of the Merchant's Guild. As the head of the Gilberta Company, I was naturally participating. Having to prepare for winter meant we were all pretty busy, but this was an important meeting where the results of the Harvest Festival were announced.

"Now then. I will announce the results of this year's Harvest Festival," the guildmaster said after discussing several preliminary topics. His eyes moved to the head of the Othmar Company, whose seat clattered behind him as he stood up. He was the guildmaster's son and Freida's father.

The Othmar Company was an old store that had dealt in the food trade before the city of Ehrenfest was even called Ehrenfest. They were allowed entry into the archduke's castle, and thus acquired information on the Harvest Festival more easily than any other commoner.

"It seems that this year's harvest was not particularly favorable. The noble provinces performed as expected, but farms in the Central District produced even less than last year."

"Again? How many years will it take for things to recover?"

Heavy sighs spread through the meeting room in response to the Othmar Company's announcement. They had all predicted it, but even so, it was a painful situation. Poor Harvest Festivals meant higher food costs, and given that everyone in the city was currently preparing for winter, this in turn meant a lot of people would barely be able to eat once the blizzards started and they were stuck inside. It was, without exaggeration, a matter of life or death for the poor people of the city. Images of Myne and Lutz, two very poor kids who had been dropping by my store, flashed through my mind.

...Are their families gonna be alright?

"I had heard that the temple was lacking in mana due to losing so many priests, but..."

"That reminds me—a few years ago, a bunch of families came to prepare for those returning priests being made into proper nobles. I wonder if that's having an impact on this?"

All of the stores that dealt with nobles shared their information, and as a result we could all predict that the political shift that occurred in the distant Sovereignty had led to the priests in the temple leaving, which meant less mana for farming towns.

"Enough theorizing—what's important is just how bad the harvest really was. We're all going to need to plan around how the prices will change," I said, and voices of approval echoed the sentiment.

"Benno is right. There's no point discussing the reason why; the nobles won't be returning either way. Could we have more details?" asked one of the merchants.

The head of the Othmar Company lowered his eyes to look at the boards in his hands. "It hasn't quite fallen by a full ten percent from last year, so things aren't extraordinarily grim. I mentioned this last year as well, but Frenbeltag to the west was deeply impacted by the political shift and their harvest has been suffering far more than ours. We are safe only because our duchy chose neutrality during the civil war."

Those gathered let out small sighs of relief at the news that the decrease wasn't enormous. Still, as far as I could tell from looking around, almost everyone were wearing hard expressions. Even the softer ones among us had been hardened by the past few years.

"Mark, how bad are things compared to ten years ago? Can you tell?" I asked Mark, who was standing beside me.

"I believe the total harvest is close to sixty percent of what it used to be," he replied. Ten years had passed without any growth in the harvest; each year it was diminishing, however slightly.

The increase in food prices meant that traveling merchants who dealt in food could freely jack up their prices to profit, and it would be harder to negotiate with them since they, too, were trying to earn as much money as possible in preparation for winter. Plus, there would unfortunately be nobles swinging their power around to demand inordinate discounts despite the situation. Large stores that did trade with nobles would suffer greatly, and survival would depend on how well they could maneuver through negotiations with nobles.

"Benno, don't traveling merchants that circle through Frenbeltag visit your store often? Do you have any news from them?" asked the owner of the Hering Company, which was outlived only by the Othmar Company. I fell into thought. Merchants lived or died based on the information they had, and they needed to provide their own information in order to get information from others. A merchant showed their skill in what information they chose to give, and how deeply they could read into the information they were given.

"I hear cities near the Ehrenfest border are growing in population; inn fees and the cost of citizenship in those cities are shooting up. Frenbeltag's Central District was hit damn hard. The traveling merchants are raising the price of their own goods, but everything might be even more expensive next year. How's Ahrensbach, though? The Hering Company gets a lot of customers from the south, yeah?"

"Not much change in Ahrensbach. Prices aren't getting too much higher, or too much lower."

Huh...? Not much change in Ahrensbach? I furrowed my brow, finding it somewhat suspicious, and in seconds all of the other store owners were listing their opinions about the southern duchy being unchanged from last year.

"The south remains the same as last year, hm? Perhaps it's time to buy our imports from them instead."

"Hold it, hold it. Switching suppliers isn't so simple. If we cut Frenbeltag off now, it'll be hard to repair relations later if something else happens."

"For how many years have they been getting worse, though? If we wait any longer, Ahrensbach may overcharge us when we're finally driven to them."

"That's true. The later we make this move, the less money we'll make."

I folded my arms, listening to the merchants who were more interested in finding new business in Ahrensbach than sticking with Frenbeltag. I could understand Frenbeltag's suffering since they had joined the civil war and lost, but Ahrensbach had exploited the political shift in their favor. Their harvests should be getting better, not remaining unchanged.

...Which piece of information was wrong?

"Hey, Benno. What's the Gilberta Company do? You do a lot of trade with the west, right?"

I stroked my chin while thinking of an answer. Everything people here knew was hearsay, which made it hard to make safe decisions. Anything could be true or false. It would be safer to sit back and gather more information before making any big moves.

"...I'm gonna keep going like I've been going. It's too early to decide whether it's a good idea to cut them off. I still owe a lot to my suppliers in the west, too."

When my father died and I inherited the store, a lot of suppliers cut ties with the Gilberta Company, saying that they had no intention of doing business with a young kid who had just barely came of age. My remaining suppliers and traveling merchants propped me up back then, and I had no intention of abandoning those who had supported me in my time of need.

...Though if their economy keeps plummeting, it might not be long before I don't have a choice.

Paying back gratitude was important, but I had no intention of bankrupting the Gilberta Company over it. I listened to the voices around me, steeling my nerves so that I wouldn't hold out for too long and miss the right time to bail.

The meeting room quieted after enough information had been exchanged. The guildmaster, having been waiting for that, stood up and clapped his hands. "Will that be enough for discussing this year's harvest? When new information comes from the castle, I'll put the documents behind the reception desk like always."

That marked the end of the meeting for today. Sensing this, the merchants all began to stand up. My nerves calmed as the tension of the meeting faded, and that was when the guildmaster looked at me and grinned.

...Just what is that geezer planning?!

I could feel my mouth harden into a frown as a bad feeling washed over me. I instinctively turned around and looked at Mark, who tapped the side of his head with a frown of his own.

The hairpins?!

By the time I realized that, it was already too late. The guildmaster held up Freida's hairpins so that all of the store owners gathered could see them.

"I would like to report my findings to all of those who assisted me. I found the hairpin craftsman I had been searching for since summer, and successfully ordered a splendid hairpin for my granddaughter's baptism ceremony. I thank all of you who assisted me in my search. And most of all, I thank the Gilberta Company, who found the craftsman and delivered my order to them," the guildmaster said with a proud grin as he held the extravagant hairpins higher. A stir arose among the merchants, a reaction even greater than what the Harvest Festival had elicited.

"Isn't that way fancier than the hairpin you were looking for?!"

"The Gilberta Company found the craftsman?!"

One could hardly blame the merchants for their surprise. The guildmaster wasn't the only one who had been greatly interested in the hairpin Myne's older sister had worn during last summer's baptism. All of the merchants knew on sight that it would be a profitable product, myself included. Especially since the guildmaster himself started investigating them afterward.

And yet, no matter how much all these big-deal store owners searched, none of them could find anything. None of them knew the kid who had worn the hairpin. They could guess it was a girl from the southern part of the city judging by her position in the rows, but the area was so poor that most rich storeowners from the north didn't have associates there.

We all tried asking the people we knew in the workshops and eateries we would personally visit, but if nobody from their family was involved in the baptism then they would just cheer on the progression from the side without joining it. Far fewer people in the middle and southern parts of town had been in a position to notice the hairpins, too, so gathering information had been a nightmare.

"Hey, Benno! How in the world did you find the craftsman?!"

I crossed my arms and fell into thought. I hadn't found the craftsman—or craftswoman, rather—through any clever searching of my own. Myne had just casually dug into her basket and brought the hairpin out, asking without any particular investment in whether it would make a good product. It had all come down to sheer luck—even when it came to our meeting...

It was only by chance that I found out about her: I was eating dinner with Corinna when Otto just happened to mention this weird girl. A bit later, he told me one of Myne's friends dreamed of being a traveling merchant, and he asked me to make him give up on it. I normally would have shot him down to save myself the time and effort, but at the time I was coincidentally low on work, and I wanted to meet that weird girl he kept talking about myself. Honestly, thinking back, I'm surprised I bothered to go at all.

Let's just say that a string of miracles happened in a row. Honestly, maybe the God of Trade brought us together.

"Ngh, not gonna tell us your source so easily, huh?"

I had just said what came to mind, but everyone else took that as me saying that no merchant would ever give up information that valuable. Some merchants stepped back with frustrated grimaces, but others bore down on me with gleaming eyes.

"Benno, I want you to sell me some of those hairpins as soon as you can. Ones just like the guildmaster has," said the head of the Hering Company. He was always deep in competition with the Othmar Company, and right now he was gearing up for business.

"Sorry, but the craftsman is busy preparing for winter. I might be able to work something out if you're fine with winter handiwork, at least."

"That's not fast enough. My niece's baptism is this winter too. It's my little sister's youngest daughter," he said, and the other merchants joined in to list off all of their friends and family who had baptisms coming up. If the Hering Company was getting new hairpins, they couldn't let themselves fall behind.

"Hold up. The hairpins I sold to the guildmaster were a special order. The craftsman won't be able to make more in time for the baptism, and there's too many of you after them."

There were more than a few merchants looking at me with hungry eyes, and I didn't want to deal with accepting some of their orders but refusing others—that would bring nothing but problems down the line.

As I worked my brain to figure out how to get out of this, the guildmaster watched on with amusement. "It seems everyone wants hairpins of their own. Are you going to deny them all? I imagine you will have to, since the hairpin craftsman was so busy with winter preparations that they don't even have the time to visit me at home."

By saying that, he deftly avoided the jealousy that would normally be sent his way by directing their dissatisfaction toward the Gilberta Company. *This freaking geezer! He's trying to make everyone pissed at me for not having any hairpins for them!*

"Master Benno, this might be incredibly important business for the Gilberta Company," Mark said from behind me, which cooled my anger in an instant. We had been working hard to get the Gilberta Company back on track after my father's death, and this was a good opportunity to show that we had fully recovered. I couldn't miss this chance.

It would be hard to get ahold of Myne considering how often she was bedridden, but Mark knew where she lived. It was precisely because winter prep required buying so many things that she might agree to make the hairpins if I offered a higher commission fee than usual.

"Alright, well... There's not enough time for everyone to get special designs, but if you all are fine with hairpins like the one from the summer baptism, I can get plenty of them for you."

"Ooh. That will do just fine, thank you."

"Just to be clear though, there's barely any time before the winter baptism, and everyone's busy preparing for winter. These are gonna be more expensive than usual and I don't know how many they'll be able to make. It's gonna be first come, first served here."

I waved a hand while looking over the gathered merchants, and Mark took out a board. The merchants wrote down their names, glaring at each other all the while.

"You have me to thank for this prosperous business, Benno," the guildmaster said with a victorious smile, as if I owed him gratitude. I touched the slip of plant paper in my pocket. The hairpins weren't the only product I had up my sleeve. I had plant paper that would someday soon flip the entire market on its head.

...*Just you wait, geezer. Don't think that smug grin on your face is gonna last forever.*

The End.

AFTERWORD

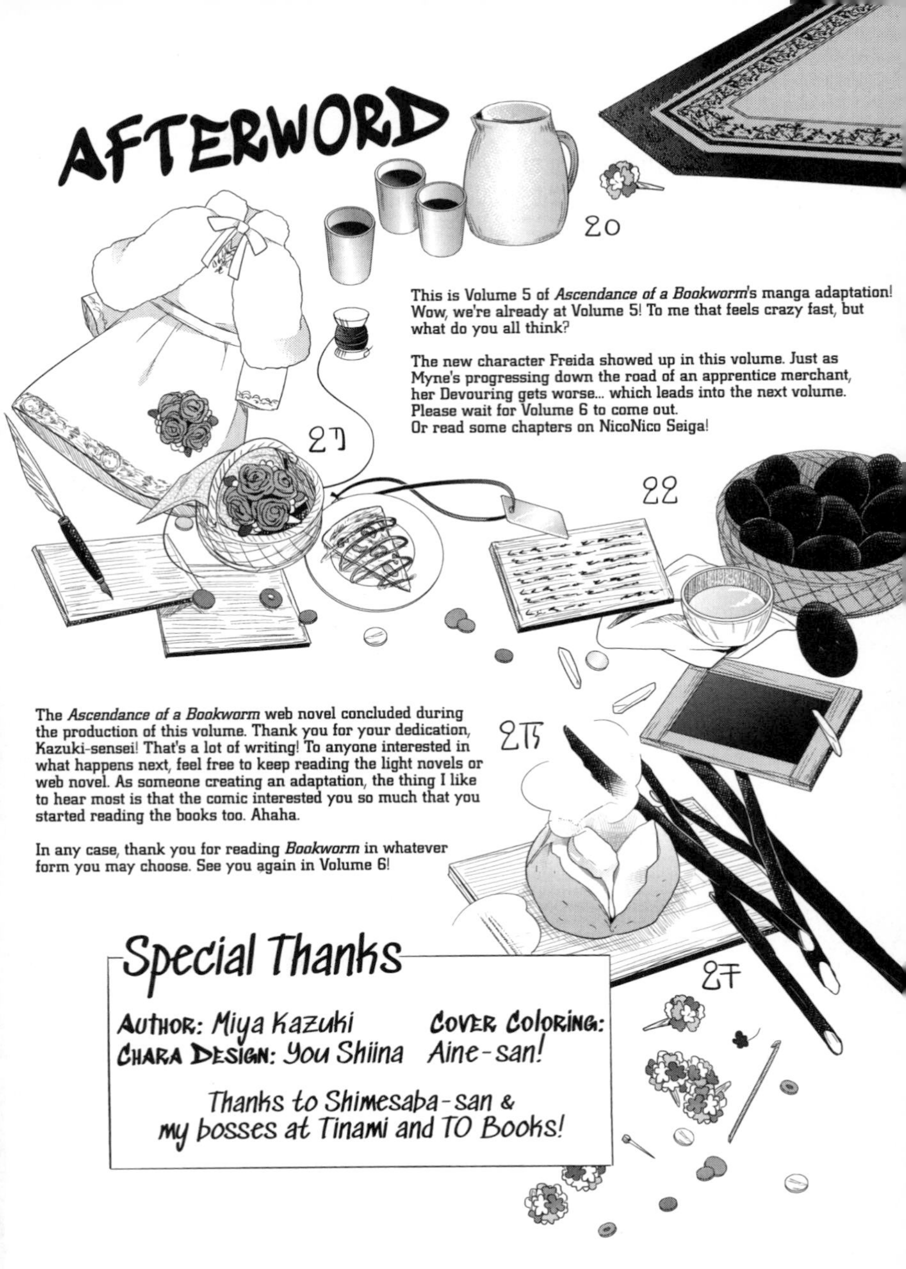

This is Volume 5 of *Ascendance of a Bookworm*'s manga adaptation! Wow, we're already at Volume 5! To me that feels crazy fast, but what do you all think?

The new character Freida showed up in this volume. Just as Myne's progressing down the road of an apprentice merchant, her Devouring gets worse... which leads into the next volume. Please wait for Volume 6 to come out.
Or read some chapters on NicoNico Seiga!

The *Ascendance of a Bookworm* web novel concluded during the production of this volume. Thank you for your dedication, Kazuki-sensei! That's a lot of writing! To anyone interested in what happens next, feel free to keep reading the light novels or web novel. As someone creating an adaptation, the thing I like to hear most is that the comic interested you so much that you started reading the books too. Ahaha.

In any case, thank you for reading *Bookworm* in whatever form you may choose. See you again in Volume 6!

Special Thanks

AUTHOR: Miya Kazuki
CHARA DESIGN: You Shiina
COVER COLORING: Aine-san!

Thanks to Shimesaba-san & my bosses at Tinami and TO Books!

Afterword

To both those who are new to *Bookworm* and those who read the web novel or light novel: thank you very much for reading Volume 5 of *Ascendance of a Bookworm*'s manga adaptation.

In this volume, Myne met Freida and began profiting from selling hairpins. Lutz has started studying in a lot of ways to grow as a merchant. He's struggling a lot, since the lives of craftsmen and merchants are so different, but he's working as hard as he can to make his dream come true. Myne and Lutz have gotten used to making paper, and as they continue to earn money by making it, Myne's Devouring grows stronger by the day.

Now then, the new character Freida is the guildmaster's granddaughter, and she's a girl that loves money (gold coins). You probably thought "Wow, isn't she like six years old? What kind of six-year-old would act like that?", am I right? Well, the truth is, I actually know someone who had a similar obsession with money when they were a kid.

Imagine a kindergarten student who spent every Sunday counting the money in their piggy bank and shaking it with a big grin on their face. One who could even do multiplication and division on the level of a third-grader when it came to money. Just imagine, and you will have an idea of what my little sister used to be like.

I always wondered what kind of genius prodigy my little sister would grow up to be, but in first grade when she was presented with problems like "There were three birds in a cage. Four flew in and two flew out. How many birds are in the cage?" she would apparently just get mad about the birds coming and going as they pleased. She wasn't a prodigy at all (haha). It's strange, too—she could have answered immediately if the question was about ten-yen coins instead.

In any case, all I did was draw a little inspiration from my little sister's weirder qualities. Freida's a cute girl in her own way. She loves making money like her grandfather does, she's fascinated by business, and she's determined to get what she wants. She will surely attract a lot of attention wearing her fancy hairpins at her winter baptism.

Suzuka drew this volume while agonizing over Freida's baptism outfit and the interior decoration of her house for me. I'm grateful that she so effectively illustrated their home based on my vague statement that "his house was fit for nobility, but only for lower-class nobles, so don't make it too fancy."

And finally, the short story in this volume was about a meeting of all of the big store owners, which was something requested while working on the web novel. It's from Benno's perspective, with there being talks of the harvest, the neighboring duchies, and the guildmaster bragging about Freida's hairpins. Please enjoy a meeting of adults not really acting like adults in a place Myne never gets to see.

Miya Kazuki

Myne's Weird #1

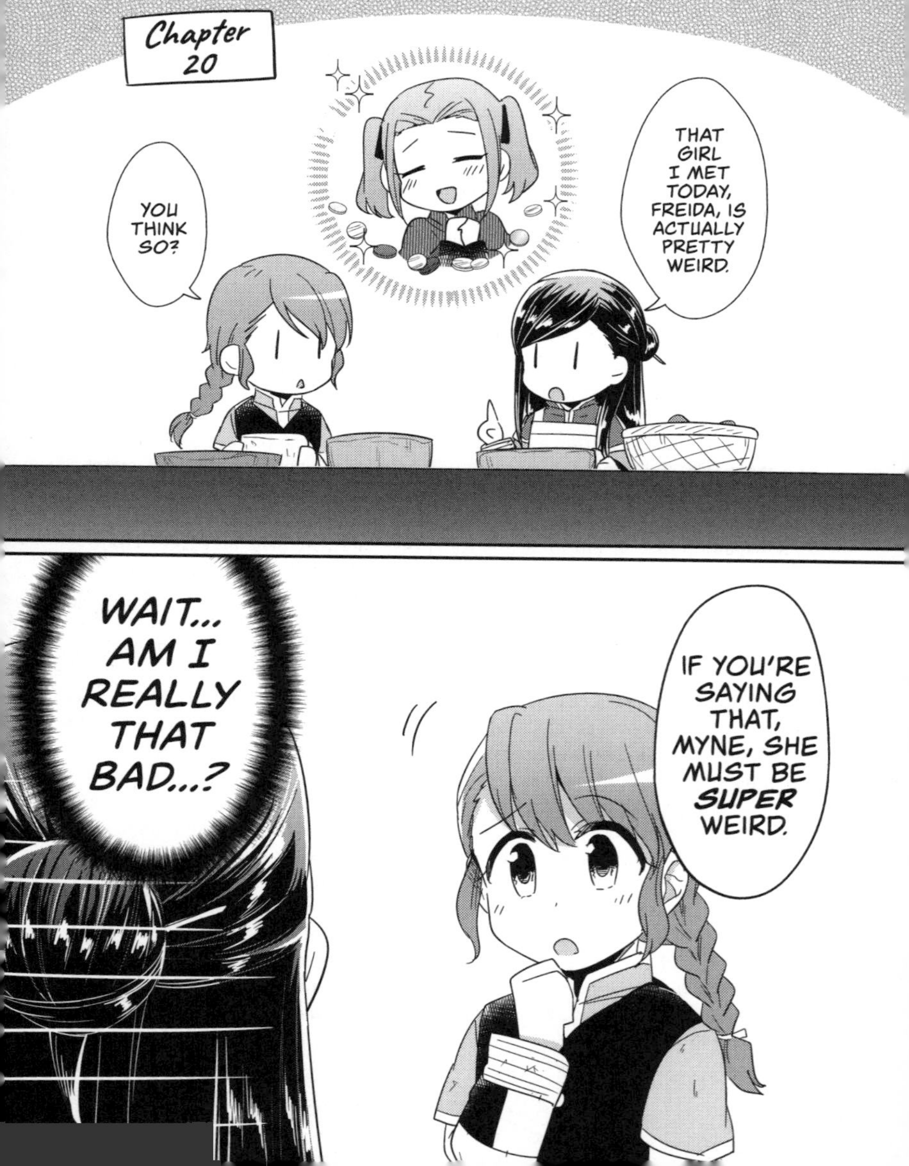
Chapter 20
THAT GIRL I MET TODAY, FREIDA, IS ACTUALLY PRETTY WEIRD.
YOU THINK SO?
IF YOU'RE SAYING THAT, MYNE, SHE MUST BE **SUPER** WEIRD.
WAIT... AM I REALLY THAT BAD...?

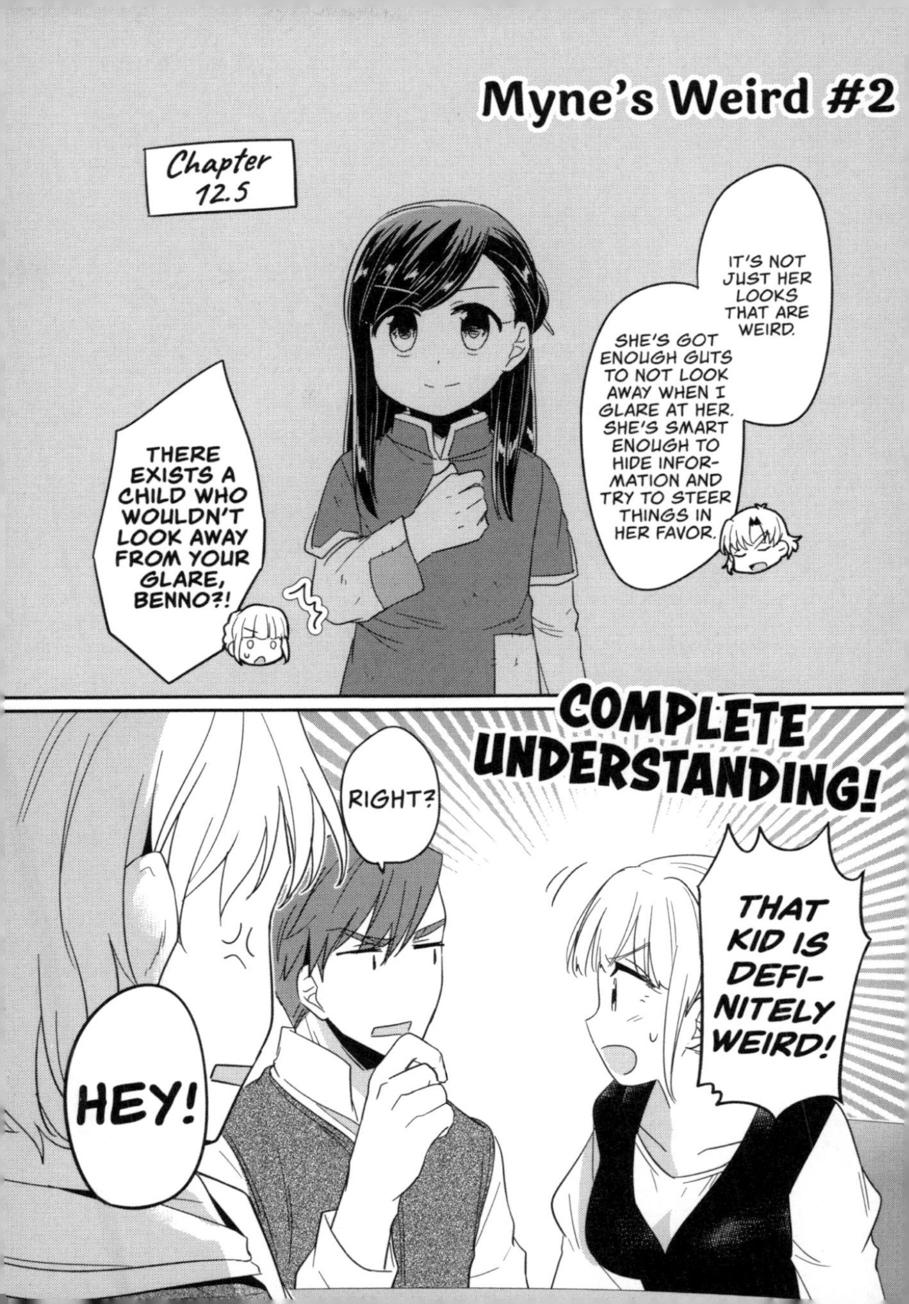
Myne's Weird #2
Chapter 12.5
IT'S NOT JUST HER LOOKS THAT ARE WEIRD.
SHE'S GOT ENOUGH GUTS TO NOT LOOK AWAY WHEN I GLARE AT HER. SHE'S SMART ENOUGH TO HIDE INFORMATION AND TRY TO STEER THINGS IN HER FAVOR.
THERE EXISTS A CHILD WHO WOULDN'T LOOK AWAY FROM YOUR GLARE, BENNO?!
COMPLETE UNDERSTANDING!
THAT KID IS DEFINITELY WEIRD!
RIGHT?
HEY!

ASCENDANCE OF A BOOKWORM (MANGA)VOLUME 5
by Miya Kazuki (story) and Suzuka (artwork)
Original character designs by You Shiina

Translated by Carter "Quof" Collins
Edited by Kieran Redgewell
Lettered by Meiru

First published in Japan in 2017 by TO Books, Tokyo.
Publication rights for this English edition arranged through TO Books, Tokyo.

Find more books like this one at www.j-novel.club!

President and Publisher: Samuel Pinansky
Managing Editor (Manga): J. Collis
Managing Translator: Kristi Fernandez
QA Manager: Hannah N. Carter
Marketing Manager: Stephanie Hii

ISBN: 978-1-7183-7254-2
Printed in Korea
First Printing: May 2021
10 9 8 7 6 5 4 3 2 1

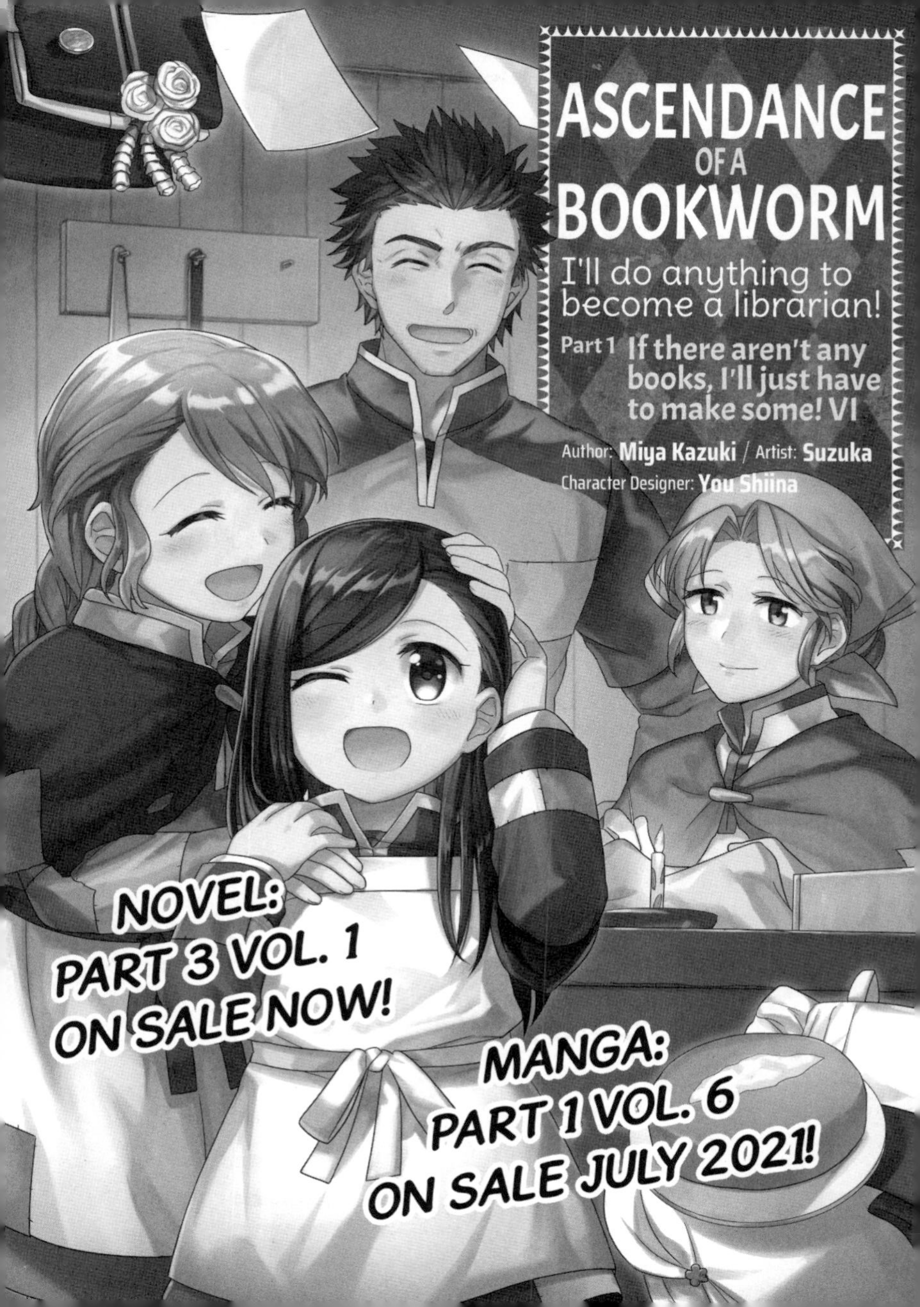
ASCENDANCE OF A BOOKWORM
I'll do anything to become a librarian!
Part 1 If there aren't any books, I'll just have to make some! VI
Author: Miya Kazuki / Artist: Suzuka
Character Designer: You Shiina
NOVEL: PART 3 VOL. 1 ON SALE NOW!
MANGA: PART 1 VOL. 6 ON SALE JULY 2021!

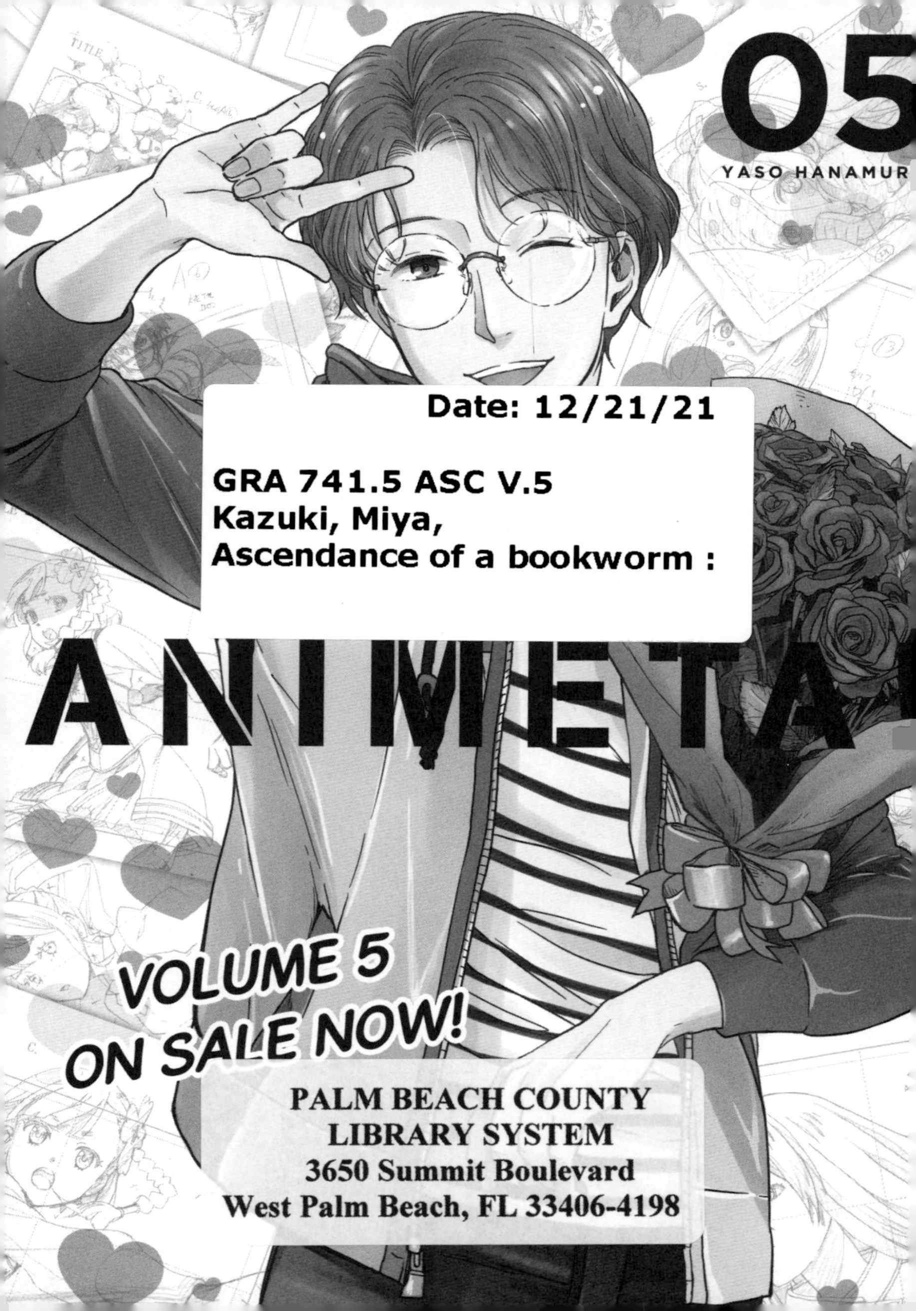
05
YASO HANAMUR
ANIMETA
VOLUME 5
ON SALE NOW!

J-Novel Club Lineup

Ebook Releases Series List

A Lily Blooms in Another World
A Very Fairy Apartment**
A Wild Last Boss Appeared!
Altina the Sword Princess
Amagi Brilliant Park
An Archdemon's Dilemma: How to Love Your Elf Bride*
Animeta!**
The Apothecary Diaries
Are You Okay With a Slightly Older Girlfriend?
Arifureta: From Commonplace to World's Strongest
Arifureta Zero
Ascendance of a Bookworm*
Banner of the Stars
Beatless
Bibliophile Princess*
Black Summoner*
The Bloodline
By the Grace of the Gods
Campfire Cooking in Another World with My Absurd Skill*
Can Someone Please Explain What's Going On?!
The Combat Baker and Automaton Waitress
Cooking with Wild Game*
Deathbound Duke's Daughter
Demon King Daimaou
Demon Lord, Retry!*
Der Werwolf: The Annals of Veight*
Discommunication**
Dungeon Busters
The Economics of Prophecy
The Epic Tale of the Reincarnated Prince Herscherik
The Extraordinary, the Ordinary, and SOAP!
The Faraway Paladin*
From Truant to Anime Screenwriter: My Path to "Anohana" and "The Anthem of the Heart"
Full Metal Panic!
Fushi no Kami: Rebuilding Civilization Starts With a Village
The Great Cleric
The Greatest Magicmaster's Retirement Plan
Girls Kingdom
Grimgar of Fantasy and Ash
Her Majesty's Swarm

Holmes of Kyoto
The Holy Knight's Dark Road
How a Realist Hero Rebuilt the Kingdom*
How NOT to Summon a Demon Lord
I Love Yuri and I Got Bodyswapped with a Fujoshi!**
I Refuse to Be Your Enemy!
I Saved Too Many Girls and Caused the Apocalypse
I Shall Survive Using Potions!*
I'll Never Set Foot in That House Again!
The Ideal Sponger Life
If It's for My Daughter, I'd Even Defeat a Demon Lord
In Another World With My Smartphone
Infinite Dendrogram*
Infinite Stratos
Invaders of the Rokujouma!?
Isekai Rebuilding Project
JK Haru is a Sex Worker in Another World
Kobold King
Kokoro Connect
Last and First Idol
Lazy Dungeon Master
The Magic in this Other World is Too Far Behind!*
The Magician Who Rose From Failure
Mapping: The Trash-Tier Skill That Got Me Into a Top-Tier Party*
Marginal Operation**
The Master of Ragnarok & Blesser of Einherjar*
Middle-Aged Businessman, Arise in Another World!
Mixed Bathing in Another Dimension
Monster Tamer
My Big Sister Lives in a Fantasy World
My Friend's Little Sister Has It In For Me!
My Instant Death Ability is So Overpowered, No One in This Other World Stands a Chance Against Me!

My Next Life as a Villainess: All Routes Lead to Doom!
Our Crappy Social Game Club Is Gonna Make the Most Epic Game
Otherside Picnic
Outbreak Company
Outer Ragna
Record of Wortenia War*
Seirei Gensouki: Spirit Chronicles*
Sexiled: My Sexist Party Leader Kicked Me Out, So I Teamed Up With a Mythical Sorceress!
She's the Cutest... But We're Just Friends!
Slayers
The Sorcerer's Receptionist
Sorcerous Stabber Orphen*
Sweet Reincarnation**
The Tales of Marielle Clarac*
Tearmoon Empire
Teogonia
The Underdog of the Eight Greater Tribes
The Unwanted Undead Adventurer*
WATARU!!! The Hot-Blooded Fighting Teen & His Epic Adventures After Stopping a Truck with His Bare Hands!!
Welcome to Japan, Ms. Elf!*
When the Clock Strikes Z
The White Cat's Revenge as Plotted from the Dragon King's Lap
Wild Times with a Fake Fake Princess
The World's Least Interesting Master Swordsman
Yume Nikki: I Am Not in Your Dream

* Novel and Manga Editions
** Manga Only

Keep an eye out at j-novel.club for further new title announcements!